Best Wishes

John D. Fowler

Mountaineers in Gray

Mountaineers in Gray

The
Nineteenth
Tennessee
Volunteer
Infantry
Regiment,
C.S.A.

John D. Fowler

The University of Tennessee Press * Knoxville

This book is printed on acid-free paper.

Library of Congress Cataloging-in-Publication Data

Fowler, John D., 1965-
Mountaineers in gray : the Nineteenth Tennessee Volunteer Infantry Regiment,
C.S.A. / John D. Fowler.—1st ed.
    p. cm.
Includes bibliographical references and index.

ISBN 1-57233-314-6 (acid-free paper)

1. Confederate States of America. Army. Tennessee Infantry Regiment, 19th.
2. Tennessee—HistoryvCivil War, 1861–1865—Regimental histories.
3. United States—History—Civil War, 1861–1865—Regimental histories.
I. Title.
E579.519th .F69 2004
973.7'468—dc22   2004010583

TO SONYA

As much a veteran of the Nineteenth as any who served.

Contents ❧

Illustrations ✺

Figures

Maps

Tables

Preface ✤

On April 26, 1865, on a farm just outside of Durham, North Carolina, General Joseph E. Johnston surrendered the remnants of the Army of Tennessee to his longtime foe, General William T. Sherman. Johnston's surrender ended the unrelenting Federal drive through the Carolinas and dashed any hope for Southern independence. Among the thirty thousand or so ragged Confederates who soon received their paroles were the men of Companies C and H of the Third Consolidated Tennessee Infantry Regiment. These seventy-eight men represented all that remained of the Nineteenth Tennessee Volunteer Infantry Regiment. Originally consisting of over one thousand men, the unit had—by four years of sickness, injury, desertion, and death—been reduced to a fraction of its former strength.

As the Rebels surrendered their arms, furled their flags, and prepared to return to their homes and families, competing emotions of sorrow and joy flooded their hearts. Many veterans openly wept at the thought of defeat, yet they all eagerly anticipated the return home to the loved ones they had left behind.

Anxiety also gripped these men. Since 1862, Federal armies had penetrated the western Confederacy and brought the Southern heartland under their control, laying waste to much of the region. Many of Johnston's veterans were haunted by fears of what they would find when they returned. What had happened to their friends and relatives? Their homes? Their farms and shops? While weighing heavily on all Rebel soldiers, these questions especially troubled the men from East Tennessee such as those in the Nineteenth. Their homeland had been a battleground for Union and Confederate armies as well as for the native unionist and secessionist guerrillas. The war had devastated the region and its people. With the capture of East Tennessee by Federal forces in the fall of 1863, the area's overwhelmingly unionist population sought to punish Rebel "traitors" and take vengeance against their secessionist neighbors for real or imagined wrongs committed under Confederate rule. Returning East Tennessee Rebels, unlike most other Confederate soldiers, would have to face the enmity of their former friends and neighbors. It was to this hostile and chaotic environment that the men of the Nineteenth returned.

Few, if any, of the regiment's veterans could have envisioned the resulting calamity as they marched off to war in 1861. Yet the conflict shattered their lives and their world, as it did those of many other Americans of that generation. The story of the men of the Nineteenth is in many ways a tragic one, yet one that provides insight into a region and its people as they faced the greatest challenge of their lives. It is a story worth telling.

This study reflects the confluence of three dynamic trends in the historiography of the Civil War. These are the use of community-based studies to examine the impact of the war on the citizen-soldiers and their families, the desire to understand the war through the experiences of the common soldier, and the increasing interest in the war in the southern Appalachians, especially Confederate loyalty in the region.[1]

Considering that literally hundreds of regimental histories already exist, one would be pardoned for thinking that this study offers nothing new to Civil War historiography. However, a closer examination of Civil War unit histories reveals a vast new field beckoning researchers. Indeed, this area of study is one of the largest military and social areas of the war left virtually unexplored.

Most regimental histories are "first-generation narratives," meaning that they were produced by, about, and largely for the members of the unit. These histories, however, are in essence memoirs and as such have limitations. The objectivity and accuracy of such works are often doubtful. Most of the authors penned the histories many years after the events they depicted, allowing time and distance to cloud memories and distort recollections. In addition, first-generation histories almost always present the unit in a favorable light. Incidents of cowardice, desertion, or ineptitude among the veterans often are not mentioned or are presented as aberrations. Along with these weaknesses, first-generation narratives, while usually offering generous hagiographical tributes to brigade and regimental officers, are woefully short of detail on the common fighting men—the real heart of all the Civil War regiments. Finally, the authors of the early regimental histories tended to treat in isolation the experiences of the unit, inadequately linking the regiment's "private" war to the larger events of the conflict. So, despite the rich information contained in the pages of such narratives, the reader is left with many unanswered questions— questions that can only be answered by a new generation of historians armed with a greater variety of sources and the techniques of modern historiographical inquiry.

The regiment was the basic building block of Civil War armies. It represented the primary object of identification for the men who fought the war. Raised and organized as a group of local companies (ten in the case of an infantry unit), the regiment consisted of neighbors, friends, and relatives, all united in a community response to the crisis. A study of these men can and should offer much more than the traditional recounting of a regiment's military exploits.

My work is part of this new approach to the study of regiments and hopefully will serve as a model for future unit histories. By combining a rich variety of primary sources such as the Official Records, the Compiled Service Records, census records, pension records, medical ledgers, newspapers, letters, diaries, and personal papers, a composite picture of the men of the regiment, the communities they came from, and the awesome impact of the war become all too apparent. The Civil War becomes less abstract and much more personal as we encounter the parades and speeches of the opening days, the fear and thrill of combat, the mangled bodies in the hospitals, the internal struggle over a commitment to "the cause" and the desire to survive, and the realization that defeat is at hand. While poet Walt Whitman despaired that the "real war" would never get into the books, regimental studies such as this one offer an excellent lens to view the era through the eyes of those who lived it.[2]

In examining a Confederate unit from East Tennessee, this study touches on another very promising yet neglected field in Civil War research: Confederate sympathy within that region. East Tennessee was one of the strongest unionist areas of the Confederacy, rivaled only by West Virginia. As early as the 1860s, inhabitants of the region wrote works attempting to explain East Tennessee's distinctive posture. This interest in the region's ardent unionism has continued to the present and has produced many valuable insights on the subject. Yet within this region of "Tories," pockets of Confederate sympathizers could be found, among whom were the men of the Nineteenth Tennessee. Why a significant minority of East Tennesseans chose to cast their lot with the fledgling Confederacy is an intriguing question and one of central importance to understanding the men who served in the Confederate units organized in the region, including the Nineteenth. By exploring antebellum East Tennessee and providing a socioeconomic profile of those who served in the regiment, this work sheds light on the origins of Confederate sympathy there.[3]

In addition to explaining why these men and their communities felt compelled to fight for Southern independence, I seek to explain the role that the Nineteenth played in the war. The regiment served from the beginning of the war to its conclusion, marching and fighting throughout the western theater and participating in every major engagement of the Army of Tennessee except Perryville. In presenting the regiment's wartime history, I explore the soldiers' effectiveness as fighting men; the thrill and fear associated with combat; the harsh and often appalling conditions of camp life; the relentless attrition through disease, desertion, and death in battle; and the specter of defeat that haunted the Confederate forces in the west. A micro-study such as this is ideal for studying and understanding the war. This approach allows not only close personal contact with a group of Civil War soldiers but also new insights and perspectives on the larger historiographical issues of the war such as the daily life of Southern soldiers, wartime military leadership, strategy and tactics, medical care, prison life, the erosion of Confederate morale, patterns of volunteering and desertion, and class stratification. Indeed, as one historian has noted, regimental studies, if properly done, create "a new arena for reinterpreting established truths about the war by synthesizing the documentary record with the testimony of participants hitherto ignored and unknown."[4]

Finally, unlike most regimental studies, mine explores the postwar experiences of the veterans. With East Tennessee under the control of unionists seeking to punish the region's Confederates, did the regiment's survivors return home? If not, where did they go? What was the postbellum period like for these men, and how did their experiences compare to those of other returning Confederate veterans? How did the war change their lives? All of these questions must be explored if we are to assess adequately the impact of the war on the men of the regiment and the Rebels of East Tennessee.

In the end, the following pages contain the stories of a group of East Tennesseans—stories of young lovers torn apart by the war, naive boys caught up in the rush of secession fever, brave charges, incredible carnage, shirkers, deserters, poor farmers, rich planters, noble beliefs, and useless sacrifices. More than anything else, however, the book contains the stories of real people coming to grips with the most traumatic event of their lives. As one historian of the Civil War has pointed out, the whole conflict may be viewed as "a composite of dozens, even hundreds, of little wars." This, then, is the Nineteenth's war.[5]

Acknowledgments ✌

As far back as I can remember, I have had a fascination with the Civil War, probably because of the powerful combination of *Gone With the Wind*, my toy soldier collection, and American Heritage's *The Golden Book of the Civil War*. This early influence engendered in me a passion for the past that would never die and would eventually lead me to become a student and a teacher of history. As I began to learn more about the war and visit the few related sites in my native Appalachia, I lamented that no major battlefields lay nearby. I assumed that somehow the war did not affect the mountains or their people. By the time I reached college, I was beginning to see the region differently. I had read about bands of loyalist guerrillas and the prevailing unionism of the mountaineers, which set the region apart from the rest of the South. But what about the Rebels? Weren't there any secessionists in Appalachia? Fortunately, this question was starting to be answered by a handful of scholars about the time I entered graduate school. Given my own interest in Appalachia's role in the war, I naturally gravitated toward such a dissertation topic. Over several years, an idea about East Tennessee Confederates grew into a dissertation and now into this book. Along the way, I learned a great deal about the Civil War, the historical profession, and life. I would like to take this opportunity to thank those who helped me along my journey.

Little did I realize how profoundly my life would be changed when I arrived at the University of Tennessee in the fall of 1994 to begin work on my doctorate. I would stay at the university for the next eight years as a student and then later as a lecturer and the assistant editor of the Papers of Andrew Jackson. During that time, I grew both as a scholar and as a person, in large part because of the many wonderful people I encountered along the way.

I was most fortunate to have met Clint Clifft, Ben Severance, and Mark Williams. Their humor, counsel, and companionship have been inestimable, and I consider them to be among my dearest friends. Kim Harrison and Penny Hamilton, the History Department assistants, became my adoptive family. I can never thank them enough for all the kind things they have done for me. They took in a befuddled graduate student and continued to guide an equally befuddled professor. I am extremely grateful to the History Department, not only for my education but also for the valuable opportunity to teach. I was fortunate to work with and learn from the many fine historians on the faculty who taught me the nuances of the profession I have chosen.

No researcher labors alone, and I have received help from a great many people who shared my interest in the Civil War and its fighting men. I especially want to mention the following people for their kind support: Dr. Jim Tumblin, Dr. Nathaniel Hughes, Violet Clark and my "sisters" at the Ellen Renshaw House Chapter #2624 of the United Daughters of the Confederacy, Sheila Johnston, Marylin Bell Hughes, Kevin Mason, John McManus, William Nelson, Richard Peuser, and Michael Musick. I owe a special note of gratitude to Dr. Jack Welsh, who in a feat of incredible generosity allowed me access to his research notes on the medical history of the Nineteenth.

I would like to thank the staffs of the Georgia Historical Society, the Tennessee State Library and Archives, the McClung Collection, the University of Tennessee's Special Collections, the University of Virginia's Special Collections, University Press of Kansas, Louisiana State University Press, Southeastern Division of the Association of American Geographers, Harper-Collins, Cumberland Gap National Historical Park, Shiloh National Battlefield, Stones River National Battlefield, Kennesaw Mountain National Battlefield, and Chickamauga and Chattanooga National Military Park. All were friendly, professional, and helpful.

I must also express my sincerest gratitude to the United Daughters of the Confederacy for honoring me with the Mrs. Simon Baruch University Award. Considering the stature of the past recipients, I am truly humbled.

I am indebted to Paul Bergeron, Bruce Wheeler, Judy Cornett, Thomas Plank, Todd Groce, and Tracy McKenzie, who took time out of their busy schedules to review the manuscript. Their critiques were invaluable and greatly improved the work. Despite their painstaking efforts and candid reviews, I alone am responsible for any errors.

I also want to thank Joyce Harrison, Scot Danforth, and the staff at the University of Tennessee Press for their belief in this project and all their hard work in bringing it to fruition.

I would especially like to acknowledge my mentor and friend Steve Ash for his patience, advice, criticism, interest, and kindness. His watchful eye guided my dissertation to completion, and he has continued to help with the creation of this book. Any contribution this study makes to the field of Civil War historiography is primarily the result of his invaluable assistance. His knowledge of the Civil War and his expertise in writing are qualities I greatly admire and hope to emulate. If I become half the scholar he is, I will consider it a great personal achievement.

Finally, I want to express my immense gratitude to my family. Ann and Art Wolfe, my in-laws and adoptive parents, have supported me in ways too numerous to count. I can never repay their love and encouragement. My most heartfelt and deepest appreciation belongs to my wife Sonya. Her patience and sacrifice over the years of graduate school reached saintly proportions. Her careful reading, editing, and word processing skills improved the quality of this manuscript immensely, while her support, understanding, and loving hand made this project possible. She is my soul mate and my best friend. Our life together is my greatest happiness. I simply could not have reached this point in my career or life without her, for which I will always be grateful.

Winner in the Mrs. Simon Baruch University Award, sponsored by the United Daughters of the Confederacy, 2001. Past winners of the Baruch Award Books are shown below.

1927   Carpenter, Jesse Thomas. *The South As a Conscious Minority 1789–1861*. New York University, 1920. University of South Carolina Press (reprinted—1991).

1929   Whitfield, Theodore M. *Slavery Agitation in Virginia, 1829–1832*. Out of print.

1931   Flanders, Ralph Betts. *Plantation Slavery in Georgia*. Out of print.

1933   Thompson, Samuel. Confederate Purchasing Agents Abroad. Out of print.

1935   Wiley, Bell Irvin. *Southern Negroes 1861–1865*. Yale University Press, 1938.

1937   Hill, Louise Biles. *Joseph E. Brown and the Confederacy*. Out of print.

1940   Haydon, F. Stansbury. *Aeronautics of the Union and Confederate Armies*. Out of print.

1942   Stormont, John. *The Economic Stake of the North in the Preservation of the Union in 1861*. Not published.

1945   Schultz, Harold Sessel. *Nationalism and Sectionalism in South Carolina, 1852–1860*. Duke University Press, 1950.

1948   Tankersly, Allen P. *John Brown Gordon: Soldier and Statesman*. Privately printed.

1951   Todd, Richard C. *Confederate Finance*. University of Georgia Press, 1953.

1954   Morrow, Ralph E. *Northern Methodism and Reconstruction*. Michigan State University Press.

1956   Cunningham, Horace. *Doctors in Gray*. Louisiana State University Press, 1958.

1957   Hall, Martin H. *The Army of New Mexico: Sibley's Campaign of 1862*. University of Texas Press, 1960.

1960 Robertson, James I., Jr. *Jackson's Stonewall: A History of the Stonewall Brigade*. Louisiana State University Press, 1963.

1969 Wells, Tom Henderson. *The Confederate Navy: A Study in Organization*. University of Alabama Press, 1971.

1970 Delaney, Conrad, *John McIntosh Kell: Luff of the Alabama*. University of Alabama Press, 1973.

1972 Dougan, Michael B. *Confederate Arkansas—The People and Politics of a Frontier State*. University of Alabama Press, 1976 (Reprinted 1991 in paperback).

1974 Wiggins, Sarah W. *The Scalawag in Alabama Politics, 1865–1881*. University of Alabama Press, 1976.

1976 Nelson, Larry Earl. *Bullets, Ballots, and Rhetoric*. University of Alabama Press, 1980.

1978 Franks, Kenny A. *Stand Watie and the Agony of the Cherokee Nation*. Memphis State University Press, 1979.

1980 Buenger, Walter L. *Stilling the Voice of Reason: The Union and Secession in Texas, 1854–1861*. University of Texas Press, 1984.

1982 McMurry, Richard M. *John Bell Hood and the War for Southern Independence*. University Press of Kentucky, 1982.

1984 Daniel, Larry J. *Cannoneers in Gray: The Field Artillery of the Army of Tennessee, 1861–1865*. University of Alabama Press, 1984.

1988 DeCredico, Mary Ann. *Patriotism for Profit: Georgia's Urban Entrepreneurs and the Confederate War Effort*. University of North Carolina Press, 1990.

1990 Nulty, William H., Jr. *Confederate Florida: The Road to Olustee*. University of Alabama Press, 1990.

1992 Willoughby, Lynn. *Fair to Middlin': The Antebellum Cotton Trade of the Apalachicola/Chattahoochee River Valley*. University of Alabama Press, 1993.

1994 Power, J. Tracy. *Lee's Miserables: Life in the Army of Northern Virginia from the Wilderness to Appomattox*. University of North Carolina Press, 1997.

2001 Fowler, John D. *Mountaineers in Gray: The Nineteenth Tennessee Volunteer Infantry Regiment, C.S.A.* University of Tennessee Press, 2004.

1 ❧

A Land Apart

East Tennessee from Frontier to Secession

Visitors entering Tennessee in the 1960s must have been bewildered by highway signs welcoming them to the "three states of Tennessee." However, such signs were entirely apt. Arguably no other state is so starkly segmented as Tennessee, and nowhere is such division more accepted and even celebrated. The state flag, for example, bears a circular crest containing three stars, one for each of the state's "Grand Divisions"—East, Middle, and West Tennessee. Indeed, Tennessee's sectionalism, predestined by geography and accentuated by subsequent economic and political differences, has been one of the most influential factors in the Volunteer State's history.

At no time has this sectionalism been more apparent and more tragic than during the Civil War era. United by politics and economic self-interest, Middle and West Tennessee overwhelmingly supported secession and alliance with the Confederacy. The majority of East Tennesseans, however, refused to abandon their allegiance to the old Union, precipitating an intrastate civil war within the national conflict. East Tennessee's stance involved more than just another chapter in the state's ongoing sectionalism, however. It also involved a rejection of the Confederate South and its values. This rejection made Tennessee's eastern counties not only a distinctive section of the state but also a distinctive region within the South.

Perhaps the most fundamental factor distinguishing East Tennessee from the rest of the state is geography. While Middle Tennessee is predominantly a land of fertile rolling hills and West Tennessee is generally flat, the eastern portion of the state is characterized by a steep and rugged landscape. Along the region's eastern border lie the Unaka Mountains. This range of lofty peaks and dense woods forms a stout barrier between Tennessee and the east. West of the Unakas lies the Great Valley of East Tennessee, which actually consists of numerous valleys and jagged parallel ridges. Along the western edges of the Great Valley rises the Cumberland Plateau—a rough mountainous area that divides East Tennessee from the rest of the state. East Tennessee's geography isolated it from Tennessee's other sections and the rest of the nation, and this isolation would greatly affect the region's future economic development.[1]

Following the War of 1812, the newly formed states west of the Appalachians experienced rapid economic change as the frontier economy based on subsistence farming gave way to commercial agriculture supplying domestic and foreign markets. However, East Tennessee lagged behind. The region's rugged topography limited the amount of agricultural land and dictated that small farms specializing in food production rather than plantations producing cash crops would be the norm. Moreover, even for those with the necessary land and interest in market production, the region's isolation hampered attempts to participate in the agricultural boom. To gain access to lucrative markets, East Tennesseans would need a cheap and efficient means to deliver their agricultural products. However, rough terrain limited the development of road construction, while obstructions in the Tennessee River below Chattanooga interfered with water transportation.[2]

East Tennessee's inhabitants hoped that railroads would solve their problem. Decades of false starts and frustration came to an end in 1855 with the completion of the East Tennessee and Georgia Railroad. This line provided Knoxville (its northern terminus) and all of lower East Tennessee a reliable and inexpensive connection to the markets of the Lower South. Three years later, upper East Tennesseans witnessed the completion of the East Tennessee and Virginia Railroad, which linked Knoxville to Bristol. When connected, the two rail lines created a route through the whole of the Valley and offered East Tennessee farmers what their parents and grandparents had dreamed of—greater access to outside markets.[3]

This access greatly affected the economy of the region. The traditional exports (corn and hogs) could now be shipped more easily, but the greatest change in the agriculture of the region was the development of a new cash crop: wheat. East Tennessee wheat proved to be of excellent quality and could command a premium in outside markets. By the mid-1850s, many Valley farmers began to shift from corn and hog production to wheat. In fact, during the 1850s, East Tennessee wheat production rose 300 percent. This wheat boom and the new transportation links that made it possible affected East Tennessee's economic development profoundly.[4]

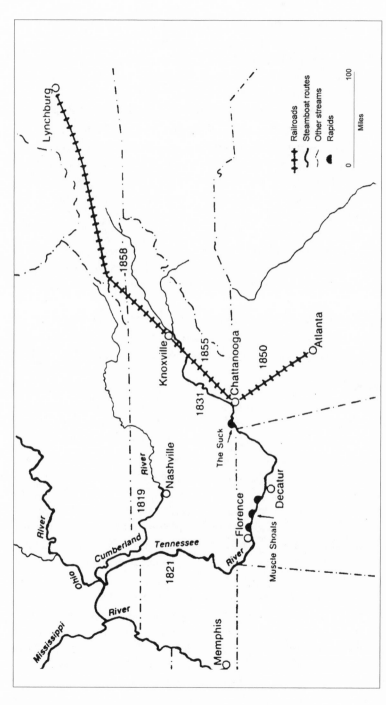

Major Transportation Connections for East Tennessee, 1800–1860. From Donald Buckwalter, "Effects of Early Nineteenth Century Transportation Disadvantages on the Agriculture of Eastern Tennessee," Southeastern Geographer 27 (1987): 31. Reproduced with permission of the Southeastern Division of the Association of American Geographers.

One major change was the growth of urban areas along the course of the new railroads. Although the urban populace of the region remained small in the antebellum era, many villages doubled or even tripled their population during the period. In addition, new communities sprang to life as a result of the railroad.[5]

These new railroad towns along with the older settlements set the stage for related development: the growth of an urban merchant and professional class. As many Valley farmers began to produce wheat on a large scale, they turned to store operators and commission merchants to sell their produce to southern markets. This relationship, similar to that between cotton factors and Lower South planters, turned the region's urban areas into trading centers where farmers bartered produce for store-bought items. In addition, the citizens of these small towns became closely linked to the economy of the wider South.[6]

Greater access to markets and the development of a cash crop also led to an increase in the region's slave population. The rapid expansion of wheat production required more labor. East Tennessee's slave population rose approximately 21 percent from 1850 to 1860. The counties with the greatest increase in wheat production (Meigs, Monroe, Polk, Rhea, and Sullivan) experienced an even greater rise (over 30 percent) in their slave population. In fact, the overall growth of the region's slave population outpaced that of whites, which was only 14 percent.[7]

Despite this increase, antebellum East Tennessee contained relatively few slaves when compared to the rest of the state or the South as a whole. In 1860 bondsmen accounted for around one-third of the slave states' population. In Middle Tennessee slaves constituted around one-quarter of the population and in West Tennessee slightly over one-third. In East Tennessee, however, slaves amounted to less than 10 percent of the population, and in no county of the region did the slave population exceed 15 percent. Moreover, the percentage of slaveholders in East Tennessee was quite small. Approximately 25 percent of white families in the South as a whole owned slaves in 1860, and the proportion in Middle and West Tennessee stood at one-fourth and one-third, respectively. But only one-tenth of white East Tennessee families held slaves.[8]

The key to a more affluent lifestyle, however, did not necessarily lie with land ownership or slave ownership but instead with commercial orientation. Farm operators producing for the market typically earned three to four times more than subsistence farmers. Why, then, did not all of the region's farmers produce for the market? While some historians argue that many antebellum farmers rejected commercial agriculture on principle in favor of the economic independence of self-sufficiency, this does not appear to be the case in East Tennessee. It was not ideology that kept more farmers from participation in the market economy but factors such as soil exhaustion and farm size, both products of the region's overpopulation. Perhaps the most significant factor, however, was high transportation costs. Only those farmers close to the region's few shipping routes, especially the railroad, could profit by commodity sales, which led to a growing economic disparity between the region's farmers. A minority near the railroad lines of the Valley became increasingly tied to the markets of the Lower South and enjoyed the financial rewards of participation in commercial agriculture, whereas the majority, inhabiting more isolated areas of the region, lived a precarious subsistence lifestyle and often suffered poverty. Indeed, as the Civil War drew near, the townspeople and commercial farmers linked to the southern economy and the subsistence farmers of the remoter areas began to view one another as different. These feelings of distinction would influence the region's response to the crisis.[9]

East Tennessee's economic isolation and the struggle for outside markets not only created internal friction but also generated a good deal of resentment toward the more prosperous sections of Tennessee. This animosity was exacerbated by the growing political power of the state's other regions, especially Middle Tennessee. As a result, a strong Whig presence developed in the eastern counties during the antebellum period in sharp contrast to Middle Tennessee's Democratic political tradition.[10]

This spirited regional rivalry was enhanced by the contrasting economic visions of the two parties, as well as by republican ideology. A product of the Revolutionary era, republicanism warned Americans that their liberty was constantly threatened by both foreign and domestic enemies. Only the vigilance of the American people provided security against despotism. Political leaders and their constituents came to view their opponents not as a legitimate opposition but as a threat to the existence of the republic and free government. The Whiggish political heritage of East Tennessee would play a significant factor in the region's response to the growing sectional crisis.[11]

With the dawning of the 1850s, brilliant statesmanship and a general willingness to settle differences by mutual concessions led to the fragile Compromise of 1850. Although most southerners, especially those of the Upper South, were generally content with its provisions, many Deep South radicals or "Fire Eaters" still believed slavery to be threatened by an ever-growing number of northern abolitionists. Southern Democrats were gradually becoming a unified political force dedicated to defending slavery.

White Tennesseans, irrespective of party, strongly endorsed slavery but generally condemned the fire-eating southern extremists. The Whigs, however, usually took a more conciliatory stance toward the North than did the Democrats, who tended to sympathize with the Lower South. This pattern would continue throughout the 1850s.[12]

The Kansas-Nebraska Act of 1854 shattered not only the Compromise of 1850 but also the second-party system. The Whig Party was the first to collapse. As northern and southern Whigs chose sides, the party disintegrated as a national force. Tennessee Whigs suddenly found themselves without a national affiliation. Like other bewildered party members, some joined the American Party. Following its collapse, many Tennessee Whigs then organized themselves as the Opposition Party. Others made a more radical choice. From the mid-1850s onward, as sectional antagonisms over slavery continued to escalate, many former Whigs switched their allegiance to the Democratic Party. Although these former Whigs may have disagreed with the Democrats' economic philosophy, they now believed this party offered the strongest protection for slavery and southern rights. Indeed, by the mid-1850s, West Tennessee, a region dominated by plantation agriculture, began to shift its political loyalty toward the Democrats. The emerging Democratic majority in the region, when added to that of Middle Tennessee, was enough to enable the party to dominate state politics for the rest of the decade.[13]

While the party system collapsed at the national level in the 1850s, it remained strong in Upper South states such as Virginia, North Carolina, and Tennessee. The surviving two-party system continued to perform a unifying function within each of these internally diverse states. However, with the tumultuous presidential election of 1860, the two-party system came to an end throughout the South.[14]

As the nation became increasingly polarized over slavery's future, four political parties contended for the presidency. The Republicans, led by Abraham Lincoln of Illinois, found widespread support throughout the North with their free-soil and free-labor ideology. However, the Republican opposition to slavery's expansion and the presence of a strong abolitionist faction in the party meant that Lincoln's name would not appear on the ballot in most Southern states. The Democratic Party, having failed to agree on a single candidate, had split in two. The moderate faction nominated Stephen A. Douglas of Illinois, while the southern-rights faction nominated John C. Breckinridge of Kentucky. The new Constitutional Union Party nominated John Bell of Tennessee; it opposed extremists on both sides and appealed mainly to Upper South Whigs.[15]

Tennessee and the rest of the country waited anxiously for the election returns. Because the states of the Lower South had pledged to secede in the event of Lincoln's election, the fate of the nation hung in the balance. On election day, Bell carried Tennessee, with his strongest support coming from the old Whig bastion of East Tennessee. He also won Kentucky and Virginia, demonstrating the conservatism and spirit of compromise that characterized the Upper South. Douglas carried less than 8 percent of Tennessee's total and managed to win only Missouri's electoral votes and part of New Jersey's. Breckinridge made a strong showing in Tennessee, losing by only forty-six hundred votes; he carried Maryland and the Lower South. Regardless of the outcome in Tennessee or the rest of the South, Lincoln was now president. The Republicans had carried every free state and won a large majority in the Electoral College, despite receiving only 39 percent of the popular vote and almost no votes in the South.[16]

True to their word, the states of the Lower South left the Union, beginning with South Carolina in December. Although no hostile action had been taken against slavery, Lincoln's election meant that after March 4, 1861, the presidency would be in the hands of a northern free-soiler. The right to own slaves and the liberty to take slave property into the territories would, the citizens of the Lower South believed, be jeopardized by a coercive central government under Republican domination. In the spirit of republicanism, they determined to leave a tyrannical and hostile Union and establish a government true to the principles of the Revolution.[17]

The secession crisis presented Tennesseans with a dilemma. While most abhorred abolitionism and supported Southern rights to property, they perceived disunion as a threat to republican government and liberty. Moreover, although Tennesseans sympathized with the Lower South's fears concerning "Black Republican" rule, the majority hesitated to support secession. After all, the Republicans had not committed a hostile act toward the South, and Lincoln had yet to assume the presidency. A cautious wait-and-see attitude on the part of the South struck most Tennesseans as the prudent course. In fact, shortly after Lincoln's election, the state leaders of both the Democratic and Constitutional Union parties urged Governor Isham Harris to call the legislature into session in the hope that that body could help organize a convention of Southern states to discuss the crisis. However, once the legislators had assembled in January 1861, Harris, a strong advocate of secession, proposed a state convention to decide if Tennessee should remain in the Union or join a new Southern republic. The legislature decided to leave that decision to the Tennessee voters, authorizing a February referendum on a convention and the election of delegates. In addition, Harris called on the legislature to adopt resolutions supporting his plan for five constitutional amendments that would forever secure Southern rights. The governor further dashed the hopes of moderates when he stated his belief that disunion could not be stopped and that Tennessee could not avoid a decision concerning its fate. "The work of alienation and disruption has gone so far," he declared, "that it will be extremely difficult, if not impossible, to arrest it; and before your adjournment, in all human probability, the only practical question for the state to determine, will be whether she will unite her fortunes with a Northern or Southern Confederacy." Harris further expressed his certainty that his fellow Tennesseans would choose the South.[18]

Harris was correct in his assertion that membership in the Union was now the key political question facing the state. Indeed, secession fever had quickly spread from the Deep South to Upper South states such as Tennessee. Loyalty to the Union proved to be the issue that led to the disintegration of the Whig-Democrat party system that had dominated state politics for twenty-five years. The *Knoxville Whig* summed up the situation when it declared, "Now let our Union people bring out able and true men, irrespective of old party associations. We have no parties but Union men and disunionists."[19]

While fear of encroaching Federal power and protection of slave property drove the Lower South from the Union, Upper South disunionists had other concerns. In Tennessee, fear of abolition could stir up secessionist support in counties with large slave populations such as those in Middle and West Tennessee. However, the potential loss of the extensive trade links with the Deep South sparked more widespread consternation. Some secessionists asserted that the Upper South could achieve greater prosperity in a new Southern republic. For example, the *Memphis Appeal* predicted that union with the Deep South would enable Tennessee to become "the chief manufacturer for the South." Disunionists further argued that the Upper South's secession could prevent a war by presenting the North with a strong united Southern front and that republican liberty could best be preserved in a Southern republic free from abolitionist demagogues.[20]

By late December, secession sentiment had become strong in substantial portions of Tennessee, especially in counties with large slave populations and Democratic tendencies. However, by mid-January, the secession wave had crested as coalitions of unionists began to preach the benefits of remaining in the old republic and the dangers inherent in joining a new Southern nation. Unionists pointed out that the Lower South's traditional support of free trade would be ruinous to the developing manufacturing interests of the state. In addition, echoing the traditional republican fear of tyranny, Tennessee unionists contended that secession was a conspiracy led by a slave-holding elite and designed to establish an aristocracy in a new Southern Confederacy. Finally, many unionists argued that secession and the war that would surely follow posed a greater threat to slavery than the Republican administration soon to take office in Washington. After all, Lincoln had assured slave owners he did not intend to interfere with slavery where it already existed. The chaos of an armed conflict, however, could destroy slavery.[21]

Upper South loyalists went on the offensive during the first two months of 1861, creating a groundswell of support for the Union. In East Tennessee a dedicated group of ex-Whigs and unionists, including attorneys Oliver P. Temple and John Fleming, newspaper editor William G. Brownlow, and Tennessee Congressman Horace Maynard, along with Democratic Senator and former Governor Andrew Johnson provided the leadership for a large unionist movement that overwhelmed the region's secessionist minority. Loyalists saturated East Tennessee with speakers, leaflets, and editorials imploring the region's inhabitants to stand behind the Union of their forefathers and warning of the antirepublican nature of a Southern nation ruled by a "slave aristocracy" determined to "overshadow and dishonor poor white men."[22]

When the votes of the February referendum were counted, Tennessee unionists had won an overwhelming victory. Although the statewide vote on the convention question was fairly close (69,387 to 57,798), votes for Union delegates accounted for over four-fifths of the total (88,803 to 24,749). The delegate vote clearly demonstrated that even if a convention had taken place, it would have been dominated by unionists. Of the three Grand Divisions, East Tennessee gave the strongest support to the loyalists, with over 80 percent of the voters rejecting the convention and approximately 85 percent voting for unionist delegates.[23]

Throughout the eight slaveholding states remaining in the Union that winter, loyalist support was strong. Kentucky, Delaware, and Maryland did not even consider holding conventions to discuss secession; North Carolina and Tennessee voters decided against conventions; and while Virginia, Arkansas, and Missouri called for conventions, voters elected a majority of unionist delegates.[24]

Many Northerners and Southern loyalists soon concluded that most Southerners, at least in the Upper South, were against secession and that the crisis facing the nation would soon resolve itself peacefully. However, the unionism of Tennessee and the rest of the Upper South was highly conditional. The continued loyalty of many unionists rested on the assumptions that Congress could devise an effective long-term solution to the slavery controversy and that the Lincoln administration would avoid any coercive actions against the seceded states. Moreover, the fragile loyalist coalition was not a true political party but a conglomeration of old Whigs and unionist Democrats, conservatives and moderates, slave owners and yeoman farmers. These diverse groups had only devotion to the Union in common, and without any other shared interests they could not develop a unifying party platform. Indeed, after the February vote, the loyalist coalition in Tennessee began to disintegrate. Decades of intense party rivalry made it difficult for old Whigs and Democrats

to continue to cooperate. In addition, in early March a squabble over the dis-
tribution of Federal patronage within Tennessee divided the loyalist coalition
along old party lines. Despite the fact that former Whigs made up the majority
of loyalists, the Lincoln administration curried the favor of unionist Democrats
by giving Andrew Johnson control of political appointments in the state. In an
effort to strengthen his own political position and retain links to the Democratic Party, Johnson ignored many Opposition office seekers and even supported a known secessionist as district attorney for East Tennessee.[25]

While Tennessee's loyalist coalition was splintering, the foundations upon
which conditional unionism stood were slowly crumbling. Upper South unionists believed that Congress would soon enact legislation or provide constitutional amendments safeguarding slavery and Southern rights, but this was not
to be the case. Even with the efforts of moderate or conciliatory Republicans,
led by Secretary of State–designate William H. Seward, President Lincoln and
the majority of his party refused to compromise on the issue of slavery in the
territories.

Despite the deadlock, Upper South unionists continued to hold out hope.
Reassured by Seward and the conciliatory Republicans that Lincoln would
maintain a "hands off" approach toward the seceded states, loyalists continued
to believe throughout late March and early April 1861 that "peaceful reunion
was possible."[26]

The Confederate attack on Fort Sumter in Charleston harbor on April
12 and Lincoln's subsequent call for seventy-five thousand volunteers to put
down the Southern "rebellion" ended any hope of a compromise. Although
a handful of die-hard Upper South loyalists continued to look for a peaceful
solution, most realized the only choice now left was to fight for the South's
independence or the Union's preservation.[27]

Most Tennessee loyalists felt they had been betrayed by Lincoln and the
Republicans and, therefore, now embraced the Confederate cause as their
own. Original and converted secessionists joined together to defend Southern
honor and republican government against the perceived oppression of a tyrannical federal government determined to subjugate them by force of arms.
Throughout Middle and West Tennessee, secession rallies were held. On the
evening of April 17, Governor Harris attended a public meeting in the capi-
tol where he informed the audience that he had just received the U.S.
Secretary of War's request for two regiments to help conquer the Rebels. Amid
cheers, the governor declared that "rather than sign such an order he would
cut his right arm from his body—rather than utter it he would tear his tongue
from its root. . . . If . . . this was treason, then before God he was a traitor." The
telegram the governor sent in response to the Secretary of War's request defi-

antly asserted that "Tennessee will not furnish a single man for coercion, but fifty thousand, if necessary, for the defense of our rights or those of our Southern brethren."[28]

The next day a group of former unionists led by John Bell published a circular that condemned Lincoln's attempt to coerce the South and declared the Union dissolved. On April 23, Bell gave a speech in Nashville in which he urged the South to action "against the unnecessary, aggressive, cruel, unjust wanton war which was being forced upon us."[29]

Secessionist leaders moved quickly to exploit the shift in public opinion caused by Fort Sumter. On April 25, only eleven days after the fort fell, the state legislature met in special session to consider taking the Volunteer State out of the Union. On May 6, the legislature declared Tennessee's independence from the United States. Anxious to demonstrate popular support for their actions, the legislators arranged for the state's Declaration of Independence to be submitted to a referendum scheduled for June 8. However, Governor Harris and the legislature, deciding not to wait for the formal public sanction of a vote, immediately began war preparations. On the same day it passed the Declaration, the legislature granted Governor Harris authority to create a state army of fifty-five thousand volunteers and authorized bonds and taxes to finance the mobilization. The next day, Tennessee signed a military alliance with the Confederacy and placed the state's military forces and defense under the direction of the Confederate president. Anticipating widespread public support of their actions, the governor and legislature had placed Tennessee into the Confederacy a full month before the people had the opportunity to voice their approval.[30]

While citizens in the rest of the state fell into the ranks of the secessionists, most East Tennesseans refused to participate in what they saw as an unjust war against the lawful national government. Brownlow spoke for the region when he declared that after having examined the situation he was for the "Stars and Stripes." Despite the fact that the June referendum was only a month away, East Tennessee loyalists believed that the unionist coalition could keep Tennessee in the Union. Surely, they thought, the people of Middle and West Tennessee would come to their senses and rise up in support of the Union cause when the time came.[31]

The immediate task of the unionist leaders of East Tennessee was to rally the region's faithful. While Horace Maynard, Thomas A. R. Nelson, and others canvassed the region, the unionist press led by Brownlow produced an incessant stream of propaganda. Local leaders organized meetings where hundreds and even thousands gathered to demonstrate their support for the Union. The speeches and writings of the unionist leaders struck a chord with most East

Tennesseans. Long accustomed to hearing about the many threats to liberty and republican government, East Tennesseans listened while loyalist leaders revealed secession to be an aristocratic plot designed to reduce the common folk to servitude in a great Southern Kingdom. In his Senate speeches, Andrew Johnson depicted the national crisis as a contest between democracy and aristocracy and labeled Confederate president Jefferson Davis a tyrant. Brownlow declared, "Let Tennessee go into this Empire of Cotton States, and all poor men will at once become the free Negroes of the Empire." He concluded that East Tennesseans "can never live in a Southern Confederacy and be made the hewers of wood and drawers of water for a set of aristocrats and overbearing tyrants." Adding weight to the conspiracy theory of the unionists was the manner in which secession was accomplished in Tennessee. Loyalists charged that Governor Harris and the legislature had established a despotism of their own by taking the state from the Union and allying with the Confederacy without first waiting for public approval.[32]

The perceived threat to republican liberty was not the only argument used by East Tennessee unionists to discourage voters from accepting the state's alliance with the Confederacy. Economic considerations also figured prominently in loyalist rhetoric. Because East Tennessee did not share the plantation economy of the Lower South and because most residents had not been engaged in the lucrative foodstuffs trade with the seceded states, unionists argued that the region had no incentive to support the South's bid for independence. Indeed, Brownlow's *Whig* asserted, "we have no interest in common with the Cotton States. We are a grain growing and stock raising people."[33]

With unionist leaders criss-crossing the region invoking visions of a tyrannical slave-owning aristocracy, the presence of large numbers of Confederate troops in East Tennessee could only add to the growing tension. East Tennessee unionists viewed the Confederates as occupation troops and proof of Southern tyranny; Rebel soldiers viewed the unionists as traitors. Confederate authorities attempted to avoid a clash with loyalists prior to the referendum, but restraining the soldiers proved difficult.[34]

Two incidents illustrate how close the tense situation came to exploding into large-scale violence. During a unionist rally in Knoxville on April 27, Andrew Johnson was addressing a crowd of supporters when two Confederate infantry companies and a military band marched toward the meeting. Believing that the approaching soldiers intended to break up the rally and perhaps seize Johnson, angry loyalists began to reach for their weapons. A bloody clash was averted when Colonel David H. Cummings, the future commander of the Nineteenth Tennessee, silenced the band and directed the Confederate procession away from the unionists.[35]

About a week later, a serious clash between Confederates and loyalists occurred at Strawberry Plains near Knoxville. Several thousand unionists had gathered on a farm adjacent to the tracks of the East Tennessee and Virginia Railroad. During the rally, a train carrying Confederate soldiers to Virginia passed by. Enraged by the loyalist gathering, a soldier on the train threw a stone at the speaker. Other soldiers seated on the roofs of the passing cars began to fire over the heads of the crowd, creating pandemonium. The unionists, many of whom were armed, fired back. Miraculously no one was injured, but the incident added to the growing animosity of the loyalists toward the Confederate cause.[36]

So great was this animosity that East Tennessee secessionists had a difficult time campaigning for the June vote. Trying desperately to convey a positive image of the Confederacy, local secessionists invited speakers from throughout the South to their meetings. Former Mississippi Governor Henry S. Foote and arch-secessionist William Yancey of Alabama joined with influential Tennessee Whigs such as Gustavas A. Henry and John Bell in extolling the virtues of the new Confederacy and labeling Lincoln a tyrant. Despite the stature of these men, they could not compete with the influence of East Tennessee unionists such as Johnson, Nelson, and Maynard. While secessionists found significant support in the southern counties of East Tennessee and in the towns and villages located along the East Tennessee and Virginia and East Tennessee and Georgia railways, the rest of the region remained adamantly loyal.[37]

The East Tennessee unionists were, however, beginning to realize that their loyalty to the old Union was not matched by the rest of the state. Therefore, in late May, a week prior to the election, loyalists convened in Knoxville to discuss their options if the vote for separation should go against them. The convention passed several resolutions condemning secession as illegal and declaring Governor Harris and the legislature guilty of conspiracy and extralegal use of power. The body then adjourned, agreeing to meet after the election if necessary.[38]

The results of the June referendum stunned East Tennessee unionists. Across the state, almost 70 percent of the voters approved the state's secession. Slaveholding Tennesseans of all sections voted overwhelmingly for secession, while nonslaveholders in both West and Middle Tennessee did the same. Only in East Tennessee did a majority reject secession. Although the region's unionist vote fell from around 80 percent in February to 69 percent in June, it was nonetheless a forceful affirmation of loyalty; voters had repudiated secession by a better than two-to-one margin. Indeed, only six of the region's twenty-nine counties (Meigs, Monroe, Polk, Rhea, Sequatchie, and Sullivan) gave majorities for secession. Nevertheless, the statewide vote carried Tennessee into the Confederacy.[39]

Convinced by the republican rhetoric of their unionist leaders that Confederate rule was tantamount to tyranny, the region's loyalists could not reconcile themselves to the election results. Nine days after the June vote, loyalist leaders convened in Greeneville to decide on a course of action. After heated debate between radicals such as Nelson and Brownlow, who advocated rebellion against the state, and conservatives led by Temple, who proposed petitioning the state legislature for separate statehood, the convention opted for the conservative approach. The General Assembly politely listened to the convention's request but refused to act upon it. East Tennessee would remain part of a state and of a nation that it had rejected.[40]

While the state and Confederate authorities hoped that the loyalists of the eastern counties would now acquiesce in secession, this was not to be the case. The region's unionists would never willingly submit to Confederate rule, and East Tennessee would soon be plunged into a state of violence and bloodshed that would not end until long after the final shots of the Civil War. Indeed, so intense was the devotion of East Tennessee unionists that over thirty thousand would join the ranks of the Federal army.[41]

This willingness to take up arms against fellow Tennesseans and Southerners clearly demonstrates the distinctiveness of East Tennessee. If the northwestern counties of Virginia can be discounted due to their proximity to the North, then eastern Tennessee was undoubtedly the Confederacy's great aberration. The uniqueness of the region was the result of several interrelated factors. First, there was East Tennessee's distinctive economy, a product of its geographic isolation. Predominantly a region of small subsistence farms and limited slavery, East Tennessee had little in common with the slave-based plantation economy that dominated most of the rest of the South. East Tennessee's distinctiveness also derived from its Whiggish political heritage that remained strong long after the Democratic Party had become the dominant force in Southern politics. This Whig Party and its leadership would form the core of the region's unionist dissenters. Finally and most importantly, East Tennessee's rejection of the Confederacy can be linked to the unionists' belief that such a government, dominated by large slave-holding aristocrats, threatened republican liberty—the very soul of the great American democratic experiment. For the loyalists of East Tennessee, the protection of republicanism required a rebellion against the tyranny of Governor Harris and Jefferson Davis.

Ironically, East Tennessee's secessionist minority also viewed the coming struggle in terms of republicanism's struggle against tyranny. For the Confederates of the region, however, Lincoln was the tyrant to be feared. Viewing the president's call for volunteers to fight against the South as tantamount to military despotism, many East Tennesseans joined their fellow Southerners in abandoning the old Union in favor of a new Southern republic that would remain true to the principles of the founding fathers. It would be in defense of these principles and this new republic that the men of the Nineteenth Tennessee would rush to arms.

2

"Southern Independence Is My Sentiment. Liberty or Death"

East Tennessee Confederates and the Men of the Nineteenth

"The Hawkins Boys took their departure from Rogersville for Knoxville. Sad and gloomy." So wrote Charlotte Phipps, a twenty-year-old Hawkins
County schoolteacher, on May 11, 1861. The Hawkins Boys she mentions in
her journal was the local volunteer company organized in response to the crisis provoked by the fall of Fort Sumter and Lincoln's call for troops to put
down the insurrection. When the company left for Knoxville, the mobilization center for East Tennessee, Charlotte's younger brother William and her
fiancé Daniel Miller, a twenty-three-year-old lawyer, were in its ranks. Anxiety
over the safety of her loved ones, as well as disappointment over yet another
postponement of her wedding, left Charlotte depressed.[1]

A week later, Charlotte's melancholy had not faded: "Times are lonely.
. . . I wish the wars were all over and my boys would come home. . . . Papa
has gone to Sinking Creek. Wish he would bring some letters for some of us.
May Heaven's choicest blessings be with my absent friends."[2] Her fiancé was
equally despondent. In a letter to Charlotte written two days after his arrival
in Knoxville, he declared:

> Well, My Love, this is a time that tries Men's souls and I am
> certain that mine was tried and that too to its utmost extent when
> I had to part with one that is dearer to me than all earth besides,
> but I hope to see you again and be happy. The little Bible that I
> received from you I will read and try to obey its injunctions and
> those that are written in the front part of it. My Dear, I can't write
> much on account of the noise that is around me, but when the

17

tug of war comes, remember that there is one in the Service that
thinks of you and will think of you in the heat of the battle. All I
have to say is may God bless you and preserve you is my whole
desire. The drum is beating and I must go.[3]

Daniel Miller was not the only East Tennessean to hear the drum's beat call-
ing him to the defense of his native South. Throughout the hollows, coves,
and villages of the region, other Daniels and other Charlottes said their fare-
wells and prepared to weather the coming storm. The long-anticipated conflict was now at hand.

By the end of May, with the referendum on independence still over a week
away, The Hawkins Boys joined some twenty other East Tennessee volunteer
companies at a makeshift military base on the old fairgrounds two miles outside of Knoxville. The encampment was named Camp Cummings in honor
of David H. Cummings, a prosperous farmer and attorney who split his time
between Eagle Bend (his thirty-five-hundred-acre Anderson County plantation) and his practice in Knoxville. A well-known and respected citizen,
Cummings had worked hard to maintain the peace between the region's unionist majority and its Confederate sympathizers in the wake of Fort Sumter's fall
and Tennessee's Declaration of Independence. His efforts had earned the admiration of many, including influential loyalists such as Oliver P. Temple and
William G. Brownlow. Indeed, Brownlow, a rabid antisecessionist, went so far
as to describe Cummings as "a gentleman, an honorable man, and a soldier as
brave as he is generous." Despite his conciliatory manner, Cummings was an
ardent Confederate and viewed Lincoln as an "infamous scoundrel" and tyrant
and the whole Republican leadership as no better than the common criminals
he had regularly prosecuted as a district attorney. Cummings's reputation, his
secessionist beliefs, and his experience as a lieutenant colonel of the Second
Tennessee Volunteer Infantry Regiment in the Mexican War thrust him into
a position of leadership in the mobilization of the region's Confederate troops.[4]

Cummings's efforts were directed by a fellow East Tennessean, Brigadier
General Richard Caswell, who commanded the newly established Military
Department of East Tennessee—one of three departments created by Governor
Isham Harris and corresponding roughly to the state's traditional Grand
Divisions. At the same time that Harris established the military departments,
he also created the Provisional Army of Tennessee to protect the state from the
anticipated Yankee invasion. The governor charged each department commander with the defense of his region as well as the organization of regiments
from volunteer companies for the Provisional Army. Working from his headquarters in Knoxville, Caswell and his staff, which included Chattanooga busi-

nessman David M. Key and former state representative James W. Gillespie, managed to organize two regiments by the end of spring.[5]

The first regiment, the Third Tennessee Volunteer Infantry, was formed on May 29 at Camp Cummings and placed under the command of the elected Colonel John C. Vaughn. Like Cummings, Vaughn was an influential citizen and a passionate defender of the South. After witnessing the surrender of Fort Sumter, he had returned to his native Monroe County, where he raised one of the first volunteer companies in East Tennessee. Vaughn's company and the rest of his regiment were shortly placed under Confederate authority. On June 2, still six days prior to the statewide referendum, the unit left the depot at Knoxville bound for Virginia, where it joined General Joseph E. Johnston's Army of the Shenandoah.[6]

Nine days later, on June 11, Caswell and his staff combined ten of the remaining volunteer companies into a second East Tennessee regiment—the Nineteenth Tennessee Volunteer Infantry. The men composing this unit came primarily from eight counties clustered in the upper and lower portions of the region. Chattanooga furnished most of the men for Company A (The Hamilton Grays) and Company I (The Marsh Blues). Men from Washington County filled the ranks of Company B, and the town of Blountville in Sullivan County provided the bulk of Company C (The Blountville Guards) and Company G. Rhea County produced the men of Company D (The Gillespie Guards), while Company E (The Knoxville Guards/Grays) was made up of men from Knox and surrounding counties. Company F came from Polk County; Company H (The Milton Guards) hailed from McMinn County; and Company K (Daniel Miller and his comrades) were from Hawkins County. The men of these companies elected David Cummings colonel of the regiment, and he began to drill his troops immediately in anticipation of a move to Virginia.[7]

Despite the best efforts of Caswell, Cummings, Vaughn, and their compatriots, however, Confederate volunteering in East Tennessee in the aftermath of Lincoln's call for war was not extensive. The two thousand or so men composing Vaughn's and Cummings's regiments represented a meager 13 percent of the disunionist vote in East Tennessee in the June referendum. Yet, by the end of the summer, with the Battle of Manassas having failed to decide the conflict, more and more Confederate volunteer units mobilized in East Tennessee. By the end of the year four additional regiments of infantry, three battalions of cavalry, and three batteries of artillery were organized. While the six thousand or so troops composing these new units still did not constitute an overwhelming display of martial strength for the Confederacy, taken along with Vaughn's and Cummings's original commands, they did represent over 50 percent of the region's pro-independence vote. East Tennessee's disunionists increasingly took up arms and demonstrated a willingness to fight for the South.[8]

But who were these disunionists and why were they willing to fight? What made them different from their loyalist neighbors? Such questions have long been ignored or relegated to the background of East Tennessee's history because of the overwhelming support for the Union in the region. Only recently have scholars begun to examine Confederate support in the Appalachian South with an eye toward understanding its origins. The question of why certain East Tennesseans chose to defy the region's unionist majority, risking their lives and fortunes in pursuit of Southern independence, lacks a simple answer. Indeed, no single answer covers every case. An examination of the historical record, including the background of the officers and men in the Nineteenth Tennessee, reveals a complex web of economic, political, social, and ideological influences.[9]

One of the more striking patterns that emerges from such an examination is the link between town residence and Confederate sympathy. Voting returns for the June 8 referendum reveal that nearly every East Tennessee township favored separation or at least exhibited significant support for the measure. This was especially true for county seats and towns located along the major avenues of transportation. What lay behind such urban support? The answer according to Oliver Temple was the newly constructed rail lines traversing the region from Virginia to Georgia. Temple maintained that the troop trains from the Deep South passing through East Tennessee on their way to Virginia triggered "the outpouring of all the disloyal people shouting and cheering," while secessionist speakers stopping at depots along the way succeeded in "stirring up the people." This turned the East Tennessee lines into "a continuous flame of secession fire."[10]

Temple's friend William G. Brownlow was closer to the mark when he pointed out the link between the region's urban trade and Confederate sympathy—a connection he labeled "the secret spring" of secession. Towns were the commercial centers of East Tennessee. It was there that the market farmers sold their crops to the agents of Deep South planters and commodity dealers and traded with local merchants. With the secession of the Lower South, the markets for most of the region's surplus produce now lay within the Confederacy. All those involved in East Tennessee agribusiness might be ruined financially, unless the region also joined the new Southern republic.[11]

The farmers, merchants, and lawyers tied to this trade network found additional incentive for secession with the end of Midwestern competition. Lying within the bounds of another country, the farms of the upper Mississippi and Ohio Valley would now be linked solely to Northern markets, leaving areas such as East Tennessee to provide for the Confederacy. Not surprisingly, the men most associated with Lower South trade became strong advocates for secession. In his socioeconomic analysis of East Tennessee Confederate leadership, Todd Groce discovered that 80 percent of his sample group lived in an urban area, while 93 percent lived on or near a major avenue of transportation, with over half of those residing along the region's rail lines. Moreover, Groce found that 56 percent of his sample were merchants or lawyers or other members of the commercial or professional classes.[12]

East Tennessee's first Confederate regimental commanders, David Cummings (a noted attorney) and John C. Vaughn (a prosperous hotel owner and merchant), exemplified these urban classes and their commitment to the South. Likewise, an analysis of the men composing the rank and file of the Nineteenth Tennessee confirms the essentially urban nature of Confederate sympathy. By using a variety of modern topographical maps, antebellum civil district maps, and census records, one can discern that the majority of the men resided in or near a town or village (often a county seat). Additionally, these towns and villages lay along the region's major transportation routes.[13]

The men of Companies A and I came mostly from Chattanooga, a regional rail hub. The men of Company B came primarily from the Washington County seat of Jonesboro, a rail town, while Companies C and G were organized in the Sullivan County seat of Blountville, five miles away from the East Tennessee and Virginia Railroad. The men of Company E came principally from Knoxville, a regional rail center, and Concord, also a rail town. Men from the areas around Ducktown and Benton, located only eight miles from the East Tennessee and Georgia Railroad, constituted most of Company F. Finally, the recruits composing Company D came primarily from the various towns and villages of Rhea County—especially Washington (the county seat), located on the Tennessee River, a longtime regional trade route.[14]

Even though secessionist support was strongest in the urban centers and along transportation routes, it was not exclusively an urban phenomenon. While Company H from McMinn County and Company K from Hawkins County were organized in their respective county seats of Athens (a rail town) and Rogersville, each company's membership was scattered throughout its county. Indeed, all the companies in the Nineteenth Tennessee recruited heavily from rural areas. Nonetheless, the enlistment pattern of the regiment demonstrates that East Tennessee's Confederates lived predominantly in and around the region's urban areas and transportation avenues.[15]

This pattern was especially true of the officer corps. Virtually every captain and field grade officer who could be located in the census records resided in or near a town and a major transportation artery. Not surprisingly, these men, like other East Tennessee Confederate leaders, came largely from the professional/ commercial classes. In addition, many of the lieutenants, noncommissioned officers, and enlisted men of the Nineteenth belonged to such classes. In all, over 19 percent of those in the regimental sample who listed an occupation came from the professional or commercial rank. They included physicians, brokers, merchants, jewelers, lawyers, and druggists, as well as the clerks and salesmen who worked for such men. Even among the regiment's skilled and unskilled laborers, significant numbers of townsfolk could be found.[16]

Because Knoxville and Chattanooga were the largest towns, the primary market centers, and the major railroad junctions for East Tennessee, it is not surprising that the companies organized in those towns (A, I, and E) had the largest proportion of men in urban-based employment. The regimental sample reveals that approximately 36 percent of the Knox and Hamilton County recruits were engaged in commercial or professional pursuits, while many more engaged in skilled and unskilled trades.[17]

Obviously, not all of these men, not even the majority of urban residents, participated in the Deep South commodity trade. However, joining the Confederacy offered benefits for the broad range of townsfolk not engaged in that enterprise. Chattanoogans, for example, desired to turn their small railroad junction into a major industrial and commercial center for the Upper South, but a severe capital shortage and indebtedness to Northern banks stood in their way. The birth of the Confederacy may have threatened the existing trade network that ran along the town's rail lines, but it also offered Chattanoogans a chance to renew their hopes. Citing Chattanooga's central location and excellent railroad connections, civic leaders and businessmen offered their town to the Confederacy as the new Southern capital or at least as a site for armories and munitions plants. Additionally, after April 1861, when the Tennessee General Assembly prohibited the collection of debts owed to Northern creditors, and later, when Confederate Congressional acts suspended such payments, the commercial classes of Chattanooga had more reasons to support the cause of Southern independence. In fact, William G. Brownlow viewed indebtedness as a major factor in Confederate support not only in Chattanooga but also throughout the region, declaring that "[w]herever a merchant is found largely indebted to the North . . . they [sic] are throwing up their hats for Jeff Davis." With the shackles of Northern indebtedness removed, Chattanoogans hoped for a bright future in the new republic.[18]

Likewise, other East Tennessee urbanites such as arch-secessionist J. Austin Sperry, editor of the *Knoxville Daily Register,* believed that new economic possibilities awaited the whole region once East Tennessee joined the Confederacy. Sperry depicted the East Tennessee of the future as "the Paradise

TABLE 1

Original Command of the Nineteenth Tennessee Infantry Regiment

Co.	Name	Rank	Age	County	Occupation	Wealth	Slaves
F & S*	David H. Cummings	Colonel	42	Anderson	Lawyer/Farmer	$64,000	18
F & S	Francis M. Walker	Lt. Colonel	33	Hamilton	Lawyer	15,000	2
F & S	Abe Fulkerson	Major	?	Washington	?	?	?
F & S	V. Q. Johnson	Adjutant	31	Hamilton	Clerk	20,000	11
F & S	Henry M. Doak	Sgt.-Major	19	Montgomery	Student	14,790	4
F & S	Joseph E. Dulany	Surgeon	30	Sullivan	Physician	25,000	12
F & S	Samuel Carson	Asst. Surgeon	25	Washington	Physician	2,985	1
F & S	Addison D. Taylor	Quarter Master	40	Hamilton	Merchant	10,800	1
F & S	David Sullins	Chaplain	31	Washington	Minister	0	0
A	John D. Powell	Captain	?	Hamilton	Merchant	?	?
B	Zadoc T. Willett	Captain	?	Washington	Student	?	?
C	James P. Snapp	Captain	35	Sullivan	Lawyer	3,150	0
D	Warner E. Colville	Captain	42	Rhea	Merchant	36,000	5
E	John W. Paxton	Captain	36	Knox	Physician	13,000	11
F	John H. Hannah	Captain	22	Polk	Post Master	0	0
G	Abraham L. Gammon	Captain	53	Sullivan	Mail Agent	5,100	3
H	William H. Lowry Jr.	Captain	34	McMinn	Lawyer	6,000	2
I	Thomas H. Walker	Captain	22	Hamilton	Student	0	0
K	Carrick W. Heiskell	Captain	23	Hawkins	Lawyer	19,400	2
MEAN			32			$14,702	4.5

Note: *F & S = Field and Staff.

of the South," foreseeing new mines, resorts, and businesses springing up throughout the region.[19]

Most East Tennessee secessionists, however, probably thought that their region's greatest opportunities for economic development lay in the traditional Deep South commodity trade. A comparison of the East Tennessee counties voting strongly for and strongly against separation suggests a relationship between secessionism and agricultural market production. Secessionist counties tended to contain larger, more valuable farms and to produce more cash crops (especially wheat) than did the pro-Union counties. An examination of the men of the Nineteenth supports the contention that market production was common among the region's rural Confederates.[20]

Of the 215 farms operated by men in the regimental sample, over 73 percent were larger than the regional average of 80 improved acres per farm. Indeed, the mean for the sample was 163.3 improved acres—over twice the regional average. Moreover, while only slightly more than 6 percent of East Tennessee's farms were 200 or more improved acres in size, almost 33 percent of the sample's farms were that large, a figure comparable to that of the plantation district of West Tennessee. Additionally, the sample's average farm value of $6,661 was almost two-and-a-half times the regional average of $2,899. Some members of the regiment or their families had agricultural holdings that were extraordinarily large and valuable by East Tennessee standards. For instance, Alexander Ish, the father of Private Benjamin Ish of Company B, owned a 678-acre Blount County farm with a value of $17,000, while Private Frederic A. Lenoir's father Albert owned a 1,214-acre Roane County farm valued at $24,000. Cornelius Miller, the father of Sergeant Willie B. Miller of Company K, owned a 4,000-acre farm in Hawkins County valued at $34,000. Colonel Cummings's 3,500-acre Anderson County property was valued at $45,000. One of the most valuable farms in the sample belonged to Alfred E. Jackson, the father of Sergeant James P. T. Jackson of Company B. This huge plantation in Washington County, consisting of more than 8,000 acres, was worth $89,400.[21]

Such large and valuable farms were clearly geared to market production. They produced great amounts of surplus crops for Deep South consumption. An examination of the men of the Nineteenth suggests the extent of such production. In Sullivan County, of the 104 households containing members of the Nineteenth, 87 included persons engaged in agricultural pursuits, and of those 87 households, 65 (74.7 percent) were producing a marketable agricultural surplus—namely swine and wheat, but also dairy products, honey, and some tobacco. The other 22 households contained farm or day laborers who most likely worked on the larger farms of their neighbors.[22]

This link between Confederate sympathy and market production was not unique to the regiment's Sullivan countians. In Washington, Rhea, McMinn, and Hawkins Counties, 44.7 percent, 46.7 percent, 71.7 percent, and 80 percent, respectively, of sample households that engaged in agriculture yielded marketable surpluses. Even in Knox and Hamilton Counties, where agricultural households were a minority, 58.3 percent and 40.7 percent, respectively, of those households generated a surplus. Only in Polk County, where mining was predominant, can a surplus-producing household not be found. Outside the eight counties that produced most of the regiment's members, the story was the same: 24 of 53 agricultural households (45.3 percent) raised a marketable surplus. In all, 211 of 372 agricultural households in the sample (56.7 percent) produced notable surpluses.[23]

While some surpluses were small (i.e., only a few dozen bushels of wheat or some extra hogs), others were extraordinary for the region. Benjamin Ish's father cultivated over four hundred bushels of wheat and close to a ton of butter in 1860, while Frederic Lenoir's family farm yielded six hundred bushels of wheat and raised over one hundred swine. James P. T. Jackson's father grew more than ten thousand pounds of tobacco in 1860, making him one of the largest producers in East Tennessee. While East Tennessee farmers grew many different surplus crops, wheat, the most valuable cash crop, was cultivated on virtually every farm engaged in market agriculture. In Washington County, for example, the family farm of Thomas D. Burson, a private in Company B, produced five hundred bushels of wheat in 1860; the neighboring farm of Private Henry Bowers raised over eight hundred bushels, making it the second largest wheat producer in the district. The family of Private James H. Morrow also grew eight hundred bushels in 1860, leading their district of Washington County. Willie B. Miller's father Cornelius generated an astonishing sixteen hundred bushels of wheat in 1860, making him not only one of the largest producers in Hawkins County but also the region. The largest wheat producer in the sample and perhaps the largest in all of East Tennessee was Colonel David Cummings, who grew forty-one hundred bushels at Eagle Bend in 1860.[24]

Closely tied to cash-crop production was slavery. Areas of strong secessionist support had experienced the greatest increase in slaves during the 1850s. While the number of slaves in East Tennessee as a whole had increased by about 20 percent between 1850 and 1860, the increase was 30 percent in counties giving 50 percent or more of their vote to independence. Although the number of slaves and masters in East Tennessee was still quite small when compared to the region's population as a whole (approximately 9 percent and 10 percent, respectively), the greater increase of slaves in counties holding large numbers of secessionists is significant.[25]

An examination of slave ownership among members of the Nineteenth offers further evidence of the connection between slaveholding and secessionism. Most of the members of the regiment came from the counties that gave strong support to separation and that had experienced the greatest increase in slave numbers over the previous decade. While only 10 percent of East Tennessee households owned slaves, over 16 percent of the regimental households did. Additionally, while the regional average was five slaves per master, the average slaveholder in the Nineteenth owned nine. Moreover, of the 87 slave-owning households in the regimental sample, 7 (8.1 percent) had 20 or more bondsmen, making the household head a planter. This figure is greater than that (3.1 percent) for all East Tennessee slaveholders who fell within this class. Additionally, 6 more regimental households had over 15 bondsmen each, close to planter status.[26]

Not only were planter households overrepresented among the men of the Nineteenth, but also these households included some of the largest slaveholders in East Tennessee. For example, Robert P. Rhea, the father of Private Robert J. Rhea of Company G, owned 32 slaves, making him the largest master in Sullivan County. Willie B. Miller's father Cornelius, who owned 29 bondsmen, was the fourth largest holder in Hawkins County. Alexander Ish owned 35 slaves, making him not only the largest slaveholder in the sample but also the largest owner in Blount County, a loyalist stronghold; and Albert Lenoir was one of the largest holders in Roane County, another staunchly unionist county. For these two households, commitment to market production for the Deep South appears to have been a stronger influence than local politics or neighborhood bonds.[27]

Note that the census figures on slave ownership may not express adequately an individual's dedication to the institution. For example, the 1860 census shows that the household of David Cummings held 18 slaves, a substantial number for East Tennessee, yet the investment of the Cummings family in black slavery went even deeper. Cummings's brother Robert of Whitehall Plantation in Lachute, Louisiana, was one of the largest slaveholders in that state (he had 111 bondsmen). Moreover, families that did not own slaves could "rent" them. There is specific evidence of such slave renting in McMinn County, where the census taker in 1860 exceeded instructions by listing renters as well as owners of slaves; the owners and renters included many of the families of the men of the Nineteenth. Analysis of the sample reveals a strong connection between slave ownership and market production. Every sample household owning slaves and engaging in agriculture produced a surplus; the greater the number of slaves, the larger the surplus.[28]

The economic interests and resources of these secessionist market farmers and their urban counterparts made them prosperous. East Tennessee Confederates as a group were much wealthier than the region's unionists, who were in many cases isolated farmers with little or no access to outside markets. Some historians have gone so far as to characterize the conflict between East Tennessee Rebels and loyalists as a "class struggle" between aristocratic merchants and planters on one hand and yeoman farmers on the other. While such a characterization is an oversimplification, there were clear class differences between the two sides.[29]

In examining The Tennessee Civil War Veterans' Questionnaires, historian Peter Wallenstein discovered that "an absolute majority" of East Tennessee unionist soldiers who completed a questionnaire came from poor families owning little or no property, especially slave property. Wallenstein also found that the vast majority of East Tennessee slaveholders who answered a questionnaire supported the Confederacy, as did the nonslaveholding farmers with other extensive property. While exceptions existed, Wallenstein concluded that "the lower third or half, or even two-thirds of the social order may have supplied more manpower for the Federal army than for the Confederate."[30]

Walter Lynn Bates's socioeconomic examination of the Third East Tennessee Volunteer Infantry Regiment, U.S.A., likewise documents class differences between East Tennessee unionists and Confederates. Bates found that the men composing this regiment were mostly poor, nonslaveowning small farmers from mountainous areas of East Tennessee. Such men were probably not engaged in market production nor were they likely to be in the future. Their vision of East Tennessee and its economic future bore little resemblance to that of the region's Confederates.[31]

Comparing the men of the Third East Tennessee to those of the Nineteenth Tennessee suggests some of the socioeconomic differences separating the region's loyalists and Rebels. For example, 27.4 percent of the Union regiment's men were over thirty years of age, while only 19.5 percent of the Nineteenth's men were that old. These figures support Todd Groce's idea of a generation gap. Groce maintains that the older citizens of East Tennessee feared that their region's political and economic influence was being eclipsed by that of both Middle and Western Tennessee. Additionally, the poor subsistence farmers of East Tennessee came to view the wealthy planter class of those other regions as a threat. However, East Tennessee's younger urban elite and commercial farmers perceived no threat from the Middle and West Tennessee agribusinessmen and sought to emulate their success through closer ties to the Deep South via the new railroads of the region.[32]

The plausibility of Groce's thesis of a gap in perception based on age is strengthened by the fact that several of East Tennessee's unionist leaders had sons who supported the Southern cause. For example, both Frederick Heiskell and Thomas A. R. Nelson had sons who joined the Nineteenth. These two instances may have been simple cases of youthful rebellion, but other such occurrences throughout the region as well as the overall age differences between Rebels and loyalists suggest a perceptual divergence concerning East Tennessee's economic future within the Confederacy.[33]

In addition to age differences, there was a definite educational disparity between East Tennessee unionists and Confederates. Bates found an illiteracy rate of 22.3 percent in a sample of the Third Tennessee—a rate higher than the Union army's average of 12 to 18 percent and the state's average of 14.5 percent for males above twenty years of age. The 1860 census classified only 29 of 602 (4.8 percent) of the Nineteenth's men as illiterate. This astonishingly low figure is supported by the work of other historians such as Fred Bailey, who found East Tennessee Confederates to be better educated than their unionist counterparts—primarily because of the Rebels' greater affluence.[34]

While age variances and literacy hint at differences in wealth, an examination of real and personal property held by members of the two regiments reveals the true extent of the economic divergence. The average household in Bates's sample held $1,960 in real and $974 in personal property. The average for the Nineteenth Tennessee was $2,992 in real and $2,711 in personal. The difference in real property, in particular, bespeaks an enormous difference in lifestyle. It is little wonder, then, that the region's unionists and later historians spoke of a "class war." Indeed, when the property (both real and personal) of the Nineteenth's members and/or their families is compared to that of East Tennesseans as a whole, one is struck by just how wealthy these Confederates were. Compared to the regional average, the sample families held 123 percent greater real wealth and 121 percent greater personal wealth. The total wealth of the sample—$3,039,873—exceeded the total wealth of fifteen of East Tennessee's thirty-one counties in 1860; in fact, in none of the region's thirty-one counties did the averages of real, personal, or aggregate wealth exceed the sample's averages.[35]

Note, however, that there were great variations of wealth within the Nineteenth. The bulk of the sample's property was held by a relatively small number of households. For example, among the Hamilton County members, 10 households (15 percent of the county sample) held 81.7 percent of the total wealth for that county's sample. In Sullivan County, 10 households (9.5 percent of the county sample) held 62.5 percent of the total; in Hawkins County, 3 households (6.5 percent of the county sample) held 39.7 percent of the total;

and in Rhea County, 7 households (9.7 percent of the county sample) held 67 percent of the total.[36]

These figures refute the notion that all East Tennessee Confederates belonged to the elite classes. The majority of the men in the Nineteenth Tennessee sample actually held modest amounts of property or none at all. Of the 533 households in the sample, 335 (62.9 percent—almost two-thirds) held less than the regional average of aggregate wealth. In fact, these households were so poor that they bring the median aggregate wealth for the entire group of 1861 recruits down to a mere $650.[37]

While protection of slave property, market production, and commercial development offered clear economic reasons for the richest one-third of the Nineteenth's men to support the Confederacy, what motivated the bottom two-thirds? This is an often-asked and much-explored question in Southern history and Civil War studies. The great majority of the men who fought, shed their blood, and gave their lives for Southern independence were nonslave-holding, noncommercial farmers from the middling or lower ranks of society. What compelled these men to make such sacrifices?[38]

In the Nineteenth's case, the factors influencing the common soldiers can be grouped into three categories: the economic and political influence of the elite, community pressures, and patriotism. But before these can be explored, two things must be noted. First, the three factors are to a certain degree inter-related; second, the last two factors influenced the elite as well as the common men.

Like the rest of the South, every community in East Tennessee contained one or more established families whose early settlement, vast land holdings, and greater educational opportunities had brought them wealth and given them influence over their neighbors. The clerks, tenants, and laborers who filled the ranks of the Nineteenth Tennessee and other Confederate regiments were tied to this elite by bonds of economic patronage. An alliance for Southern independence between the rich and the less affluent made perfect sense to both parties. While the elite hoped to protect and expand their economic ties to the Lower South, their tenants and employees and humble neighbors hoped to secure their livelihood and perhaps build a better future for themselves and their families in the Confederacy.[39]

But what about the yeoman farmers and artisans who made up the bulk of the regiment? They were not tied to the elite by economic bonds. Why did they fight? For many small, independent farmers, access to the Lower South's foodstuff markets, albeit on a small scale, proved an inducement to enlist in the Confederate cause. Likewise, artisans in the region's small urban centers may have envisioned a more prosperous future for themselves as the region grew in importance to the new Southern nation. Such economic considerations are quite plausible and similar to those in other areas of the upland South. However, perhaps stronger motivating factors were the elites' political influence, Southern patriotism, and a desire to defend the local community.[40]

The lower and middling classes traditionally looked to the wealthy and educated for guidance on state and national issues. Therefore, the large-scale farmers, merchants, and lawyers who composed the local elite not only controlled their community's major agricultural and commercial enterprises but also provided political leadership to the deferential populace.[41]

In the crisis of 1861, pro-Confederate members of this elite took the lead in organizing their neighbors into the volunteer companies that formed the Nineteenth Tennessee. For example, Abraham Looney Gammon, who organized and captained Company G, hailed from a well-known and influential family. When Gammon represented Sullivan County in the Thirty-Second General Assembly, he was following a family tradition. His father, George Gammon, a prosperous merchant, had served as a state senator while his grandfather, Richard Gammon, also a merchant, had not only served as a representative in the Third and Fourth General Assemblies but had also represented Sullivan County in the state constitutional convention of 1796. Almost certainly, Abraham Gammon used the power and prestige of his family to help fill the ranks of his company.[42]

Gammon was aided in his endeavor by a distant relative, Samuel Rhea, who was one of the leading merchants of Blountville and whose son James served as Gammon's first lieutenant. The Rhea family could trace its Sullivan County roots to John Rhea, an Irish-born lawyer who settled in East Tennessee in 1778. Like Abraham Gammon's grandfather, Rhea had served as a member of the first Tennessee constitutional convention. He also served in the House during the First and Second General Assemblies and went on to hold a variety of local, state, and national offices—including nine terms as a U.S. congressman.[43]

Another prominent Sullivan countian and one of the leading attorneys of Blountville, James P. Snapp, organized Company C. He was aided by his friend and roommate Charles St. John, another distinguished member of the local bar, and by William Gammon, a wealthy Blountville merchant whose son William Jr. served as sergeant in Company C.[44]

In Hawkins County, the situation was much the same. Carrick White Heiskell, who organized Company K, came from a prominent family. His father Frederick had been a noted newspaper editor and a state senator, as had his brother Joseph. Joseph Heiskell would also serve two terms as an East Tennessee representative in the Confederate Congress. Carrick Heiskell's uncle William Heiskell and cousin Samuel Gordon both served in the General Assembly.[45]

Another prominent Hawkins County family that played a leading role in forming the Nineteenth was the Powells of Rogersville. Robert D. Powell, a newspaper editor, served Captain Carrick W. Heiskell as first lieutenant of Company K. His brother Samuel served as second lieutenant and another brother, Thomas, only eighteen years old, joined as a private. The Powell brothers' father, George Rutledge Powell, was a banker worth over eight thousand dollars. He had served in the Twenty-First General Assembly prior to holding the local offices of circuit court clerk and clerk and master of the Chancery Court. The brothers' uncle, Samuel Powell, also served in the General Assembly and was instrumental in organizing the Twenty-Ninth Tennessee Infantry Regiment, a unit he also commanded. The Powell family's tradition of political service could be traced back even further, to the brothers' grandfather, also named Samuel, who served as a Tennessee Supreme Court justice and a member of Congress, and to their great-grandfather, General George Rutledge, who was a member of the Tennessee Constitutional Convention of 1796 and later a member of the General Assembly.[46]

The most influential Knox County Confederate associated with the organization of the Nineteenth was noted physician, philanthropist, and secessionist leader John W. Paxton. He recruited and captained the Knoxville Grays.[47]

Warren E. Colville, a wealthy merchant, organized the first of Rhea County's Confederate volunteer companies and was subsequently elected captain of the unit. In addition to being one of the leading citizens of the town of Washington and overseeing a personal fortune of $35,000, Colville held local political posts including county trustee. Colville's third lieutenant (or ensign) was Samuel Josiah Abner Frazier, who came from a distinguished legal family. Frazier, who was valedictorian of his class at East Tennessee University in 1860, had just begun his study of law when the war came. His father, Samuel Frazier, a prominent lawyer and one of the pioneer settlers of Rhea County, had served as a district attorney for more than twenty-one years. Moreover, Samuel J. A. Frazier's great-grandfather was a Revolutionary War veteran, a prominent member of the 1796 state constitutional convention, state senator in the first three General Assemblies, and a district attorney. Lieutenant Frazier's family also included a great uncle (Julian Frazier), three uncles (Nicholas Gibbs Frazier, Beriah Frazier, and Constantine Frazier), and two distant cousins (Joseph G. Frazier and Nicholas P. Frazier) who all served in the Tennessee state legislature.[48]

Kentucky native Francis Marion Walker was among the most prominent Hamilton County Confederate leaders. Governor Harris asked this ex–district attorney to form a volunteer company that became Company I of the Nineteenth. Walker was elected captain of the unit, but he handed over this post to his brother-in-law when he became lieutenant colonel of the regiment. Walker's counterpart was John D. Powell, a Chattanooga merchant who organized and led Company A.[49]

Not only did this old elite organize and captain the volunteer companies forming the Nineteenth, but also they served as lieutenants, noncommissioned officers, and privates. For example, among the leading citizens of Sullivan County serving in the Nineteenth was Dr. Joseph Dulany, the regimental surgeon. Dulany's kinsman, Elkanah Dulany, had been among the founding citizens of Blountville, had served as a state representative, and had established the family's tradition of medical service in the community.[50]

Two wealthy and notable Hawkins countians were Jacob Miller (father of Daniel C. Miller) and Richard G. Fain. Miller, a successful merchant, banker, and farmer, served as county sheriff before becoming a representative in the Twenty-Seventh General Assembly. Fain, a member of a widespread and distinguished East Tennessee family, had two sons, Nicholas and Samuel, who served in the Nineteenth. He was the president of the Rogersville and Jefferson Railroad, a fourteen-mile spur of the East Tennessee and Georgia Railroad. The elder Fain also served as clerk and master of a local court in addition to working an extensive farm.[51]

Among Captain John Paxton's men in Company E were the sons of several prominent local officeholders and businessmen including Shade Calloway, who served as census taker and assistant marshal; C. W. Nelson, the clerk of the superior court; William Craig, the clerk of the city court; and Felix W. Earnest, a route agent for the East Tennessee and Georgia Railroad.[52]

John Blair III of Washington County sent his son Robert L. and his son-in-law David Sullins off to war with the Nineteenth—Robert L. as a private in Company B and Sullins as the regimental chaplain. The elder Blair was not only a prosperous lawyer and hotel owner, but also a merchant and manufacturer. He also had served as a state senator and representative and was a six-term U.S. Representative. Blair's father John Jr. had also been involved in politics, serving in the North Carolina legislature before representing Washington County in Tennessee's First General Assembly.[53]

Other notable Washington countians associated with the Nineteenth were First Lieutenant Joseph A. Conley and Corporal James Crawford of Company B, whose fathers both held the post of county court clerk. Private John B. Mason's father A. G. served as constable, while Private Robert C. Crouch's father William was both census taker and postmaster. Perhaps the most prominent Washington County family linked to the Nineteenth was that of Congressman Thomas A. R. Nelson. Although an outspoken unionist, Nelson failed to convince his son Alexander to remain loyal. The younger Nelson cast his lot with the men of Company B.[54]

Among Captain John Powell's officers and men were many of Chattanooga's most prominent citizens, such as Second Lieutenant Daniel Kennedy, a well-to-do druggist, and Third Lieutenant Francis M. Foust, whose family was among the earliest settlers in East Tennessee. Also serving in Company A was Summerfield Key, the son of attorney David M. Key, a member of General Caswell's staff and one of the chief figures in the mobilization of East Tennessee's Confederate forces. The company also included Private George Pierce Massingale, whose father Henry White Massingale was one of Chattanooga's leading citizens, having held the office of mayor several times as well as being a successful businessman. Other prominent Chattanoogans in the Nineteenth included First Lieutenant Beriah F. Moore of Company I, a noted attorney; V. Q. Johnson, the regiment's adjutant; and Addison D. Taylor, a dry goods merchant whose commercial expertise led to his appointment as regimental quartermaster.[55]

These members of East Tennessee's Confederate elite, like their compatriots throughout the region, had a political as well as economic connection to the Deep South: by and large, they belonged to the Democratic Party. At first glance it may appear odd that the large-scale farmers and urban elite who composed the Confederate leadership were Democrats. Traditionally, such professions, residence patterns, and market orientation were associated with Whig ideology. However, antebellum party affiliation cannot always be explained in tidy generalizations. It had as much to do with intangibles such as community and family heritage, oratorical ability and charisma of political leaders, the party preference of rivals, and the influence of elite families as it did with ideological and political issues. Though pinpointing the reasons behind such affiliation is difficult, the region's Confederates clearly had a strong affinity for the Democratic Party.[56]

In his analysis of East Tennessee disunionists, Todd Groce found that almost 80 percent of the officers leading the region's Rebel troops belonged to the Democratic Party. Both John C. Vaughn and David Cummings were Democrats, and among the officers of the Nineteenth the party of Jackson predominated. For example, Captain Carrick White Heiskell was a lifelong Democrat, as was Abraham L. Gammon; Captain James P. Snapp actually chaired a Democratic states' rights meeting in Blountville prior to the outbreak of hostilities.[57]

Not all Whigs were loyalists, though, nor all Democrats disunionists. Democrats in the First Congressional District, for example, followed the lead of Andrew Johnson and remained loyal. In fact, across East Tennessee three-fifths of the Democrats voted against separation in the June referendum. Conversely, perhaps one-fifth of the region's former Whigs became Confederates. Nonetheless, Confederate support clearly was strongest among the region's Democrats. An examination of the returns for the June referendum reveals that all but one of the East Tennessee counties voting for separation had a Democratic tradition (Sequatchie County was too new to classify). In addition, the separation vote exceeded 40 percent in Marion, McMinn, Washington, Hawkins, and Hamilton Counties—all of which contained a large Democratic constituency.[58]

Not surprisingly, the officers and men of the Nineteenth came primarily from these Democratic counties. While it is impossible to ascertain the political affiliation of every member of the regiment—especially the enlisted men, who left few records—their residence in traditionally Democratic areas of East Tennessee offers suggestive evidence of party preference. The large number of the men and their family members who bore the Christian names of Democratic icons such as James K. Polk, Martin Van Buren, Andrew Jackson, Thomas Jefferson, and John C. Calhoun lends additional weight to such a supposition.[59]

This Democratic heritage assured that the party's rhetoric concerning the North's violation of Southern rights and Lincoln's despotism struck a responsive chord. East Tennessee Confederates, like their counterparts throughout the South, believed their communities, their homes and families, their liberty, and even republicanism itself to be in jeopardy. As the threat of the Yankee invasion loomed ever larger, the region's Confederate leadership began to organize volunteer companies to meet this challenge. While the economic and political influence of the community's leading citizens strongly influenced the recruits, loyalty to their family, friends, neighbors, and community influenced them as much if not more.[60]

Because volunteer companies represented a community's determination to protect itself, the members of these units saw their enlistment not only as a chance for adventure and glory but also as a sacred responsibility. Likewise, the local citizens viewed the unit as an extension of themselves and their resolve. Nowhere is this more clearly illustrated than in the flag ceremonies that christened the new companies. Leading ladies of the community presented their handmade flag to the local unit in a public ceremony. Such presentations became the highlight of Chattanooga's social life, with the women of the town finally exhausting their supply of silk and cotton in producing the banners. These ceremonies became public spectacles designed to demonstrate the community's strength, patriotism, and resolve. Speeches generally followed, along with martial band music and perhaps a picnic or banquet. The centerpiece of the ritual, however, was the flag, which was an emblem not only of the volunteer company but also the community. This banner linked the new soldiers to their community as they marched off to face the Yankees. Indeed, the flag became a symbol of everything the men held dear. In the ensuing struggle few things would be more significant to companies and regiments than advancing their flag and protecting it from capture while at the same time endeavoring to capture their opponents' banners.[61]

Along with flags, most communities also attempted to provide the uniforms, arms, and other equipment the company would need. Whether donations came from the populace as a whole or from some wealthy citizen, the communities made every effort to equip the soldiers with the necessary accoutrements. For example, the ladies of Hawkins County made the uniforms worn by Daniel Miller and William Phipps when they left a distraught Charlotte and marched off to face their new lives as soldiers. Patriotic citizens donated the light gray uniforms worn by the Hamilton Grays, and Edward Marsh, a wealthy Chattanooga businessman, gave the Marsh Blues their uniforms, equipment, and name.[62]

Undoubtedly, such demonstrations of solidarity roused the community loyalties of the new soldiers. But other local influences could command greater affection and sense of duty. One was the bond of kinship. The ranks of Civil War volunteer companies were filled not only with friends and acquaintances but also with relatives. Fathers, sons, brothers, uncles, nephews, and cousins all joined together in defense of the community and the family. Virtually every Confederate volunteer company included men related to one another, and the Nineteenth was no exception. In many cases, all the males in a household joined their local company. The regimental sample includes forty-five sets of brothers and ten sets of father and son. A detailed genealogical analysis for the entire sample is beyond the scope of this work, but an examination of one family—the Rheas of Sullivan County—reveals a kinship web of vast proportions. In addition to the previously mentioned links between Samuel Rhea's sons and Captain Abraham L. Gammon's family, there were Rhea family connections to the Lynns, Walkers, Fains, Powells, and many others. These families sent members not only to the Nineteenth but also to other East Tennessee Confederate units, such as the Sixtieth and Sixty-Third Tennessee Infantry Regiments. In all, close to sixty persons in the Rhea family kinship network fought for the Confederacy, including six who served in the Nineteenth. Undoubtedly, the desire to protect one's kin, coupled with a sincere belief that a Northern invasion threatened the survival of the community, inspired such enlistments.[63]

Women also played a pivotal role in Confederate volunteering. While males felt pressures from many quarters to enlist, the desire to protect women and win their admiration proved one of the most compelling. Likewise, females felt considerable community pressure to encourage and support the enlistment of family members, husbands, and friends. The *Knoxville Daily Register,* for example, exhorted the region's women to place their arms about the necks of their male relatives and urge them to vote for separation and representation. In the same issue, "A Tennessee Woman" urged the men of East Tennessee to don their armor in defense of their country. The ardor of female Confederates could be quite intense. Regimental Chaplain David Sullins remembered his wife as being "about the worst rebel among us."[64]

This enthusiasm for secession and war was maintained, despite the emotional or financial hardships such actions brought to their lives. Whether it was postponement of a wedding, as in the case of Charlotte Phipps, or the absence of a father of nine children, as in the case of Private John Alaway of Company F, the women of the South had to accept their losses and demand that their menfolk enlist to avoid the social stigma of cowardice or disloyalty.[65]

Unionist Oliver Temple saw such feminine influence as one of the key factors contributing to Confederate sympathy:

> With the first sight of a uniformed soldier, and the sound of the first tap of the drum, or note of the fife, they enthusiastically espoused the Southern cause. The young ladies were first in manifesting this feeling; then followed the mothers, then the brothers and lovers, and finally the father had to yield. Thus was many a head of a family and devoted friend of the Union led to join the Southern cause. . . . The zeal and the enthusiasm of these ladies were intense. Base and craven, indeed, was the young man, in their estimation, often expressed in words, who did not promptly enlist. . . . With the all-powerful influence of the women on the side of secession, few were the young men in our towns who did not take up arms in its behalf.[66]

If the urging of patrons, community, family, and women were not enough to encourage East Tennessee's disunionists to fight for the South, the weight of God's injunction could also be added. Secession and the Confederacy won widespread support among Southern ministers, and no political or economic argument could carry more persuasive force than the approval of the Almighty.[67]

In East Tennessee, influential religious organizations such as the Holston Methodist Conference and the Presbyterian Synod of East Tennessee took a pro-Confederate stance. This is not to say that the region's Methodists or Presbyterians or members of any other denomination all supported the Confederacy. East Tennessee's churches, like its populace, divided on the issue of independence. Methodist minister William G. "Parson" Brownlow, for example, was a staunch unionist. Nonetheless, within the communities favoring separation, the clergy were generally pro-Confederate, and the pastoral messages heard by the region's disunionists undoubtedly convinced them that God was on their side—a comforting notion. Indeed, the men of Companies C and G from Sullivan County implored the local circuit-riding Methodist preacher, David Sullins, to accompany them to Camp Cummings and minister to their spiritual needs. While at the camp, Sullins became the chaplain of the Nineteenth Tennessee, and his sermons proclaimed the righteousness of the Southern cause. Other ministers in the regiment, such as Robert T. Howard and Andrew Johnson (both Baptists), aided Sullins in his efforts, and while at Knoxville, local ministers conducted religious services for the men every Sunday morning and afternoon. The *Knoxville Daily Register* reported in early May 1861 that "Many of the volunteers . . . go into this conflict fully impressed with the righteousness of their cause [and with the] belief that the Lord of Hosts will conduct them to a glorious victory."[68]

The region's Confederates, including the men of the Nineteenth Tennessee, envisioned themselves in a holy crusade against foes who threatened their world—a world ordained and blessed by divine providence. They considered marching off in defense of these blessings as a great duty and privilege. Perhaps the most sacred blessing to be protected was that of self-government. Patriotism exerted a tremendous influence on members of the Nineteenth. Like other Confederates throughout the South, they were convinced that they were fighting to preserve the liberty their forefathers had fought for and won in the Revolution.[69]

As discussed in chapter 1, Americans viewed themselves as the beneficiaries and guardians of the revolutionary heritage, and the fate of the nation's experiment in republican government rested upon their shoulders. While East Tennessee unionists and their Northern counterparts fought to preserve the Union as the "last best hope" for representative government, East Tennessee Confederates envisioned themselves engaged in a struggle to secure their liberty from a tyrannical federal government—a government that not only sought to curtail the expansion of slavery and hence new economic opportunity but also, after the fall of Sumter, intended to force the seceded states back into the Union. Such an act of aggression would turn the Southern states into conquered provinces and destroy the liberty and self-government bequeathed by the revolutionary generation. The Confederates of East Tennessee, like their counterparts elsewhere in the South, prepared to resist such tyranny in the spirit of their ancestors.[70]

So compelling was this perceived parallel between the revolutionary past and the current crisis that Southerners envisioned themselves engaged in the Second American Revolution. After reviewing the volunteer companies at Camp Cummings, J. Austin Sperry spoke for his pro-Confederate readers when he wrote in his *Knoxville Daily Register*, "We congratulate the volunteers of our mountain district upon their near prospect of sharing in the glory of this, the second War of Independence." Sperry, in true revolutionary spirit, also labeled Lincoln a despot and reminded the region's unionists that "[t]hose who would betray Tennessee into the power of the unholy military despotism of the North, are Tories, and will bear the stigma of Tories." The *Register* also pointed out that the Confederate Constitution assured every citizen of all the rights enjoyed under the old Constitution while the Confederate nation protected Southerners against the encroachment of Northern tyranny. Sperry exhorted his readers to support the new Southern republic and praised the troops coming to Knoxville, who were "willing to volunteer and meet Lincoln's thievish and mercenary forces, if they should attempt to pollute the soil of East Tennessee with their unholy feet."[71]

Among those associated with the Nineteenth Tennessee, such spirit also ran high. Captain Hannah's men from Polk County marched to a drum used at the 1781 siege of Yorktown and boldly proclaimed that it would beat again at a charge on Washington, D.C.—to which the *Nashville Republican Banner* replied with a toast: "Victory again, say we, to the drum and the gallant fellows who follow it in its second mission for Independence." Daniel Miller and his compatriots in the Hawkins Boys received a patriotic poem from an admirer; published in the *Knoxville Daily Register*, it read in part, "For braze and daring are those souls/who in freedom's cause engage/they shrink not from the cannonballs/when the battles fiercely rage."[72]

Freedom's cause was precisely what Charlotte Phipps's brother William had on his mind when he closed a letter to his sister with the spirited epigram, "Southern Independence is my sentiment. Liberty or Death." While William's comrades in the Nineteenth would undoubtedly have agreed with his sentiment, none could have foreseen just how difficult the struggle for that independence would be or how prophetic the young Rebel's statement would prove for many members of the regiment.[73]

3 ❧

"We Are the Pick Regiment of Tennessee"

From Knoxville to Shiloh

On a warm June morning in 1861, William Phipps searched for a shady spot among the tents of Camp Cummings and sat down to write Charlotte. Although his second stint at sentry duty had left him so tired he could barely hold his eyes open, he fought off sleep in an effort to tell her all the camp news and to inquire about his family. Phipps was especially anxious to hear how his elderly father, James, was managing the farm now that his son was gone. Family was important to William. The young Rebel had been in Knoxville for less than a month, but homesickness had plagued him since his arrival. However, despite the longing to return to his loved ones, William had focused his efforts on becoming a good soldier. Over the past weeks, he had begun to acclimate himself to military life and had developed a strong sense of pride and identity with his regiment. This *esprit de corps*, like that manifested by thousands of other Civil War soldiers, flowed into his letters home. Phipps proudly boasted to Charlotte that as new volunteer companies arrived in Knoxville they sought to join his outfit because "we are the pick regiment of Tennessee."[1]

Such youthful ardor belies the difficult transition experienced by William and his comrades as they left behind the comforts of home and family to pursue the life of a soldier. The men of the Nineteenth, like Civil War recruits everywhere, had enthusiastically volunteered with visions of a brief war full of adventure and glory. After a short time in camp, however, the novelty of army life wore off and such dreams faded. Instead of daring battlefield exploits, the men faced a monotonous daily routine of idleness, mealtime, and drill while enduring primitive living conditions and frequent illness.[2]

Upon arriving at Camp Cummings, Charlotte's fiancé Daniel probably echoed the sentiments of many of the men when he remarked, "I dread camp life since I saw the way we had to live." The old fairgrounds contained only a few structures, forcing the regiment to live in tents. Groups of four to six enlisted men, called messes, shared a tent. Once the commissary issued rations, it was the responsibility of each mess to prepare its own food. William found the situation bearable, declaring that "[t]here have been some very disagreeable nights since we have been in our camps; but our [his and Daniel's] tent is made of good cloth, we rest as comfortable as at home; I still get plenty to eat." Phipps's youth may have helped him accept his new situation. Most members of the regiment undoubtedly found their messmates' cooking barely edible and the lack of privacy both in the tents and on the communal bathing trip to the Tennessee River less than idyllic.[3]

While trying to adjust to their new surroundings, the recruits confronted one of the most despised aspects of army life: drill. For men anxious to test their courage on the battlefield, the incessant marching seemed unbearable, and practicing the manual of arms without muskets could be confusing and humbling. Nonetheless, the intricate maneuvers of nineteenth-century warfare, which used column and linear formations for movement and battle, required soldiers to deploy quickly and change facing while maintaining cohesion, even if under enemy fire. Veteran troops often had trouble performing such tasks, so it is hardly surprising that raw recruits such as the men of the Nineteenth were left positively bewildered. Most of the men found drill difficult, exhausting, and often embarrassing, and they generally loathed it. After weeks of practice, however, Phipps finally began "to understand the military movements tolerably well." Daniel, however, could only complain about his and William's plight, telling Charlotte, "I have no idea that you will know us if we ever shall meet you again; the sun, oh, how it burns us viz. those that have been used to shade and ease."[4]

The five hours of daily drill were hardly enough to turn these citizen-soldiers into an effective combat unit. Moreover, the quality of their instruction left much to be desired. In most Civil War units, the recruits' lack of military knowledge and skill was exacerbated by equal ignorance on the part of their officers—a situation one historian has labeled "the ignorant leading the uneducated." Few of the company-grade officers of the Nineteenth had any military training or experience. Fortunately, the Nineteenth possessed a small cadre of commissioned and noncommissioned officers with the ability to bring some semblance of order to the mob of enlistees in their charge. For example, the regiment's sergeant major, nineteen-year-old Henry Doak, had studied light infantry and artillery tactics at college prior to enlisting. Colonel Cummings, a

Mexican War veteran, immediately put Doak to work drilling both the men and their officers. Lieutenant Colonel Francis Walker also had served in the Mexican War and had some military training at Transylvania College in his native Kentucky. Likewise, Captain John D. Powell had served in Mexico and was a graduate of the South Carolina Military Institute (the Citadel). Other officers with prior military training included Captain Zadoc Willett, who forwent his graduation at the United States Military Academy to raise a volunteer company in Jonesboro, and Major Abraham Fulkerson, who graduated from the Virginia Military Institute. This handful of men had the responsibility of turning the Nineteenth into a disciplined combat unit in a short time.[5]

The citizen-soldiers' general disregard for military discipline added to the officers' difficulty in training their troops. The men filling the ranks of Confederate regiments such as the Nineteenth were highly individualistic. In true republican spirit, they viewed themselves as "free men" engaged in a struggle to preserve a democratic society based on individual liberty. Consequently, they deeply resented any attempt, even by superior officers, to curtail their freedom of action or impose rules on them.[6]

By modern military standards, the discipline of these volunteer regiments was shockingly lax. The recruits, however, viewed any attempts to regulate their behavior as draconian. For example, Phipps found unbearably harsh Captain Heiskell's threat to limit recruits' letter writing to parents only. Miller also thought Heiskell quite rigid when the captain would not allow his messmates to care for him during a bout of fever. Clearly, Captain Heiskell, like the rest of the regiment's officers, faced a formidable task in turning strong-willed and often spoiled individuals into an effective fighting force that would respond to orders without hesitation.[7]

Another factor contributing to the common soldiers' resentment and disregard for orders was the traditional practice of electing regimental officers, both commissioned and noncommissioned. Given that the men themselves placed their leaders into power, they were not inclined to humble themselves before them. Another factor complicating command was social class. Members of the elite generally garnered officer positions and were given some measure of deference based on past social standing. However, the close civilian relationships that had existed between many of the officers and men could compromise that deference. Additionally, members of the elite who served in the ranks often resented taking orders from their social equals or inferiors.[8]

The link between social class and rank so prevalent in the Confederate army was well demonstrated by the elections in the Nineteenth. The elected company commanders and their lieutenants were the same members of the mountain elite who had organized the companies, while the field officers were some of the region's most influential citizens. Even at the noncommissioned level the men continued to elect members from the upper classes. Daniel Miller, for example, who was elected first (orderly) sergeant of Company K, came from a wealthy commercial farming family that owned huge tracts of land and a considerable number of slaves. Indeed, the wealth held by the Nineteenth's officer corps (commissioned and noncommissioned) was considerable. The households of the original officers in the regimental sample held almost 37 percent of the sample's aggregate wealth. When compared to East Tennessee households as a whole, those of the regiment's officers held, on the average, almost 560 percent more aggregate wealth. This great wealth was often tied up in slaves. Close to 40 percent of these officers' households owned bondsmen. Like other Confederate officers throughout the South, the men leading the Nineteenth into battle primarily came from the prominent families of their county and region.[9]

The elite status of the regiments' officers and their interest in slavery could be seen in their living arrangements. While virtually all the members of the regiment lived in tents and washed in the Tennessee River, these upper-class soldiers often brought personal servants to attend to their needs. For example, Captain John D. Powell of Company A had an elderly slave named Munger who, when not caring for his master, often entertained the camp with his fife playing. Daniel Miller's father sent a slave boy to cook for his son and William—much to their delight and undoubtedly to their compatriots' jealousy.[10]

When not eating or drilling, the men faced long hours of idleness. While some chose to use such time to write letters, read, talk, or attend religious services, others opted for more controversial diversions such as gambling and drinking—even on the Sabbath. Daniel Miller got so weary of the drunkenness about him that he hoped the regiment would leave Knoxville. Several recruits found the tediousness of army life so unbearable that they deserted— in some cases only days after enlisting. William Phipps wrote of one such fugitive who deserted his post while on guard duty and headed home, but was tracked for some twenty-five miles, caught, and tried for his life. Although a record of the trial does not exist, the man was probably dishonorably discharged and released, as were other deserters at this time.[11]

While the handful of erstwhile patriots who forsook their oath and abandoned their comrades undoubtedly dampened the regiment's morale, the exodus of soldiers because of illness probably affected morale even more. Beginning in May and lasting the rest of the year, disease swept the ranks of the regiment. This was not at all uncommon; most new Civil War regiments experienced outbreaks of contagious childhood diseases almost immediately on arrival at their camp of assembly. The prewar isolation of the recruits, especially those from rural areas, had shielded them from measles, mumps, whooping cough, and diphtheria. No sooner had the men begun to recover from these ailments than the camp diseases appeared—typhoid, diarrhea, and dysentery. These later illnesses primarily resulted from contaminated food and water. In addition, a host of related "fevers," generally paratyphoid or pneumonia, plagued the men.[12]

Lacking adequate medical facilities at Camp Cummings, Dr. Dulany sent serious cases home to recuperate. Miller's bout with "fever" resulted in a curtailment of duty and eventually a furlough. Instead of returning to his father's farm near Rogersville, he convalesced at the Montvale Springs Resort. Undoubtedly Miller was ill, but his prolonged stay in such a posh environment led to rumors of cowardice. When Charlotte Phipps wrote him, concerned over this indictment of her fiancé, the irate Miller vigorously defended himself and promised to return soon to the regiment—which he did. The regiment, however, was no longer at Camp Cummings.[13]

By late June, concern for the region's defense against both internal and external threats prompted General Caswell to deploy elements of the Nineteenth throughout East Tennessee. Companies C and K went to Loudon, Tennessee, to guard the railroad bridges against loyalist guerrilla raids, and detachments under Colonel Cummings, Lieutenant Colonel Walker, and Major Fulkerson sealed off the major points of access into the region from Kentucky: Big Creek Gap, Cumberland Gap, and Jamestown, Tennessee. Although this single regiment hardly could be expected to cover the entire 120-mile Kentucky/Tennessee border within the East Tennessee Department, Caswell hoped by patrolling those key thoroughfares to guard against a major invasion and prevent the smuggling of arms to loyalists. During June, the Nineteenth Tennessee provided the bulk of organized Confederate infantry in East Tennessee. The situation was potentially dangerous, given the size of the loyalist population. However, Governor Harris, anxious to placate East Tennessee's unionists and calm their fears about military despotism, urged President Jefferson Davis to limit the number of Confederate troops in the region and to employ only Tennessee regiments. Although the region's unionists were already organizing and drilling militia companies and attempting to procure weapons, Harris still hoped to win them over to the Confederate cause.[14]

Part of the governor's conciliatory plan involved the appointment of Brigadier General Felix K. Zollicoffer as the new head of the Department of East Tennessee. Citing the general's extensive political background and great influence among old Whigs, Harris successfully urged President Davis to name Zollicoffer to this command. Both Harris and Davis hoped that Zollicoffer's

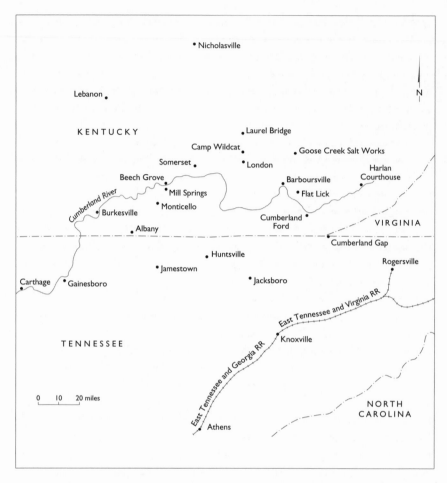

East Tennessee and Eastern Kentucky. Drawn by William Nelson.

past association with many of East Tennessee's Whig leaders would help bring them into the Confederate fold and end the threat of unionist rebellion. This hope, however, would not be realized.[15]

Arriving in Knoxville in late July, the general attempted to appease the populace by tolerating their unionist sentiments as long as they took no overt action against the Confederate government. Despite his political qualifications and friendly relations with Knoxville loyalists, Zollicoffer was a poor choice for such an important post. His excessive leniency toward the unionists in East Tennessee was seen by them as weakness, and his lack of proper military training would prove disastrous to the soldiers under his command.[16]

In fairness to Zollicoffer, it must be noted that he lacked the resources to perform his duties adequately. The Confederate War Department had charged him with protecting the vital East Tennessee railways, suppressing unionist guerrillas, and defending the Kentucky/Tennessee border—with only the Nineteenth and a few independent infantry and cavalry companies. New regiments eventually arrived to bolster his strength, but many were unarmed and all were poorly equipped and trained. Such a weak force could do little more than garrison the major towns and mountain passes, guard the railroad, and sporadically patrol the numerous coves of the region. It could not stop determined unionist activity.[17]

By July, the Nineteenth was reunited at Cumberland Gap and ordered to fortify the pass against possible attack. Daniel Miller, now apparently healthy, rejoined his comrades. The rest of the regiment, however, was not as fortunate. His future brother-in-law William Phipps contracted typhoid and was furloughed. Meanwhile, an epidemic of measles and mumps spread throughout the ranks, incapacitating virtually the entire command. At this point, Miller's health failed again. Stricken with typhoid, he joined Phipps, who was convalescing in Hawkins County. Although both soon returned to the army, Miller remained weak.[18]

Those members of the regiment who were fit for duty continued to build breastworks and participate in daily drill. The Gap was critical to the defense of Upper East Tennessee, and the encampment soon became a major base of operations for cavalry patrols as well as a magnet for "sutlers," Confederate sympathizers, and visitors. Several recruits joined the regiment while it was at the Gap, augmenting its depleted ranks. Despite months of soldiering, the men were still novices at war, and many mishaps and accidents occurred. On more than one occasion, stray animals wandering near the camp at night were challenged and then fired on by nervous sentries. After such a false alarm, the men would often wait in battle array for hours for an attack that would not come. Carelessness with firearms led to several accidents. In fact, the regiment's first casualty was a young sergeant who shot himself through the hand, and Lieutenant Colonel Walker proved himself as careless as his men when he shook a box of percussion caps, sparking an explosion that injured his hand badly. Clearly, the Nineteenth needed all the preparation and training it could get before it faced the enemy.[19]

The state's congressional and gubernatorial elections in early August revealed that, despite the efforts of Governor Harris and General Zollicoffer, the East Tennessee loyalists desired to remain in the Union. Harris was reelected, but in the eastern counties he lost by a wide margin to his opponent William H. Polk; moreover, the region's unionists defiantly elected four representatives to the U.S. Congress. One of those new congressmen, Thomas A. R. Nelson, was captured by Confederate cavalry while trying to sneak into Kentucky and was delivered to Lieutenant Colonel Walker at Cumberland Gap. Through the efforts of the Reverend Sullins, Nelson was briefly reunited with his son Alexander, a private in Company B, before he was taken to Knoxville and eventually Richmond, Virginia.[20]

The election results embarrassed and angered Harris and Zollicoffer, and both thereafter displayed a markedly less conciliatory attitude toward East Tennessee's unionists. Throughout the region, Confederate troops began to break up loyalist organizations and arrest their leaders. Major Fulkerson led one such expedition from Cumberland Gap into the surrounding East Tennessee counties, rounding up unionists and forcing them either to take an oath to the Confederacy or face arrest.[21]

Fulkerson's efforts were soon halted. In early September, a Confederate force under Major General Leonidas Polk seized Columbus, Kentucky, ending that state's tenuous neutrality and provoking Union authorities to send troops of their own into the state. In order to shore up his now-exposed defensive line, General Albert Sidney Johnston (commander of Confederate forces in the western theater) moved the bulk of his command from Nashville to Bowling Green, Kentucky, and ordered Zollicoffer's brigade to Cumberland Ford (modern-day Pineville, Kentucky). Zollicoffer immediately sent three regiments (including the Nineteenth) to the ford, where they established Camp Buckner. He then concentrated all other available forces at Cumberland Gap as a prelude to joining the advance into Kentucky. While the regiment was at the ford, disease continued to sap its strength. Daniel Miller again succumbed to typhoid and diphtheria and was furloughed for the third time.[22]

The inhabitants of eastern Kentucky were as hostile to the Confederacy as those of East Tennessee, and Zollicoffer feared that Home Guard units would contest his presence in the state. On September 18, he ordered Colonel Joel A. Battle of the Twentieth Tennessee to take a mixed force of some eight hundred men (including Companies B and K of the Nineteenth) to Barbourville, Kentucky, and destroy Camp Andrew Johnson, a training facility for East Tennessee and Kentucky unionist militia. Arriving at dawn, the Confederates surprised some three hundred "bushwhackers." After a brief exchange of gunfire, the unionists fled, leaving Colonel Battle's men in possession of the camp and its meager supplies.[23]

Although a few of Battle's men were wounded, only one was killed: Lieutenant Robert Powell of Company K. This insignificant action at Barbourville was the first engagement of the Civil War fought in Kentucky, and it resulted in the first Confederate battle death in the western theater. This was also the first battle death for the Nineteenth. Powell's death touched not only his comrades in the Nineteenth but the whole of Zollicoffer's command. Decades later, veterans vividly remembered their first comrade to fall under enemy fire—an event that brought home to them the reality of war.[24]

Still fearful of Home Guard activity and a Union army offensive, Zollicoffer sent out a constant stream of cavalry patrols. Aggressive by nature, the general concluded that the best defense was offensive action against Federal and Home Guard posts in eastern Kentucky. Therefore, in late September, Zollicoffer launched a daring two-pronged raid perilously close to the Federal base at Nicholasville (Camp Dick Robinson). One force, under Colonel James E. Rains of the Eleventh Tennessee, would attack Laurel Bridge in Laurel County, destroying the Home Guard encampment and clearing the route toward Camp Dick Robinson and central Kentucky. The second force, under Colonel Cummings, would proceed with a convoy of wagons to the Goose Creek salt works in Clay County to procure salt.[25]

On September 25, Rains's detachment started for Laurel Bridge. There it routed the enemy troops. Cummings's force (the Nineteenth plus a cavalry escort) started for the salt works the same day and arrived after a grueling three-day march over poor roads in pouring rain. The men traveled without tents, and Cummings worried that the already sickly and weakened regiment would now suffer from exposure. Indeed, the men were cold, wet, and generally miserable, which perhaps explains why the colonel allowed the men to indulge themselves with liquor and stolen honey and geese. The situation at "Camp Drunk" (as they later called it) eventually got out of hand. One soldier rode a stolen mule through the ranks while holding an old, torn umbrella above his head, much to his comrades' delight. Inebriated soldiers, especially young William Vestal, a private in Company E, began wildly flinging muddy geese about. A brawl erupted. Cummings sent Sergeant Major Doak to stop it. As the young Doak attempted to break up the fight, he was assaulted by F. M. Dempsey, an ex-prize fighter known to the men as "Big Dempsey." Angry and unable to handle the giant, Doak put his pistol to Dempsey's head, but fortunately for both men the rain-soaked weapon misfired. Doak later remembered an enraged Colonel Cummings yelling "God Damn," knocking him out of the way and ending the free-for-all. The next day, the command started for Camp Buckner with two hundred barrels of salt that Zollicoffer had authorized Cummings to receipt for. However, the local farmers would receive no compensation for the stolen foodstuffs, much to their chagrin and the disgust of General Zollicoffer, who promised severe punishment to the thieves in the ranks.[26]

Despite the success of both raids, Johnston wanted Zollicoffer to avoid further advances into Kentucky. However, Zollicoffer let his aggressive nature get the best of him. Disregarding orders, he planned another strike against Union forces. On October 16, he marched his entire available force from Camp Buckner ten miles north to Flat Lick. While in camp that night, he decided to continue northward along the Wilderness Road the next day and attack Camp Wildcat. His command was not in good condition for a fight. Supply shortages and sickness had taken a toll on the men. Zollicoffer's advancing column numbered only about four thousand soldiers; two thousand of their comrades failed to join the expedition because of illness, furlough, or detail duty. In mid-September, the Nineteenth's fit-for-duty personnel had numbered around seven hundred. By the end of the month, it had fallen to around six hundred. Cummings lost another one hundred men on the Goose Creek expedition; he worried that these men would not be fit for duty until April.[27]

Nonetheless, Zollicoffer eagerly pressed ahead, force-marching his men along the Wilderness Road. The column covered some eighty miles in three days, arriving at the ford of the Rockcastle River on October 20. Along the way, Zollicoffer's green troops endured Federal patrols sniping at them and otherwise disrupting their progress. Near Camp Wildcat, Federal harassment increased, leading to heavy skirmishing. The Nineteenth was bloodied, losing six killed and twenty wounded. Pushing the Federal scouts back, Zollicoffer's men discovered felled trees designed to block their advance. After having his troops clear these obstacles, Zollicoffer reconnoitered the Federal position. He found Camp Wildcat to be a fortified hillock at the head of a gorge about a quarter of a mile wide. The rough, broken terrain, thick forest, and extensive entrenchments made the position quite formidable. Nonetheless, Zollicoffer was determined to "feel" the Federal position.[28]

The next morning around 9:00 A.M., Zollicoffer deployed skirmishers and sent the Eleventh and Seventeenth Tennessee Infantry forward to storm the hill. The Nineteenth was assigned to guard the Confederate camp, although it appears that several volunteers, including Sergeant Major Doak, participated in the assault. The attack met with some initial success as Federal units gave ground. However, the terrain prevented all the Confederate assault force from engaging all at once, leading to piecemeal attacks that were finally beaten back. After probing the defenses for some three hours, Zollicoffer was convinced that the position could be taken only with heavy casualties if at all, and he abandoned the assault. Losses were light—fewer than one hundred casualties on each side. During the night, Zollicoffer's men left their campfires burning and began the long retreat to Camp Buckner in the darkness.[29]

News of the Confederate repulse at Camp Wildcat excited East Tennessee's unionists, who now anticipated Federal "liberation" of their region. In fact, East Tennessee's loyalist leadership had been in secret discussions with authorities in Washington about just such a move. Plans were under way for a unionist rebellion to coincide with a Federal invasion.[30]

Although unaware of the planned rebellion, Zollicoffer was concerned about an invasion. Toward the end of October, the general received reports that a strong Union force under Brigadier General George Thomas was planning to enter East Tennessee somewhere between Cumberland Gap and Bowling Green. To meet this new threat, Zollicoffer began to shift his forces rapidly. His brigade evacuated Camp Buckner and returned to Cumberland Gap, where it improved the fortifications. Leaving a large garrison at the Gap, Zollicoffer moved the rest of his command (including the Nineteenth) southward into Tennessee. He marched his foot-sore regiments across the Cumberland Plateau, fortifying the mountain passes and deploying small detachments as he went.[31]

Zollicoffer became convinced that the turnpike between Albany, Kentucky, and Jamestown, Tennessee, would be Thomas's invasion route. Endeavoring to beat the Federals to the area, he force-marched most of his command (including the Nineteenth) to Jamestown. The rapid march, poor food, and cold weather combined to dampen the troops' morale, leading to outbreaks of drunkenness and subsequent temperance crusades on the part of chaplains such as the Reverend Sullins. Regardless of the strain on his men, Zollicoffer was determined to find Thomas and strike him before Thomas learned of his presence.[32]

News of the impending invasion panicked East Tennessee's Confederates. Many of the region's leading secessionists begged Richmond for reinforcements, predicting the capture or destruction of the railroads. In early November, loyalist guerrillas attacked and burned several key railroad bridges in anticipation of the Federal advance. The "revolt" soon collapsed in the face of Confederate reinforcements under Brigadier General William Carroll and the absence of Federal troops. While his subordinates struggled with the loyalists' rebellion, Zollicoffer informed General Johnston that with the mountain passes between Cumberland Gap and Jamestown now fortified and garrisoned, he planned to seize the initiative from the Federals and secure a position on the Cumberland River before winter.[33]

Leaving Colonel William B. Wood, post commander of Knoxville, and General Carroll to handle the situation in East Tennessee, Zollicoffer moved cavalry, artillery, and several regiments of infantry (including the Nineteenth) into Kentucky. With the weather worsening rapidly, Zollicoffer's engineers searched for a suitable location for winter quarters. The site chosen was the tiny hamlet of Mill Springs on the south bank of the Cumberland River. Besides offering access to grist and saw mills, the new camp could be supplied by steamboat from Nashville if the river could be kept clear of Federal troops.[34]

Arriving in late November, Zollicoffer's troops were sorely in need of rest. In the past month, they had marched more than 250 miles over some of the worst roads imaginable, often in bad weather. Rest, however, would have to wait. Reacting to Zollicoffer's advance, Major General Don Carlos Buell, commander of the Federal Army of the Ohio, sent a brigade under Brigadier General Albin Francis Schoepf to Somerset, ten miles from Mill Springs, to prevent Zollicoffer from crossing the Cumberland and advancing into central Kentucky. After the two forces had skirmished, Zollicoffer made an ill-advised decision to cross the river and occupy the north bank at Beech Grove. With a river prone to flash floods at his back and an enemy capable of concentrating superior forces at his front, Zollicoffer had violated a basic tenet of warfare and set in motion a chain of events that would imperil his small brigade. Upon crossing most of his men to Beech Grove, Zollicoffer set about fortifying his position. With creeks protecting the flanks and breastworks and *chevaux de frise* protecting the front, "Camp Beech Grove" appeared so formidable that General Schoepf withdrew eight miles past Somerset.[35]

Yet the apparent strength of Beech Grove was merely a facade. The entrenchments were inadequate to stop a determined attack, and, even worse, Zollicoffer's troops were in no condition to man them effectively. Sickness still held his effective force to around four thousand men. Many were suffering from the effects of poor sanitation and exposure, and the onset of winter promised only to increase their misery. Within the Nineteenth, medical furloughs multiplied, slowly eroding the regiment's strength. Daniel Miller had avoided the suffering of his compatriots in Company K. Since his furlough in early September, he had been attached to the quartermaster's department and provost marshal's post, first in Knoxville and later in Rogersville (his home), ostensibly until he could recover his health. Apparently Miller had received the aid of Captain Heiskell in obtaining this position. On December 8, Dr. Dulany discharged Miller from active service; he had been absent with a variety of ailments for four out of the six months that the regiment had been in service. Miller would continue to hold his present position in Rogersville, although he wanted a full discharge from the army. While he was obviously weakened by his illnesses, his shivering and hungry comrades at Beech Grove undoubtedly resented the wealthy young man's connections and comfortable assignment.[36]

The men fit for duty remained poorly trained and disciplined. Most, like the men of the Nineteenth, had received only the rudiments of drill. Also, they had experienced only small unit actions and were not prepared for a battle in which entire regiments would be engaged and integrated with cavalry and artillery units.[37]

To make matters worse, Zollicoffer's soldiers were still poorly equipped and supplied. Basic gear such as blankets and coats were lacking, as were such items as entrenching tools. Perhaps most disturbing, the majority of the general's troops still carried antiquated firearms. Zollicoffer also lacked enough artillery pieces and ammunition. Finally, his men faced short rations because of the barrenness of the surrounding country and Federal efforts to cut his river supply line. Zollicoffer remained oblivious to all these handicaps and dangers, however, and unrealistically assumed that his men would be capable of offensive operations as soon as mild weather returned.[38]

By mid-December, the Davis administration decided to replace Zollicoffer as commander of the Department of East Tennessee with Major General George Crittenden. On learning of Zollicoffer's position on the north bank of the Cumberland, Crittenden immediately ordered him to withdraw to Mill Springs. But throughout the remainder of December, as snow fell on his shivering troops, Zollicoffer continued to hold his position. He even had his troops strengthen his earthworks and construct huts for winter quarters—still on the north shore.[39]

By the time Crittenden arrived at Mill Springs in early January to assume command, the situation was critical. Heavy rains had swollen the Cumberland River to flood stage, making a crossing difficult and increasing the danger that the brigade would be destroyed if the Federals decided to attack.[40]

Such a decision had already been made. On January 1, Federal forces under General Thomas moved out of Lebanon, Kentucky, and headed for Somerset. Luckily for the Confederates, the same rain imperiling them also slowed the Federal advance. By January 17, Thomas had reached the settlement of Logan's Crossroads (now Nancy, Kentucky), ten miles north of Beech Grove, where he paused to allow his strung-out column to form up and to await the arrival of General Schoepf's brigade.[41]

Meanwhile Crittenden busied his men building flatboats to transport his artillery, horses, and wagons to the south bank. On January 10, he sent the Nineteenth out on a reconnaissance in force. The regiment returned to camp without encountering anything but freezing rain and muddy roads.[42]

On January 15, Carroll arrived from Knoxville with another brigade, albeit a poorly trained and equipped one. Crittenden now had a change of heart. Carroll's brigade raised his strength to that of a small division and convinced him that he was strong enough to challenge Thomas. He therefore moved Carroll's force across the river to Beech Grove, hoping to attack Thomas before Schoepf could ford the high waters of Fishing Creek and join his commander. As a cold rain fell on the night of January 19, the men of the Nineteenth, like their comrades throughout the division, drew and cooked three days' rations, received ammunition, and waited restlessly for their first real battle.[43]

About 11:30 P.M., with two cavalry companies forming a vanguard, Zollicoffer's brigade filed out of the Beech Grove entrenchments in the following order: the Fifteenth Mississippi Infantry, Rutledge's Battery, and the Nineteenth, Twentieth, and Twenty-Fifth Tennessee Infantry. Around midnight, Carroll's brigade began to follow Zollicoffer's muddy trail. For the next six hours, the shivering, thinly clad Rebels trudged along the Mill Springs Road, braving an icy rain and muck sometimes more than a foot deep. The artillery caissons frequently became mired, and every step for the infantrymen became a struggle.[44]

Crittenden's plan called for an assault at first light to surprise the sleeping Federals, but the bad weather and roads slowed the Confederate advance to a crawl. As dawn came, most of Crittenden's troops were still toiling along in a column strung out for nearly three miles. The general would have no time to close up his force and position it for attack, however. Sometime around 6:00 A.M., gunfire shattered the morning stillness—Zollicoffer's cavalry had encountered the enemy's pickets. Crittenden had now lost the element of surprise and would have to commit his regiments piecemeal.[45]

While Carroll's brigade double-timed up the muddy road to join the battle, Zollicoffer deployed the Nineteenth Tennessee and the Fifteenth Mississippi to drive back the Federal pickets. The contending forces engaged in a running skirmish for about a quarter of a mile as the pickets slowly gave ground. Approaching a ridge, the pickets attempted a stand at a log house on the west side of the road, but they were driven up the ridge by superior numbers. Zollicoffer halted at the base of the ridge to organize his brigade into a line of battle. The Fifteenth Mississippi deployed on the right of the Mill Springs Road with the Twentieth Tennessee in support. The Nineteenth deployed across the road and to its left with the Twenty-Fifth Tennessee in support. As the brigade struggled to get into position for attack, some in the Nineteenth began to discard excess gear in a persimmon thicket. Once his troops were ready, Zollicoffer started his brigade up the ridge, driving the Federals slowly backward. As the Nineteenth crested the ridge, more Federal infantry arrived to reinforce the pickets, and the enemy fire intensified. As the Federal units formed their lines, one officer remembered seeing the Nineteenth bearing down on them with "their treasonable colors flaunting in the breeze."[46]

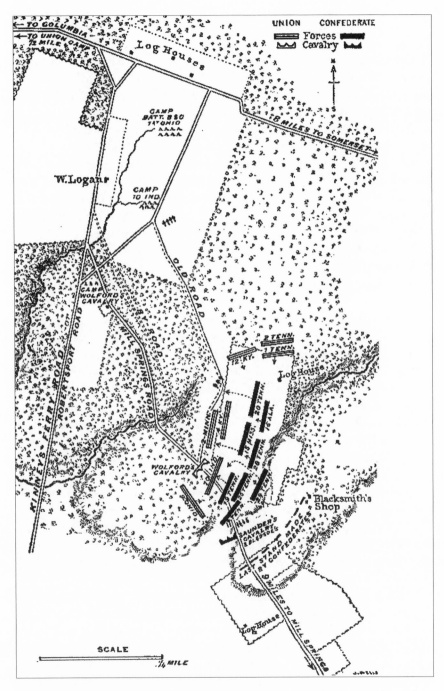

Battle of Mill Springs. Robert U. Johnson and Clarence C. Buel, eds., Battles and Leaders of the Civil War, *4 vols. (New York: Century Company, 1884–87), 1:388.*

On the Confederate right, the Fifteenth Mississippi and Twentieth Tennessee were also encountering enemy infantry, pinning them in the woods along Logan's Field. Meanwhile, the Nineteenth and Twenty-Fifth Tennessee charged and drove the opposing Federals across a field into thick woods. At this point, however, the Confederates stalled. The heavily wooded and broken terrain disrupted command and control. The Nineteenth was losing contact with the Fifteenth Mississippi; Cummings ordered Lieutenant Daniel Kennedy of Company A and Sergeant Major Doak to find the right flank of the regiment and connect it to the Mississippians' left—a difficult maneuver for the raw recruits. Adding to the chaos, a heavy rain was falling, punctuated by claps of thunder and streaks of lightning. The dark overcast along with the smoke of battle and a thin mist filtering through the tall trees and thick undergrowth of dogwood and blackjack created a murky, surreal atmosphere.[47]

The Nineteenth was heavily engaged with Union infantry when Cummings ordered the regiment to cease fire because the smoke obscured the enemy. In the eerie gloom and haze, Zollicoffer rode forward. The nearsighted general became convinced that the Nineteenth was firing into the Fifteenth Mississippi. Adding to his confusion were the blue uniforms worn by several Confederate companies in the Fifteenth and Nineteenth. Zollicoffer ordered Cummings to continue to hold his fire and then rode forward toward the Federal line, believing it to be the Mississippians and intending to stop their firing. Many members of the Nineteenth broke ranks to follow him. Riding into the lines of the enemy, Zollicoffer did not realize his mistake until one of his aides began firing his revolver. Before the general could escape, a fusillade blasted him from the saddle, leaving his lifeless body in the mud. The fire of the enemy, coupled with the shock of Zollicoffer's death, panicked the Nineteenth. The regiment began to fall back in disorder.[48]

Learning of Zollicoffer's death, Crittenden rode to the front and gave command of Zollicoffer's brigade to Cummings, who was struggling to readjust the regiment's lines. The Federals now began to advance against the Confederate left. As the Nineteenth fell back, the Twenty-Fifth Tennessee came to its aid. However, Federal pressure on its front and flank forced the Twenty-Fifth to fall back as well.[49]

Trying to hold the line, Crittenden ordered Carroll to bring up his brigade, and to ease the pressure on his left he ordered the Fifteenth Mississippi to charge the Union center. Carroll sent his Twenty-Eighth Tennessee in support of the Fifteenth Mississippi's attack. Elements of the Twenty-Eighth also helped shore up the Confederate left, aiding a counterattack by the Nineteenth Tennessee that checked the Federal advance and won control of a rail fence, where the regiment halted and exchanged fire with the Union line. Crittenden also deployed some artillery, but the cannon fire proved ineffectual.[50]

The failure of the artillery was unfortunate because the Nineteenth, like other Confederate regiments on the firing line, was losing a battle of firepower with the Federals. Most of General Thomas's regiments had recently been issued new, highly accurate Enfield rifles, which the motley assortment of Confederate arms simply could not match. Adding to the disparity in the quality of arms was the rain. Wet powder in the firing pan often caused the old flintlock muskets and country rifles to misfire. One Confederate officer estimated that nearly one-half of the Confederate weapons would not fire. Several members of the Nineteenth became so enraged that they broke their worthless flintlocks over the fence. Riding along the lines, Carroll witnessed many of the men abandoning the field, unable to use their weapons.[51]

As the Federals continued to attempt to flank the Confederate left, Carroll ordered the Nineteenth to disengage with the enemy to its front and shift to the left. Misunderstanding the order, the regiment again became confused. Lieutenant Colonel Francis Walker, now commanding the regiment, began to move back and forth among the companies, settling the men and moving them to their assigned spot. Meanwhile, the Fifteenth Mississippi's drive on the Federal center and right was repulsed. The fighting all along the battlefront was fierce, with the Confederates desperately attempting to hold their line in the face of increasing Federal pressure.[52]

At 9:00 A.M., Thomas ordered one of his regiments to fix bayonets and charge the Confederate left. The Twenty-Fifth Tennessee and the Nineteenth broke and fled in confusion. Carroll directed the Twenty-Ninth Tennessee to repel the charge, but when its colonel fell, it too broke. At about the same time as the collapse of the Confederate left, a flanking attack on the right forced back the Fifteenth Mississippi and Twentieth Tennessee. Panic now reigned. Tired, frightened Rebels ran from the field in the face of a renewed Federal advance all along the front.[53]

In the wild scramble back down the Mill Springs Road, the Confederates abandoned haversacks, cartridge boxes, weapons, and even their comrades. Regimental musician William J. Worsham and some of his companions in the Nineteenth carried a mortally wounded friend to the yard of a log cabin that served as a Confederate aid station. As the Federals approached, Worsham and his companions began to fall back. Decades later, Worsham could still remember the look on the man's face as he lay on a blanket staring at his comrades who were leaving him alone to die. Others, however, including regimental surgeon Dulany, refused to leave the wounded and dying. Dulany was captured (but later released) by the pursuing Federals.[54]

The first true battlefield experience for the Nineteenth had proven to be a disaster. But why? Why had the regiment and the Confederate force as a whole been routed? Certainly, inadequate firearms and poor leadership were factors. Furthermore, the long night's march in numbing cold left the men of the Nineteenth exhausted and vulnerable to sustained enemy pressure. The lack of support also undermined the regiment's morale. Civil War soldiers generally could carry on intense firefights for only a half hour or so. If not relieved by then, they would begin to drift from the battle line to search for water or ammunition or to rest and clean their weapons. Given these factors, along with the regiment's poor training, the Nineteenth's collapse at the Battle of Mill Springs is understandable.[55]

Confederate cavalry screened the routed troops, but fortunately General Thomas did not launch an immediate, all-out pursuit. Around 3:00 P.M., the exhausted and demoralized Confederates trudged into the Beech Grove defenses soaked to the skin. Within an hour, some of Thomas's artillery arrived and began an exchange of fire with Confederate artillery that lasted into the night. Despite the cannonade, members of the Nineteenth settled into their cabins to dry off, prepare a hot meal, and recuperate from their ordeal. Soon, however, the order came to abandon the camp. Crittenden and his lieutenants had concluded that an immediate retreat across the river to Mill Springs was the only way to save the army. Throughout the night, a small stern-wheel steamboat, the *Noble Ellis*, with two flatboats lashed to its sides, ferried the disheartened little army across the river. As dawn came, Sergeant Major Doak sat on the bank and gazed across the river at the troops still at Beech Grove. He saw frightened members of the Nineteenth shoving their way past other men who were clamoring to board the boats. Cavalrymen rode back and forth, yelling and whooping in an unsuccessful effort to cajole their mounts to swim the flooded river—the horses having better sense than the foolhardy soldiers who tried to swim and were drowned or swept away. Frightened soldiers had to be beaten off of the overloaded boats to keep them from being swamped. Amid all the chaos, Federal shells continued to fall.[56]

As the sun came up, Crittenden had the *Noble Ellis* burned and began to organize the long retreat southward along the Cumberland River to Gainesboro, Tennessee, where the troops could be supplied. They would have little to subsist on during the retreat, for Crittenden had had to abandon most of his commissary stores and camp equipment, along with almost all of his artillery, many small arms and much ammunition, more than one hundred wagons, and around one thousand horses and mules.[57]

The shattered force began the dismal eighty-mile trek toward Gainesboro. Along the way, the men had little to eat. On one occasion, the day's ration consisted solely of cornmeal. Without utensils, the men improvised, cooking their "dough" on boards placed near the fire. On another occasion, the hungry men mixed flour, lard, and salt into a paste, rolled it into a pencil-shaped string, and wrapped it around their ramrods to cook over an open fire. This miserable diet, the incessant sleet and snow, the lack of tents, and the fear of enemy pursuers resulted in widespread desertion. Many officers and men simply headed for home, having had their fill of war. Among the deserters was Private Jacob Carmack of Company I of the Nineteenth. After his father, Isaac, was killed at Fishing Creek, the young Rebel decided to return home to care for his mother and six siblings. He no doubt felt that his family had sacrificed enough for "the cause." Adding to the gloom surrounding the retreat was the drunkenness of both Crittenden and Carroll, which forced a disgusted Colonel William Wood of the Sixteenth Alabama, the third-ranking officer, to lead the withdrawal. Years later veterans of some of the hardest fighting and toughest conditions in the western theater remembered the retreat from Mill Springs as their worst experience of the war.[58]

On Sunday evening, January 26, a week after the disastrous battle, the remnants of Crittenden's division reached Gainesboro, where a steamer from Nashville unloaded badly needed food, clothing, and tents. Two weeks later, the men moved to Camp Fogg near Carthage. Although Crittenden had suffered only some five hundred casualties at Mill Springs (thirty-five from the Nineteenth) and his division was now rested and resupplied, the men's spirit had been broken by the rout and the ordeal of the retreat. The division would need time to rebuild morale before taking the field again.[59]

Two captains in the Nineteenth, Zadoc Willett of Company B and John Powell of Company A, took this time to try to recruit a regiment of their own in East Tennessee. Apparently dissatisfied in the Nineteenth, or perhaps wanting to put their military education to better use and to rise in the ranks, the two officers advertised for weeks but garnered few recruits. Confederate volunteers from the region were becoming scarce, especially with the possibility of Union invasion threatening the families of secessionists. The news of Crittenden's defeat had panicked East Tennessee's Confederate population. There was fear of an immediate strike by Thomas and open rebellion by the loyalists. Colonel Cummings tried to reassure his wife that the Tories would not harm her and the children, but he and the rest of the regiment certainly worried about the safety of their loved ones back home.[60]

While at Camp Fogg, Crittenden's men learned of the fall of Forts Henry and Donelson and of General Johnston's evacuation of Nashville. The general was headed southward to Murfreesboro, and he ordered Crittenden's division to rendezvous with him there. The Confederate front in the western theater had collapsed, and Johnston was retreating fast. Although the men in the Nineteenth read newspapers that ridiculed Johnston and blamed him for the recent disaster, they retained confidence in him.[61]

When Crittenden's force reached Murfreesboro, some of the stragglers and deserters from the Mill Springs retreat rejoined it. Perhaps the most unexpected face among the returning troops of the Nineteenth was that of William Vestal of "Camp Drunk" fame. He had been shot through the bowels at Mill Springs, the ball exiting near the spine; believing the wound to be mortal, his comrades had left him in Monticello, Kentucky, as they fled southward. Captured by the pursuing Federals, Vestal was taken to a hospital, where he summoned the strength to escape and return to the regiment. In sharp contrast to Vestal's dedication to duty stood the apathy of Daniel Miller. He settled into a comfortable post in the Quartermaster's Department in Knoxville and married Charlotte. His bride remained in Hawkins County during this time, and Daniel wrote her news of William and other mutual friends.[62]

In Murfreesboro, Johnston organized his combined force into three divisions under Generals William J. Hardee, Gideon Pillow, and Crittenden. The Nineteenth remained in Crittenden's division. However, Colonel W. S. Statham replaced Cummings as brigade commander, and Cummings returned to the regiment.[63]

Meanwhile, in West Tennessee and northern Mississippi, General P. G. T. Beauregard was building a new Rebel army, and he requested that Johnston join him. At dawn on February 28, 1862, Johnston marched his men southward from Murfreesboro, while he evaluated his options. Over the next two weeks, his troops plodded along the muddy roads of Middle Tennessee and northern Alabama to the town of Decatur. The march was largely uneventful except for the terrible weather. The men were buffeted by heavy rains, occasional snow, and high winds. One member of the Nineteenth recalled a particularly miserable night near Athens, Alabama, when the tents and camp equipage were sent ahead of the regiment. As a torrential rain pelted the soldiers, they were forced to sleep sitting with their backs against trees or prostrate in the oozing mud. Later, when tents were available, the soldiers remembered having to hold on to them while they slept lest the wind blow them away.[64]

Even as they cursed the horrible weather, however, the men were cheered by the civilians along their route. Citizens displayed Confederate flags and yelled encouragement to the soldiers as they filed past. Along the way, Johnston issued better weapons to his men, including new Enfield rifles from England. The Nineteenth, however, did not receive Enfields but were instead rearmed with reconditioned rifled muskets—still a great improvement.[65]

Johnston at last became convinced that he should join Beauregard at Corinth, Mississippi. On March 15, the Nineteenth, along with the rest of Johnston's weary troops, left Decatur. They arrived at Corinth on March 20. There Beauregard and Johnston combined their forces into the Army of the Mississippi, organized into four corps under Generals Hardee, Polk, Braxton Bragg, and John C. Breckinridge. Breckinridge, a former vice president of the United States, had replaced Crittenden when the latter (along with General Carroll) was arrested for drunkenness. Breckinridge's reserve corps (in reality a division) consisted of Colonel Robert Trabue's brigade of Kentuckians, Brigadier General John S. Bowen's brigade of Tennesseans and Arkansans, and Statham's brigade, composed of the Fifteenth and Twenty-Second Mississippi and the Nineteenth, Twentieth, Twenty-Eighth, and Forty-Fifth Tennessee.[66]

After organizing the army, Beauregard and Johnston formulated a strategy to recapture the initiative in the west. Their plan was a surprise attack on Major General Ulysses S. Grant's Army of the Tennessee, which was positioned near a small riverboat stop called Pittsburg Landing. If Grant's army could be attacked before General Buell's Army of the Ohio could join him, the Confederates might be able to defeat the two Federal forces in detail and perhaps liberate West and Middle Tennessee.[67]

Johnston left the formulation of a battle plan to Beauregard, who designed an assault of successive waves to sweep the enemy from the field, each wave consisting of a corps. He did not foresee that the four corps would become hopelessly intermingled. In addition, Beauregard's timetable was unrealistic. He allowed only one day for the corps commanders to assemble their scattered units, march some twenty miles, and get into position for an attack the next morning. Poor roads, bad directions, and green troops would all combine to make a one-day march impossible.[68]

To make matters worse, on the morning of April 4 (the time designated for the attack), a torrential rain began falling, turning the roads into thick mud. By that time, the operation was twelve hours behind schedule, and Johnston was forced to postpone the attack until the following morning. However, that night the rain continued to fall, and the already bad roads became quagmires with muck a foot deep. By late afternoon of the fifth, Polk's and Bragg's corps were still not properly deployed, and Breckinridge's tired, mud-splattered troops (designated as the army's reserve) were still far to the rear. The attack was again postponed.[69]

Late that night, Breckinridge's corps stumbled to its line of departure for the next day's battle. The men lay down on the wet grass and got what rest they could. Many were hungry. The soldiers had lived on a few biscuits and small pieces of meat since the march began. Although exhausted, many could not sleep; thoughts of tomorrow's battle weighed heavily on them. Surely, some members of the Nineteenth must have thought about the coming dawn and the eerie similarities between this and their last experience in battle. It was raining and cold then, too, and it was also the day before the Sabbath.[70]

As dawn approached, Johnston worried that Buell might send reinforcements to Grant by river. If these troops landed in the Confederate rear near Hamburg, the Rebels would be caught in a vise. To safeguard against such a disaster, Johnston personally ordered Colonel George Maney, commander of the First Tennessee Infantry, to take his battalion, the Nineteenth Tennessee, and Colonel Nathan Bedford Forrest's independent cavalry regiment to Greer's Ford on Lick Creek. From that point, Maney could survey the river and the Confederate rear. Once Maney was satisfied that Buell's men were not going to land at Hamburg, he could join the assault.[71]

Around 5:00 A.M., the crash of musketry announced the Confederate onslaught. All through the morning, the soldiers of the Nineteenth waited

The Nineteenth at Shiloh. Drawn by William Nelson (see next page.)

A. 4/6: predawn–10:00 A.M. *As part of Colonel George Maney's force, the Nineteenth guarded the Lick Creek ford.*

B. 4/6: about 2:30 P.M. *Leaving Lick Creek, the Nineteenth joined in Colonel Maney's charge across Sarah Bell Field to the Manse George cabin and beyond toward Bloody Pond.*

C. 4/6: 4:00–5:00 P.M. *Released from Maney's command, the Nineteenth rejoined Statham's brigade, participating in the collapse of the Hornet's Nest. There General Prentiss may have surrendered to Colonel Francis Walker commanding the regiment. D. 4/6: about 7:00 P.M. At dusk, the Nineteenth, along with the rest of Statham's brigade, halted at General Grant's last line of defense at Pittsburg Landing.*

E. 4/6: P.M. *Breckinridge withdrew his regiments (including the Nineteenth) to the camps of General McClernand's division, where there was widespread looting.*

F. 4/7: about 8:00–11:00 A.M. *Breckinridge moved his units (including the Nineteenth) toward the sounds of fighting as General Nelson opened his attack on the Confederate right. The Nineteenth fought in the area of the Sunken Road.*

G. 4/7: early afternoon. *The Nineteenth as part of Statham's brigade was driven from Duncan Field and forced back with the rest of the Confederate Army.*

H. 4/7: 3:00–5:00 P.M. *Breckinridge's corps formed the core of the Confederate rear guard as Beauregard's battered army retreated.*

I. 4/7: P.M. *Breckinridge's men camp at this position before moving to Mickie's farm and eventually Corinth.*

nervously. Ahead of them, in the tangled forest and farmers' fields, the battle raged with increasing fury. A crescendo of musketry and cannon echoed along Lick Creek, and still they waited. In the distance, the men could see ambulances rolling along with their bloody cargo. When anyone passed by,

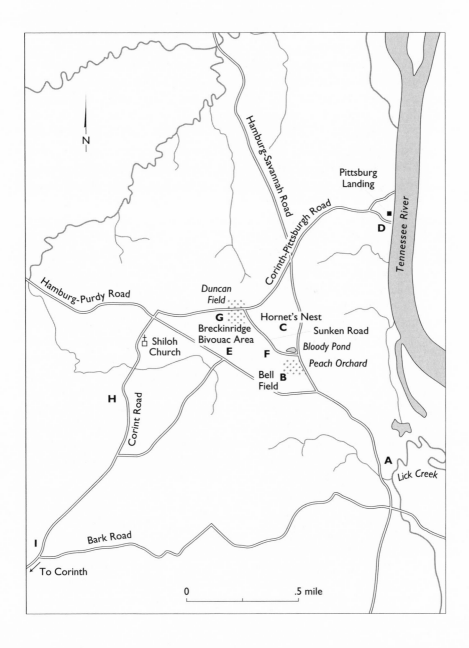

the soldiers eagerly sought news from the front. It was all good. The Yankees were falling back, abandoning their camps. It appeared that a great victory was at hand.[72]

By 11:00 A.M., Maney was convinced that Buell would not land at Hamburg, and he released the Nineteenth and Forrest's cavalry from his command. Both units, along with Maney's, began to advance toward the front. Marching at the double-quick up the Hamburg-Savannah Road toward the sound of battle, the men of the Nineteenth began to shed their knapsacks and blankets. As they neared the front, they passed fields strewn with the dead and wounded of both sides. Wounded Rebels cheered—happy to see reinforcements no matter how meager. Stragglers, exhausted or frightened by the morning assaults, regained their strength and joined the ranks of these fresh units.[73]

As Maney approached Sarah Bell's Field, he was overtaken by his division commander, Major General Frank Cheatham, who ordered him to take units of his choice and attack a Federal battery blocking the Confederate advance near the George Manse cabin at the center of the so-called Hornet's Nest, where Federal troops were making a strong stand. Maney selected his own First Tennessee Battalion, the Ninth Tennessee Infantry, the Sixth and Seventh Kentucky Infantry, and the Nineteenth Tennessee. Deploying the regiments in a battle line, Maney placed the First Tennessee on the left, the Ninth Tennessee in the center, and the Nineteenth Tennessee on the right, with the Sixth and Seventh Kentucky in support.[74]

At 2:30 P.M., Maney began to move his troops forward. As the men of the Nineteenth crossed an open field, they could see their comrades in Statham's brigade falling back after a failed attempt to pierce the Federal defenses on the left of the Hornet's Nest. To their front, troops of Colonel Zacariah C. Deas's Alabama brigade began to fall back into the advancing line. Maney's regiments opened their ranks to allow the exhausted and bloodied Alabamians to pass to the rear. Some of the advancing soldiers sneered at the perceived cowardice of Dea's men, yelling "flicker, flicker" at them—a reference to the yellow hammer, a bird native to Alabama. But not all of Maney's troops themselves were brave. A member of the First Tennessee remembered seeing a man shoot off his own finger rather than cross the field.[75]

Bearing left, the charging East Tennesseans crossed a cornfield and approached the Manse cabin. There the Federal fire intensified, tearing into the Nineteenth's ranks and killing and wounding many. Among those were Colonel Cummings, who lost a finger, and Captains Willett and Walker, who died leading their companies. Storming the cabin and gaining the woods to the west of the field, near the Sunken Road, Maney's men came under a crossfire. They lay down and commenced a heavy exchange with the enemy.[76]

Once his troops were under cover of woods, Maney released the Nine-teenth to return to Statham's brigade. Sometime between 3:00 and 4:00 P.M., during a lull in the fighting, the regiment rejoined the brigade. By 4:00 P.M., Breckinridge launched Statham's and Bowen's brigades along with two brigades of Bragg's corps in a fierce assault on the left flank of the Hornet's Nest. Both sides suffered heavy casualties as the wave of Confederates, scream-ing the defiant Rebel yell, slammed into the Federal lines. The heavily wooded and broken terrain was covered with acrid smoke. As at Mill Springs, com-mand and control proved virtually impossible to maintain. Regiments and companies broke into small groups of men rushing forward, firing, reloading, and rushing forward again.[77]

By 5:00 P.M., the Hornet's Nest began to collapse. The Federal lines slowly crumbled under the pressure of Breckinridge's forces on the left and Bragg's on the right. Rushing through the shattered Federal line, the Nineteenth linked up with the Crescent Regiment of New Orleans coming from the opposite direction. By 5:30 P.M., the remnants of the defending forces surrendered and Federal resistance in the Hornet's Nest ended. As the prisoners were being dis-armed, many members of the Nineteenth eagerly exchanged their altered flintlocks for Federal Enfield rifles. The regiment may have claimed an even greater prize of war. At least two veterans of the Nineteenth and a Confederate Congressman maintained that Brigadier General Benjamin M. Prentiss, com-mander of the Hornet's Nest's defenders, surrendered his sword to Lieutenant Colonel Walker.[78]

Following the collapse of the Hornet's Nest, the Confederates pushed ahead, anticipating a complete rout of the Federal army. Grant in the mean-time had established a strong line of artillery near Pittsburg Landing as a last-ditch defense. Rebel units trying this line found the rifle and cannon fire unbearable and retreated in disorder. By 6:00 P.M., with dusk approaching, Bragg hastily organized various brigades for one final assault on the Federal left. Brigadier General Breckinridge, with Statham's and Bowen's brigades, prepared to support the charge. Unexpectedly, General Beauregard, who since Johnston's death that afternoon had commanded the Rebel army, sent word to call off the assault. Believing the Yankees to be in retreat and his own men in need of rest, he saw no value in a frontal attack against the strong Federal posi-tion. The tired, hungry, and bloodied foot soldiers facing the wall of cannon undoubtedly agreed.[79]

As the sky grew dark, Statham's and Bowen's brigades retired to the Federal camps overrun that morning and began helping themselves to the spoils of war. Men in the Nineteenth satisfied their hunger with captured bacon, sugar, and crackers. Frightful images must have crept into their minds now that they had time to reflect on the events of the day. One soldier remembered vividly the sight of a busy aid station with dead men lying all about "and the long line of wounded and dying men on the way to the surgeon's station; the trickling blood from the improvised stretchers; the white upturned face still streaked with powder . . . the quick breath and far-away look; the amputated legs and arms laid in a tangled heap. . . ."[80]

After filling their stomachs, the men looked for a place to rest, whether in the captured tents or at the roots of trees. Unfortunately, Federal gunboats firing intermittently into the Confederate lines made rest virtually impossible. To make matters worse, around 10:00 P.M. the heavens unleashed a deluge on the armies. Lying in the rain, the soldiers could hear the cries of the wounded and the boom of Federal cannon all through the night. Most thought they had won a great victory. Little did they expect what the next morning would bring.[81]

Unknown to most of the Rebels, during the night the Federals were reinforced by General Buell's army and a fresh division of Grant's army, giving the Federals a great numerical advantage. Far from retreating, Grant and Buell planned to sweep Beauregard's army from the field the next morning. Around 3:00 A.M., the thunderstorm began to subside. Just before dawn, the combined Federal armies, some forty-five thousand strong, advanced cautiously toward the Confederate camps. Beauregard hastily set about locating and deploying his scattered troops. The commingled Confederate corps had not been separated during the night, meaning the Confederate generals would have to take command of separate sectors of the battlefront in order to restore some semblance of command and control. Only Breckinridge had managed to keep his corps intact.[82]

Breckinridge's men assembled and moved toward the front, deploying along the old Hornet's Nest front. There they encountered Buell's troops, sparking a heavy engagement along the East Corinth and Corinth Roads. Meanwhile, to the west, Grant's army, recovered from yesterday's beating, began to exert heavy pressure on the Confederate left flank. The outnumbered and exhausted Rebels began to slowly give ground.[83]

Posted on the right-center, in woods near the Sarah Bell Field, the Nineteenth became the unwilling recipient of the stray Federal shells. The men were ordered to take cover. Sergeant Major Doak was lying down behind a giant oak when Benjamin Ish of Company E joined him and began to crowd the sergeant major away from the safe middle of the tree. Whether through fear or a lifelong affliction, the young private began to stutter: "Di-Di-Doak, I n-n-never knew vally o' t-t-timber afore. Di-Di-Dam' fever I g-g-gru-ub-grub-'nother s-s-sup-pprou-out's long's I live."[84]

Federal troops advanced from the woods surrounding Bloody Pond toward the George Manse cabin and across Sarah Bell Field. There they were met by heavy Confederate artillery fire and by an intense volley of musketry delivered by elements of Bowen's and Statham's brigades, including the Nineteenth, which had emerged from the underbrush. Unable to withstand the heavy fire, the Federals withdrew. Major General Hardee ordered a counterattack, using Bowen's brigade to spearhead the assault. Federal cannons stopped the Confederate charge cold.[85]

The Yankee infantry then advanced once more, breaking the Rebel line and overrunning a battery of the Washington artillery. The Confederates rallied in the woods along the Purdy-Hamburg Road and charged again to recapture the cannon. When the Crescent Regiment from Louisiana engaged in a desperate hand-to-hand struggle for control of the guns, Breckinridge asked his staff if any of his regiments could aid them. Lieutenant Colonel Walker, who was within earshot, replied that the Nineteenth could. Screaming the Rebel yell, the Nineteenth charged into the melee along with the other regiments of Statham's brigade. Fighting hand-to-hand, they helped push the Federals back. Both sides continued to attack and counterattack. Sergeant Major Doak remembered participating in three separate charges against a Federal battery before a rifle ball mangled his left hand and he had to leave the field.[86]

Toward noon, the counterthrusts of the weary Confederates holding the right flank began to lose momentum, and their line began to crumble in the face of renewed Federal assaults. Situated in a thicket of white oaks near Duncan Field, the men of the Nineteenth watched as long lines of Federals approached. Much to their delight, a Yankee regiment to their front remained in column formation, giving the Nineteenth a huge undefended flank to fire into. The men released a devastating fusillade and then participated in an intense firefight that Union Brigadier General William Tecumseh Sherman recalled being "the severest musketry fire I ever heard." The remnants of the enemy regiment staggered back. The Nineteenth's success was only temporary, however. The regiment, along with the rest of Breckinridge's corps, was driven from Duncan Field to the southwest toward Shiloh Church, leaving behind a great number of killed and wounded.[87]

Doak's hand was being treated by a captured Federal surgeon when Breckinridge's line began to break. The surgeon warned Doak to escape while he could. Taking a shot of brandy, the young Rebel left the hospital, deftly avoiding the advancing Federal columns. As Doak fled, he was sickened by the sights and sounds of the battlefield—the groans of the wounded, dead men littering the ground, and a wandering horse with half its shoulder torn away.

Entering another aid station far to the rear, he became ill at the sight of amputated feet, fingers, and toes. On the verge of vomiting, he staggered out of the
tent and joined other soldiers headed rearward.[88]

The whole Confederate line was now collapsing. By 2:00 P.M., it was apparent to Beauregard that his men could endure no more, and the army would
have to retreat. By 3:00 P.M., he had organized a five-thousand-man rear guard
on a ridge south of Shiloh Church along the Corinth Road. Breckinridge's
brigades made up the bulk of the force. This line held the Federals at bay until
about 5:00 P.M., allowing the battered Southern army to withdraw. Breckinridge
then moved his command to the intersection of the Corinth and Bark Roads,
camping for the night. The next day the corps moved to Mickie's (Micky's)
Farm, eight miles from Corinth. Breckinridge held this position until the April
8, allowing Beauregard to make good his army's escape and to organize a defense
at Corinth. With the rest of the army safe and the Federals advancing, the
Nineteenth, along with the rest of Breckinridge's men, abandoned Mickie's and
retired to Corinth.[89]

The battle of Shiloh was over, but its effects on the men of the Nineteenth and the populace of both nations were far-reaching. This was the costli-
est battle in the conflict to date (twenty-three thousand combined casualties);
more Americans died in this single battle than in all of America's previous
wars together. Beauregard placed Southern casualties at approximately 25 percent of his total force. The Nineteenth lost approximately that proportion of
its strength. It would never fully recover from this blow.[90]

Nor would the communities that sent the men of the Nineteenth to war
recover. Upon hearing that eight members of his Sullivan County congregation
had been killed, the Reverend Sullins remarked that "[t]he war has reached old
Sullivan now." Sullins's attachment to the men of the regiment went well
beyond the Sullivan countians:

> I had helped to enlist them all and knew their homes and loved
> ones. No chaplain ever had a sadder part than I. For these troops
> in the Nineteenth Tennessee were enlisted in the East Tennessee
> portion of the Holston Conference, and I had been a pastor in
> nearly every town from which they came—Chattanooga, Athens,
> Knoxville, Jonesboro, Blountville, Bristol, etc. I had enjoyed the
> Christian hospitality of many of their homes, and knew their
> families. And when the name of one was called and no response,
> I thought of some loved one, father or mother, brother, sister, wife,
> or child, to whom the news of his death would with crushing
> weight bring heartache and tears.

Sullins was especially saddened by the death of Captain Willett. When told that the captain's body was in a box ready to be shipped to Washington County, the clergyman "felt a great thud at my heart as I thought of his beautiful young wife, Rettie Lyle, my dear old pupil up in the hills by Jonesboro. . . ."[91]

Most of the regiment's losses, however, were wounded. The hospitals, pub-lic buildings, and private homes in and around Corinth were full of broken and maimed soldiers. Having escaped the Federals and survived a dismal march, Sergeant Major Doak reported to a makeshift hospital at the Old Female Seminary. There Sister Agatha of the Sisters of Mercy cared for his wounded hand and the inflammation and fever caused by erysipelas. Although gravely ill, Doak was fortunate in being within Confederate lines. Other members of the regiment had been wounded and left on the field. Searching the battlefield the night of the second day's fighting, the Reverend Sullins managed to avoid the Yankees but could not find his brother-in-law, Second Lieutenant Robert L. Blair of Company G. Months later, Sullins learned that Blair had injured his ankle in one of the charges of the Nineteenth on the morning of April 7. Unable to walk, Blair had been captured and sent to Johnson's Island Prison in Ohio. Lieutenant J. M. Sims of Company F was also seriously wounded, unable to walk, and captured by Federal troops. Sims was luckier than Blair, however. His brother, B. M. Sims, searched the battlefield and, finding the wounded Sims in a Federal hospital, slipped him out of the tent and carried him about five miles; the pair was rescued by a detachment of Forrest's cavalry.[92]

As irreplaceable as the casualties were to the Nineteenth and the South as a whole, perhaps the worst loss the Confederacy suffered at Shiloh was its optimism. Morale in Beauregard's army plummeted in the wake of the battle. A New Orleans journalist captured the mood of the Southern people when he said, "after Shiloh the South never smiled again." In fact, the war would never be viewed the same way again. The men in the Nineteenth, like their fellow Southerners, realized that the collapse of Johnston's western front and the hor-rific losses at Shiloh foretold a much longer and harder road ahead if inde-pendence was to be attained. The first year of the war was over, and the clerks and farmers who had marched and fought from eastern Kentucky to the Tennessee River, who had seen comrades killed and wounded, who had starved and frozen, who had endured illness and fatigue, found that the war had irrevocably changed them. Their innocence and arrogance were now gone, replaced by a ruggedness of mind and body, painful memories, and ques-tions about their commitment to "the cause"—a commitment that would be sorely tested in the months ahead.[93]

4 ❧

"Fortunes of War"

From Corinth to Stones River

May 1862 found General Beauregard's battered Army of the Mississippi entrenched near the railroad junction of Corinth, Mississippi. Several weeks had passed since the bloody Confederate repulse at Shiloh, and the situation appeared desperate. Beauregard's thinned ranks had been augmented by the recent arrival of Major General Earl Van Dorn's Army of the West and by troops rushed from elsewhere in the western theater. These combined forces numbered some seventy thousand in the face of over one hundred thousand Union troops slowly advancing toward Corinth.[1]

Yellow flags belonging to the Confederate hospital corps decorated the town's hotels, public buildings, schools, churches, and larger homes. These makeshift hospitals overflowed with over twenty thousand sick and wounded. Groaning men smeared in filth and blood lay on the sidewalks, porches, and railroad platforms awaiting care or death. A shortage of physicians and medical supplies only exacerbated the situation.[2]

Along with these horrors, epidemics of typhoid fever, erysipelas, dysentery, malaria, and measles raged through the army camps. The officers of the Nineteenth, who had about three hundred men fit for duty after Shiloh, watched as their sick list increased daily and the death toll mounted. As if all this were not enough, a severe shortage of food, especially fresh vegetables, was producing malnutrition and scurvy. The men of the Nineteenth subsisted on flour, sugar, molasses, a little beef, and rye for coffee. Water, too, was in short supply, and what was available was contaminated. One veteran in the regiment remembered the men having to dig holes in the ground to allow "seep water" to fill a pit, where it was drunk eagerly by the thirsty soldiers. With latrines nearby, it is little wonder that dysentery and typhoid plagued the men. After a day or two, "wiggletails" would infest the water hole, and new sources would have to be dug out of the swampy ground.[3]

For those lucky enough to avoid illness, the weeks after Shiloh were filled with the dull routine of camp life and mind-numbing drill punctuated by occasional skirmishes with Yankee patrols. Statham's brigade (including the Nineteenth) spent most of its time on provost duty in and around Corinth. Given the horrendous conditions faced by these men, it is surprising that morale held up as well as it did. While there were desertions, for the most part a grim determination prevailed in all the Rebel ranks. This was partly due to their commitment to independence, but the men now also felt they had little choice. With the upcoming expiration of the twelve-month enlistment term for scores of volunteer regiments, the Confederate Congress resorted to an extreme measure. On April 16, it passed the first national conscription act in American history, declaring that all white males between eighteen and thirty-five not legally exempt were subject to service in the Confederate army for three years unless the war ended sooner. All soldiers then serving had to continue for an additional three-year term. Even those already in the army whose ages fell outside the conscript age were required to remain in service for ninety days or until suitable replacements could be found.[4]

A revolution to protect personal liberty had now taken a radical turn. The morale of the twelve-month men fell immediately. After nearly a year of disease, privation, and the hardships and horrors of a soldier's life, the volunteers eagerly anticipated a return to the comforts of home. They now were asked to sacrifice more blood and sweat for the Southern cause. This would be a severe test of their patriotism.[5]

The act allowed the men to elect new officers for their additional three-year period of service. Elections were scheduled for May; the entire Confederate force at Corinth was to be "reorganized." Would the old officers be reelected, or would new ones take their place? It is generally accepted that the Confederate officer corps came from the elite of Southern society. This was undoubtedly true in the spring of 1861, when traditional community leaders led their neighbors off to war. However, as death, wounds, resignation, and capture removed officers, were they replaced by members of the same class? The election results of the Nineteenth at Corinth suggest answers to such questions and shed light on the dynamics of small-unit leadership in the Confederate army.[6]

There was considerable turnover among the commissioned officers in the regiment. Colonel Cummings declined to run for reelection, most likely because of his age, a wound suffered during the Mexican War that left him lame, and the

TABLE 2

Disposition of the Original Officer Corps of the Nineteenth
Tennessee in the Regiment's Reorganization at Corinth, May 1862

Unit	Name	Outcome
Field Officers	Col. David H. Cummings	Resigned (Wounded)
	Lt. Col. Francis M. Walker	Promoted to Colonel
	Major Abraham Fulkerson	Not Reelected (Wounded)
	Adjutant V. Q. Johnson	Not Reelected
	Sgt. Maj. Henry M. Doak	Not Reelected (Wounded)
	Surgeon Joseph E. Dulany	Remained in Position
	Quartermaster A. D. Taylor	Remained in Position
	Chaplain David Sullins	Resigned (Promotion)
Company A	Capt. John D. Powell	Not Reelected
	1st Lt. V. Q. Johnson	Not Reelected
	2nd Lt. Daniel Kennedy	Promoted to Captain
	3rd Lt. Francis Foust	Promoted to 1st Lt.
Company B	Capt. Zadoc Willett	Killed at Shiloh
	1st Lt. Joseph Conley	Killed at Mill Springs
	2nd Lt. Nathan Gregg	Resigned (Wounded)
	3rd Lt. James G. Deaderick	Promoted to Captain
Company C	Capt. James P. Snapp	Not Reelected
	1st Lt. Charles St. John	Resigned (Illness)
	2nd Lt. George W. Hull	Died
	3rd Lt. John M. Jones	Not Reelected
Company D	Capt. Warner E. Colville	Resigned
	1st Lt. Peter Miller	Resigned (Illness)
	2nd Lt. James A. Wallace	Resigned
	3rd Lt. Samuel J. A. Frazier	Promoted to 1st Lt.
Company E	Capt. John W. Paxton	Resigned (Illness)
	1st Lt. John M. Miller	Not Reelected
	2nd Lt. J. K. Graham	Resigned
	3rd Lt. William W. Lackey	Promoted to Captain
Company F	Capt. John H. Hannah	Remained in Position
	1st Lt. Parley C. Gaston	Not Reelected
	2nd Lt. Jesse M. Sims	Promoted to 1st Lt.
	3rd Lt. J. C. Holms	Not Reelected
Company G	Capt. Abraham L. Gammon	Remained in Position
	1st Lt. James A. Rhea	Remained in Position
	2nd Lt. Robert L. Blair	Not Reelected (Captured)
	3rd Lt. James Carlton	Not Reelected

TABLE 2 (CONTINUED)

Unit	Name	Outcome
Company H	Capt. William H. Lowry	Not Reelected
	1st Lt. U. L. York	Not Reelected
	2nd Lt. Dimmon A. Wilkins	Not Reelected
	3rd Lt. Thomas Maston	Not Reelected
Company I	Capt. Thomas Walker	Killed at Shiloh
	1st Lt. Beriah F. Moore	Promoted to Lt. Col.
	2nd Lt. Warren Hooper	Resigned
	3rd Lt. John Lovejoy	?
Company K	Capt. Carrick W. Heiskell	Remained in Position
	1st Lt. Robert D. Powell	Killed at Barbourville
	2nd Lt. Samuel Powell	Not Reelected
	3rd Lt. Samuel Spears	Not Reelected

hand wound received at Shiloh. He was replaced by Francis Walker, the regiment's former lieutenant colonel. Walker's election was part of a pattern of previous officers being elevated in rank. For example, the regiment's new lieutenant colonel, Beriah F. Moore, was formerly a lieutenant and captain in Company I.[7]

However, not all of the old officers were reelected. Of the forty captains and lieutenants who officered the various companies at their conception in 1861, only eleven held a position after the reorganization. Many of the original officers had been killed, seriously wounded, captured, or promoted. Others had resigned during the last year, and a few simply were not chosen by their men. For example, the men of Company H replaced all their original command. Whether this was due to poor combat performance, overly strict discipline, or some other source of unpopularity is not clear.[8]

All the officers who were not reelected left the regiment, seeking election to positions in other units or attempting to organize new companies and regiments. Major Abraham Fulkerson, for example, who was not present at the reorganization because of a groin wound and failed to win an office, went back to East Tennessee and helped organize another regiment, which became the Sixty-Third Tennessee. Likewise, Sergeant Major Doak was not at the reorganization. He was in Knoxville recuperating from his hand wound. Although recommended for a commissioned officer's position in the regiment, Doak attempted to raise a volunteer company in Washington County. Unable to garner enough recruits, the young man obtained a lieutenancy in the Marines with the help of his father. While some officers such as Fulkerson and Doak managed to maintain or improve their rank, others faced the prospect of becoming privates—a dishonor they preferred to endure in another unit.[9]

Most of the newly commissioned officers in the regiment had been privates. In all, nineteen of the new lieutenants were former privates as well as three of the new captains: Ward C. Harvey of Company C, Joseph Frazier of Company D, and W. Paul McDermott of Company H. Among the field officers, Rufus A. Jarnigan, the unit's new major; Arthur Fulkerson, the new sergeant major; and William Bowles, the new adjutant, had been privates. Eight of the new company-grade officers had been noncommissioned officers, as had one of the field officers. However, veteran officers commanded seven of the regiment's ten companies, and both the new colonel and lieutenant colonel possessed command experience. Though the men were willing to elect privates as junior officers, they generally wanted experienced men as company commanders and field officers. The past year's combat had taught them the value of experience.[10]

Respect for social class was equally apparent. The new commissioned officer corps of the Nineteenth by and large came from the elite classes of East Tennessee in terms of both occupation and wealth. While several of the new officers could not be located in the census, enough were found to confirm the upper-class background of the regiment's new leaders. Like the original officer corps, these men came from wealthy, slaveholding, commercial farming families or those of urban professionals.[11]

There were a few exceptions, such as Thomas Carney and Nicholas P. Nail (former privates and now lieutenants in Company A). Carney, a journeyman tailor, listed $27 in aggregate wealth in the 1860 census, while Nail, a tinner, listed $150. Interestingly, both men were much older than the regimental average of twenty-six years—Carney was forty-four, Nail thirty-eight. Perhaps their age can explain their election; other possibilities include combat performance, personality, or even prewar occupation. As artisans living in Chattanooga, both men probably had daily contact with many of the men in the company, several of whom were close neighbors. Certainly wealth, social class, and experience were very influential in determining the new officers, but other factors were also at work, as exemplified by Carney and Nail.[12]

Unfortunately, the Compiled Service Records do not provide enough information on new noncommissioned officers to allow any firm conclusions to be drawn. However, based on what evidence does exist, it appears that social class was also a factor in the election. Although the average wealth of the noncommissioned officers was below the regional average—meaning that these men were obviously not members of the elite—the higher the rank, the more wealth the sergeant's or corporal's family possessed.[13]

TABLE 3

Reorganized Command of the Nineteenth Tennessee Infantry Regiment, May 1862

Co.	Name	Rank	Age	County	Occupation	Wealth	Slaves
F & S*	Francis M. Walker	Colonel	34	Hamilton	Lawyer	$15,000	2
F & S	Beriah F. Moore	Lt. Colonel	25	Hamilton	—	10,800	0
F & S	Rufus A. Jarnigan	Major	22	Anderson	Student	26,000	14
F & S	William Bowles	Adjutant	?	?	?	?	?
F & S	Arthur Fulkerson	Sgt.-Major	25	Hawkins	Teacher	15,000	9
F & S	Joseph E. Dulany	Surgeon	31	Sullivan	Physician	25,000	12
F & S	Addison D. Taylor	Quartermaster	41	Hamilton	Merchant	10,800	1
F & S	Apparently not filled	Chaplain	—	—	—	—	—
A	Daniel A. Kennedy	Captain	21	Hamilton	Druggist	8,000	0
B	James G. Deaderick	Captain	26	Washington	Lawyer	450	1
C	W. C. Harvey	Captain	?	?	?	?	?
D	Joseph G. Frazier	Captain	26	Rhea	Officer	2,500	0
E	W. W. Lackey	Captain	?	?	?	?	?
F	John H. Hannah	Captain	24	Polk	Postmaster	0	0
G	Abraham Gammon	Captain	54	Sullivan	Mail Agent	5,100	3
H	William McDermott	Captain	27	McMinn	Lawyer	9,000	8
I	J. D. Lively	Captain	?	?	?	?	?
K	Carrick W. Heiskell	Captain	24	Hawkins	Lawyer	19,400	2
MEAN			29			$11,312	4

NOTE: *F & S = Field and Staff.

With its reorganization complete, the Nineteenth, like the rest of General Beauregard's regiments, waited to see how their commander would respond to the deepening crisis at Corinth. They would not have to wait long. On May 25, 1862, with his army much reduced by disease and a vastly superior foe threatening to overwhelm him, Beauregard decided to abandon Corinth and retreat southward along the Mobile and Ohio Railroad to Tupelo, Mississippi, fifty-two miles away. That same morning, the Nineteenth boarded railroad cars and headed eight miles southward, where they would guard a vital bridge on the army's route of withdrawal. For about a week, the men lived in a swampy creek bottom with "scarcely enough ground above water to lie down." On May 30, Beauregard's main body evacuated Corinth and passed the sentinels of the Nineteenth on its way to Tupelo. Around noon on June 2, the Nineteenth gratefully boarded cars for its trip southward to rejoin the army.[14]

At Tupelo, the army received yet another shock. On June 20, Beauregard was replaced by General Braxton Bragg. The men of the Nineteenth had little time to get acquainted with the new commander because they, along with the rest of Breckinridge's division, joined Van Dorn's forces rushing to the defense of Vicksburg. The Mississippi River citadel was threatened by Union navy and army forces. Van Dorn's mission as new departmental commander in Mississippi and Louisiana was to protect Vicksburg at all costs, preventing Union control of the Great River and maintaining the tenuous link between the western and trans-Mississippi theaters.[15]

Arriving by train from Jackson, Mississippi, on July 1, the men of the Nineteenth were struck by the great wealth and beauty of Vicksburg, with its many fine houses and gardens. The regiment's encampment was about two miles from the city, but the men usually spent five days and nights of each week on picket duty along the city's levees. Within a few days, the novelty and charm of the city wore off as daily drill and inspection were initiated and the men were exposed to intermittent shelling. As the old enemies of boredom and monotony set in, the men sought any diversion. One especially unusual and dangerous pastime was to wait for the town's sandy soil to absorb a large-caliber projectile from the Union gunboats and then gather around the hole for the subdued explosion and a shower of dirt. A less peculiar but still dangerous activity was to sit on the housetops to observe the shelling and maneuvering of the enemy flotilla. On one occasion, a group from the regiment caught the attention of the gunboats. Shells began to rain down close to the house; the men scattered just before it was demolished by a direct hit.[16]

Although the local citizens were grateful for the protection afforded by the thousands of Confederate soldiers occupying the city, quite naturally some began to resent the presence of the troops near their homes because of the fire drawn from the Union fleets. The Nineteenth generally spent one to two afternoons and nights each week on the lawn of a large estate belonging to an Englishman. Being in plain view of the Union fleet, the camp was often shelled. The exasperated host could not force the men to leave, so he attempted to deflect the fury of the Yankee warships by flying the Union Jack above his house. The ploy failed. Vicksburg residents were also annoyed by the garrison troops' habit of freely taking whatever they needed, especially food. As time passed, orchards were depleted and livestock disappeared. As food became more scarce, prices soared, and many came to view the ragged troops as a barbarian horde. Nevertheless, most residents felt gratitude and sympathy for the men holding the Yankees at bay.[17]

As the Rebels endured day after day of shelling without being able to strike back, feelings of helplessness weighed heavily on them. When two Federal mortar boats moored on the east bank of the Mississippi, the Nineteenth had its chance for revenge. On a hot, muggy July 4, Statham's brigade was ordered to march four miles into the swamps south of the city to drive away any troops or boats that might have crossed the river. The oppressive heat sapped the men, forcing many to drop out along the way. Passing through a swamp full of knee-deep mud and thick cane, they reached a levee, beyond which lay the river and the mortar boats. The crews of the vessels, sleeping on the bank and playing cards, were oblivious to the danger. Deploying for battle and then advancing, the Rebels emerged from a cane brake and fired two volleys into the surprised Yankees. The mortar boats escaped, however, and a nearby Federal gunboat responded quickly, unleashing a heavy fire on the Rebels. The brigade advanced to a point where the gunboat's cannons could not be depressed enough to fire on them. There for about an hour the men exchanged fire with the vessel. Evidently the gunboat maneuvered itself into firing position and was joined by other vessels. The Federal fire became intense, forcing the Rebels to retreat into the swamps as trees splintered about them. Several men lost their shoes in the ooze and one his pants in the swamp as the disorganized troops fled. The attack had failed, yet casualties had been light. The Nineteenth lost only two killed and two wounded, and the men remained in high spirits following their "adventure."[18]

While Yankee gunboats could not break the men's spirits, a more sinister foe soon did: disease. On arriving at their camps, the men began to use a contaminated pond for a water source. The water was so full of scum and "wiggletails" that it had to be strained before use. This swampy environment was also an ideal breeding ground for mosquitoes, which infested the camps and led to outbreaks of malaria. Here, as at Corinth, sickness began to ravage the regiment. As the weather grew hotter and "fever" spread throughout the ranks, the men began to look for a way out of Vicksburg, the regiment, and, indeed, even the army. Many found their escape through death. Among those succumbing to the fever was the popular Brigadier General Statham, the brigade's commander. He was replaced by Brigadier General Charles Clark, an unknown entity to the men.[19]

Those not taken ill sought to leave the unhealthy environment any way they could. Several enterprising individuals in Company H managed to forge transfer papers. Others simply lied their way out. The Compiled Service Records for the regiment reveal that almost 100 soldiers received discharges in July 1862. Given that the total effective strength of the unit just prior to that month probably stood at around 250, this blow was severe. Interestingly, the two reasons most often given for these discharges were the expiration of the soldier's term of service and age. As to the term of service, the Nineteenth, like all the other regiments at Corinth, presumably had reenlisted back in May. Possibly many of the men had refused to reenlist and now wished to return home. Most of those discharged for reason of age claimed to be either under or over the eighteen-to-thirty-five limits prescribed by the conscription act. Such claims are consistent with the provision of the act that required those over or under the conscription ages to wait up to ninety days to be discharged. Because the act went into effect April 16, mid-July would have been the right time for such discharges to occur. Indeed, discharges for age were the catalyst for Captain William Lackey's advertisements in the *Knoxville Daily Register* during the summer. Lackey hoped to replenish his company by appealing to the patriotism of East Tennesseans and offering transportation to Vicksburg to join his hard-fighting "veteran" unit. The captain cautioned that, "[n]one will be received but those of good fighting character." He had little to worry about—few if any responded to his offer.[20]

Interestingly, when the discharged soldiers' ages as listed at Vicksburg are compared to the ages given in the 1860 census, there are discrepancies. Many of those claiming to be older than thirty-five would not have been so, even if two or three years' leeway is granted to the census age. Those claiming to be under eighteen either had lied to enlist or were now lying to get out. While there were legitimate age-related discharges, such as that of Private James Tyner of Company I, who had enlisted in 1861 at the tender age of fifteen, or Private Daniel Knox of Company D, who was fifty-one at his discharge, a good number were patently fraudulent—suggesting that Dr. Dulany, who processed the discharge papers, may have winked at the men's falsehoods out of sympathy for their plight. Given the epidemics of malaria, dysentery, measles, and

other diseases, and the feeling on the part of many that they had done their
duty after twelve months of service, it is little wonder that so many men
attempted to get out of the regiment.[21]

For the wealthy, another avenue of escape existed: substitution. The conscription act provided that any man wishing to be free from military service
could bring a proxy to his camp of instruction. If the proxy was found to be
lawfully exempt from military duty and physically fit for service, the "principal" providing the proxy was entitled to a certificate of discharge. Enticing the
proxy was left to the principal's ingenuity. Although Congress had intended
substitution as a way to mollify the harshness of the draft, such a system
favored those best able to hire replacements.[22]

According to the Compiled Service Records, it was June 1862 before any
members of the Nineteenth took advantage of the provision. Although the
records are not complete, they do offer some insight into the process of substitution. Eight men secured substitutes between April and August, of whom five
could be located in the 1860 census. All five were young and came from elite
households. The fathers of Private Thomas Crawford of Company H and
Private Wade P. Rutledge of Company G were wealthy commercial farmers
worth $51,000 and $20,000, respectively, and each owned eleven slaves.
Private Powell H. George's father was the McMinn County court clerk. Private
James Smith of Company D held $8,000 in real property and lived with a
planter owning $58,000 in aggregate wealth. Sergeant Nathan Galloway of
Company G, the poorest of the group, came from a household with $3,250 in
aggregate wealth—still 79 percent above the regional average. As for their substitutes, little information beyond name and residence can be found. Interestingly, at least two were from states other than Tennessee, suggesting they might
have been obtained in or around Vicksburg.[23]

The case of Sergeant F. D. Faulkner of Company I is particularly intriguing.
Although Faulkner could not be located in the census, and thus his wealth and
occupation are unknown, he procured two substitutes from his own company.
One potential proxy was John McNabb, a sixteen-year-old who had joined
Company I with his seventeen- or eighteen-year-old brother Aaron in the
summer of 1861. The boys' mother was a washer woman, listing $50 of aggre-
gate wealth in the 1860 census. Obviously, substitution offered a potential
windfall for such a destitute family. Both McNabbs received a discharge in July
because of their age. It appears, however, that John did not remain Faulkner's
substitute for long because Faulkner soon obtained the services of another comrade in Company I, William J. Tate. Tate, like McNabb, was sixteen and now
subject to a discharge. He too came from a single-parent household. His

mother, a domestic with five younger children, listed $50 in aggregate wealth in 1860. For this family, too, substitution offered a potential financial boon. Tate served for Faulkner until the following October, when he deserted. Although he would return, he continued to desert periodically throughout the war and eventually disappeared from the records. The other substitutes who served in the regiment followed that pattern. As was the case throughout the Confederate army, most substitutes proved unreliable.[24]

Late in July the Federals called off the campaign against Vicksburg. The naval vessels steamed away with the army forces on board. The first prolonged assault on Vicksburg was over, and the Confederate flag still flew over the city's bluffs. General Van Dorn was not willing to sit idly waiting for the next assault. On July 26 he ordered Breckinridge to assemble those of his division well enough to travel and proceed southward to Camp Moore in southeastern Louisiana. There Breckinridge was to link up with Brigadier General Daniel Ruggles's force of about one thousand. The combined force would then march eighty miles to Baton Rouge and attempt to retake the city. Van Dorn's objective was twofold: to protect the flow of supplies from the trans-Mississippi via the Red River and to secure a staging area for a future assault on New Orleans.[25]

Breckinridge, whose regiments were decimated by the fever, had a difficult time fielding a force. General Clark ordered all who were fit for duty in his brigade to prepare to move out immediately. The Nineteenth, weakened by discharges as well as sickness, could muster fewer than one hundred effectives.[26]

On July 27, Breckinridge's division minus Bowen's brigade left the Vicksburg railroad depot with fewer than four thousand men. The soldiers changed trains at Jackson for the long trip southward. On the evening of the twenty-eighth, the stiff and weary Rebels climbed out of the cars at Camp Moore. Breckinridge conferred with Ruggles and learned that the latter's troops were in as bad shape as his own. Heavy rain and hot, humid weather had sent hundreds to hospitals already crammed with malaria and dysentery cases. Breckinridge's troops added even more to the sick lists. The general had brought along only those who seemed well enough to campaign, but many broke down from exertion or malaria on the way. Almost half of his original force was now too ill to participate in the assault on Baton Rouge.[27]

Breckinridge learned from Ruggles that the Federal garrison at Baton Rouge numbered around five thousand—considerably more than his own force. He wired Van Dorn that if the C.S.S. *Arkansas* could drive the Federal gunboats away from the city, he was still willing to attack. Van Dorn wired back that the Rebel ironclad would be at Baton Rouge on the morning of August 5. Confident of the *Arkansas*'s arrival and his own troops' elan and

ability, Breckinridge prepared for the assault. To simplify the command structure, he reorganized the troops into two divisions of two brigades each. Clark
and Ruggles would each command a division.[28]

The Nineteenth, like so many other units, was by now a regiment in name
only. Most of the men were too sick to stand; the healthy ones numbered less
than a regulation company. Thus, the Nineteenth was consolidated with the
Twentieth, Twenty-Eighth, and Forty-Fifth Tennessee to form a battalion in
Colonel Thomas B. Smith's brigade of Clark's division.[29]

With an effective strength of around thirty-six hundred, Breckinridge left
Camp Moore at daybreak on July 30. The Rebels presented a pitiful sight as
they marched off to battle. Nearly one-third of the force lacked shoes. Many
lacked coats and shirts, and some were almost naked. They carried no tents
and had only two days' cooked rations in their haversacks.[30]

As the march progressed, the troops suffered greatly. The weather was
hot and humid. Fresh water was scarce. The men drank from stagnant, scum-
covered ponds. Sickness also began to take a toll. Weakness, headaches, nau-
sea, and vomiting plagued many, and exhaustion, fever, and chills forced
some to fall by the wayside. Worse still, some suffered from the bloody evac-
uations associated with dysentery and struggled to keep up with their comrades. Houses along the way were converted to hospitals as Breckinridge's
force began to disintegrate. By the time the army reached the Comite River
on August 4, ten miles from Baton Rouge, only twenty-six hundred effectives
remained, and many of those were gravely ill. William W. Etter, a lieutenant
in Company K of the Nineteenth, refused to leave his comrades despite his
high fever and violent, uncontrollable shaking caused by chills. His case and
countless others demonstrate the gallantry and fierce determination that
Breckinridge was counting on so heavily.[31]

At 11:00 P.M., the Nineteenth, along with the rest of the Rebel force,
crossed the Comite River and marched along the Greenwell Springs Road
toward Baton Rouge. Just before dawn, the little army arrived on the outskirts
of the city. A thick fog blanketed the terrain, reducing visibility to less than
"20 steps." In the eerie atmosphere, Breckinridge deployed his two divisions,
placing Ruggles's men to the south (left) of the Greenwell Springs Road and
Clark's men (including the Nineteenth) to the north (right). The depletion of
the ranks precluded the standard double line of battle. Instead, a single thin
line preceded by skirmishers would have to overcome Yankee resistance. At
about 4:30 A.M., the sounds of wild yells and musketry echoed through the fog
as the Confederate skirmishers began to drive back the Union picket line.[32]

The advancing Rebel line was slowed by fences, hedges, gardens, and
ditches, but Clark's division managed to mount a charge that drove a Union

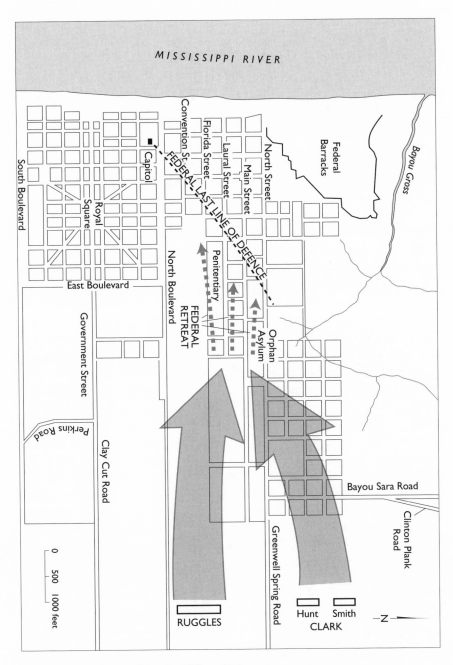

Battle of Baton Rouge. Map by William Nelson.

regiment from its camp. Through a mistake in orders, some of the advancing Confederate units withdrew, but Smith's brigade (containing the Nineteenth) apparently continued to hold its position on the extreme Confederate right. Breckinridge then commanded Ruggles and Clark to regroup their divisions for another assault. Among the troops who went forward was Smith's brigade, which charged headlong into the Union line only to be met by a storm of musketry and enfilading canister rounds. Smith was forced to order a hasty retreat. Breckinridge kept up the pressure on the Federals, however, and for the next hour, both sides poured heavy fire into one another's ranks without either giving way. Eventually, however, the Federals yielded the field, retreating to a previously prepared defensive line around the city's arsenal and barracks.[33]

The exhausted Rebels mounted a spiritless pursuit. It was now around 10:00 A.M. They had marched all night, had been fighting since dawn, and were now out of water. Looking over his troops, Breckinridge estimated that only one thousand would be available for another assault—and that assault would have to be made against a formidable Federal line, protected by several well-placed batteries and by Union gunboats that even now were shelling his forces. He decided that without the *Arkansas* to drive away the Federal flotilla, he could not risk another attack. The need for water compelled the general to move his men back to Ward Creek, three miles from the city. Lacking transportation, he ordered that the captured Federal supplies and equipment be destroyed. The army found no water fit to drink at Ward Creek, and the exhausted men marched back to Baton Rouge to search the cisterns in the suburbs. They found little water. Disheartened, they sought a place to rest to wait for the *Arkansas* and the next assault. Neither would come.[34]

Citizens helped the Rebels gather their dead and wounded. Among the latter was Lieutenant J. M. Sims of Company F, who was wounded in the same leg that had been injured at Shiloh. The wounded were made as comfortable as possible, but the poorly equipped Confederates lacked even picks and shovels with which to bury their comrades.[35]

In the late afternoon, Breckinridge learned that the *Arkansas* had run aground and could not aid his next assault. Without it, Breckinridge was convinced, his mangled army could not storm the new Federal position. He gave orders for a retreat to the Comite River. The Battle of Baton Rouge was over.[36]

General Breckinridge was understandably proud of his men. They had fought fiercely, pushed the Federals to their limit, and captured (temporarily, at least) most of the city. The general can perhaps be forgiven for boasting that ". . . no troops ever behaved with greater gallantry and even reckless audacity." He attributed the Confederate success to ". . . sublime courage inspired by a just cause . . .". Without a doubt, patriotism did spur the men. However, the determination of a tired, sick, thirsty, and angry infantryman to best his enemy cannot be overlooked. Private William J. Worsham noted that while the Nineteenth's ranks were thin, it could boast of "grit and nerve." The regiment, reduced to less than the strength of a company, did perform well. Colonel Walker was cited for gallantry in Breckinridge's official report of the battle. Lieutenant Colonel Beriah F. Moore had his horse shot out from under him while rallying the men. The whole regiment had displayed the dogged combativeness, perseverance, and confidence that became hallmarks of the Rebels in the western theater.[37]

Following the action at Baton Rouge, Breckinridge occupied Port Hudson, Louisiana. This strong position on the Mississippi enabled the Confederates to control the mouth of the Red River. Anticipating another attack by the Rebels, the Federals abandoned Baton Rouge on August 18. Breckinridge would not have a triumphant entry into the Louisiana capital, however, because on the same day that the Yankees evacuated, Van Dorn directed him to turn over command of Port Hudson to Ruggles and transport his Kentucky and Tennessee regiments northward to Jackson, Mississippi.[38]

General Bragg (commanding the Western Department) was planning an invasion of Kentucky to coincide with an advance by his subcommanders (Generals Van Dorn and Sterling Price) into West and Middle Tennessee. Aware of the political implications of a move into Kentucky and of Breckinridge's considerable influence and popularity in his home state, Bragg requested Van Dorn to order Breckinridge to move his Kentucky and Tennessee troops to East Tennessee in time to participate in the offensive. Bragg's subsequent appeal to Breckinridge that he come immediately was greeted with hearty approval by the general.[39]

Shortly after arriving in Jackson, Breckinridge discovered that Van Dorn planned to include Breckinridge's troops in the invasion of West and Middle Tennessee. Van Dorn directed the Kentuckian to reorganize and rest his weakened division and prepare to advance as soon as possible. Through the rest of August, Breckinridge's men recuperated in Jackson, receiving new clothing and provisions. The fever patients left at Vicksburg and the other towns and hamlets of Mississippi and Louisiana began to trickle back to their units.[40]

While at Jackson, Breckinridge directed his regiments to sew the names of all of their engagements onto their battle flags. The soldiers in the Nineteenth proudly stitched "Fishing Creek," "Shiloh," "Vicksburg," and "Baton Rouge" onto the large, frayed stars-and-bars banner they had carried for so long. As an emblem of the unit's achievements and sacrifices, this flag was the object of fierce devotion among the veterans of the Nineteenth.[41]

Also while camped at Jackson, the men drew eleven months' pay in the form of large, uncut sheets of paper notes. In true army fashion, payday turned into an occasion for gambling. Private Jake Williford set up a chuck-a-luck game near the paymaster's tent and cleaned out many of his comrades before they even got back to camp.[42]

In early September, Van Dorn was ready to strike at Memphis and ordered Breckinridge to move his division to a camp about sixteen miles north of Holly Springs, Mississippi, in the area of Grand Junction, Tennessee. Transportation was scarce, and Breckinridge was forced to ship his men in cattle cars. The Nineteenth, part of the Third Brigade, left on the morning of September 10 in a train that the men declared "filthy beyond description." With no room to lie down inside the cars, many of the soldiers endured heavy rains to stretch out on the roofs. When they disembarked at Grand Junction, the men were wet, dirty, and agitated.[43]

Around September 15, Van Dorn agreed to release Breckinridge to join Bragg by way of East Tennessee. Breckinridge moved his men back to Jackson and on to Meridian, where he reorganized. Colonel Walker took command of the new Second Brigade, consisting of the Nineteenth, Twentieth, Twenty-Eighth, and Forty-Fifth Tennessee and McClung's Battery. While at Meridian, the Nineteenth received news that their brigade was ordered to Knoxville. They were going home.[44]

As they boarded the cars for the long roundabout journey, the men sang and danced in anticipation. The celebration stopped suddenly when they discovered that one of those enjoying the spectacle, Private Andrew Flenor of Company C, had apparently choked to death while eating. Flenor's brother, Pete, had died just a few months earlier at Corinth. The men of the Nineteenth had become accustomed to battlefield deaths and fatal illnesses, but accidental deaths weighed heavily on them—particularly this one, which occurred before Flenor could return home to a family still grieving over his brother's death.[45]

The brigade traveled a circuitous route across the heartland that the men had been fighting so long to defend. From Meridian they went to Mobile, then to Montgomery, West Point, Atlanta, Dalton, and finally Chattanooga, where they arrived early on the morning of September 30. There Companies A and I were dropped off to begin a six-day furlough. The Hamilton Grays proceeded to march proudly down the streets of Chattanooga, the martial music of their band awakening the town. The rest of the regiment disembarked at Knoxville, where the men scattered to their homes, anxious to find their loved ones and thankful to have survived to see this day.[46]

While the men of the regiment reveled in their homecoming, their officers busied themselves with recruiting. Sixteen months of hard service had depleted the Nineteenth's ranks from over 1,000 at its inception to a current strength of perhaps 150. When Civil War regiments fell below 250–300 men, they could not function effectively and were often either disbanded or consolidated with other understrength units. The Nineteenth desperately needed recruits in order to survive as an independent unit.[47]

Obtaining replacements in East Tennessee at this time would be difficult. Since the initial outpouring of Confederate volunteers in 1861, the number of enlistees from the region had declined precipitously. By the summer of 1862, only four new infantry regiments had been formed, and one of those had been disbanded because of the disloyalty of some of its members. Two primary factors account for the dwindling supply of recruits: a small pro-Confederate population and unionist guerrilla activity. Half of the voting age secessionists went off to war in 1861, more followed in 1862, and those still remaining were not eager to leave their families. Conditions in East Tennessee in 1862 were quite chaotic. The animosity between the region's loyalists and Confederates had escalated into acts of partisan violence. Only the presence of Confederate troops kept the unionists in check. Yet these forces lacked the numbers to pacify the eastern counties. Across the region, unionist guerrillas threatened Confederates, burned and looted their homes and businesses, and even beat or murdered them in a calculated campaign to drive the secessionists from East Tennessee.[48]

Adding to the Nineteenth's difficulties in obtaining new men was the second conscription act, passed in September 1862. The new act raised the upper draft-age limit from thirty-five to forty-five. On the surface, such legislation would appear to be an aid to rebuilding the regiment. However, the act caused difficulties for the Nineteenth and other preexisting units. Recruits rushed to newly formed units instead of veteran ones. Several factors explain the surge in the organization of new units. Although the first conscription act had been suspended in East Tennessee as a conciliatory gesture toward the region's unionists, the second was not suspended. Confederate sympathizers unwilling to serve in the army (who also had benefited from the suspension) now faced the stigma of being drafted if they did not quickly enlist. Furthermore, many of the new recruits hoped that the new units being formed would remain in East Tennessee for home defense, keeping them close to their families. Finally, the prospect of advancement and higher rank drew many to the new units. The infantry units formed in 1862 contained many men who had served in the region's earliest regiments. These were in many cases former officers who had failed to win reelection at the army's reorganization or otherwise had been discharged.[49]

Two field-grade officers in the new Sixtieth Tennessee, Lieutenant Colonel Nathan Gregg and Major James A. Rhea, had both served as lieutenants in the Nineteenth, and First Lieutenant Nicholas Fain, Captain Joseph R. Crawford, and Captain James C. Hodges were also ex-officers in the regiment. Major

James P. Snapp of the new Sixty-First Tennessee had organized and led Company C of the Nineteenth until the new elections at Corinth. In the new Sixty-Third Tennessee were Lieutenant Colonel Abraham Fulkerson (a former major in the Nineteenth), adjutant Uriah L. York (a former lieutenant), and Second Lieutenant Thomas W. Powell (a former private).[50]

Another obstacle to reconstituting the Nineteenth was the drafting of unionists. While these men could be forced into the army, only constant supervision could keep them in it. Such recruits were more trouble than they were worth.[51]

Despite these problems, the Nineteenth began to rebuild its strength. Even before the regiment's arrival in East Tennessee, notices appeared in the local papers advising members on detached service or absent without leave to return to their companies immediately or face punishment. Among those returning was Daniel Miller, who reluctantly left his position in the provost marshal's office to rejoin his old comrades. Captain Heiskell tried to use his brother Joseph's influence as a congressman to secure all the conscripts from Hawkins County for his company—to no avail. Heiskell's company, like all the others from East Tennessee, would receive only a designated portion of the new men.[52]

By the end of the fall of 1862, the Nineteenth had increased its numbers to over 380 effectives. One hundred eight of the 161 new recruits found in the Compiled Service Records were also found in the 1860 census. This permits a socioeconomic comparison with the original enlistees and offers insight into the make-up of the reconstituted regiment. Interestingly, despite the increase in the conscription age limit, the average age of the new men was twenty-four, two years younger than that of the original group—perhaps demonstrating the link between youth and Confederate support discussed in chapter 2. The average aggregate wealth of the recruits was $3,062. This was 19.2 percent above the regional average but much less than the original group's $5,703. Also, 79 of the 108 households of the new recruits (73.2 percent) held aggregate wealth below the regional average, meaning that the wealth of this group, like that of the volunteers of 1861, was concentrated in the hands of a few families. Indeed, the median aggregate wealth of the 1862 recruits was only $250 compared to $650 for the original group. In contrast to the 1861 volunteers, however, the new recruits came primarily from the households of yeoman and tenant subsistence farmers; only a few commercial agricultural families and slaveholders were part of the group. One plausible explanation is that the wealthier families were such committed secessionists that all of the military-aged men had already entered service; thus, the remaining pool tended to be from the lower classes. Finally, 11 of the recruits had brothers who had joined the regiment in 1861, revealing a not surprising family connection within the unit.[53]

The Nineteenth's rebuilding benefited from a fortuitous turn of events that allowed the regiment to remain in East Tennessee much longer than planned. On October 2, three days after Walker's brigade arrived in Knoxville, General Breckinridge arrived and began preparations to move his division into Kentucky. However, Major General Samuel Jones, acting commander of the Department of East Tennessee in Major General E. Kirby Smith's absence, became concerned over Federal threats to his department from Middle Tennessee. Jones therefore assumed command of Breckinridge's Tennessee regiments, including the Nineteenth, planning to use them to defend East Tennessee or even to strike into Middle Tennessee.[54]

Meanwhile, Breckinridge moved with his Kentucky units to join Bragg, only to learn that the invasion was over and he was to take his forces to Murfreesboro, where Bragg planned to concentrate his entire army. Regaining some of the Tennessee units, Breckinridge moved toward Murfreesboro in mid-October. The Nineteenth, however, stayed in Jones's command.[55]

On October 15, the regiment moved to Loudon, where it guarded the railroad bridges and continued to recruit. Daniel Miller returned to a soldier's life, again bitterly complaining. Two days after the regiment's arrival, he told Charlotte that "The Hawkins Boys are played out. Only about one dozen of them is any account at all. . . . [First Lieutenant Isiah] Huffmaster, *the coward*, is our Commander. . . . I am sorry that I joined the company. . . ." His primary source of dissatisfaction was the officers, and his comments reveal not only his lack of confidence in them but also class antagonisms at work in the unit. In a letter to Charlotte written two days later, Miller declared:

> I am completely outdone with our officers. . . . Huffmaster is a consumate fool and a big headed Dutch scoundrel. None of the elite of the company likes him at all and looks upon him with contempt. Wiley [Second Lieutenant Willie B. Miller] you know is the best of fellows but his knowledge of military tactics is quite limited—Etter [Second Lieutenant William W. Etter] is not with us—how he will do is yet to be tested. Colonel Moore [brigade commander] (Walker being absent) is a pretty good officer, but a man devoid of all principles, he treats men like slaves. Our Major [Rufus A. Jarnigan] is an ignorant bragidocio, but I must quit my complaints.

Daniel did not stop complaining, either about the officers or about the daily drill, the lack of blankets and proper shoes, or the poor rations. Perhaps the real source of his complaints was having to submit to authority. Compared to many other Civil War officers, Lieutenant Colonel Moore was a disciplinarian. He expected his men to obey orders without question and to perform their duties without hesitation. Moore even went so far as to arrest a sentry for not challenging him. Such strict adherence to military procedure, along with the deprivation and physical exertion of infantry service, did not appeal to Daniel Miller.[56]

Miller continued to seek provost duty. When his friend Captain Heiskell was again assigned as the provost marshal at Knoxville, Miller got his wish and on October 23 left William Phipps and the rest of the unit. Heiskell and Miller were not alone in their preference for provost duty. Captain Abraham Gammon resigned his commission on October 15 (citing poor health from fever contracted in the swamps of Vicksburg) and became a deputy provost marshal in charge of the First District of East Tennessee. Likewise, W. E. Colville, ex-captain of Company D, took charge of District Nine. The elite of the regiment were in a position to secure such comfortable assignments through their or their families' influence. The war was becoming a poor man's fight.[57]

One week after Miller's departure, the Nineteenth reluctantly left East Tennessee to join Bragg's army at Murfreesboro. For the next six weeks, the regiment moved toward its destination, periodically stopping for days at a time at camps along the way. Part of the delay was the result of Bragg's efforts to reorganize the newly created Army of Tennessee. Although the men believed they were still part of Walker's brigade in Breckinridge's division, apparently no one else did. At one point, the regiment disappeared altogether from the army's table of organization. Eventually it was assigned to Brigadier General Patton Anderson's division, but then that unit was broken up. Finally, in mid-December, the regiment became part of General Polk's corps, General Cheatham's division, Brigadier General Alexander P. Stewart's brigade (consisting of the consolidated Fourth/Fifth and Thirty-First/Thirty-Third Tennessee as well as the Twenty-Fourth Tennessee and Stanford's Battery). Also at this time, Colonel Walker returned to the regiment, having been relieved of brigade command in the reshuffling of officers and units.[58]

Although the men in the Nineteenth may have anticipated a quiet winter in which to acclimate themselves to their new surroundings and new command, this would not be the case. On December 26, the Union army under Major General William Rosecrans left its Nashville stronghold and advanced against Bragg's army, which was assembled some thirty miles away in and around Murfreesboro.[59]

Lacking adequate cavalry to scout the Federals, Bragg was slow to react to the advance. By December 30, the Federal dispositions became clear. After an agonizing day spent waiting for an attack that never came, Bragg decided to

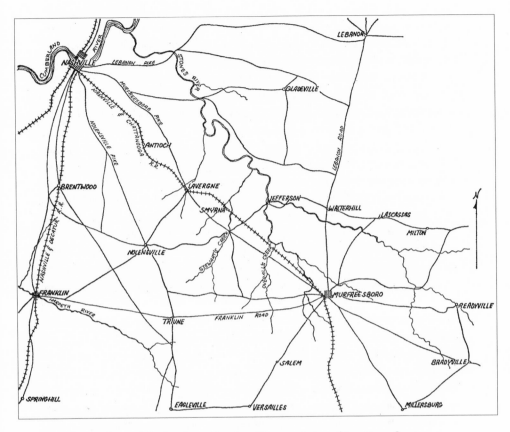

The Approaches to Murfreesboro. Reprinted by permission of Louisiana State University Press from Autumn of Glory: The Army of Tennessee, 1862–1865 *by Thomas Lawrence Connelly. Copyright © 1971 by Louisiana State University Press.*

seize the initiative and strike first. He summoned his corps commanders and outlined a simple yet daring battle plan. At dawn the next day, his strong left wing would attack in echelon, executing a giant wheeling movement designed to push the Federals back past the Nashville Pike and against Stones River. Confederate cavalry would then cut off Rosecrans's army from its supply base at Nashville, leading either to its surrender or its destruction.[60]

While the plan was simple in theory, a wheeling movement of that size and complexity over heavily wooded and broken terrain in the face of enemy resistance would be a difficult challenge. Another potential problem for the Confederates concerned General Polk's rearrangement of his command structure on the eve of battle. Originally, Major General Jones Withers's division, which formed the front line of Polk's corps, was to move forward as a solid line, while Major General Benjamin Cheatham's division followed in support. However, the rough terrain in front of Withers and Cheatham prevented the generals from being able to supervise adequately their long battle lines.[61]

Polk directed the two generals to split up their commands. Cheatham was to command the two left brigades in Withers's front line as well as his own two left brigades in the supporting line. Likewise, Withers would lead the two right brigades of his division plus the two right brigades of Cheatham's command (including Stewart's). This arrangement gave each general a two-brigade front with two brigades in reserve. This was sound structuring, but it could prove confusing for the brigade and regimental officers who had never served together yet who now needed to cooperate closely.[62]

The icy rain that had fallen all day continued into the night, and a northerly wind picked up and whistled through the dark cedar thickets and across the empty cotton and corn fields where tomorrow's battle would be fought. As the soldiers bedded down to get what rest they could, the military bands of both armies began to play their favorite tunes. The music carried through the wintry night to both sides of the line, and a contest of sorts developed. The challenge of "Yankee Doodle" was answered by "Dixie," and "The Bonnie Blue Flag" was followed by "Hail Columbia." Finally, one by one, the Confederate bands joined the Federal musicians in the playing of the familiar and heart-touching "Home Sweet Home." Soldiers on both sides joined in singing. Private William J. Worsham of the Nineteenth recalled many years later how deeply the moment affected him and his comrades: "During the stillness of the night, each soldier of both armies, was holding communion with his own soul, his mind occupied with the thought of what tomorrow would bring, whether wounds or death, and would he ever see home again, when the notes of this inspiring tune came floating on the stillness of the night." Soon the music faded away, the chorus stopped, and the opposing forces who had just joined voices to sing of home and family lay down to await the dawn, when they would raise their voices together once again—this time in the shouts and curses of combat.[63]

As dawn broke, fog blanketed the fields and forests, and a cold drizzle continued to fall. At 6:22 A.M., Major General John McCown's division advanced through the mist toward the Federal right. Five hundred yards behind it came Major General Patrick Cleburne's men. Only when contact was made with the Union pickets did the forest echo with the taunting sound of the Rebel yell. Bragg had attacked first, and the struggle for Middle Tennessee had begun.[64]

The two Confederate divisions swept everything before them. Panic filled the Union ranks. McCown and Cleburne drove the Yankees back for nearly

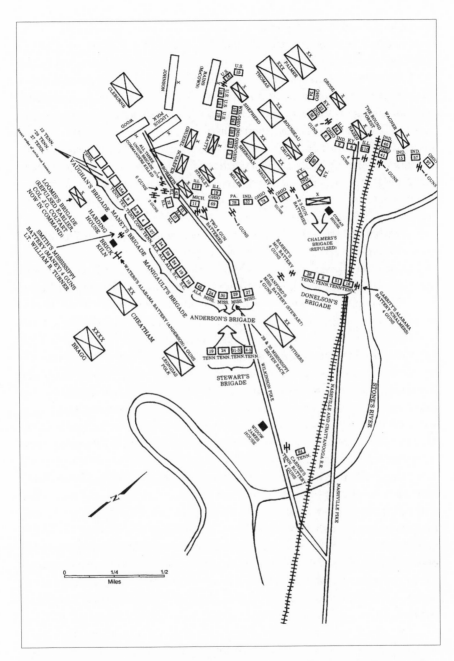

The Confederate Assault at Murfreesboro. From Christopher Losson, Tennessee's Forgotten Warriors: Frank Cheatham and His Confederate Division *(Knoxville: University of Tennessee Press, 1989), 86.*

two miles through the cedar brakes toward the Nashville Pike, where a strong defensive line was being hastily established. There the Confederate advance lost its momentum and ground to a halt.[65]

Cheatham sent his division forward about 7:00 A.M. to support McCown and Cleburne, but his piecemeal assault was repulsed. At 8:00 A.M., General Stewart, acting on his own initiative, ordered his brigade to advance in support of General Patton Anderson's brigade of Withers's division. Stewart wheeled left to bring his men under cover of the forest for protection from Federal fire. The brigade arrived at earthworks of loose stone and timber made on Sunday by Anderson's men and temporarily halted. For the next half hour, the men were exposed to heavy artillery fire from an unseen battery. While members of the Nineteenth were lying behind the wall, a shell struck it. Jagged bits of metal and shattered rock rained on the ranks, seriously wounding six men of Company I and demoralizing the regiment.[66]

Stewart soon had the brigade advancing toward Wilkinson Pike. The men saw two of Anderson's regiments falling back in disorder as the Confederate front line collapsed. They crossed the pike and moved toward some woods, where they saw the evidence of earlier fighting. The ground was strewn with wounded and dying men, maimed horses, and small arms and other equipment. As Stewart's men entered the woods, the Nineteenth overran the battery that had shelled them and pushed ahead. Surging forward, the regiment was hit by a fusillade from Federals concealed among the trees. The color bearer was killed. Ignoring the danger, Corporal John Mason of the color guard picked up the battle flag and held it aloft in the forefront of the regiment. This inspired his comrades; joined by the whole brigade, they blasted the Union line with rapid and accurate fire. The Federals began to fall back.[67]

Relentlessly moving forward, Stewart's and Anderson's brigades captured more cannon and scores of prisoners. Before long they linked up with other Confederate brigades and regiments, pushing the scattered pockets of Union resistance before them. One of these pockets, consisting of a brigade of U.S. army regulars deployed in a cedar forest, put up a stiffer resistance than the others. The regulars were flanked on the left by the Eighth Tennessee and on the right by the whole of Stewart's brigade. Although broken within twenty minutes, the regulars slowed the Rebels and decimated Stewart's brigade in the process.[68]

The advancing Rebels halted at the edge of the woods in front of a cotton field full of fleeing Federals. Beyond this lay the Nashville Pike, where the Federals had established a formidable last line of defense. The Confederates sensed a complete victory if the pike could be taken. Flushed with the day's success, the Nineteenth and other regiments moved into the open field.[69]

Almost immediately, Federal batteries deployed along the pike and near a small cedar thicket known locally as the "Round Forest" unleashed a furious barrage of canister. Undaunted, the Rebels pressed ahead and began to exchange fire with the Federal infantry dug in along the pike. As the Nineteenth surged forward, Orderly Sergeant Joseph Thompson of Company I ran after the Yankees who were still fleeing toward the pike, seizing one and dragging him back as a prisoner. Before the young Rebel could get his prize to the rear, the Federal was cut down by a stray bullet. Angry and determined, Thompson pursued and captured another man, whom he managed to return safely to the rear.[70]

Although the broken men retreating across the field could offer no resistance to the advancing Rebels, the units along the pike forced the Confederates back with heavy loss of life. Rejoining the brigade, the Nineteenth took a position along the edge of the woods. The unobstructed cotton field between the Confederate and Federal lines became a "no man's land" where none but the most daring entered.[71]

With the Nashville Pike and a complete victory within their grasp, the Confederates' attack had petered out. The weary and bloodied Rebel brigades needed help to make a final assault. Around 2:00 P.M., Bragg ordered some of his fresh troops to attack the Round Forest—the strongest position on the battered Union line. The attack failed, and by late afternoon the fighting ended.[72]

As nightfall approached, Stewart had his men gather up abandoned Federal arms and equipment. Then, leaving a strong picket force, the brigade retired about 100 yards rearward into the woods and bivouacked. The brigade needed food and rest. It had been heavily engaged throughout the morning and had suffered grievously. In the Nineteenth's camp, the men finally had an opportunity to reflect on the day's events. The regiment had fought well against a determined enemy, driving all before it, including vaunted regular troops, until reaching the final Federal line. The men had captured fifty of the enemy, including Sergeant Thompson's hard-won prisoner. They had overrun several batteries and collected 300 small arms, along with much ammunition and other equipment. The success came with a heavy price, however. The Nineteenth suffered 136 casualties out of 382 men engaged—well over a third of its strength. Indeed, the regiment suffered more casualties than any other in Stewart's mangled brigade. Its strength was now close to what it had been before the recruiting efforts of the fall. The Nineteenth was bleeding to death.[73]

Despite the high losses, the Nineteenth had maintained its discipline and fighting spirit throughout the day, being one of the few units courageous enough to attempt an assault against the Federal line along the Nashville Pike. The regiment's performance and elan were in no small part the result of the

outstanding leadership of its officer corps, both commissioned and noncommissioned. First Sergeant Joseph Thompson was cited for gallantry in the after-
action reports, as were First Sergeant Amos C. Smith of Company B and
Sergeant George N. Richardson and Corporal John Mason of Company K. The
cost was high, however. Fourteen noncommissioned officers were wounded and
two killed. Six commissioned officers were wounded, including Lieutenant
J. M. Sims, who was knocked down and disoriented by a bullet that grazed his
head. Three commissioned officers were killed: Major Rufus A. Jarnigan,
Captain Joseph G. Frazier of Company D, and Lieutenant S. G. Abernathy of
Company E.[74]

As the men began to drift off into a fitful sleep, a mist covered the battlefield. It was New Year's Eve, and while people in both nations celebrated, the
men of the Nineteenth, having endured the slaughter of the day's battle, now
endured a night of freezing rain and high winds. Instead of band music, this
night would be filled with the groans and cries of the wounded left in the forest and the fields and the creaking of ambulances carrying their gruesome
cargo. The well-clad Federal dead presented the men with a source of badly
needed items. The Yankee corpses were literally stripped naked. Food, coats,
shoes, blouses, and trousers were taken by the Rebels. One enterprising member of the Nineteenth boasted of gathering three blankets during the cold
night—a rich treasure.[75]

Upon hearing reports that the Federals were retreating, Bragg prepared to
follow Rosecrans's shattered army back to Nashville, and he telegraphed Richmond with news of a great victory. The general, however, was badly mistaken.
Although mauled, Rosecrans had decided to stay and "fight or die."[76]

At daybreak on January 1, the Nineteenth, along with the rest of Stewart's
brigade, moved to the edge of the cedar woods and found the Yankees still dug
in and ready to renew the struggle. Bragg ordered Polk to prod the Federal line
around mid-morning. The Confederates moved into the abandoned Round
Forest and skirmished heavily but went no further. Although Bragg expected
Rosecrans to withdraw, the Federals entrenched, and both sides now warily
watched one another. That night the men of the Nineteenth returned to their
camp and huddled around their fires, thankful to have been spared the bloody
day they had expected.[77]

By January 2, the Confederates had pulled back and established a strong
defensive line, still waiting for the Federals to withdraw. Unable to wait any
longer, Bragg planned an assault against the Union left flank. When reconnaissance revealed that the Federals now controlled high ground that allowed
them to enfilade the Confederate line with artillery fire, Bragg ordered
Breckinridge to seize the heights. The resulting attack was a failure.[78]

Another miserable night of sleet and freezing temperatures followed. Wet clothes froze to the skin of the shivering soldiers. By the morning of January 3, Bragg became convinced that Rosecrans was not going to retreat and was even being reinforced. Around 10:00 A.M., Bragg reluctantly ordered a withdrawal.[79]

During the afternoon, baggage and ordnance trains headed south towards Shelbyville along with most of the wounded. Some of the more badly wounded, however, would be left behind. All through the night, sleet fell as the Army of Tennessee abandoned Murfreesboro and plodded southward. Unsure of his destination, Bragg continued to ponder his options while sending Polk's corps (including the Nineteenth) to Shelbyville. After days of indecision and countermarching, Bragg decided to establish a defensive line on the ridges of the Duck River Valley.[80]

The army suffered greatly during the march southward, enduring incessant rain, frigid temperatures, and short rations. Morale was low; the men were sullen. Most of the soldiers believed that they had won a great victory. Yet they had abandoned the field and their winter quarters to the Yankees. To the men in the ranks, it seemed that Bragg's incompetence had led to this disaster, and their confidence in his ability began to ebb.[81]

On the Duck River across from Shelbyville, the Nineteenth settled into its new winter camp. As the men gathered around their fires, buffeted by the cold January winds, their thoughts certainly turned to the new year and the prospects for them and their families. The Battle of Murfreesboro had been the bloodiest day for the regiment thus far in the war. The regiment's numbers were now about what they were when it arrived in Knoxville, before reconstituting its strength. Replacing these recent casualties would be virtually impossible. Back home the supply of patriots was now depleted, leaving only conscripts—most of whom were unionists hoping to desert—and shirkers such as Daniel Miller.

Charlotte Miller's brother William endured the cold and hunger at Shelbyville. Her husband, however, lived a life of comparative luxury in Knoxville, oblivious to the suffering of his brother-in-law and former comrades. Planning a visit home to Hawkins County, Miller informed his wife, "I suppose that the Captain [Heiskell] can let me off. He won't of course be so hardhearted as to not let me off." Later, after shipping sixty unwilling conscripts to East Tennessee units, Daniel took a moment to write Charlotte: "I am doing pretty well now. Charlotte, we have Back Bone, spareribs, sausages and Rye coffee, occasionally a little milk and butter but who cares for anything else when we have those 'Big Fat' sausages. I would be glad to see you, My Dear, but the fortunes of war are such that I will not be able to come up until next Saturday. . . . I can manage C. W. H. [Captain Carrick W. Heiskell] pretty much as it suits me."[82]

While Daniel looked forward to a visit home and more fat sausages, his comrades in the Nineteenth contemplated the prospect of a lean winter followed by renewed Federal advances in the spring and the likelihood of more costly battles such as Murfreesboro. Despite such grim visions, however, they did not despair, for the news elsewhere in the Confederacy was good. To most it appeared that the South might still win its independence. The events of the coming year would tell.

5 ❧

"A Nobler Spirit Has Not Been Sacrificed for Human Liberty or Southern Freedom"

The Chickamauga and Chattanooga Campaigns

The spring of 1863 was a time of dissension in the ranks of the Nineteenth Tennessee. The roots of such discord stretched back to October of the previous year when Captain Abraham L. Gammon, commander of Company G, resigned his office because of age and a slow recovery from typhoid fever contracted at Vicksburg. Gammon was placed on detached service as a quartermaster in East Tennessee. He turned over command of the company to the next ranking officer, First Lieutenant Robert L. Blair, and thus began the turmoil.[1]

At the organization of the company in June 1861, Gammon had been elected captain; James A. Rhea, first lieutenant; Robert L. Blair, second lieutenant; and James Carlton, third lieutenant. At the reorganization in Corinth in the spring of 1862, Carlton and Blair were not reelected. Although popular with the men, Blair had been captured at Shiloh and was unavailable. As a result, while Gammon and Rhea retained their offices, Gammon's son, James K. P. Gammon, won Blair's second lieutenancy, and Hiram D. Hawk became the company's new third lieutenant.[2]

In early October 1862, just before Captain Gammon resigned, Blair rejoined the Nineteenth (then at Loudon Bridge in East Tennessee) after being exchanged. About this same time, First Lieutenant Rhea left the regiment to become the major of the Sixtieth Tennessee Infantry, one of the new units forming in East Tennessee. Standard military practice dictated that Second Lieutenant James K. P. Gammon and Third Lieutenant Hiram D. Hawk move up a grade in rank if an examining board found them qualified for promotion. However, it appears that the officers and men of the company, including Abraham Gammon and his son, requested that Blair become the company's new first lieutenant, and they asked Lieutenant Colonel Moore (acting regimental commander in Colonel Walker's absence) to see to the appointment. In order for Blair to assume the office, Second Lieutenant Gammon and Third Lieutenant Hawk sent written waivers to the department commander, Major General Samuel Jones, for approval. The approval was granted.[3]

Sometime after the battle of Murfreesboro, Moore sent a letter of inquiry to the Adjutant and Inspector General's Office in Richmond to ascertain the legality of Blair's promotion. New regulations stipulated that special appointments such as Blair's required the consent of the president as well as the department commander. The Inspector General's Office informed Moore that if he forwarded to Richmond written waivers of the company officers involved, the army would consent to Blair's appointment. At this point, however, Lieutenant Gammon apparently had a change of heart and refused to give his consent, while his father, although no longer an officer in the regiment, began to use his influence to have his son appointed first lieutenant of Company G. The elder Gammon undoubtedly realized that whoever held this office would eventually become the unit's captain, an office he coveted for his son.[4]

In a letter to Tennessee senator Landon C. Haynes, Abraham Gammon claimed that Blair had been "appointed" by Moore in violation of military law and that, although the young Gammon had agreed initially to waive his rights to promotion, he now understood such an act to be illegal and was determined "to insist upon his rights—and go up by promotion." In addition, Captain Gammon maintained that Blair had been persistently absent, forcing his son to shoulder the responsibility of company command without the privilege of rank. Senator Haynes, anxious to aid a wealthy and influential constituent, appealed to the secretary of war, James Seddon.[5]

Responding to a letter from the War Department, Moore defended Blair's promotion, and in the process he revealed tears in the fabric of the regiment's cohesion as well as his own resentment toward the manipulation of rank and assignment in favor of those with wealth and influence. Moore reviewed the case, pointing out that General Jones, and not a regimental officer, had appointed Blair. Furthermore, Moore declared that if the present department commander, General Bragg, refused Blair's claim to the first lieutenancy, then Gammon would be ordered before a board of examination immediately to determine his suitability for the position. However, Moore obviously believed that promoting Gammon would be a mistake, and he took exception to the sympathetic assertions of Senator Haynes, who had told the War Department that the young Gammon had served with his company throughout its long and arduous service and was, therefore, most deserving of a promotion. Moore declared that "[f]rom some time previous to the battle of Fishing Creek until after the Battle of Shiloh and the Reorg. of the Regt. Lt. Gammon we are informed and believe was in the Quartermaster Department and receiving pay as an active [combat soldier] to the amount of $50.00 per month. He has been on but few long marches and only in one engagement with his Company." The lieutenant colonel went on to state that Gammon "is one of those many Boys with influential fathers, who obtained details in the Quartermaster's Department" and "The Hon. L.C. Haynes is certainly mistaken when he states that Lt. Gammon 'has the merit of having seen much hard service during the war.' Probably being a Congressman he knows not what 'hard service' is." Moore continued his tirade, maintaining that Lieutenant Gammon, not Blair, was guilty of chronic absenteeism and that Gammon had no reason to complain, because he had been fully instructed as to the legalities of Blair's promotion. Finally, Moore offered an impassioned appeal for Blair's retention:

> After having done much to enforce discipline and good order
> in the Company, after having commanded it in the battle of
> Murfreesboro with the same gallantry which at Shiloh won for
> him the praise of his men and officers and more than all after
> having relinquished his expectations of office elsewhere [i.e., in
> the new East Tennessee regiments formed in the fall of 1862], it
> would as we consider be a great injustice for him to be deprived
> of his position through the false statements of an old man
> [Abraham Gammon] and fickleness and bad faith of a boy.[6]

Moore's appeal apparently convinced the War Department and President Davis. Blair remained first lieutenant and was soon promoted to captain. Blair's adversary, James K. P. Gammon, became the company's new first lieutenant, and while he may have remained ambitious for promotion and may even have considered transferring to another regiment, he continued to serve with the Nineteenth. Gammon would eventually become the company's captain when wounds forced Blair to retire in the fall of 1864.[7]

Such a squabble within the Nineteenth demonstrates that personal honor and ambition often overshadowed self-sacrifice for the Southern cause. Moreover, it mirrored an even more serious disruption among the Army of Tennessee's senior officers. Following the retreat from Murfreesboro, bitter quarrels among Bragg and his corps and division commanders destroyed the high command's esprit and threatened the effectiveness of the Confederacy's principal army in the western theater. Between January and June, Bragg and his generals engaged in a war of words. They forwarded official reports to Richmond that contained accusations of incompetence and dereliction of duty during the 1862 Kentucky invasion and the Murfreesboro campaign. Buttressed by support from General Joseph E. Johnston, the western theater commander, and President Davis, Bragg endeavored to consolidate his hold on the Army of Tennessee and rid it of the "anti-Bragg" coalition that had formed. Bragg struck first at General John C. McCown, having that outspoken critic court-martialed. Bragg's action elevated General Alexander P. Stewart to command of McCown's division. Stewart's old brigade, containing the Nineteenth, remained in Cheatham's division of Polk's corps, and Brigadier General Otho F. Strahl became its new commander. Bragg then turned his wrath on the influential and popular John C. Breckinridge and Benjamin F. Cheatham, and finished by attacking his corps commanders, Hardee and Polk. He ultimately vanquished his detractors and managed to secure his position as the Army of Tennessee's commander. However, his denunciations fueled his generals' animosity and added to his unpopularity with the rank and file, especially among Kentucky and Tennessee units.[8]

Bragg's position within the army may have been secure, but the same could not be said of the army's strategic situation. Following the retreat from Stones River, Bragg established his headquarters at Tullahoma, some forty-five miles south of Murfreesboro. He then established a defensive line forward of the Duck River, deploying Polk's corps around Shelbyville. There, Polk constructed formidable entrenchments. To prevent a Federal turning movement, Bragg extended his already lengthy fifteen-mile front between Shelbyville and Wartrace by screening his flanks with cavalry, resulting in a seventy-mile line. But the Rebels simply lacked the numbers to cover every possible route of a Federal advance on Tullahoma.[9]

To make matters worse, Bragg's army, already badly outnumbered, was shrinking. After the Battle of Murfreesboro, Bragg rebuilt the army through rigorous enforcement of conscription. However, the War Department sent more than eleven thousand of his new recruits to Mississippi in a vain attempt to defend Vicksburg. This left the Army of Tennessee with around forty thousand effectives. The Federal host he now faced numbered twice that.[10]

The Nineteenth was among the units receiving replacements. Although the exact number joining in 1863 is not known, the Compiled Service Records for the regiment list 121 names. By matching these names to the 1860 census, it is possible to create a socioeconomic profile of the new men that can be compared to that of the 1861 and 1862 enlistees.[11]

At first glance, it appears that the new recruits, like their 1861 counterparts, belonged to the region's upper classes. The average aggregate wealth for

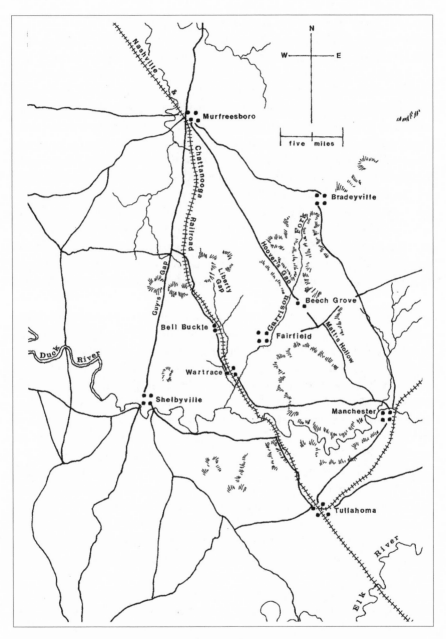

The Tullahoma–Shelbyville Line. Reprinted by permission of Louisiana State University Press from Soldier of Tennessee: General Alexander P. Stewart and the Civil War in the West by Sam Davis Elliot. Copyright © 1999 by Louisiana State University Press. Map by Blake Magner.

the 1863 group was $3,510. This was 36.6 percent above the regional average and 14.6 percent higher than the aggregate wealth of the 1862 sample. However, the 1863 average, like that of 1862, fell far short of the average wealth of the original enlistees. In addition, almost 80 percent of the 1863 group's total wealth was concentrated in the hands of only six households. If these prosperous families are removed from the calculations, the remaining households average only $781 in aggregate wealth—less than a third of the regional average of $2,569. Indeed, the median aggregate wealth for the 1863 recruits was only $100 compared to $650 and $250 for the 1861 and 1862 recruits, respectively. Obviously, many of the men joining the regiment in 1863 came from the poorest households of East Tennessee. Furthermore, over half of the new men were heads of families, compared to around 25 percent in the 1861 and 1862 groups. They were also generally older, averaging twenty-eight years of age, compared to twenty-six in 1861 and twenty-four in 1862. Being older, the heads of households tended to have larger families.[12]

The economic burden of military service placed a great strain on the families of these new recruits, most of whom were probably poor subsistence farmers. Such strains, along with the absence of an economic link to the rest of the Confederacy based on commercial farming and the fact that they were forced into the army, diminished this group's commitment to Southern independence. Not surprisingly, desertion became common among these new recruits.

One of the new men arriving at the Nineteenth's camp in Shelbyville bears mentioning. Eighteen-year-old Private Wiley B. Moseley was a free mulatto. Although tens of thousands of African Americans served in the Confederate army, virtually all held a support position such as cook, musician, teamster, or laborer. Moseley, however, was a combat soldier—one of the very few black men who bore arms in the Rebel ranks. Unfortunately, little information exists concerning Moseley's service. He joined in April 1863 and apparently fought at Chickamauga before disappearing from a hospital in November. As to what motivated this young man to fight for the Confederacy, few clues remain. Generally, free blacks or mulattos were not conscripted, so Moseley may have been a volunteer. He had worked as a laborer on a large commercial farm owned by William Perry. Perry owned one slave, a nineteen-year-old male. While it is possible that Moseley was somehow related to the farm owner and wished to fight in defense of Perry's property, such a supposition lacks any evidence. More likely, Moseley was conscripted. The Tennessee General Assembly passed an act in June 1861 authorizing Governor Harris "at his discretion to receive into the military service of the State all male free persons of color, between the ages of 15 and 50, or such numbers as may be necessary who may be . . . capable of actual service." If the state failed to obtain a "sufficient number" of volunteers, the governor was authorized to press them into service. As the supply of East Tennessee white manpower evaporated, the authorities may have rounded up free blacks.[13]

Regardless of who they were or where they came from, Bragg was happy to get all the recruits he could. He had a difficult time feeding them, however. Another reason for the scattered deployment of the army was the need to forage. Not only was Bragg's army inadequately supplied by the government, but also his transportation system teetered on the verge of collapse. A shortage of teams and wagons curtailed food-gathering and left many soldiers hungry.[14]

While the Army of Tennessee may have been able to cope with all of these problems, one it could not overcome was the high command's lack of strategic foresight. By squandering six months feuding, instead of designing an effective strategy for the defense of Tennessee, the Army of Tennessee's high command proved itself unworthy of the soldiers it led.[15]

Equally disturbing was the manner in which the generals spent their six-month hiatus. When not engaged in intrigues against Bragg, the army's senior officers organized and attended a series of gala social events designed to eliminate the monotony of army life. Officers in crisp uniforms with fine sashes and polished boots danced and flirted with local belles, apparently oblivious to the Federal minions less than two days' march away.[16]

Grim witnesses to the collapse of the army's leadership, the common soldiers enjoyed an uneventful winter and spring. The lull gave the men an abundance of free time, and while the routines of camp life could become monotonous, they were always preferable to the horrors of combat and the hardships of campaigning. Many grew accustomed to this new life of ease. Private William J. Worsham remembered that during those months "we . . . scarcely thought of war save only when we were at the front on picket duty."[17]

Bragg was determined that his army not lose its combat edge during this long period of idleness. He therefore insisted on the enforcement of rigid discipline reinforced by frequent inspections and abundant drill. Indeed, visitors to the Army of Tennessee at this time remarked on its good training and discipline. The enlisted men who were repeating the seemingly endless and mind-numbing drills were less enthusiastic. Private Worsham recalled the winter and spring of 1863 as a period when "[o]ur time [was] occupied in drilling both in regimental and brigade [formations], inspections, dress parades, and our big revivals."[18]

The "big revivals" Worsham mentioned became a significant factor in the lives of many of the soldiers in the Nineteenth as well as the rest of the army. Revivals began in the Army of Tennessee late in 1862 as part of a wider movement originating in the Army of Northern Virginia. This new religious spirit would remain with both armies, waxing and waning in intensity until the close of the war. The deep spiritual feelings experienced by many of the Rebel soldiers reflected the growing ferocity of the conflict as well as the precarious nature of a soldier's existence. Whether through enemy fire, disease, or accident, death was a constant companion. Enduring combat and the ghastly sights of the battlefield and hospital required an inner strength often bolstered by religion. Christianity's promise of salvation and eternal life offered reassurance and consolation to those facing death daily. Also, as defeats began to multiply, Rebel soldiers increasingly looked to God's grace as the South's last hope.[19]

By late spring of 1863, the men in the Army of Tennessee would sorely need such spiritual succor. Rosecrans was preparing to launch his campaign for the capture of Middle Tennessee and the strategic rail hub of Chattanooga. In early June, Bragg responded to cavalry reports of a Federal buildup by ordering Polk and Hardee to inch their corps toward Murfreesboro to ascertain the enemy's intentions. When convinced that Rosecrans was going to advance, Bragg directed his corps commanders to fall back to their camps at Shelbyville and Wartrace. Throughout the month, Federal activity increased. On June 15, a Yankee probe collided with the Nineteenth along the Shelbyville-Manchester Pike, resulting in a heavy skirmish. Although they held the field at the end of the day, the men of the Nineteenth remained apprehensive of future enemy movements.[20]

Had the men in the regiment known the Federal battle plans, their apprehension would have grown. On June 23, Rosecrans put the Army of the Cumberland into motion, executing a grand turning movement. Bragg, completely deceived by the deft movements of the Federal columns and fearing the entrapment of his army, ordered Hardee and Polk to fall back to Tullahoma. At dawn on June 27, as a heavy rain fell, the Nineteenth along with the rest of Strahl's brigade abandoned the camps on the Shelbyville-Manchester Pike and marched into Shelbyville. The regiment entered the town around 8:00 A.M. and helped burn the last of the military stores there, to prevent their capture. They then distributed to grateful townsfolk the food that could not be transported to Tullahoma. The regiment soon was slogging its way southeastward along the muddy Shelbyville-Tullahoma Road, passing mired vehicles and exhausted teams. The deluge continued for the next two and a half weeks. Although it added to the misery of the retreat by turning the roads into paste, it proved to be a blessing in that it slowed the Federal advance.[21]

The regiment trudged into Tullahoma late on the evening of June 28. The next day the men strengthened unfinished entrenchments around the town in anticipation of the Federal assault. All that day and night they manned the muddy trenches in the pouring rain with nothing to eat. General Cheatham's presence among the troops of his division lifted their sagging spirits. Private Worsham remembered seeing the general sitting on a stump in the driving rain with one shoe off and his big toe protruding from his worn sock, a sight that endeared him to his Tennessee troops.[22]

Morale, however, was about to receive another sharp blow. As Rosecrans continued to advance, Bragg decided to abandon Tullahoma. At daylight on July 1, the Nineteenth along with the rest of Cheatham's division left the trenches. By noon, the regiment and the rest of the Army of Tennessee were across the Elk River and heading for Cowan, Tennessee, at the foot of the Cumberland Mountains. Although the terrain around Cowan offered an excellent defensive position, Bragg ordered the army to proceed to Chattanooga.[23]

Cheatham's division was the last to begin the long ascent up the Cumberlands, camping at University Place on the night of July 3. The next evening the division brought up the rear of the army, which had reached the Tennessee River. The soldiers slowly began to cross—some by the railroad bridge at Bridgeport, others, including the Nineteenth, on a pontoon bridge at the mouth of Battle Creek. On July 7, the last of Bragg's ragged army entered Chattanooga. The long retreat was, for now at least, at an end.[24]

The loss of Middle Tennessee, coming on the heels of the fall of Vicksburg and Robert E. Lee's bloody repulse at Gettysburg, shook the Southern republic to its core. All these disasters resulted from poor leadership at critical moments, but arguably the Army of Tennessee was the most badly handled. At a cost of fewer than six hundred Federal troops and without a significant engagement, Rosecrans had maneuvered Bragg out of Middle Tennessee. The psychological blow to the army was profound. As the soldiers plodded along the sloppy roads toward Chattanooga, hundreds of deserters, mostly Middle Tennesseans, fell out of the ranks. These Rebels had little faith that the Army of Tennessee would return to their region and saw no reason to fight for a nation that had abandoned their homes and families to the advancing Federals. The morale of those who remained in the army was weakened further. They had been led poorly, and they knew it.[25]

Bragg deployed the bulk of Polk's corps around Chattanooga, where the troops hastily constructed earthworks. The Nineteenth positioned itself on a ridge above the town's landing; there the men dug in and awaited the Federals.[26]

In early August, the Confederate War Department merged Major General Simon Buckner's Department of East Tennessee with Bragg's Department of Tennessee. This move increased Bragg's troop strength, but also gave him the responsibility of defending the region all the way to Knoxville—a situation that would cloud his strategic thinking during the whole of the forthcoming

Chattanooga campaign. Bragg converted Buckner's force into another corps for his army. Bragg also received reinforcements from Joseph Johnston in late August under the command of Major General W. H. T. Walker. Walker's men became another corps in the Army of Tennessee. Even with these reinforcements, however, Bragg was badly outnumbered.[27]

Rosecrans designed another turning movement to force Bragg from Chattanooga. Part of his plan involved a bombardment of the town. On Saturday, August 21—which President Davis had designated as a day of prayer and fasting throughout the Confederacy to beseech God's favor—shells began to rain down on the Confederate fortifications guarding the town. Whether by accident or design, shells also exploded in the streets of Chattanooga, inflicting civilian as well as military casualties. One crashed into the First Presbyterian Church on Market Street, badly frightening the throng of civilians and soldiers who were listening to the prayer of the Reverend B. M. Palmer, a visiting minister from New Orleans. Palmer continued to entreat the Almighty for aid as the congregation quickly exited. When he had finished, only a handful of his audience remained, including newly promoted Major Carrick W. Heiskell and several other members of the Nineteenth.[28]

The earnestness displayed by Heiskell and others in seeking God's aid for Chattanooga reflected the regiment's strong commitment not only to the town but also to East Tennessee as a whole. Two of the regiment's companies had been recruited in the town, and every member of the Nineteenth knew that the fall of Chattanooga would leave most of the region under Yankee occupation, cutting the men off from their homes and families. The Federal bombardment was a vivid sign of the danger facing the Rebel patriots of East Tennessee.

The Federal shelling was also responsible for an affair of honor involving Lieutenant Colonel Beriah F. Moore. One of the first shells to land in the town wounded a little girl. She was taken to the home of Moore's father, Antipasse, who lived on Missionary Ridge, out of range of the Federal cannon. However, the elder Moore's home was already full of refugees. When Moore refused to admit the child, Brigadier General Preston Smith, one of Cheatham's brigade commanders, made "unkind remarks" to the elderly gentleman. Lieutenant Colonel Moore heard of the incident and demanded an explanation from Smith. Unsatisfied with the general's response, Moore challenged him to a duel. However, the quick intervention of Major Heiskell and an apology from Smith averted an encounter.[29]

Federal artillery continued to shell Chattanooga intermittently for the next two weeks, wreaking havoc. Meanwhile, Rosecrans sent the bulk of his army across the Tennessee at four points southwest of the town. On September 6,

Bragg realized that Rosecrans's army was behind him and that the Army of Tennessee would have to abandon its fortifications or be cut off. Two days later, the Rebel army marched toward Rome, Georgia, where Bragg planned to concentrate his army.[30]

As the long Confederate columns headed southward, many soldiers, especially East Tennesseans, began to drift from the ranks. Like the Middle Tennesseans who had abandoned the cause earlier, these men were unwilling to continue fighting now that their homeland had fallen to the Yankees. Even before the evacuation of Chattanooga, deserters—including members of the Nineteenth—began to slip away in the night. Disgusted with Bragg, doubtful of Southern victory, and perhaps hopeful of returning home and putting the war behind them, these soldiers chose to surrender to the Yankees. On the night of September 5, three such men of the Nineteenth swam the Tennessee River and turned themselves over to Federal sentries. The three then offered information on the state of the Rebel army.[31]

These men were neither the first nor the last to abandon their comrades in the regiment. Beginning in June 1861 and continuing until the general surrender in North Carolina, the Nineteenth suffered from absenteeism and desertion. The regiment was certainly not unique in this regard. High rates of absenteeism and desertion occurred in all Confederate units, especially after the military disasters of 1863 and 1864. While absenteeism hurt the combat effectiveness of the regiment, the eventual return of the perpetrators confirmed their commitment to the cause. Desertion, however, not only sapped the regiment's strength but also demonstrated an abandonment of, or lack of dedication to, Southern independence and, therefore, presented a graver threat to the republic's survival. Why did men of the Nineteenth desert? Who were those most likely to do so? How did their departure affect the unit? Exploring these questions sheds light not only on the experience of the Nineteenth but also on the crucial historiographical issue of why the South lost the Civil War.[32]

As to why certain members of the Nineteenth deserted, a myriad of possibilities exists. First, conditions in the Confederate Army, especially the Army of Tennessee, were appalling. Lack of proper food, clothing, and shelter undoubtedly drove many to leave the ranks in order to survive. In addition, illness and wounds weakened many soldiers to the point they could no longer endure the Spartan environment of camp life. Certainly, too, the horrors of combat motivated some men to abandon the army. While these factors certainly contributed to the unit's desertion, it appears that the most significant motivating factor was familial concerns. Historians have long recognized that Confederate deserters generally came from the middle and lower classes of

Southern society. The families of these men often teetered on the edge of economic ruin. A soldier's absence from home inflicted severe hardships on such
households, which were desperate for labor. Because few of these men benefited from slavery or commercial agriculture, in many cases they came to perceive the conflict as a rich man's war but a poor man's fight. Under such conditions, family responsibility overshadowed patriotic duty, and many left the
army for home—especially conscripts, who had been forced into service in the
first place.[33]

There is abundant evidence that this factor was at work among the
Nineteenth's deserters. Data from the Compiled Service Records and the 1860
census provide a socioeconomic portrait of the regiment's deserters and reveal
distinctions between the volunteers of 1861 and later recruits, who were mostly
conscripts. The Compiled Service Records list 158 deserters out of 1,009 1861
enlistees, or about 15.6 percent of the total. One hundred twenty-one of those
deserters in 117 households have been located in the 1860 census. The average
aggregate wealth for these men was $2,785—only 8.4 percent higher than the
regional average and 51 percent less than the 1861 regimental average.
However, the disparity in wealth between the deserters and the rest of the Nineteenth was even greater than these numbers indicate. The majority of wealth
held by the deserters was concentrated in only a few households. The richest
10 households held 54.5 percent of the deserters' wealth. If these 10 households
are removed from the calculations, the average aggregate wealth of the 1861
deserters falls to $1,387, or 54 percent of the regional average. The median
aggregate wealth of these men was only $250, $400 less than the total 1861
sample. Clearly, the regiment's 1861 deserters were among East Tennessee's
poorest residents.[34]

The 1862 group was even poorer. The Compiled Service Records list 35
deserters out of 161 recruits in 1862, or 21.7 percent of the total. Thirty-four
of these deserters in 32 households have been located in the 1860 census. The
average aggregate wealth of the group stood at $1,088, only 42 percent of the
regional average. Again, the majority of the group's wealth was concentrated
in a few households. In fact, the 5 richest households held almost three-fourths
of the group's total wealth, and if they are removed from the calculations, the
remaining 27 households averaged only $325 in aggregate wealth. This figure,
coupled with a median aggregate wealth of $225 for the group, demonstrates
the abject poverty confronting these men.[35]

The 1863 deserters present a similar picture. The Compiled Service
Records list 61 deserters out of 121 recruits, or slightly over 50 percent. Forty-
one of those men in 39 households have been located in the 1860 census. The
average aggregate wealth of the group was $2,691, slightly over the regional

average of $2,569. Yet again the wealth of the group was concentrated. The 4 richest households of the group held almost 86 percent of its total wealth. If those 4 are taken out of the calculation, the remaining 35 households average only $428 in aggregate wealth. The median aggregate wealth for the group was a mere $87.50. Obviously, such households represented East Tennessee's lowest classes.[36]

Equally telling, none of the deserter groups contained many slaveholders. The 1861 group contained 14 slaveowning households, or 12 percent of its total. The 1862 group contained only 1 slaveowning household, or 3.1 percent of its total. The 1863 group had 4 slaveowning households, or 10.3 percent of its total. Likewise, few of the households engaged in market agriculture—24.8 percent of the 1861 group, 23.5 percent of the 1862 group, and 23.1 percent of the 1863 group—and in most cases farm surpluses were small. Interestingly, the number of households with a member of the regiment as head increased with each group—30.8 percent for the 1861 group, 38.2 percent for the 1862 group, and 51.3 percent for the 1863 group. Most of these men had wives and children, and, given their poverty, the household would have been hardpressed to make ends meet without the labor of the deserter.[37]

While the household's economic condition certainly influenced the decision to desert, other familial concerns also appear to have been a factor. For example, Privates Robert E. Depew and Samuel P. Depew of Company G deserted together after the death of one brother and the discharge of another—perhaps believing that their family had done enough for the cause. Likewise, after the death of their brother Thomas at Shiloh, Privates William Leath and Alexander Leath of Company E left the regiment. (As these and other examples illustrate, desertion was often a joint decision of kinsmen.) Moreover, many of those leaving the ranks were the only sons of aging parents. Private James F. M. Newport of Company D, for example, was the only son of Asa and Elizabeth Newport, both fifty-seven years old. Private Robert P. Short, also of Company D, had left his seventy-year-old mother alone when he joined the army in 1861.[38]

Concern for loved ones rose dramatically in 1863 when Union forces occupied most of East Tennessee. Confederate families throughout the region were now at the mercy not only of Federal troops but also of unionist guerrillas who were anxious to punish East Tennessee's Rebels. Not surprisingly, a correlation exists between the Federal invasion of the region and desertion in the Nineteenth. The great majority of the regiment's deserters—70.3 percent of the 1861 group, 79.4 percent of the 1862 group, and 95.1 percent of the 1863 group—left the army in the fall of 1863, most of them in September as Bragg's army evacuated Chattanooga.[39]

Making desertion an even more attractive option in this period was Lincoln's Proclamation of Pardon and Amnesty, issued in December 1863. Under this lenient policy, apostate Rebels could have their U.S. citizenship rights restored simply by taking an oath to support the Constitution and federal legislation concerning slavery. This proved most inviting, especially to poor subsistence farmers with no direct stake in slavery. Generally, if a Confederate deserter's home lay within Federal lines, he was to be permitted to return home. However, by 1864, abuses of the lenient Federal policy had apparently convinced Washington to release East Tennessee deserters north of the Ohio River. In addition, because so many deserters later rejoined the Confederate Army, Federal officials began subjecting new deserters to rigorous examinations designed to determine suitability for release. Those found unsuitable were sent to prisoner of war camps. Many of these men were undoubtedly earnest in their desire to change their allegiance but lacked "indisputable proof" of their integrity. One was Private Joseph E. Spurgin of Company G, who wrote the following letter to Edwin P. Stanton:

To his Excelency,

The Honorable Secretary of War. Sir I address you a few lines this evening concerning my welfair. Mr. Secretary I wish to take the Oath of Allegiance to the United States and become a loyal citizen, Sir I am not a captured man I threw down my arms come across the southern lines reported as a deserter, I was informed the Oath would be administered in Nashville Tenn when I arrived there no one was permitted to take the Oath unfortunately I was brought to Rock Island Prison and held as a prisoner of war, Mr. Secretary having no friends to assist in getting me out of prison I now appeal to you knowing you have the power, Sir I am a conscript when conscripted I resolved to desert, the first opportunity having do so I think it nothing more than right I should be released, Sir if it pleases your honor to release me or to have it done it will be a favor one never to be forgotten, Sir I think my remarks are plain and satisfactory. I never want to be exchanged, nothing more I will close.

I will remain respectfully yours

Joseph E. Spurgin[40]

Although the deserters would not be forced to fight against their former compatriots, they were not free from military obligation. They could be enrolled in the

Union Army and sent west to frontier posts where their presence would free other Federal troops to join the war effort against the Confederacy. It does not appear that any of the Nineteenth's deserters were drafted into such service. However, many volunteered. The Compiled Service Records identify thirty-eight members of the regiment (including Joseph E. Spurgin) who joined the Federal forces—either units slated for frontier service, new army units being raised for use against the Confederacy, or the Union Navy. While most of these "galvanized Yankees" were deserters who had joined the Nineteenth in 1862 or 1863 and hence were probably conscripts, almost half were 1861 enlistees. Clearly these men had lost faith in the Confederacy's ability to win its independence. They and thousands like them who bolstered the Federal ranks, along with the other thousands of deserters who simply went home or wandered the countryside, offer compelling evidence of the Confederacy's internal collapse.[41]

Desertion withered the Nineteenth. As a result, the combat effectiveness of the regiment, like that of all Confederate units, ebbed just as the Federals mounted their most determined effort to subdue the rebellion. The absence of these men from the battlefield unquestionably hastened the death of the Confederacy. With fighting spirit lacking in so many Confederate soldiers, it is a testament to the fighting spirit of those remaining in the ranks that the Southern republic lasted as long as it did.[42]

Confederate authorities tried, though with little success, to curtail desertion. In the beginning, it was hoped that peer pressure would suffice. The names of deserters were published in local papers, and rewards were offered for the return of such men. For example, while captain of Company K, Carrick W. Heiskell offered twenty-five dollars of his own money in addition to the thirty dollars paid by the government for the apprehension of Privates Alvin P. Underwood and John A. Martin. Both men were returned to the regiment, but later they disappeared again, and in fact Underwood joined the enemy. Punishments inflicted by Confederate authorities on captured deserters included branding, lashing, hard labor, confinement, public humiliation such as bucking and gagging, and ultimately death by hanging or firing squad. The Nineteenth's deserters appeared to have avoided such sentences. Although in several instances the death penalty was decreed, in each case the subject received a reprieve—only to desert again and, fortunately, not be recaptured.[43]

While most of the deserters thinning the ranks of Bragg's bedraggled army in the fall of 1863 were simply war-weary men anxious to return home, others were decoys sent out by Bragg to mislead the Federals. He hoped that these men, bearing tales of the army's disintegration, would encourage Rosecrans's overconfidence and lead the Federals to commit a careless act that would allow the Confederates an opportunity to strike back.[44]

Early on the morning of September 12, Bragg received reports of isolated Union troops at Lee and Gordon's Mill in North Georgia. He ordered Polk to take Cheatham's division at Rock Spring Church, six miles southeast of the mill, and move against the Yankees. But Polk ignored the order to attack,

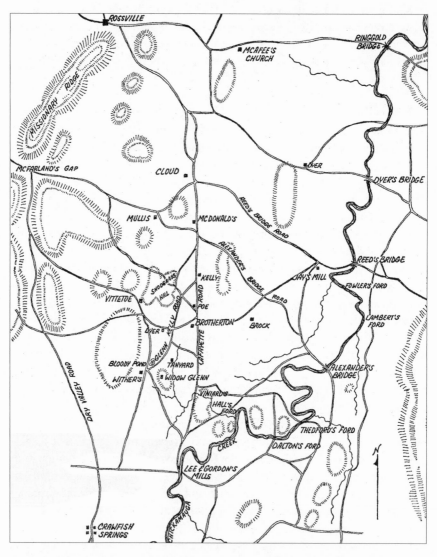

The Chickamauga Front. Reprinted by permission of Louisiana State University Press from Autumn of Glory: The Army of Tennessee, 1862–1865 *by Thomas Lawrence Connelly. Copyright © 1971 by Louisiana State University Press.*

citing concerns over the size and strength of the forces to his front. Anxious that an opportunity not be lost, Bragg sent reinforcements to Polk's aid and again ordered Polk to attack. However, when Bragg arrived at the front on the morning of September 13, he found that a whole Federal corps had taken position on the west bank of Chickamauga Creek.[45]

Polk, still cautious, did not move until 9:00 A.M. He then sent Strahl's brigade toward the mill to find the Federal line. As the brigade moved forward, Colonel Moore ordered Major Heiskell to deploy a skirmish line for the Nineteenth. Around noon, the men advanced to within earshot of the Yankee line. After a brief skirmish, the brigade fell back. Polk had hoped to entice the Yankees to strike at his strong defensive line, but the Federals had no such intention.[46]

An exasperated Bragg pulled his forces back from Lee and Gordon's Mill. Disappointment over his lieutenants' failures was somewhat offset by the prospect of immediate reinforcements, especially two divisions of the Army of Northern Virginia under Lieutenant General James Longstreet. Believing that he had perhaps one last opportunity to crush Rosecrans before the Army of the Cumberland could coalesce, Bragg decided to strike even before all of Longstreet's men had arrived. On the morning of September 18, elements of Bragg's army crossed Chickamauga Creek. Sporadic fighting throughout that day proved inconclusive, and Confederate delays and indecision gave the Federals time to bring more troops onto the field.[47]

The Nineteenth did not participate in the fighting on September 18. It, along with the rest of Cheatham's division, spent the day marching along the east side of Chickamauga Creek and maneuvering into position for an early crossing the next morning to support units already on the other side. Although the regiment did not march far, the men were hungry and irritable, and they bedded down with stomachs full of apprehension and little else.[48]

The division broke camp before dawn as echoes of musketry filtered through the thickets lining the creek. Cavalry under Forrest, along with supporting infantry from Walker's reserve corps, had encountered the Yankee line. When Federal counterattacks threatened to push the Confederates back across the Chickamauga, Walker requested reinforcements. Bragg ordered Cheatham's division to rush to Walker's aid. The division had already crossed the creek around 7:00 A.M. at Dalton's (or Hunt's) Ford and positioned itself behind Buckner's corps as support. After receiving Bragg's dispatch at 11:00 A.M., Cheatham moved his Tennesseans quickly toward the front and the sound of battle.[49]

By noon, Cheatham had maneuvered his division into position on Walker's left flank, south of the Winfrey Farm. There he paused to arrange his

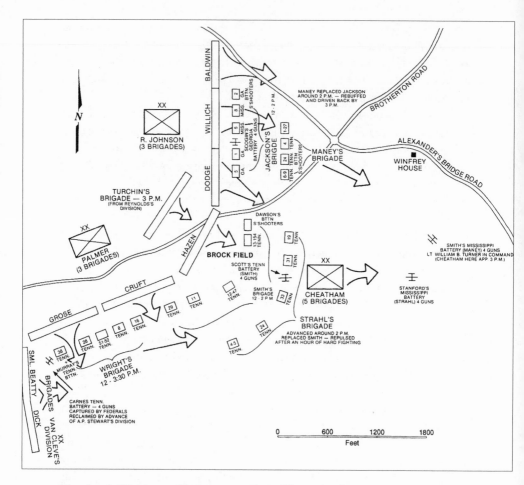

Cheatham's Division at Chickamauga. From Christopher Losson, Tennessee's
Forgotten Warriors: Frank Cheatham and His Confederate Division *(Knoxville:
University of Tennessee Press, 1989), 105.*

command. The brigades of Brigadier Generals Marcus Wright, Preston Smith,
and John Jackson were stretched out almost a mile left to right forming the
division's line of battle, with Strahl's and Maney's brigades forming the reserve.
Once set, the division lurched forward. Marching at the double-quick, the
Rebel regiments lost cohesion in the dense underbrush and broken terrain.
Cheatham paused again to allow his commanders to straighten their lines and
rode along, encouraging his men. Passing near the Nineteenth, he yelled his
familiar cry, "Give them hell, boys, give them hell." He had not passed from

sight when the equally excited yet more dignified Polk arrived, urging the Tennesseans to "Give them what General Cheatham says, we will pay off old chores today." As Polk passed the regiment, a shell crashed into Company A, wounding two men and signaling the beginning of what was to be another bloody day for the Nineteenth.[50]

As the Confederates struggled through the undergrowth, Private Worsham saw so many wounded Rebels retreating that it appeared they outnumbered their advancing comrades—a discouraging sight. Within minutes, Cheatham's front brigades encountered the Yankee line and were heavily engaged. The Rebels soon overwhelmed the Federals and drove them back into breastworks completed the previous night. There, however, the Confederate advance stalled as the battered forward brigades ran low on ammunition and Federal reinforcements appeared. Unable to sustain their fire, the brigades of Jackson and Smith withdrew and requested immediate support. Struggling to stabilize his line, Cheatham ordered his reserve units forward around 1:00 P.M. Maney's brigade moved to replace Jackson's, while Strahl's relieved Smith's.[51]

Such maneuvering in rough terrain and under enemy fire was difficult. Because Maney's and Strahl's movements were not properly coordinated, the Confederate line was crooked and riddled with gaps, a situation inviting disaster. As Strahl advanced, he discovered that his right flank was exposed and thus ordered his men to shift right. Around 2:00 P.M., Strahl's men approached Brock Field in line of battle still looking for support to their right. The Nineteenth occupied the extreme right of the line. As the regiment entered the field, it received the fire of an entire Federal brigade to its front and enfilading fire from the exposed right flank. In less than fifteen minutes, 75 of the unit's 242 men were struck down.[52]

Strahl watched in horror as the officers in his right-flank regiments were all unhorsed. In the Nineteenth, the steady nerve of the officers, especially Colonel Walker and Lieutenant Colonel Moore, held the regiment together. Such courage carried a heavy price. Captain William W. Lackey of Company E was killed instantly by a bullet in his head. Captain S. J. A . Frazier, leading Company D, fell with a wound to his windpipe. As he lay on the ground clutching his throat, two of his men dashed to his aid only to be cut down themselves. The enemy fire was so intense that the captain received two more wounds as he writhed on the ground struggling to breathe. Lieutenant J. M. Sims of Company F suffered yet another wound, his fourth since joining the regiment, and Major Carrick W. Heiskell received a crippling wound to his foot. The command of Company G was especially hard hit. Captain Robert L. Blair, Second Lieutenant Hiram D. Hawk, and the new third lieutenant, young John

H. Rhea, all were wounded in the space of a few minutes. A Rebel cannoneer observing the scene declared that he had never seen "so many men fall on so small a space of ground."[53]

Unwilling to endure the withering musketry any longer, Strahl ordered his whole brigade to fall back a short distance and regroup. As Strahl and his officers struggled to calm their men and reform their lines, General Alexander P. Stewart's division moved into place on Cheatham's left flank, protecting it from a Federal turning movement. Cheatham's right flank, however, was in trouble. Maney's brigade was breaking due to pressure in front and from both flanks. His regiments were giving way just as Strahl rallied his brigade at the edge of Brock Field. It was now around 3:00 P.M. Determined to form a new line near the Winfrey House, Maney appealed to Strahl for help in closing the gap between the two brigades. Strahl immediately ordered the Nineteenth to change its front to the north and charge across the gap while the Thirty-First and Thirty-Third Tennessee moved into Brock Field in support.[54]

Despite Strahl's best efforts, Maney could not hold his position against the Union advance. His brigade crumpled, and he withdrew further to the rear. The Nineteenth then endured more enfilading fire, as Maney's withdrawal again left Strahl's flank exposed. Strahl found himself in an untenable position and ordered his men to retire about 3:30 P.M., abandoning Brock Field to the enemy. Learning that Smith's brigade was to his right rear, he instructed his regiments to form up on its left flank.[55]

The Rebels now paused to catch their breath. After its initial success, Cheatham's division had been driven back slowly all afternoon until it now stood near its original line of departure. Exhausted and low on ammunition, the men watched and waited. As the Federals advanced perilously close to the weak Confederate line, Rebel batteries unleashed a barrage of canister into the Yankee line. The assault lost momentum, and the Yankees retreated.[56]

Artillery had saved Cheatham's division, and Cheatham's division in turn had saved the Confederate right, although at a frightful cost. The Nineteenth alone had eight killed, sixty-six wounded, and twenty missing—almost 40 percent of its total strength. Not since Murfreesboro had the regiment or the Army of Tennessee experienced such a bloodbath, and it showed no sign of ending. As Cheatham's stunned Tennesseans held their ground, the battle still raged around them. Determined to turn the Federal left, Bragg continued to feed units into the fight. Throughout the late afternoon, the sounds of heavy fighting reverberated through the forests as the Nineteenth waited.[57]

Near twilight, Patrick Cleburne's division advanced for one final assault, which was to be supported by Cheatham. Strahl ordered his men to fall in. The Confederates struck the Federals hard, driving them back. However, as darkness fell, stiffening resistance and confusion caused the attack to sputter out. Some of Cheatham's troops joined in the attack, but Strahl's brigade was not engaged. As the musketry subsided, Strahl brought his brigade forward through the woods to Brigadier General James Deshler's line near Brock Field. There, close to the scene of the afternoon's carnage, the men bivouacked in line of battle. The long day was finally over.[58]

That night a cold northerly wind whistled through the scrub oaks and pines along Chickamauga Creek. Temperatures plunged to near freezing. The proximity of the Yankees prevented the use of campfires, and the warm day and the exertions of combat had left the men wet with sweat, intensifying the chill. The soldiers huddled in their blankets. The thick gunsmoke and the heavy foliage created a murky, stifling environment, and passing clouds generally obscured the quarter moon. In the darkness, the men of the Nineteenth recuperated. Some slept, others whispered, and others lay quietly reflecting on the horrors they had witnessed. The sounds of skirmishing pickets and wounded men crying out in pain reinforced the surreal nature of the scene. Perhaps the most ominous sounds penetrating the night air were those of axes and shovels at work along the Union line, as the enemy strengthened earthworks in anticipation of the coming day.[59]

The Federals' late-night entrenching suggested that Rosecrans had adopted a defensive posture for tomorrow's action. The opposite was true of Bragg. He believed his army had come close to crushing the Federal left, and he was anxious to finish the job. The arrival of Longstreet along with the intermingling of the army's units during the day's action led Bragg to reorganize the army's five corps into two "wings." Longstreet would command the left wing and Polk the right, which included Cheatham's division. Bragg held late-night meetings with both wing commanders and outlined his plan for the next day. At first light, Polk would send his divisions against the Federal left flank. As the pressure of the assault began to turn the Union flank, Longstreet would send his divisions forward.[60]

Polk's attack the next morning was delayed, but finally, around 9:30 A.M., he ordered his troops into action, holding Cheatham's division in reserve. Throughout the morning and early afternoon, Polk sent in brigade after brigade in futile, disjointed attacks against the Federal earthworks. Meanwhile, the Nineteenth and the rest of Cheatham's Tennesseans remained idle, menaced only by occasional shelling. Exasperated at Polk's failure to break the Federal line, Bragg ordered Longstreet into action. Around 11:00 A.M., a mix-up in orders caused a Federal division to pull out of the Union center just as Longstreet's wing surged forward. As screaming Rebels poured into the gap, Rosecrans's line splintered and the Yankees panicked.[61]

Meanwhile, Polk was struggling to get his units into position for a renewed effort against the Federal left. Around 2:00 P.M., he ordered Cheatham to move his division to the extreme right of the Confederate line. The men reached Reed's Bridge Road, where they deployed in line of battle and waited. They had a long wait. Polk did not advance his troops until around 5:00 P.M.— far too late to support Longstreet. Nevertheless, by twilight, the Federal army had retired from the field, except for some units holding out along Snodgrass Hill and Horseshoe Ridge. These soon retreated as Rebel yells reverberated through the forests. Some of Cheatham's units had been engaged in the late afternoon assaults, but Strahl's brigade and the Nineteenth had been spared. Nonetheless, they were as elated as any of the other Rebel troops on the field. The long-suffering Army of Tennessee finally had its great victory.[62]

Though some of his generals advised a quick thrust against the shaken Federals, Bragg demurred, pointing out that the army still faced a serious shortage of food and transportation and had suffered enormous casualties. Instead, the Rebels spent September 21 scouting for the enemy, collecting abandoned equipment, burying the dead, and searching for wounded. Among those found was Private Thomas Wright of Company E. Wright had been shot once in his right side and twice in the chest during the first day's fighting near Brock Field. Miraculously he survived the wounds and the frigid nights and was rescued by his astonished comrades.[63]

As Bragg's army cleared the battlefield, reports came in indicating that the remnants of Rosecrans's army were evacuating Chattanooga. On the morning of the twenty-second, Bragg ordered Cheatham's division, accompanied by Governor Isham Harris, to make a reconnaissance in force into the town. After Maney's and Smith's brigades cleared Missionary Ridge of Yankee troops, Cheatham reported that the enemy appeared to be retreating toward East Tennessee. However, when Bragg arrived with the rest of the army the next morning, he discovered that the Yankees had actually dug in.[64]

Bragg did not believe his army could storm the town's fortifications. Neither did he believe that his men were capable of an offensive beyond Chattanooga. He therefore chose to force Rosecrans to move by laying siege to the town. Now, he reasoned, Rosecrans must either retreat or starve.[65]

If Bragg lacked the combativeness to drive the Federals from their stronghold, he exhibited more than enough to assail his own generals. Shortly after Chickamauga, he suspended from command both Polk and Major General Thomas C. Hindman, ostensibly for their failures in the recent campaign. Several of the army's most prominent generals retaliated by petitioning President Davis for Bragg's removal. Again, as after Murfreesboro, the Army of Tennessee's leadership ignored the Federals and engaged in an internal power struggle. Jefferson Davis traveled to Bragg's headquarters in mid-October intending to rid the army of its dissension. Instead, he only made it worse. After hearing the candid recriminations of both sides, Davis chose to sustain Bragg. Bragg used the president's declaration of support as an opportunity to rid the army of his enemies. The vindictive general relieved both D. H. Hill and Simon Buckner and received Davis's permission to restructure the army. Officially, Bragg's decision to break up established divisions and reshuffle their brigades was intended to mitigate the effects of battlefield losses on a particular state or region. Unofficially, it was intended to destroy the anti-Bragg cliques in his divisions, especially those of Breckinridge and Cheatham.[66]

Cheatham's division, the largest in the army, consisted primarily of Tennesseans. They were devoted to their native-son commander. Cheatham was equally fond of the men, and protective of his reputation. When he learned of the impending reorganization, he tendered his resignation and went on leave. He returned, however, when the secretary of war refused his resignation. But the division he returned to bore little resemblance to the one he left. Only one of his old brigades remained; the rest were all transferred. This brigade realignment coincided with the reorganization of the army into three corps commanded by Hardee (who replaced Polk), Breckinridge, and Longstreet. Strahl's brigade now belonged to Alexander P. Stewart's division of Breckinridge's corps. No doubt Bragg hoped that his efforts had finally quashed his opposition. They had not. Many of his officers still loathed him.[67]

The squabbling among the army's high command affected the men in the ranks. The dismembering of units eroded morale and faith in Bragg. Many soldiers abandoned the army and the Southern cause rather than serve under their despised commander. It was not only the reshuffling of brigades that drew their wrath. The supply situation, critical after Chickamauga, had deteriorated further. When President Davis reviewed the army in October, he was met with cries for food from the thin, ragged ranks. Although accustomed to privation, the men had never endured such a shortage of rations, clothing, and shelter. The Nineteenth, for example, was issued what the men called "sick flour." Lacking oil or shortening, the men had to make biscuits using only salt and water. The nauseating mixture gave the flour its name. Later the biscuits grew so hard that several soldiers bored holes in them, inserted powder, and blew them apart to make a point and generate laughs. Such humor may have helped the men cope with their lack of food, but the army's condition was far from laughable. Thousands of soldiers grew weak from fever brought on by hunger and exposure. Some foraged for game, horse fodder, rats, or anything else edible. Others, such as Private J. P. Edwards of Company A, attempted to raid commissary stores. Edwards was caught, tried, and sentenced to wear a barrel shirt with a placard labeled "Government Bacon Thief." As a deterrent to future raids, he was paraded before warehouse guards for five consecutive days and then marched before the regiment for three additional days.[68]

The suffering of the Federal army, however, matched or exceeded that of the Confederates. The siege was working. Stretched out in a seven-mile semi-circle from the base of Lookout Mountain to the south bank of the Tennessee near East Chickamauga Creek, the Confederate lines cut nearly every route into Chattanooga. It appeared that if the Army of Tennessee could hold on a bit longer, Rosecrans would have to retreat—that is, if he could not be rein-forced. To prevent the Union forces in upper East Tennessee from coming to Rosecrans's aid, Bragg dispatched Major General Carter Stevenson's and Cheatham's divisions to Sweetwater in October. (At this point, Strahl's brigade was still under Cheatham's command, although Cheatham was then absent.) The two divisions did little while on this excursion into East Tennessee. Though the men of the regiment did not realize it at the time, this would be the Nineteenth's last visit home until the end of the war.[69]

Bragg should have shifted his concerns to his other flank. The new Federal commander, Major General Ulysses S. Grant, realized that the seizure of Lookout Valley and Brown's Ferry at the foot of Lookout Mountain would open up a supply route to Bridgeport and relieve the beleaguered garrison. Using recently arrived reinforcements, the Federals struck early on the morn-ing of October 27. They surprised and overwhelmed the Confederates. With the famous "cracker line" now open, the siege could not succeed. Bragg, how-ever, continued the siege and then proceeded to make the situation worse by ordering Longstreet and his two divisions into East Tennessee to defeat the Federal army at Knoxville. This left Bragg badly outnumbered. Nevertheless, he clung to the illusion of besieging Chattanooga.[70]

After the loss of Lookout Valley, Bragg endeavored to adjust his lines and bolster his crumbling left flank. Hardee's corps would now be responsible for holding Lookout Mountain and the portion of Chattanooga Valley on the west side of Chattanooga Creek. Breckinridge's corps would deploy from the east bank of the creek and along the base of Missionary Ridge from north of the Rossville Road to near Tunnel Hill, where Cleburne's division guarded the Confederate right. After a bit of maneuvering, the Nineteenth, along with the rest of Stewart's division, settled into its soggy position in the valley and waited for the rains to stop or the Federals to move. They would not have to wait long for either.[71]

On November 24, the Federals struck both Confederate flanks, storming Lookout Mountain and nearly taking Tunnel Hill. That night, Bragg ordered the army to pull back to a position atop Missionary Ridge. Hardee's corps would hold the right around Tunnel Hill while Breckinridge would hold the center and left to the Rossville Road.[72]

During the night Confederate divisions began moving from the valley toward the summit of Missionary Ridge. However, instead of concentrating their forces at the crest, Bragg and his corps commanders split their strength between rifle pits along the ridge's base and newly dug entrenchments further up the steep slope. This illogical deployment created several potentially disastrous problems. First, if the Federals broke the first line of resistance along the base, the retreating Rebels would be mixed in with the advancing Yankees, blocking the fire of their comrades further up the ridge. Second, because they would be spreading their small army over two, or in some cases three, successive rows of entrenchments, the Confederate commanders would have few or no troops left for a tactical reserve to plug any breaks in their line. Moreover, although Breckinridge had started to fortify the ridge on the twenty-third, more breastworks would have to be built that night, and supporting artillery would have to be placed in the dark, without proper sighting. To make matters worse, the Confederates wound up placing most of the hastily dug entrenchments without regard to proper fields of fire or the elevation of the ridge, creating blind spots that would allow the enemy to reach the top nearly unmolested while the defenders would have to expose themselves to get a clear shot.[73]

In the dark hours of the morning of November 25, Strahl moved his brigade from the valley toward Missionary Ridge. He placed the Thirty-First and Thirty-Third Tennessee in the rifle pits at the base of the ridge to act as skirmishers as the rest of his men climbed the slope. Near the top, Strahl established his main line, deploying the Twenty-Fourth Tennessee on the left and the Nineteenth on the right. He held the consolidated Fourth and Fifth Tennessee in reserve. Later, Strahl moved the Fourth and Fifth to a secondary defensive line about two hundred yards in front of his main line, giving him three rows of entrenchments to hold. Like the rest of the Rebel units along Stewart's sector of the front, Strahl's brigade would have no reserve force.[74]

The day dawned clear and cool and with it came a Federal assault aimed at the Confederate right. The struggle lasted until mid-afternoon, ending in failure for the Yankees. As the sounds of battle drifted from the Confederate right, Breckinridge's front remained quiet. However, around noon, increased Federal activity in the valley caught the Rebels' attention. Fearing an attack, Breckinridge repositioned his men. He shifted the divisions of Stewart and Brigadier General William Bate to the right, closing a dangerous gap between them and General Patton Anderson's division. Confusion reigned as the Confederate brigades realigned themselves. Strahl's brigade moved right and

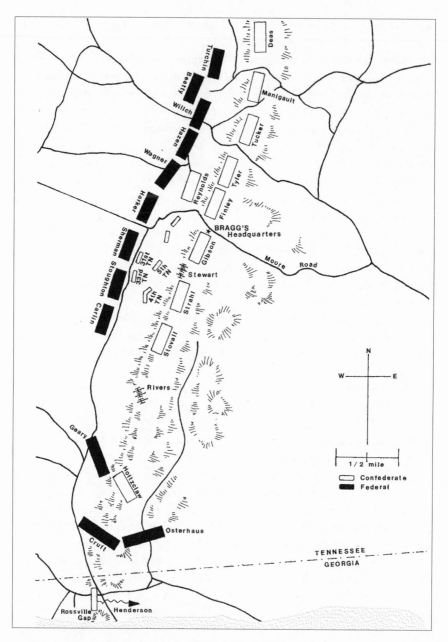

Missionary Ridge. Reprinted by permission of Louisiana State University Press from Soldier of Tennessee: General Alexander P. Stewart and the Civil War in the West *by Sam Davis Elliot. Copyright © 1999 by Louisiana State University Press. Map by Blake Magner.*

then retraced its steps back to allow Colonel Randall Gibson's brigade to slide into line. Strahl's men finally occupied a position next to their original line.[75]

Lieutenant Colonel Moore distanced himself from the Nineteenth and the chaos of the moment. He sat entranced, gazing at the familiar landscape before him. The regiment's entrenchments lay across his father's farm, and to his right he could discern the orchard surrounding his boyhood home—now Bragg's headquarters. As Moore stood reflecting on this twist of fate, his father appeared. At one point in their meeting, Moore placed all his personal effects in the old man's hands—perhaps because he had had a premonition of his fate.[76]

Meanwhile, moving along his regiment's line, Colonel Walker surveyed the position. Despite the afternoon's realignment, the Thirty-First and Thirty-Third Tennessee still guarded the brigade's front at the base of the ridge while the Fourth/Fifth Tennessee held a second line behind them. The Nineteenth and Twenty-Fourth Tennessee and a section of Stanford's battery held the third (or main) line. To the left of the Twenty-Fourth stood Brigadier General Marcellus Stovall's brigade of Georgians; to the right of the Nineteenth stood Gibson's brigade; to Walker's right rear stood another section of Stanford's battery. Although Walker worried about the strength of the hastily dug and incomplete breastworks that his men occupied, the position would prove as strong as any along the thinly manned ridge.[77]

By 3:30 P.M., the better part of four Federal divisions had assembled in the valley below. The dress-parade formations awed the Rebel defenders. A six-gun cannonade echoed across the valley, and a blue wave advanced. For a few moments, the Yankees marched unmolested. Then the thunderous peal of Confederate artillery pierced the silence. John Gold in the Twenty-Fourth Tennessee remembered that when Stanford's batteries opened fire, the ear-splitting sound was "terrible to endure." Despite the frightening noise, the shelling proved largely ineffective. The Rebel artillerymen overshot their targets.[78]

As the Federals approached the base of the ridge, confusion and panic gripped the Rebel defenders in the rifle pits. Unsure of their mission as skirmishers, some attempted to hold their position while others simply fired a volley or two and scampered up the slope, allowing their steadfast comrades to be flanked and routed. Before long, all the rifle pits had fallen to the Yankee assault, and hundreds of scared Rebels were scrambling toward the main line. Among the throngs of fleeing men were members of the Thirty-First and Thirty-Third Tennessee, who headed toward the Nineteenth to try to reform behind their entrenchments.[79]

Colonel Walker's attention was momentarily diverted from the battle below when he discovered a gap of over one hundred yards between his right flank and Gibson's brigade. He immediately informed General Stewart, but Stewart failed to recognize the seriousness of the problem, assuming that whatever gap there was must be small and could be covered by Stanford's battery. Besides, Stewart had no reserve with which to plug any gap. Walker reported that the battery had retreated after expending its ammunition, and although he promised to direct his right wing's fire into the gap, he doubted its effectiveness. Stewart should have paid more attention to Walker's report. Unknown to the general, Bragg had shifted Gibson's men to the right to close another interval and protect his headquarters.[80]

While the Federals consolidated their hold on the base of the ridge, artillery and small arms fire from higher up ripped into their ranks, taking a deadly toll. Instinctively and without orders, the Union troops emerged from the trenches and advanced. Private Worsham recalled that "the enemy came on, crawling up the steep ascent like bugs, and were so thick they were almost in each other's way." To the front of the Nineteenth, a Federal surge gained the flank of the Fourth/Fifth Tennessee, which soon broke and scattered in disarray. Many survivors fled toward the crest of the ridge, where they joined the Nineteenth. As the enemy approached Strahl's main line, the Nineteenth and Twenty-Fourth unleashed a withering fire that forced the attackers back several times. At one point, the Twenty-Fourth actually charged, forcing the Yankees back down the ridge. Federals to the front of the Nineteenth could advance no closer than fifty yards from the Rebel earthworks before being cut down by the rapid and accurate fire. Although momentarily successful, Walker knew his position was far from secure. The men were down to their last few cartridges, and their right flank was still dangerously exposed. The regiment's right wing could only slow the Federal advance through the gap; it could not stop it.[81]

Before long, the remnants of Strahl's brigade and the defenders of other parts of the Rebel line began to give way. On Walker's right, charging Federals overran Gibson's brigade, and the colonel soon counted three stands of enemy colors on his flank. Again, as at Chickamauga, a deadly enfilade tore into the Nineteenth. Lieutenant Colonel Moore had his horse shot from under him— the fourth since the war began. In quick succession, he was shot in the hand and then struck down by a mortal wound. His brother Nicholas, a private in Company I, fell wounded near him and was captured by the onrushing Yankees. Both brothers lay within sight of their home. Their blood flowed onto their father's farm—land they had fought so hard to protect.[82]

Moore's death was a great blow to the regiment. Although he had been a demanding officer and a strict disciplinarian, he had improved the unit and won the respect of his men. He had fought in all the regiment's engagements, had earned the praise of superiors for his bravery, and had proven himself devoted to the Southern cause. Following Moore's death, Colonel Walker wrote, "No purer patriot or higher loved and esteemed man has given his life to his country in this war. . . ." Likewise, General Strahl eulogized the fallen officer, stating, "A braver man and truer patriot has not fallen, and a nobler spirit has not been sacrificed for human liberty or southern freedom." The Nineteenth, and indeed the Confederacy, could not afford to lose such men.[83]

With the Nineteenth disintegrating and the Federals threatening to gain his rear, Strahl ordered the Twenty-Fourth and Nineteenth to fall back some three hundred yards and re-form, placing skirmishers on the flanks. The men quickly redeployed and replenished their cartridge boxes. All about them, Stewart's line had collapsed, giving the Federals control of large portions of the ridge. When a large enemy force advanced on Strahl's left, he ordered his men to retreat to a small hill some five hundred to six hundred yards behind the ridge. Skirmishers again fanned out right and left to prevent the brigade from being flanked. Spotting Yankees on his right this time, Strahl determined that with both flanks unsupported his shaken men could not hold, and he ordered the brigade to retire toward Bird's Mill on South Chickamauga Creek.[84]

At the creek, Strahl's men encountered hordes of panic-stricken stragglers and found wagons jamming the bridge. General Stewart ordered Strahl to form his brigade into a line of battle across the Bird's Mill Road "to protect as much as possible the confused and disorganized mass." Stewart then directed Strahl to reconnoiter the opposite bank and find a strong position. Later the brigade crossed the bridge and took up that position. The brigade was now the army's rear guard, ordered to defend the crossing as long as possible to allow the shattered army to escape and then destroy the bridge to prevent its capture. That evening and into the night, the men of the Nineteenth watched the sad, broken remnants of the Army of Tennessee file past. Around 2:00 A.M. on November 26, Strahl decided he could wait no longer and ordered the bridge destroyed. The creek, swollen by recent rains, offered a formidable barrier. Within a short time, the sound of tramping feet announced the arrival of the Federals. Fortunately, they were content to hold their position. Strahl sent a detachment to watch a ford about a mile to the south, but no Yankee threat materialized there. The rest of the night passed quietly.[85]

The brigade continued to hold its position until around 10:00 A.M., when Breckinridge ordered Strahl to move it to Chickamauga Station. There it joined Brigadier General Joseph Lewis's brigade of Kentuckians. Together the two units protected the army's rear as it headed into Georgia. The station was deserted and most of the army stores had been removed or destroyed, but several railroad cars full of corn remained and had to be burned. Such a waste of food, however necessary, must have angered men who had practically starved for months.[86]

As members of the Nineteenth torched the cars, they observed several dead Rebels littering the ground, victims of Federal artillery. Years later, Private Worsham recalled that it was at this moment he realized just how callous he and his comrades had become: "They still remained lying on the ground when we left, and if they were taken care of by our men we never knew, nor did we know who they were or to what regiment they belonged. How indifferent we become towards our dead in times of war; we pass them, cast a glancing look and go on, with but little more feeling than if they were hogs." This was a reaction far different from that in the early days of the war, when the whole regiment had been stunned and saddened by the death of Lieutenant Powell at Barbourville. Like all soldiers through the ages, the veterans of the Nineteenth had been hardened by their experiences. The violent death of a handful of men, strangers at that, could not shock men who over the last two and one-half years had witnessed the killing fields of Shiloh, Murfreesboro, and Chickamauga.[87]

The brigades left the station around 11:00 A.M. and marched along the road to Ringgold, where they were to rendezvous with the rest of the army. The column had not gone a mile when rapidly advancing Federals forced Strahl to deploy his men in line of battle. They repulsed the attack and resumed the march. Strahl finally halted the brigade about a mile outside of Ringgold. It was midnight, and his foot-sore soldiers had been in action for nearly three days with little food or sleep. Strahl allowed them four hours of rest before starting them out again in the predawn darkness.[88]

At Ringgold Gap, General Cleburne's division relieved Strahl's brigade as the army's guard. But before the brigade could rejoin Stewart's division, Bragg directed Strahl to place his men in support of Cleburne lest the Federals break through the gap. Fortunately, Cleburne's masterful stand made it unnecessary to call the brigade to action. Finally, on the night of November 27, Strahl's spent men rejoined Stewart's division. The agonizing retreat, however, would last three more days—finally ending at Dalton.[89]

There a dejected Bragg tendered his resignation, turned command of the broken army over to Hardee, and departed. Few if any were sad to see him go. Almost a year had passed since Bragg and his army had stood on the banks of Stones River facing Rosecrans. The past months had witnessed a brutal struggle for control of Tennessee—a struggle that left the Army of Tennessee crippled and a Union army poised to invade the Confederate heartland. For the men of the Nineteenth, the past year had been especially harsh because of the enemy invasion of East Tennessee. With their homes and families now under occupation and at the mercy of the region's militant unionists, many chose to abandon the cause. Others, however, chose to fight on. These diehards would be fighting not only to save the Confederacy but also for the right to return home. Their fate and that of the Southern republic now largely depended on the ability of one man: Joseph E. Johnston.

Daniel C. Miller.
Born into wealth and privilege, Miller had a tough time acclimating himself to army life. He joined Company K, "The Hawkins Boys," in June 1861. He spent most of his military career serving in the provost and commissary departments. He survived the war and eventually moved his family to Virginia, where he served as school superintendent, lawyer, and county judge. Miller Family Papers (#10287), Special Collections, University of Virginia Library.

Henry Melville Doak.
At the age of 19, Doak enlisted in June of 1861 as a private in Company E, the "Knoxville Guards." Because of Doak's knowledge of military drill obtained while in college, Colonel Cummings assigned "Sergeant-Major" Doak the task of drilling the regiment. Doak served with the regiment until wounded at Shiloh. Obtaining a commission as a lieutenant in the Confederate Marines, he served out the remainder of the war in various ports along the Atlantic coast. After the war, he became a successful editor for several city newspapers. Clement A. Evans, ed., Confederate Military History.

Francis Marion Walker.
Kentucky native Francis Marion Walker was among the most prominent Hamilton County Confederate leaders. A Mexican War veteran, Walker was the Nineteenth's original lieutenant colonel and obtained the rank of brigadier general shortly before being killed in action at the Battle of Bald Hill. Worsham, Old Nineteenth.

William Worsham.
One of the original recruits to enlist in 1861, Worsham served as a regimental musician. He survived the war and wrote a history of the regiment. This photo was taken sometime around the turn of the century. Source: Worsham, Old Nineteenth.

David Sullins.
Reverend Sullins served as the regiment's chaplain before becoming a division chaplain and quartermaster in 1862. He survived the war to write his memoirs. Worsham, Old Nineteenth.

Carrick White Heiskell.
Although the son of a prominent unionist newspaper editor, Frederick S. Heiskell, the younger Heiskell and his brother Joseph chose to support the Confederacy. While Joseph served in the Confederate Congress, Carrick joined Company K of the Nineteenth as its captain. Heiskell continued to rise in rank until he became colonel of the regiment in 1864. He survived the war and moved to Memphis, where he resumed his prewar law practice. He became both a circuit judge and city attorney. Worsham, Old Nineteenth.

Columbus Etter.
Etter joined the "Hawkins Boys" of Company K in 1861 with his brother William. He was killed in action at Shiloh. Worsham, Old Nineteenth.

William E. Etter.
Etter joined the "Hawkins Boys" of Company K in 1861 with his brother Columbus. A few months after Columbus was killed at Shiloh, William was elected second lieutenant of Company K at the regiment's reorganization in Corinth. He rose to first lieutenant and continued to serve with the regiment until the general surrender of the Confederate forces in 1865. He died in Palarm, Arkansas, in 1898 at the age of sixty. Worsham, Old Nineteenth.

John H. Hannah.
Hannah joined Company F from Polk County with his seventy-nine-year-old father and four brothers in 1861. At the regimental reorganization in 1862, Hannah became captain of the company. He was later promoted to major, serving until the regiment surrendered in 1865. After the war, he married and operated a successful wholesale business in Louisville, Kentucky. Worsham, Old Nineteenth.

Abraham Fulkerson.
A graduate of the Virginia Military Institute, Fulkerson was elected major of the regiment in 1861. At the reorganization in Corinth in 1862, Fulkerson left the Nineteenth to become colonel of the Sixty-Third Tennessee. Worsham, Old Nineteenth.

James G. Deaderick.
*Originally the third lieutenant
of Company B from
Washington County,
Deaderick would steadily
rise through the ranks due
to attrition. At the close of
Hood's campaign, he was
made lieutenant colonel of the
regiment. Deaderick returned
to East Tennessee after the
war, where he married and
began a family. In 1882,
he resettled in California.*
Worsham, Old Nineteenth.

Hiram D. Hawk.
*Hawk joined Company G in
June 1861 as a private with
his brothers James and
William. At the regiment's
reorganization in 1862, he
was elected third lieutenant
of Company G. He became
second lieutenant in 1863.
Hawk was wounded three
times—in the left leg at
Shiloh, in the right leg at
Chickamauga, and in the
right shoulder at Franklin—
yet survived the war.*
Worsham, Old Nineteenth.

S. J. A. Frazier.
Elected third lieutenant of Company D in 1861, Frazier eventually became captain. He received a ghastly throat wound at Chickamauga, where he was captured. Studying law while in prison, he survived the war, returned to East Tennessee, and became a successful attorney and real estate developer.
Worsham, Old Nineteenth.

James H. Havely.
Havely joined the "Hawkins Boys" of Company K in 1861. He survived the war.
Worsham, Old Nineteenth.

R. P. James.
James was a tinner by profession, living in Chattanooga when the war began. For some reason, he joined Company K from Hawkins County. He served with the regiment throughout the war, receiving a severe wound at Franklin. Worsham, Old Nineteenth.

6 ✍

"A Wise & Just Providence"

The Campaign for Atlanta

On December 27, 1863, General Joseph E. Johnston arrived at Dalton and assumed command of the Army of Tennessee. He was shocked by what he found. President Davis had led Johnston to believe that despite its defeat at Missionary Ridge the army remained fit and capable of immediate offensive operations. Nothing could have been further from the truth. Johnston took charge of a force of fewer than twenty-seven thousand effectives. Inadequate transportation and a severe supply shortage also plagued the Confederates. The men Johnston encountered—huddled around campfires, lacking food, clothing, and blankets—could hardly have been called an army.[1]

A regimental invoice compiled that winter by the Nineteenth's ordnance sergeant, Edward F. Lyons, suggests the urgency of the situation. Lyons inventoried the unit's equipment, which consisted of sixty-one rifles, thirty bayonets, twenty cartridge boxes, and four thousand rounds of ammunition. Even with a full complement of commissioned officers, the Nineteenth's effective strength was probably little more than one hundred—the regulation strength of a company. Although the unit continued to recruit, the Compiled Service Records reveal that only a handful of new men joined in 1864; and given the Confederacy's manpower shortage, the best the regiment could hope to do was maintain its current strength. In a letter to his father, Captain Richard W. Colville of Company H voiced his concern and resentment at the situation. Several members of the regiment had attached themselves to a cavalry unit and were resisting returning to the Nineteenth: "We have 18 men present in our company now. I do not know why Col. Walker has not sent after Cy Henry and the rest of them. He has been threatening to send after them ever since we have been here [Dalton]. Lt. [Thomas] Carny got a detail to go after them a while back, and I give [sic] him their names and the command they were with, but he did not go."[2]

The fiasco at Chattanooga had not only sapped the army's strength but also damaged morale and undermined discipline. Famished soldiers plundered local farms and supply depots. Many regiments no longer conducted roll calls or drills, and their men wandered freely. Fighting, drinking, and gambling were common in the Nineteenth's camp. Private William Vestal of "Camp Drunk" infamy engaged in repeated brawls. The Army of Tennessee was becoming a mob.[3]

Before facing the Federals, Johnston would have to rebuild his army. Throughout the winter and spring of 1864, he worked tirelessly. More and better rations along with new clothing began to arrive. To improve discipline, he issued General Orders No. 5, which reestablished reveille, drill, and taps. He also received permission from the president to restore the order of battle that had existed prior to Bragg's reshuffling. The reuniting of old commands won Johnston immediate praise from his generals and their men, especially Cheatham and his Tennesseans. In February, the Nineteenth and the rest of Strahl's brigade rejoined Cheatham's former units, thus reestablishing their old division, which was in Hardee's corps. As part of the army's reorganization, newly promoted Lieutenant General John B. Hood joined Hardee as commander of one of Johnston's two infantry corps.[4]

With the shuffling of brigades, Strahl's men left their winter quarters west of Dalton for Cheatham's camps east of the town. The brigade moved in next to the men of Brigadier General John K. Jackson's brigade of Walker's division. As Strahl's men settled into their new cabins, they were appalled by the sight of men imprisoned in stocks in Jackson's camp. On the night of their arrival, about one hundred of Strahl's soldiers, including members of the Nineteenth, resolved to free the prisoners and destroy the pillory. A sentry sounded the alarm, and several of the men were captured and placed under arrest. The next morning, when Jackson's men refused to release the culprits, the Nineteenth prepared to storm their camp and "shoot if necessary." Fortunately, the captives were released. The incident demonstrated the difficulty in restoring discipline to the ranks. Johnston, however, had initiated the use of the pillory and was determined to maintain order. A month later, stocks appeared in the Nineteenth's camp.[5]

In late February, the Rebels got the opportunity to fight someone besides one another. A Federal raid aimed at the important supply center of Meridian, Mississippi, prompted the local department commander, General Polk, to appeal to Johnston and the War Department for reinforcements. President Davis, anxious to protect the town and its arsenal, ordered Johnston to send three of Hardee's divisions (Cheatham's, Cleburne's, and Walker's) to Demopolis, Alabama, where they would join Polk's forces.[6]

On the morning of February 20, Cheatham's six thousand veterans boarded two trains for Atlanta, the first stop on their journey. The next day, about one-third of Strahl's brigade decided to enjoy their visit to the city and "took on a high 'Tight.'" They chased the equally intoxicated Cheatham from street corner to street corner, begging "Mars Frank" to make a speech. The awkward, drunken general was unable to oblige and merely said, "Ah, go away, my boys . . . come along boys, you are all my boys," and wandered away. The strong bond between Cheatham and his men, whether formed in battle or on a drinking binge, moved Private Worsham to write that "[i]f there ever was a General and his men, of whom it could be said, the men belong to the General, and the General belong to the men, it was Gen. Cheatham and his division."[7]

The next morning, the hungover troops traveled to West Point, where the penitent attended church. The division then passed through Montgomery and Selma before arriving in Demopolis. However, the Rebels spent only a few days in the town. The Federal raid was over, and Johnston wanted his men back in Dalton in case the Union forces around Chattanooga moved against him.[8]

The men of the Nineteenth returned to their camp to find their shanties partially demolished. Most believed that Jackson's brigade was responsible, but they did not retaliate. Instead, they repaired their cabins and resumed the monotony of camp life.[9]

Eager for a diversion, Cheatham's Tennesseans hunted, drank, gambled, and frequented prostitutes. The primary pastime for many men, however, was joining in the revivals that were again sweeping the army. The religious fervor of the Army of Tennessee reached its zenith at Dalton. After the disasters of 1863, the Confederacy's only hope of victory appeared to lie with God; even if victory proved beyond reach, salvation was possible. Christianity consoled and shielded the men and allowed them to accept the slaughter of the past three years as part of a divine plan. This conviction helped believers control their fear and face their fate. In this sense, religion enabled the soldiers not only to justify the terrible human cost of the war but also to offer further sacrifices.[10]

Each of Cheatham's brigades built a "brush arbor" or chapel where the men gathered each day for devotionals. At night, the singing and shouting of the faithful and repentant filled the air. In late April, a tragedy occurred that greatly disturbed the men. While preparing the arbor of Maney's brigade, the soldiers swept some trash against a large hickory tree and burned it. Apparently the fire damaged the trunk. One night as the soldiers knelt in prayer, the tree toppled without warning, killing ten men. Private Worsham recalled that "[t]his came like an explosion in the deep world of thought, and the soldiers whose hearts of adamant had not been moved for years, began to show signs of unrest, and began to look forward beyond the sunset of this life and to think of life over there." Worsham may have exaggerated the religious impact of the tragedy, but it is certain that mishaps such as this haunted even the toughest veteran. As the ambulances carried the victims to their graves, the soldiers lined the route, "their stout hearts bowed in deep sorrow."[11]

More pleasant memories were generated by that year's late snowfalls. A particularly heavy one in March provided enough ammunition for a snowball fight between Cheatham's and Walker's men. With martial music blaring and flags waving, thousands of soldiers threw themselves into a sham battle that lasted for hours and left several with black eyes. In the end, Cheatham's men won the battle and celebrated victory by plundering Walker's camps.[12]

This was not the last sham battle the Rebels participated in. As the spring campaign drew near, Johnston conducted maneuvers around Dalton. These exercises, along with target practice, sharpened the combat edge of the army. Likewise, a grand review boosted the soldiers' esprit. Although Johnston continued to resist Richmond's call for an invasion of Tennessee, by May 1864 he had not only rebuilt the army's strength to around forty-four thousand effectives but also had revived its faith in itself. Captain Richard W. Colville of Company H expressed his enthusiasm in another letter to his father.

> We have orders to be ready to march at a moments warning and it is reported that the enemy are advancing in force and probably before this reaches you we may be engaged in deadly strife with the enemy.
>
> I have no fear about the result. I believe we are as certain to whip them as we fight, and if we once get them started back like we did at Chickamauga, Johns[t]on will follow them up and drive them out of Tenn. The whole army is in better health and spirits than I ever saw them.

This faith was about to be tested.[13]

During the first week of May, Johnston's scouts reported that Sherman's army was moving. Unsure of the enemy's objective, a nervous Johnston wired Richmond and Polk for reinforcements. The War Department authorized Polk to send all "available" units, but surprisingly Polk headed to Dalton with almost his entire force.[14]

The Army of Tennessee had spent the winter strengthening the Dalton defenses, part of which ran along a chain of hills west of town known as Rocky Face Ridge. Except for several gaps that would need to be guarded closely,

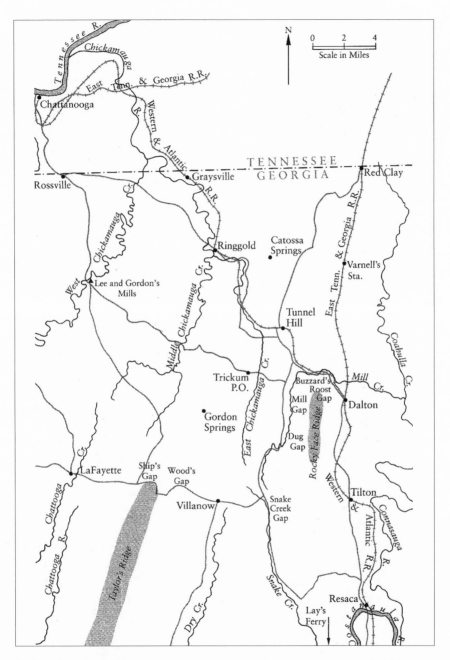

Dalton Area. From Decision in the West: The Atlanta Campaign of 1864, *by Albert Castel, published by the University Press of Kansas © 1992. www.kansaspress.ku.edu. Used by permission of the publisher.*

Johnston's twenty-mile line appeared to be impregnable. Therefore, he did not believe that Sherman would attack. Instead, he correctly surmised that the Federals would attempt to outflank him, probably by moving on Rome, Georgia, some forty miles southwest of Dalton. However, the Dalton line could not be abandoned until Sherman's intentions were clear, and by May 6 all Johnston knew for sure was that the Federals were at Tunnel Hill, only two miles from his entrenchments.[15]

The next day, the Nineteenth and the rest of Cheatham's division left their winter quarters and positioned themselves on Rocky Face Ridge at the extreme left of Hardee's line. The division's left rested on Mill Creek Gap (Buzzard's Roost), and its brigades extended northward along the ridge about one mile before bending eastward to connect with Major General Carter Stevenson's division entrenched in the valley north of Dalton. Cheatham's men quickly fashioned crude breastworks from rocks. Shortly after their arrival, the Rebel picket line was engaged by advancing Federals. The division repulsed two Federal assaults that afternoon. Skirmishing followed, lasting into the evening.[16]

Meanwhile, Johnston received ominous reports of Yankee columns moving southward west of Rocky Face. Still unsure of Sherman's intentions, he waited. On May 8, sketchy reports of Federals south of Dalton filtered into Confederate headquarters. Around 4:00 P.M., a strong Yankee force attacked Dug Gap. Johnston immediately ordered Hardee into action. Strahl's brigade marched at the double-quick to the gap some five miles away. The winded Rebels scampered up the ridge overlooking the gap and formed a line of battle at its crest. They arrived just in time to block the charging Yankees. Throughout the rest of the evening, Strahl's brigade held its position under a heavy artillery bombardment.[17]

The next morning, Cleburne's division relieved Strahl's men, who returned to their old position. There they repulsed at least five attacks aimed at the angle where Cheatham's and Stevenson's divisions joined. These and other attacks along the Rocky Face line blinded the Confederate high command to the real threat southward. While sporadic fighting continued at Rocky Face, a strong Federal force slipped through Snake Creek Gap, threatening to capture Resaca and thus sever the Rebel supply line to Atlanta via the Western and Atlantic Railroad. Only Union timidity and Rebel luck allowed Confederate forces to reach Resaca in time to block the Federal drive.[18]

Amazingly, Johnston still did not perceive Sherman's objective and continued to hold the bulk of his army at Dalton. Over the next three days, he shifted Cheatham's division and his other forces to meet threats both real and imagined. Finally, on May 13, he ordered Hardee and Hood to move their entire

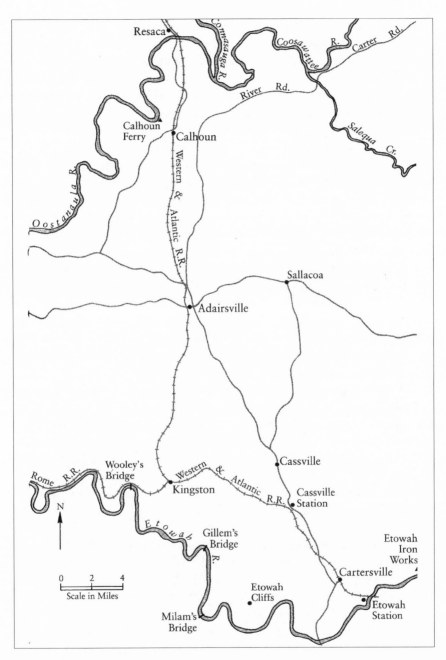

The Region from the Oostanaula River to the Etowah River. From Decision in the West: The Atlanta Campaign of 1864, *by Albert Castel, published by the University Press of Kansas © 1992. www.kansaspress.ku.edu. Used by permission of the publisher.*

corps to Resaca, where they linked up with advance elements of Polk's army. Johnston was overjoyed to see Polk and his men, and he immediately incorporated them into the Army of Tennessee, designating them as a third corps.[19]

Johnston's delayed reaction to Sherman's move on Resaca gave him little time to establish a new defensive line. In fact, his army could not cross the Oostanaula River before the Federals consolidated. Therefore, they had to make a stand at Resaca. Johnston formed a strong line on a range of hills along Camp Creek covering Resaca and his all-important railroad line. Polk's corps anchored the Confederate left on the Oostanaula River, Hardee's protected the center, and Hood's deployed on the right to the Conasauga River. Near the center of the Rebel position, the Nineteenth, along with the rest of Cheatham's veterans, erected breastworks while under constant fire from Federal skirmishers and artillery. The fighting intensified, and the Confederates beat off several strong probing actions.[20]

Fighting began at dawn on the fourteenth and went on throughout the day as the Federals continued to probe the Confederate line for weaknesses. On the following afternoon, Union troops bridged the Oostanaula, threatening the army's supply line. Although the Rebels held them until nightfall, Johnston realized that his position was untenable and abandoned Resaca. Around midnight, the Nineteenth and the rest of the army crossed the river and headed for Calhoun.[21]

Along the way, additional units from Polk's command bolstered the army, but Johnston did not believe his men could contest the Federal crossing of the Oostanaula, nor did he believe the terrain favored a stand at Calhoun or Adairsville. However, as Johnston examined the topography of the region, he developed a bold plan. Below Adairsville, two diverging roads led to Cassville. To expedite his army's movement, he would split it between the two routes and then reassemble it at Cassville. If Sherman did likewise—and Johnston believed he would—the reunited Rebel force could strike and annihilate one Federal column before help could arrive from the other.[22]

To give the Confederate army time to reassemble at Cassville, Cheatham's division, including the Nineteenth, would hold the advancing Federals near Adairsville. As the rest of the army headed southward on May 17, Cheatham's men deployed on both sides of the Calhoun Road and waited. In the late afternoon, a light drizzle and forward elements of Sherman's army interrupted the Rebels' supper. Skirmishing gradually intensified as more Federals arrived. The Rebels held their position until midnight and then quietly withdrew.[23]

The division rejoined Hardee's corps and prepared to assault Sherman's divided army. However, on May 19, exaggerated reports of Yankee cavalry to the Confederate rear led Johnston to call off the ambush and entrench his

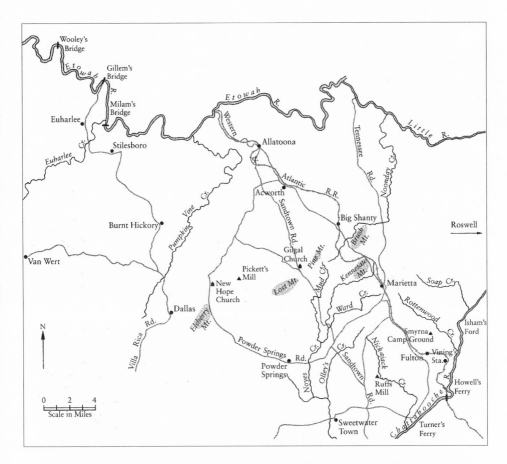

The Region from the Etowah River to the Chattahoochee River. From Decision in the West: The Atlanta Campaign of 1864, *by Albert Castel, published by the University Press of Kansas © 1992. www.kansaspress.ku.edu. Used by permission of the publisher.*

army on high ground near Cassville. On the night of May 20, fearing that their lines could not hold a determined assault, the Rebels retreated across the Etowah River to Allatoona Pass. Although the Allatoona defenses were formidable, the Federals could flank them easily by crossing at any of several fords to the west. Luckily, on May 23, Confederate cavalry discovered a Union force crossing the Etowah near Stilesboro, well to the rear of the left flank. Johnston immediately ordered his army to intercept the Yankees.[24]

On May 23, the Nineteenth and the rest of Cheatham's division headed for Dallas. The next day, the men marched and countermarched as the

Confederate high command sought to make contact with the Federals. That evening, the tired soldiers halted and deployed near New Hope Church, a strategic crossroads about two miles from Dallas. By morning, Johnston had spread his army over a wide front, blocking Sherman's advance. Cheatham's division separated from the rest of Hardee's corps, which was on the left, and positioned itself on the right center between Polk's and Hood's. The fighting late that afternoon was intense and lasted until a thunderstorm broke. Although the main Federal effort was directed at Hood's corps, Cheatham's skirmish line was heavily engaged. That night, soldiers on both sides dug into the red mud and fortified their lines.[25]

The crackle of rifle fire began again at dawn and continued unabated throughout the day. However, neither side launched a major assault. That night Cheatham was ordered to drive the Federals from Elsberry Ridge, a rise to the left of his line. The men awoke at 3:00 A.M., marched to the left, and formed a battle line for the dawn attack. Strahl's brigade, with the Nineteenth in front, was joined by Brigadier General Alfred J. Vaughan Jr.'s brigade. The brigades of Maney and Wright were in reserve. A fierce see-saw fight ensued, and the Rebels seized the ridge and linked up with General William B. Bate's division on their left. However, a gap of almost a mile existed on Cheatham's right, inviting Federal attempts to envelope his exposed flank. Cheatham extended his division to the breaking point before Brigadier General James Cantey's division of Polk's corps finally sealed the gap around mid-afternoon. Although the Confederate hold on the ridge was now secure, constant skirmishing continued throughout the day along this part of the front.[26]

On May 28, Johnston's scouts detected a Federal movement toward the Western and Atlantic railroad. As Sherman shifted his army eastward, Johnston matched his movements, always probing for weaknesses. By June 2, all of Hardee's corps had moved to the right, leaving Cheatham's Tennesseans to hold the Confederate left. The division skirmished daily, but no other major engagement occurred in the area. Sherman reached the railroad on the sixth, and Johnston fell back, searching for more defensible terrain. As Federal dispositions became clearer, the Confederates consolidated to their front. By June 8, Hardee's corps was at Gilgal Church south of Pine Mountain, Polk just behind Pine Mountain, and Hood east of the railroad.[27]

At this point, the pace of the campaign slowed. The terrain the two armies occupied was rugged and densely forested, with hills and ravines. Only a handful of roads traversed the area. Moreover, the late spring of 1864 had been unusually wet. The daily rains from late May until the third week of June turned the roads into quagmires and slowed the Federal columns to a crawl.[28]

Sherman's men slogged forward across a broad front. On June 10, they ran into Hardee's men near Pine Mountain and skirmished for several days. When

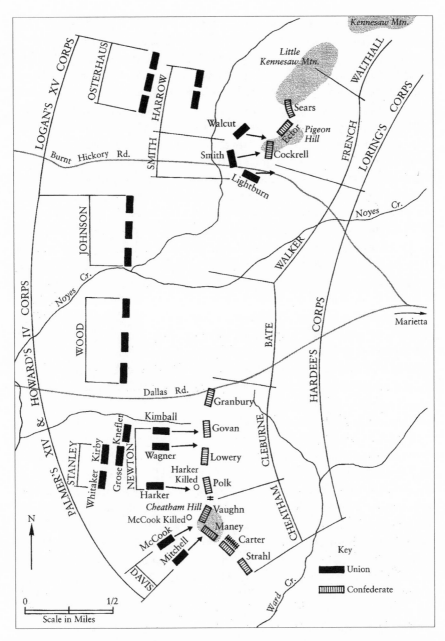

The Battle of Kennesaw Mountain. From Decision in the West: The Atlanta Campaign of 1864, by Albert Castel, published by the University Press of Kansas © 1992. www.kansaspress.ku.edu. Used by permission of the publisher.

threatened with a turning movement, Hardee requested that Johnston visit
Pine Mountain and determine if it could be defended. On the overcast morning of June 14, Polk joined Johnston and Hardee, and the generals rode to the
front to reconnoiter the enemy positions. They stopped to confer near the
entrenchments of the Nineteenth. There, a throng of soldiers gathered around
the commanders. Federal artillery bombarded the inviting target. As everyone
scampered for cover, a shell fragment hit General Polk, killing him instantly.
The news of the general's death spread quickly and seriously demoralized the
army. Though Polk was not a great tactician, he had always been popular with
the men. Private Worsham believed that the army had "sustained a loss not to
be easily filled. Gen. Polk was a brave officer, a good man and a Christian soldier." Johnston placed Polk's senior division commander, Major General
William W. Loring, in temporary command of the corps and, now convinced
that Pine Mountain could not be held, abandoned it.[29]

The next day, Colonel Walker took temporary command of Maney's
brigade. As part of the new arrangement, the Nineteenth left Strahl's brigade
and joined him, and the Forty-First Tennessee was transferred from Walker's
new command to Strahl's. The Nineteenth was now brigaded with the consolidated First and Twenty-Seventh Tennessee, the consolidated Sixth and Ninth
Tennessee, and the Fourth, Twenty-Fourth, and Fiftieth Tennessee. With
Carrick W. Heiskell, the regiment's new lieutenant colonel, in East Tennessee
recovering from his Chickamauga wound, Major James G. Deaderick took command of the Nineteenth.[30]

Under increasing Federal pressure, the Rebels were forced back to the
region's dominant geographical feature—Kennesaw Mountain. On the rainy
night of June 18, the men in the Nineteenth and the rest of the army trudged
up the muddy slopes of Kennesaw. There, the hungry and exhausted men dug
trenches and built breastworks. By dawn, Johnston's army had turned the two-
mile long ridge into a fortress. The Confederate defenses stretched in a six-
mile arc, guarding the approaches to Marietta as well as the railroad. Hardee's
men entrenched in front of Noyes's Creek and John Ward Creek.[31]

Virtually everyone expected Sherman to continue his flanking moves, but
he had other plans. On June 27, the Federals launched a two-pronged attack
at the Confederate center. The first assault was aimed at Pigeon Hill, where
Loring's and Hardee's corps converged. The well-entrenched Confederates
easily repulsed the charge and inflicted heavy casualties, but the main Union
effort was still to come. Fortunately for the Rebels, the strike hit the section of
the line held by Cheatham's and Cleburne's divisions, arguably the toughest in
the army. Moreover, both divisions had built strong fieldworks and had been
alerted to Federal intentions by a preassault bombardment.[32]

The weakest point in the Confederate defenses was a salient on a hill (known today as Cheatham's Hill) occupied by Walker's (Maney's) brigade. Unlike the rest of the Confederate line, the salient lacked adequate abatis, and, more importantly, the entrenchments had been placed along the topographical rather than the military crest of the hill. As had been the case on parts of Missionary Ridge, the defenders now had a blind spot close to their line where the Yankees could gather before the last rush to the trenches.[33]

While the Confederates easily repulsed the attack along most of the line, the fighting at Cheatham's Hill, especially where Walker's brigade occupied an angle (now known as Dead Angle), became desperate. The full weight of two Federal brigades fell against the consolidated First and Twenty-Seventh Tennessee and the Nineteenth. The Nineteenth waited until the last possible moment and then unleashed a fusillade that staggered the Yankees. However, the Federals recovered, and for the next two hours the thin Rebel line along the hill endured repeated assaults.[34]

Private Sam Watkins of the First Tennessee recalled the savagery of the fighting: "a solid line of blazing fire right from the muzzles of the Yankee guns . . . poured right into our very faces, singeing our hair and clothes, the hot blood of our dead and wounded spurting on us, the blinding smoke and stifling atmosphere filling our eyes and mouths, and the awful concussion [from the firing of nearby Rebel batteries] causing the blood to gush out of our noses and ears, and above all, the roar of battle, made it a perfect pandemonium." Private Worsham, likewise blinded by smoke and deafened by noise, remembered that "all along the line the fighting was desperate and beyond description."[35]

Under a blazing sun, with temperatures over one hundred degrees, the men fired their rifles so rapidly they became almost too hot to hold. Behind the trenches, Rebel batteries fired double shots of canister into the advancing enemy. The Federals reached the fortifications, where vicious hand-to-hand combat ensued. The Rebels used rifle butts, bayonets, and even rocks against the Yankees. On at least two occasions the Federals planted their colors above the trenches, only to be driven back at great cost. Walker feared the line would collapse and sent the Sixth and Ninth Tennessee to reinforce the First/ Twenty-Seventh. Unable to penetrate the Rebel works, the Federal attack waned, and the Yankees fell back to the edge of the ridge to regroup.[36]

For the men on Cheatham's Hill, the past hours had seemed like an eternity. As Private Watkins recalled:

> When the Yankees fell back, and the firing ceased, I never saw so many broken down and exhausted men in my life. I was sick as a horse, and as wet with blood and sweat as I could be, and many of

our men were vomiting with excessive fatigue, over-exhaustion, and sun stroke; our tongues were parched and cracked for water, and our faces blackened with powder and smoke, and our dead and wounded were piled indiscriminately in the trenches. There was not a single man in the company who was not wounded, or had holes shot through his hat and clothing.

Beyond the Confederate works lay a writhing mass of wounded Federals and their dead comrades. The carnage was beyond Private Worsham's descriptive powers. "[L]anguage," he wrote, "would fail to picture this field of butchery with its dead and wounded." The suffering continued, however. Repeated efforts by the Rebels to aid the wounded drew Federal fire, enraging the Confederates and leading to protracted firefights.[37]

Despite the repulse of the Federals, Cheatham's position along the hill was still precarious. The Yankees entrenched along the hill's military crest, a stone's throw from the Rebel line, and the next two days and nights saw incessant skirmishing. The Federals even burrowed toward the Nineteenth's works, hoping to plant explosives underneath and blast a hole in the Rebel line. The proximity of the enemy strained the nerves of the men on both sides, and the slightest movement or sound, especially at night, provoked a firefight. At least two veterans recalled that a luminescent display by fireflies on the night following the Federal assault caused a jittery sentry to fire his weapon—resulting in an intense exchange of musketry between the two sides.[38]

On June 30, the Federals asked for a truce near Dead Angle to collect their dead. The corpses had decayed badly after three days of exposure in the summer heat, creating nauseating sights and smells. The men of both sides emerged cautiously from their trenches. Some soldiers fraternized with the enemy, trading coffee and tobacco or just chatting. When Cheatham appeared, Federal troops even pressed him for an autograph.[39]

When the truce ended, the men returned to their works and the skirmishing resumed. The Confederates were especially cautious of the Federal sharpshooters. So intense and accurate was their fire that, in Private Worsham's words, "a hat raised on the end of a stick . . . would be filled with bullet holes in less than a minute." Confederate marksmen, likewise, were vigilant for careless Yankees.[40]

As he avoided sniper fire in the trenches, Worsham no doubt reflected on the change in the style of warfare since the opening of the campaign at Dalton. It is unlikely that the young private fully comprehended the impact of mass citizen armies, steam power, and rifled muskets on the development of warfare, but he surely now understood the futility of open frontal assaults on an entrenched enemy. While the Army of Tennessee had seen fieldworks before, it was in the Georgia campaign that their construction became a fine art. In fact, by 1864 troops on both sides and in both major theaters saw fortifications as a necessity and dug in as a matter of course. Worsham noted that "[t]he country all around was cut up with entrenchments and honeycombed with rifle pits, and the woods looked as dreary and as desolate as if it had been swept by a tornado."[41]

By 1864, using axes, spades, picks, bayonets, and bare hands, the men of the Nineteenth and their fellow soldiers could create elaborate fieldworks in an hour or so. A standard entrenchment consisted of a broad trench several feet deep surmounted by a three- to four-foot-high breastwork covered in front by dirt. Above this, a head log resting on supports created a narrow slit through which the troops took aim at an advancing enemy. In front of this, abatis consisting of felled trees, branches, *chevaux de frise,* or other obstructions slowed the enemy advance. Frontal assaults against such positions were a risky proposition—a fact underscored by the piles of Federal dead at Cheatham's Hill.[42]

Another aspect of the changing nature of warfare apparent to Worsham and his comrades was constant contact with the enemy. Instead of the customary pitched battle followed by weeks or months of inactivity, the army now experienced combat every day. Indeed, Worsham recalled the month from the New Hope–Dallas line to Kennesaw Mountain as "one continuous battle."[43]

With enemy entrenchments always nearby, the men had little time to relax. Constant sniper fire and artillery barrages exhausted them mentally and physically. Moreover, this small-scale warfare was, in the long run, just as bloody as a pitched battle, and the soldiers had to endure the sight of continual battlefield casualties. For example, at Kennesaw the regiment witnessed the gruesome death of John White of Company E, who was nearly torn in half by an exploding shell. His comrades removed a jagged two-pound piece of shrapnel from his bowels while a look of "anguish and despair . . . rested on his sad face." The next day John Spears of Company K collected canteens and went for water. A Federal shell blew off the top of his head. His sickened comrades buried him at the home of his aunt in Marietta. The grief-stricken woman invited the men to dinner, and they eagerly accepted. "Nearly two long years had gone by since we had eaten in a house or at a table," Worsham recalled. "We were sorry for her, poor, sad, but kind-hearted woman . . . but we were too busily engaged just then to think of the dead." The callousness Worsham had noted after Missionary Ridge was clearly increasing as he and his comrades endured the mental fatigue of modern warfare. How could he feel sad for one death, Worsham reasoned, when "there were thousands of dead left on the blood-stained fields of this Kennesaw region." One historian of the

Atlanta campaign described the soldiers as "a horde that ha[d] been hardened by war to the point where they regard[ed] suffering, their own and others', with varying mixtures of scorn, despair, and utter indifference. In other words, they [did] not give a damn."[44]

A good portion of the blood shed in that campaign belonged to the men of the Nineteenth. The fighting from Dalton to Kennesaw had cost the regiment twenty men killed and sixteen wounded. Of course, the Nineteenth was no stranger to high casualties. Shiloh, Murfreesboro, and Chickamauga each had inflicted losses of 25 percent or more. Indeed, by this point of the war, the surviving members of the regiment could look back with mingled horror and pride at their combat record, which included most of the major battles of the western theater. They had seen their ranks decimated again and again—and the bloodbath of Hood's Middle Tennessee debacle was still to come.[45]

Yet just how extensive were the casualties in the Nineteenth, and how unique was the regiment in this regard? In his 1902 reminiscences, Worsham recalled that 1,297 men served in the Nineteenth. Of those, 200 (15.4 percent) were killed, 292 (22.7 percent) died in hospitals, and 552 others (42.6 percent) were wounded. Altogether, therefore, 1,046 (80.7 percent) of the men suffered death or injury. Worsham's data (which are presumably based on now-lost regimental records) reflect a familiar story of attrition in Civil War units. Commands organized in 1861 were depleted as the war progressed, and by 1864, unless new recruits joined, they were either disbanded or consolidated with other weakened units.[46]

An examination of the Compiled Service Records reveals more of the regiment's medical history. However, significant differences exist between the C.S.R. and Worsham's data. According to the C.S.R., 1,436 men served in the Nineteenth. Of those, 103 (7.2 percent) were killed or mortally wounded, 141 (9.8 percent) died otherwise, and 172 others (12 percent) were wounded. The records also show that 90 (6.3 percent) retired or were discharged because of their medical condition, 180 (12.5 percent) were listed as sick at one time or another, and 157 (11 percent) were at some point sent to the hospital without any recorded explanation.[47]

The incomplete nature of the records of the regiment makes it impossible to know which version is more accurate. However, in both cases the critical depletion of combat strength is evident. The C.S.R. do offer considerable data on illness. This information is vital to understanding the Nineteenth's experience, for disease was an even more dangerous threat to the men than combat.[48]

The Confederate recruits of 1861 almost always experienced outbreaks of childhood diseases shortly after their unit's organization. Chicken pox, mumps, whooping cough, and measles plagued the soldiers. Most recovered from this initial bout of sickness but then had to face the wave of "camp diseases" that usually followed. Among the most serious of these was typhoid, which accounted for about one-fourth of all disease-related deaths among Rebel soldiers. By far the most deadly camp diseases, however, were diarrhea and dysentery (alvine flux). Brought about by malnutrition, fatigue, exposure, and fecal contamination, these intestinal disorders ravaged Confederate ranks, killing more men than the enemy killed and severely debilitating many thousands of others. So perplexed were medical personnel by these two afflictions that some even advocated cauterization of the anal opening as a treatment. Moreover, because Confederate troops continually suffered from poor rations, filthy camp conditions, exposure, and infestations of vermin, they experienced a variety of other camp diseases ranging from the uncomfortable to the deadly. Camp itch, scurvy, bronchitis, tuberculosis, rheumatism, pneumonia, and malaria decimated Rebel units. Additionally, "self-inflicted" diseases such as syphilis and gonorrhea plagued the Southern army throughout the conflict.[49]

Although complete medical profiles for every member of the regiment do not exist, medical ledgers from Atlanta's Fairground Hospitals One and Two covering the period from February 1863 to November 1864 offer a glimpse of the unit's medical woes. During the nearly two-year span, those two hospitals treated ninety-one patients from the Nineteenth. Six of those were listed without a complaint. Among the rest were eighteen cases of recurring fever; seventeen of diarrhea; thirteen of debility associated with diarrhea and dysentery; four of icterus; three of rheumatism; two each of gonorrhea, syphilis, and pneumonia; and one each of dysentery, typhoid, pleuritis, nephritis, neuralgia, bronchitis, and arrhythmia.[50]

Some of the Nineteenth's patients had a persistent condition that necessitated frequent hospital visits. Private Benjamin F. Woods of Company F, for example, repeatedly sought treatment for syphilis in the period covered by the ledgers. Others, such as Private Thomas R. Carlton of Company K, were hospitalized for successive ailments. In February 1863, Carlton was treated for malarial fever contracted at Vicksburg. During April and May of that same year, he was back in the hospital, suffering from general debility. Having apparently recovered his vigor, Carlton returned to the hospital in June with gonorrhea. In September, he was back with a gunshot wound.[51]

The Atlanta hospital ledgers disclose fourteen other instances of gunshot wounds and one amputation. Given the Nineteenth's combat record, battlefield casualties were a significant part of its medical history. Wounded men made up the vast majority of such casualties, and gunshot wounds were by far the most common sort of wound. The large-caliber, low-velocity bullets used during the war created frightful tissue damage and often splintered bone.

Abdominal, chest, or head wounds were generally fatal and often not even treated by medical personnel. Nineteen-year-old Private Samuel D. Moore of Company B was a rare exception. As recounted in his pension application, he survived a ghastly facial wound at Kennesaw Mountain caused by a ball that entered near the left side of his nose and exited under his right eye, leaving him horribly scarred, totally blind in his right eye, and partially blind in his left eye.[52]

Pension and service records reveal that other members of the regiment suffered equally terrible wounds. For example, Private Joseph Britton of Company K was shot in the right shoulder at Murfreesboro. The ball eventually migrated to his spinal column and paralyzed his right arm for life. At Franklin, Private George W. Roller of Company G received a shot to the right side of his head that cut off part of his ear and blinded his right eye. Atop Missionary Ridge, Private Thomas Ensminger of Company H received a grisly wound when a minié ball tore away half of his lower jawbone, passed down through his neck, and exited between his shoulders. Amazingly, Ensminger survived.[53]

Many of the men endured multiple wounds. Private John Basket of Company H was shot in his left wrist and arm at Murfreesboro and lost part of his foot at Resaca. Private Allen Christian of Company K was wounded in the knee at Murfreesboro and in the chest at Chickamauga. Private Silas Riggins of Company H was loading his rifle at Shiloh when a ball ricocheted off his weapon and passed through his left arm and chest. At Franklin, Silas was hit again, this time in the right eye, blinding it. Hiram D. Hawk, who eventually rose to the rank of second lieutenant in Company G, survived three wounds— one in the left leg at Shiloh, one in the right leg at Chickamauga, and one in the right shoulder at Franklin.[54]

These men were lucky in that they survived not only their wounds but also their treatment. Given the primitive state of nineteenth-century medicine, serious limb wounds necessitated amputation. If one lived through the shock of such an experience, the unsterile conditions at aid stations and hospitals invited lethal postoperative infections. Staphylococcus, tetanus, septicemia, toxemia, pyemia, osteomyelitis, and gangrene were widespread.[55]

The Confederacy endeavored to maintain clean, efficient, and well-supplied hospitals, but wartime shortages and huge casualties often overwhelmed the fragile system. After the spring of 1863, the Army of Tennessee's sick and wounded had the good fortune of being under the supervision of Samuel H. Stout, the army's superintendent of hospitals. Stout's hospitals were among the best in the Confederacy and continued to receive patients from the Nineteenth until the end of the war.[56]

In the early years of the war, before an effective hospital system was established, physicians often furloughed seriously wounded or ill patients. However, as absenteeism and desertion grew, the practice became less frequent. The C.S.R. for the Nineteenth list sixty-one cases of desertion from a hospital or failure to return from a medical furlough.[57]

In the war's initial stages, men whose wounds or illnesses prevented their return to active duty often were discharged. However, as a manpower shortage gripped the Confederacy, medical discharges became harder to obtain. For example, in the summer of 1863, Second Lieutenant A. B. Hodge of Company D received the approval of the regimental surgeon and Colonel Walker to resign his commission because of recurring bouts of "fever." However, the chief surgeon of Cheatham's division denied the request, and Lieutenant Hodge was retained. Alternatives to discharge, such as provost marshal duty or assignment to the Invalid Corps, became more common. Daniel Miller's bout with typhoid in 1861 ostensibly was the reason for his posting to provost duty in East Tennessee. While one could speculate that family connections played a role in Miller's reassignment, few would question Captain Robert L. Blair's transfer to the Invalid Corps. A medical examining board declared Blair unfit resulting from a serious gunshot wound received at Dalton. Crippled by a ball that remained in his chest, Blair was assigned provost duty in East Tennessee.[58]

While disease and combat accounted for most of the regiment's fatalities and injuries, soldiering during the Civil War held other dangers. For example, First Lieutenant Robert J. Tipton of Company B was killed by unionist guerrillas while he was on recruiting duty in his native Carter County in the summer of 1863. Lewis Rowe, Company A's color sergeant, was killed in a railroad accident near Murfreesboro in January 1863. Rowe's comrade in Company A, Private James Powers, was murdered by Private Thomas Stevens, also of Company A. Private J. T. Barnes was injured at Loudon, Tennessee, when a storm blew down his tent, crushing his left side and permanently disabling his left arm. Privates N. P. Frazier of Company D and Michael Wagner of Company B received injuries while constructing breastworks during the Atlanta campaign. Frazier hurt his back, incapacitating him for months, and Wagner suffered a double hernia. Privates Henry A. Parrott of Company G and William R. Stewart of Company F were ruptured during the war, and Private Richard Lions of Company G badly injured his right testicle while scaling a fence during the rout at Fishing Creek. Privates William H. Patterson of Company H and H. B. Mullins of Company C succumbed to sunstroke.[59]

Whether by microbe, bullet, or accident, death and disability withered the Nineteenth's ranks, leaving only the healthiest or luckiest to finish the war.

Were the dangers evenly spread throughout the regiment? Did a particular group suffer a higher incidence of death, injury, or illness? Casualties appear to be spread fairly evenly among the ten companies. However, the officer corps of the regiment differed markedly from the privates in several regards. The C.S.R. reveal, for one thing, that commissioned and noncommissioned officers were less likely than privates to die from disease. Of the 258 officers who served at one time or another in the regiment only 13 (5 percent) died of disease, compared to 128 (10.9 percent) of the 1,178 privates. While the officers' educational and intellectual advantages may account for the difference, their access to better shelter, clothing, food, and medical care is a more likely explanation.[60]

Privates also were more likely to receive wounds than officers. Among the privates, 150 of 1,178 (12.7 percent) were wounded compared to 22 of the 258 officers (8.5 percent). Interestingly, however, the officer corps had a fatality rate much higher than that of privates: 32 of the 358 officers (12.4 percent) were killed compared to 71 of the 1,178 privates (6 percent). The ideals of honor and gallantry current in the nineteenth-century South influenced enlisted men as well as officers to expose themselves to danger without flinching. But officers were expected to lead by example and thus felt even greater pressure to demonstrate their courage and masculinity. This fact, coupled with the necessity for Civil War regimental officers to exercise command at the point of contact with the enemy, probably accounts for the comparatively higher number of officer deaths in the regiment. Often mounted and conspicuously uniformed, officers made inviting targets for enemy sharpshooters.[61]

Finally, the C.S.R. reveal that officers had a much greater chance than privates of obtaining a discharge or being retired. Only 60 (5.1 percent) of the 1,178 privates received medical discharges from active duty compared to 30 (11.6 percent) of the 258 officers. A likely explanation for this is the greater wealth, power, and influence of the officer corps.[62]

These dry medical statistics cannot fully describe the frightful carnage experienced by the men of the Nineteenth over the course of the war. But the death, suffering, and sacrifice they allude to were the lot of many a Confederate regiment. Awareness of such horrors, however imperfectly they are reflected in the historical record, helps historians understand the plague of desertion that crippled the Nineteenth and other Civil War commands. It also helps historians appreciate the deep commitment to Southern independence and defense of home that motivated those who endured until the end. What that end would be was still in doubt as Worsham and his comrades peered from their breastworks atop Cheatham's Hill.

Throughout the rest of the rainy month of June, the two armies continued skirmishing. On July 1, the rains finally stopped, and the weather turned

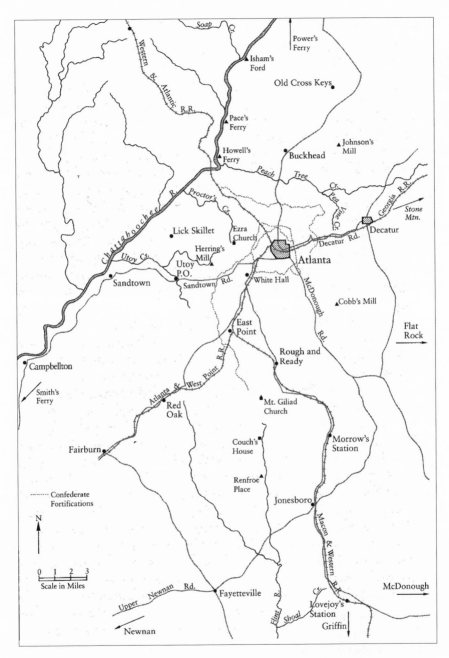

The Atlanta Area. From Decision in the West: The Atlanta Campaign of 1864, by Albert Castel, *published by the University Press of Kansas* © 1992. *www.kansaspress.ku.edu. Used by permission of the publisher.*

hot. As the roads dried, Confederate cavalry discovered Federal columns heading southeast from Kennesaw. On the night of July 2, Johnston blocked the Federal advance by moving his army to the old Methodist campgrounds near Smyrna. Sherman, however, quickly turned the Confederate left flank, forcing the Rebels to retreat again.[63]

On July 5, Johnston's men occupied extensive fortifications on the northern bank of the Chattahoochee. However, between July 5 and July 9 the Confederates lost touch with the Federal army. When Rebel cavalry reestablished contact, Johnston discovered the Yankees had crossed the Chattahoochee at two points upriver, rendering his defensive line on the north bank untenable. Johnston responded by abandoning the river line and retreating toward Atlanta, less than ten miles away.[64]

With the Federals poised to capture one of the South's last major transportation and industrial centers, Jefferson Davis felt he had to act. On July 9, he dispatched his military advisor, Braxton Bragg, to Atlanta, ostensibly to discuss strategy with Johnston. In reality, Bragg's mission was to ascertain if Johnston planned to fight for the city. By July 17, Davis was convinced that Johnston would not do so. He therefore relieved Johnston of command and replaced him with Hood.[65]

Historians debate the impact of Johnston's removal on the morale of the Army of Tennessee. Many of the army's generals regretted the change in command and questioned Hood's ability. Hardee felt humiliated since he was senior in rank to Hood. Dissension again invaded the army's high command. The rank and file were even more dissatisfied. Some soldiers even advocated mutiny or desertion. In the Nineteenth, "the news of the change came to the men like a clap of thunder from a clear sky," and many openly wept. In his postwar memoirs, Private Worsham declared that "[t]o us, Johns[t]on was removed without sufficient cause." The members of the regiment had approved Johnston's Fabian strategy, believing that his "idea of warfare did not consist in butchery or useless sacrifice. With his small army he acted on the defensive and only fought when he was certain of doing the most good with the least loss of life. No one else could have done more with the means at his command than he." Worsham perceived, in retrospect, that the appointment of the young and reckless Hood was the "death knell of the Army of Tennessee."[66]

Two days after assuming command, Hood assembled his corps commanders to hear his plan for a bold strike at Sherman. Having learned of a wide gap between two wings of the Federal army, Hood wanted the corps of Hardee and recently appointed Lieutenant General Alexander P. Stewart to drive one wing into Peachtree Creek while Cheatham and the rest of his forces prevented the other wing from sending aid.[67]

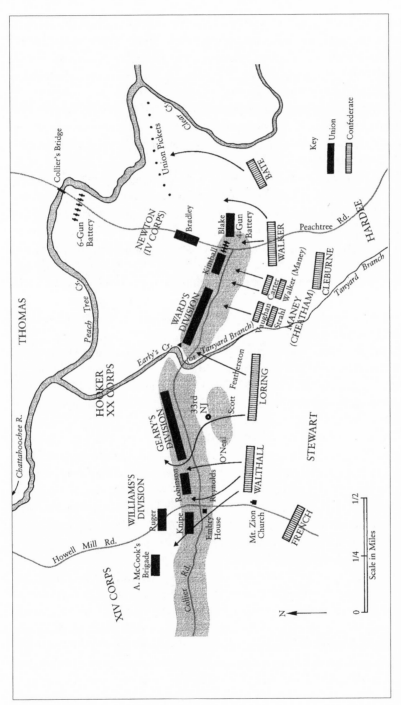

The Battle of Peachtree Creek. From Decision in the West: The Atlanta Campaign of 1864, by Albert Castel, published by the University Press of Kansas © 1992. www.kansaspress.ku.edu. Used by permission of the publisher.

Hood's plan was in the tradition of the audacious maneuvers he had witnessed in the Army of Northern Virginia. Unfortunately, neither he nor his subordinates possessed the same organizational ability, discipline, and battlefield skill found in Robert E. Lee and his officers. Ultimately Hood's attempts to emulate Lee's success would prove catastrophic for the Army of Tennessee.[68]

Hardee deployed his divisions for attack about 3:00 P.M. on July 20. The Nineteenth and the rest of Cheatham's division, now under Maney, held the corps' left. Colonel Walker again assumed command of Maney's brigade, leaving Major Deaderick to lead the regiment.[69]

Because Hardee did not properly reconnoiter the ground between his line of battle and the Federal positions, the attacking Rebels had little idea of what awaited them. Maney sent his men forward at 4:00 P.M. with the brigades of Vaughan and Colonel John Carter in front and Strahl's and Walker's men following. The dense underbrush along Peachtree Creek slowed the progress of Maney's Tennesseans. Encountering intense small arms and artillery fire, the front brigades advanced to within one hundred yards of the enemy entrenchments but could go no further. When Strahl's and Walker's brigades came up, they could do little more than take cover behind the crest of a hill and exchange fire with the Yankees.[70]

Elsewhere, the Rebel assault was equally ineffective, and Hardee ultimately called off the attack. The men of the Nineteenth skirmished with the Federals into the night. Around 10:00 P.M., they and the rest of Maney's division gathered their dead and wounded and withdrew to their line of departure. The Battle of Peachtree Creek was over.[71]

Maney's tired men would have little time for rest. The next morning, pressure from the other Federal wing advancing via Decatur prompted Hood to order Maney's men to reinforce the beleaguered Rebels near Bald Hill (now known as Leggett's Hill). Marching under a scorching sun, many soldiers collapsed from sunstroke and exhaustion. Once at Bald Hill, the Nineteenth and the rest of the division dug entrenchments and skirmished with the enemy. Around midnight of July 22, they were ordered to disengage and return to Atlanta, where Hardee was reassembling his corps.[72]

That day Colonel Walker received word of his promotion to brigadier general, effective the next day. Since February of the previous year, several men had advocated Walker's promotion, including East Tennessee Congressmen Joseph B. Heiskell and William G. Swan, as well as Generals Strahl, Stewart, Cheatham, and Hardee. Walker had served as a temporary brigade commander on several occasions since 1863 and impressed his superiors each time. Heiskell told the secretary of war that "[i]f merit is to be the test of promotion no man deserves it more," and Strahl noted that although the citizens of Walker's congressional district petitioned him to resign his commission in 1863 to run for the House of Representatives he declined, preferring to remain with his command. Strahl, moved by such self-sacrifice, remarked that "Col. Walker is an able, efficient, and experienced officer—a high toned and honorable gentleman, and a desent [sic] and humble Christian—There are few officers whose claims for promotion are so numerous, and none who are more worthy and deserving." Walker, now a general, continued to command Maney's brigade until he could be reassigned as the new commander of Vaughan's brigade. That reassignment would never take place.[73]

Hood now planned to strike the Federal force near Decatur. He ordered Hardee's corps to hit the Yankee's left flank near Cobb's Mill. Having arrived in Atlanta, the men of the Nineteenth had to pass through looting mobs panicked by the sight of the army in apparent retreat. It was 3:00 A.M. before Maney's Tennesseans set out for Cobb's Mill, marching along dusty roads in the humid night air.[74]

The attack had been planned for daybreak, but it was dawn before Hardee's men arrived at Cobb's Mill. It took hours to rest, feed, and organize the corps. Hardee did not deploy his divisions until around noon. The Nineteenth and the rest of Walker's (Maney's) brigade were taken from Maney to bolster Bate's division. Walker's men were still searching for Bate's headquarters when Hardee launched the attack. Again, however, Hardee had failed to reconnoiter the field, with disastrous results. Rough, wooded terrain disrupted cohesion, and hidden Federal entrenchments took the Confederates by surprise. Although the Rebels launched several assaults that penetrated the Union line, they could not break it.[75]

As the sun set, the battle reached a crescendo. Hardee had time for one last assault, and he aimed it at Bald Hill, the linchpin of the Yankee line. Brigadier General Daniel C. Govan's brigade was ordered to strike the hill to the south, while Walker's (Maney's) and Brigadier General Hugh W. Mercer's redeployed brigades attacked it from the rear. As the Nineteenth and the rest of Walker's (Maney's) and Mercer's brigades crossed a cornfield, they encountered an intense fire of small arms and artillery that tore swaths in their ranks. Walker's Tennesseans reached the base of the hill, but Mercer's men took cover one hundred yards from the Union line and refused to advance further. As a result, Walker's men were exposed to "a terrific hail of bullets and cannon shot" from the whole Federal line. When the Nineteenth reached an angle in the enemy line, its color bearer, Sergeant John Mason, raced ahead of the regiment and planted the unit's battle flag on the Union works. The Rebel charge gained the Federal works, but at a terrific cost. Walker, who was moving among his men brandishing his sword and encouraging them to hold their

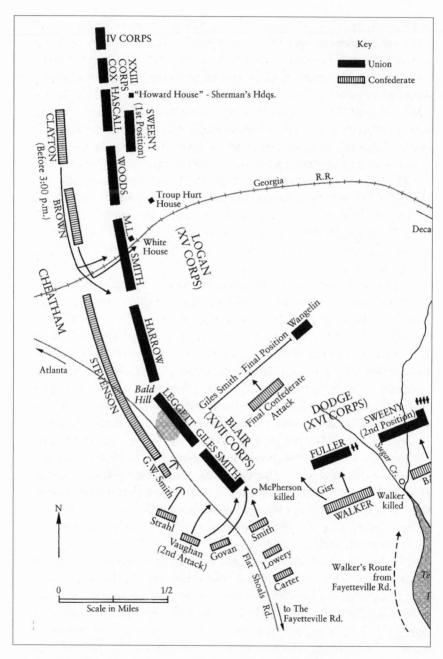

The Battle of Bald Hill. From Decision in the West: The Atlanta Campaign of 1864, *by Albert Castel, published by the University Press of Kansas © 1992. www.kansaspress.ku.edu. Used by permission of the publisher.*

ground, made an inviting target. A ball struck him in the chest; he slumped to the ground on one knee as if in prayer, and died. Yet another beloved and irreplaceable officer had fallen while leading the men of the Nineteenth. A Federal counterattack drove the Tennesseans back, again inflicting heavy casualties. Company H of the Nineteenth lost its captain, Paul McDermott, and its orderly (first) sergeant, John Richards. Altogether, Walker's (Maney's) brigade suffered fifty-three killed and eighty-seven wounded—the highest casualty total among all the Tennessee brigades. About a score of those came from the Nineteenth. Walker's repulse doomed Govan's assault. Sporadic fighting continued into the night, but for all purposes the Battle of Atlanta had ended.[76]

Hood's army had lost at least nine thousand men since July 17. However, among the ranks were five thousand replacements—former clerks, musicians, teamsters, convalescents and the like, as well as five thousand militiamen, mostly old men and boys—bringing the army's strength to around fifty-five thousand, slightly over half the strength of Sherman's force. Among those bolstering the ranks of the Nineteenth were Lieutenant Colonel Heiskell (the regiment's new commander) and Daniel C. Miller. The desperate need for manpower apparently had drawn both men from their provost duty in East Tennessee. Heiskell, however, was on crutches and Miller lacked the stamina for campaigning.[77]

Growing dissension in the high command added to the army's problems. Hardee, angry at both Hood and President Davis, wanted to be relieved of his command. A new corps commander, Lieutenant General Stephen D. Lee, did arrive, but he replaced Cheatham, who returned to his old division. Jefferson Davis insisted that Hardee retain his position. The petty squabbling among the army's leadership continued.[78]

For several days after the Battle of Atlanta, both armies waited to see what the other would do. Then, in late July, Sherman maneuvered his army around the western defenses of Atlanta in an attempt to cut the Macon and Western Railroad, the city's only remaining supply line. Heavy fighting at Ezra Church and along Utoy Creek stalled the Federal drive. Throughout most of August, Sherman remained in place and intensified the bombardment of Atlanta. Private Worsham recalled daily barrages, including incendiary shells that sparked numerous fires. Grimly, the men of the Nineteenth and the rest of the Confederate army held on.[79]

Sherman eventually tired of pounding the defiant city, and in late August he resumed his effort to cut the Macon and Western, this time aiming for the small rail town of Jonesboro, twenty miles south of Atlanta. Hood dispatched Hardee and Lee to Jonesboro to protect the army's supply line. He instructed Hardee to assume overall command and drive the Federals into the Flint River

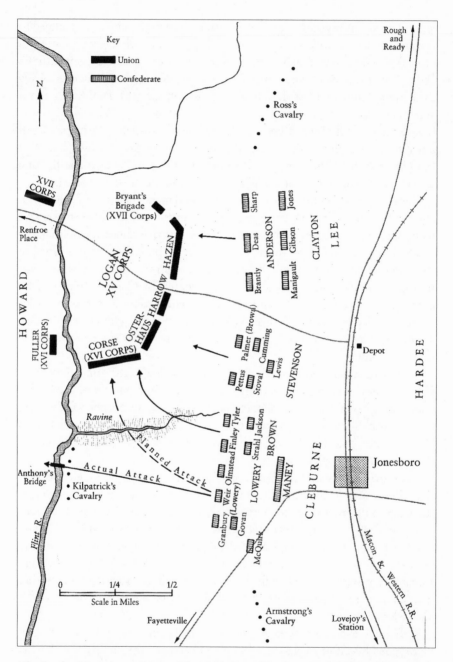

The Battle of Jonesboro, August 31, 1864. From Decision in the West: The
Atlanta Campaign of 1864, *by Albert Castel, published by the University Press of
Kansas © 1992. www.kansaspress.ku.edu. Used by permission of the publisher.*

if possible. If unsuccessful, Hardee was to hold Jonesboro to allow Hood to evacuate Atlanta's defenses.[80]

Hardee's and Lee's men arrived at Jonesboro on the thirty-first. After preparing defensive works, the Rebels deployed for battle around 3:00 P.M. and then moved forward. The assault degenerated into a fiasco. Lee's corps was decimated by heavy federal fire and Hardee's (under Cleburne) lost cohesion and failed to make contact with the enemy. With his troops hopelessly disorganized, Hardee ended the attack.[81]

On learning of the repulse at Jonesboro, Hood ordered Lee's corps to return to Atlanta and Hardee's men to hold Jonesboro. At daylight, September 1, the men of the Nineteenth took position behind their works, but the expected attack did not come. The Rebels, therefore, had time to strengthen their defenses. Finally around 4:00 P.M., the Federals struck Hardee's right and broke the Rebel line, but a counterattack sealed the breach and threw the Yankees back. Hardee then received word of a Federal force to his rear and redeployed Cheatham's division (now under Brigadier General John C. Carter) to the northeast to counter the threat. Once there, the men of the Nineteenth and the rest of the division frantically constructed breastworks. Facing an overwhelmingly superior enemy force, Hardee ordered a retreat that night toward Lovejoy's Station.[82]

Hardee's daylong stand allowed Hood and the rest of the army to escape Atlanta. Among the Confederates fleeing the city that night was Lieutenant Colonel Heiskell, whose foot wound still prevented him from joining his regiment. Riding along in the darkness, he observed the explosions of abandoned ordnance that lit up the night sky. "The pyrotechnics were fearful in grandeur," he later recalled. "The lurid glare of licking flames, the mighty boom of bursting shells, broke upon the gloomy desolation and oppressed the soul with awe and sadness." The next morning, Federal forces took possession of the city, and Hood telegraphed Richmond, blaming his officers, especially Hardee, for the loss of the city. Meanwhile, Sherman pursued the battered Army of Tennessee to Lovejoy's Station but soon decided to pull his victorious troops back to Atlanta. The campaign was over.[83]

On September 8, Sherman and Hood concluded a truce to protect the evicted civilian populace of Atlanta as it fled the city. Among those watching the stream of refugees was Daniel Miller. Enraged and horrified by what he saw, he wrote Charlotte that "Sherman has put into execution his diabolical plan of dispossessing all Southern men and placing in possession the loyal of the Federal government. . . . Such conduct cannot much longer be tolerated by a wise & just Providence and that is one reason why I think that our cause will finally result in a glorious peace and an independent Confederation."[84]

Only "a wise and just Providence" could save the South now. Miller described the condition of the Nineteenth, stating that "[t]his company [K] is nearly played out but with few good men being left. We have about only one hundred guns left and about thirty officers [in the regiment]." Amazingly, the Nineteenth, through recruitment and the return of absentees, had finished the

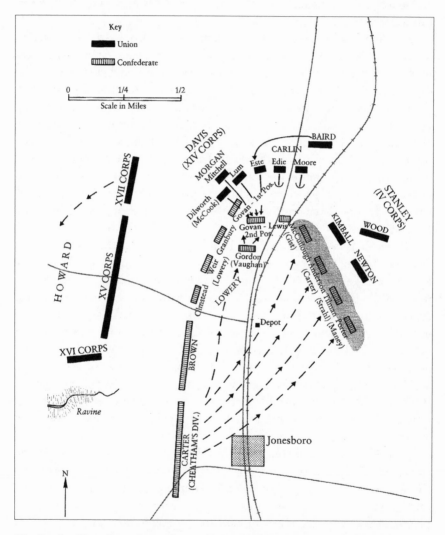

The Battle of Jonesboro, September 1, 1864. From Decision in the West: The Atlanta Campaign of 1864, *by Albert Castel, published by the University Press of Kansas © 1992. www.kansaspress.ku.edu. Used by permission of the publisher.*

Atlanta campaign with as many if not more men than when it started. These soldiers, however, represented a pathetic remnant of the regiment.[85]

Now that Atlanta had fallen, Miller and his compatriots awaited the army's future campaign. Rumors and speculation filled the regiment's camp. Miller believed that "we will remain in Georgia during this fall and winter." In this, he was partly correct. Hood moved his army to Palmetto on the Atlanta and West Point Railroad and waited for the arrival of President Davis to discuss plans for the Army of Tennessee's future. With Atlanta occupied and the Confederacy teetering on collapse, the South desperately needed a brilliantly conceived and well-executed campaign from the Army of Tennessee. It would have neither.[86]

7 ✎

"A Black Page in the Memory of Our Lost Cause"

From Hood's Invasion to Johnston's Surrender

On a rainy September 25, 1864, Jefferson Davis arrived at Palmetto, Georgia, for his last visit with the Army of Tennessee. The fall of Atlanta had severely shaken Southern morale, and the president was touring the Confederate heartland, trying to strengthen the public's resolve. He hoped to revive the esprit of Hood's army, on which so much now depended. Davis spent three days visiting the troops, conferring with his generals, and developing a strategy to reverse the tide of war in the West.[1]

The army Davis found in the muddy camps at Palmetto was in appalling shape. Much of its commissary, quartermaster stores, and ordnance had been lost in Atlanta, leaving the men without adequate food, clothing, and ammunition. Winter was approaching, and thousands of soldiers were still without shoes. Moreover, the carnage of the battles around Atlanta had destroyed the men's faith in Hood's leadership. As the president reviewed the bedraggled troops, cries for Johnston's return reverberated through the ranks. When a member of Davis's entourage, Howell E. Cobb, delivered a patriotic speech, a disgruntled private yelled out, "a shell or two would knock all the sweetness out [from the eloquent words] in less than no time." Rhetoric was not what the soldiers needed.[2]

Nor could such patriotic effusions end dissension within the high command. All three of the army's corps commanders, Hardee, Lee, and Stewart, advised Davis to replace Hood, preferably with Johnston. Hardee and Hood continued to blame one another for the capture of Atlanta, and Hardee asked again to be relieved if Hood was not removed. The humbled Hood tendered his resignation, but Davis refused it. Instead, the president sustained Hood and

161

reassigned Hardee to the Atlantic coast. This elevated Cheatham to corps command. However, the public outcry over the fall of Atlanta forced Davis to rearrange the command structure in the West. Unwilling to restore Johnston, Davis assigned his old nemesis, Beauregard, to command the newly created Military Division of the West. Ostensibly, Beauregard now controlled all Confederate forces in the western theater, including the Army of Tennessee. In reality, however, Davis intended for the position to be mostly advisory and supervisory. Unfortunately for the men of the Nineteenth and the rest of the army, John Bell Hood would still lead them.[3]

The question of where Hood would lead them was decided at Palmetto. Davis approved Hood's proposal to move against Sherman's supply line—the Western and Atlantic Railroad. Once the Rebels were astride the railroad, Sherman would be forced to attack Hood or head south to open up a new supply line on the Gulf or Atlantic coasts. If the Federals attempted to clear the railroad, Hood would fight on ground of his choosing or draw the Yankees northward. If Sherman pushed southward, the Rebels would shadow him, striking when and where they could inflict the most damage. Davis bid Hood move quickly. On September 29, two days after the president's departure, the Army of Tennessee began crossing the Chattahoochee, heading northeast. The Confederacy's last great offensive was under way.[4]

Among those plodding along the muddy Georgia roads were the men of the Nineteenth. With Cheatham's promotion to corps command, Major General John C. Brown now commanded Cheatham's old division of Tennesseans, which included the Nineteenth. However, following the death of Francis Walker and the retreat from Atlanta, the regiment had been transferred back to Strahl's brigade, where it was consolidated with the understrength Twenty-Fourth and Forty-First Tennessee under the command of Colonel James D. Tillman. Carrick Heiskell apparently was promoted to colonel around this time, although the regiment's strength of around one hundred clearly did not warrant such rank. Heiskell's foot wound, however, prevented him from joining his men. This left newly promoted Major John Hannah as the Nineteenth's ranking officer.[5]

On October 2, Hood's army seized the railroad north of Atlanta and moved northward, demolishing track and capturing Yankee garrisons. By the end of the first week of October, Hood's plan had worked perfectly; Sherman was now in close pursuit of the Rebel army. For the next several weeks, Hood drew the Federals northward, frustrating Sherman's attempts to engage. However, by mid-October, as Hood approached Gadsden, Alabama, he began to rethink his strategy. Instead of establishing a strong defensive position and baiting the

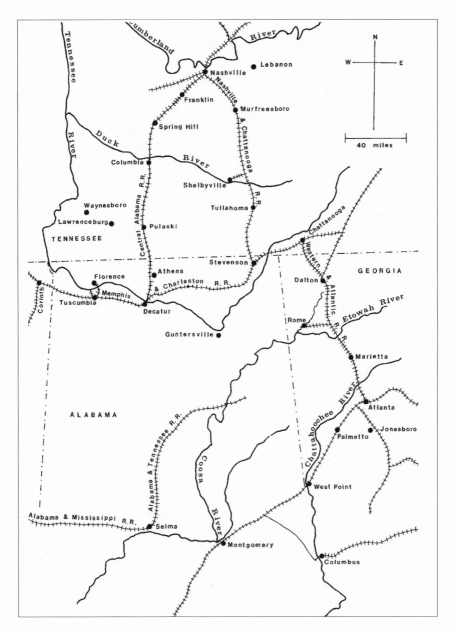

Hood's Tennessee Campaign. Reprinted by permission of Louisiana State University Press from Soldier of Tennessee: General Alexander P. Stewart and the Civil War in the West *by Sam Davis Elliot. Copyright © 1999 by Louisiana State University Press. Map by Blake Magner.*

Federals to attack, he envisioned pulling the Federals even further north. In fact, Hood now planned to cross the Tennessee River and strike Sherman's depots at Stevenson and Bridgeport, Alabama. Surely, he reasoned, the Federals would follow. However, by the end of October, Sherman's patience had reached its limit, and he ended the chase. Intent on executing his "march to the sea," he returned to Atlanta; but to keep an eye on Hood, he sent a portion of his army under Major General George Thomas to Tennessee.[6]

The Confederates did not learn of Sherman's redeployment until November 17. By then, Hood had moved his army to Florence, Alabama, taking it well out of position to follow Sherman. Hood was not overly concerned, however. His plan now was to cross the Tennessee, capture Nashville, and invade Kentucky. Davis tacitly approved the new plan.[7]

Searching for a suitable crossing point, Hood led his troops across northern Alabama all the way to Tuscumbia. There the army waited three weeks for reinforcements and supplies. In the meantime, the mild weather of October gave way to a November of rainy days and frigid nights. Adding to this misery was the serious logistical problem created by Hood's tramp across Alabama—the ramshackle railroads and broken-down wagon trains could not supply his men adequately. Still without shoes, Cheatham's shivering troops tied freshly cut cowhide around their feet and tried to ignore the smell.[8]

On November 15, the Nineteenth and the rest of Brown's division crossed a pontoon bridge as bands played and Rebel yells echoed across the icy river. The regiment moved to a point past Florence, where the men pitched camp and waited. Within a week, Hood established contact with Nathan Bedford Forrest, whose cavalry would spearhead the army's advance. On Monday morning, November 21, still woefully short of supplies, the army set out from Florence toward Nashville. As the thinly clad Rebels trudged forward, it began to snow. Private Worsham recalled that "[t]he wind blew almost a hurricane in our faces, and with the snow, was almost blinding. All day long we plodded through the storm, so slow we could hardly keep warm." Bonfires lined the roads, and every few hundred yards the freezing Rebels would huddle for warmth before moving on to the next fire.[9]

Hood sent each corps by a different route. He himself rode with Cheatham's men, who covered only twelve miles that day before camping at Rawhide near the Tennessee-Alabama border. The bone-numbing cold and slushy roads had exhausted the men. The winter storm intensified the next day, but Cheatham pushed the troops from sunrise to dark, covering eighteen miles and camping only fourteen miles from Waynesboro. As the soldiers struggled on through the wind and snow, they passed under a canvas banner stretched from two trees across the road on the Tennessee state line. The sign read "Tennessee, A Grave or a Free Home." Such was the spirit of the shivering veterans in the Army of Tennessee.[10]

On November 23, Cheatham's corps entered Waynesboro, which was deserted and in ruins. When the men prepared their camp that night, they had little food. Cheatham's wagon train had broken down, and for the next several days the troops subsisted on three biscuits a day.[11]

On the twenty-fourth, Hood's army was reunited along the Waynesboro to Mount Pleasant Pike. Forrest had warned Hood that a Federal force under Major General John M. Schofield was moving northward from Pulaski, Tennessee. Hood planned to beat Schofield to Columbia, Tennessee, where the road to Nashville crossed the Duck River. This would place the Rebels between Schofield and whatever forces were in Nashville.[12]

On the evening of the November 26, the Rebels reached Columbia and found entrenched Federals waiting for them on the north bank of the Duck. Schofield had won the race. However, Hood still believed he could maneuver his army between Schofield and Nashville. Leaving part of his forces to hold Schofield, he would send the rest (including Cheatham's corps) three miles east, where they would ford the Duck and move behind the Federals to Spring Hill. Remembering the fiasco of Hardee's flanking march at Atlanta, Hood decided to direct this one himself. He would begin at dawn on November 29.[13]

Mild temperatures had returned, and the day grew warm as the flanking column cleared the Duck River. Fearing an attack on his flanks, Hood directed Cheatham to deploy Brown's division as skirmishers on both sides of the main column. Struggling through woods and muddy fields, Brown's men, including the Nineteenth, became exhausted.[14]

Meanwhile, Forrest's troopers rode ahead and made contact with Yankee infantry at Spring Hill. Hood ordered the cavalry to hold its position while he brought the flanking column into position. It was becoming clear that at least part of Schofield's force was retreating toward Spring Hill.[15]

Around 3:00 P.M., the head of the Confederate flanking column arrived at Rutherford Creek, about two and a half miles from Spring Hill. Hearing the crackle of small arms fire in the distance, Hood rode ahead to view the situation. When he saw Federal forces moving northward along the Columbia Pike, he realized that the road would have to be seized to prevent Schofield from escaping the trap. Hood returned to Rutherford Creek and outlined a plan to Cheatham. Hood would personally lead Cleburne's division across the creek and move it toward the pike. When all of Bate's men had assembled, Cheatham would lead them to Cleburne's support. Finally, Hood would return to the creek and send Brown's men forward. Stewart's corps would remain at the creek in reserve.[16]

However, as Cleburne moved toward the Columbia Pike, contact with a strong Yankee force on his right led him to swing his entire division northward toward Spring Hill, well short of the pike. At this point, Cheatham and Hood began issuing contradictory orders. Cheatham failed to conduct Bate to the battlefield, but when Bate wandered forward, he encountered Hood, who ordered him to advance on Cleburne's left and seize the pike. Later, as Bate's men pushed to within a few hundred yards of their objective, Cheatham ordered the division to pull back from the pike and move northeast to close up on Cleburne's left. When Brown's division moved up, Cheatham ordered it northward to support Cleburne's right flank.[17]

After sending Cheatham's corps to seize the pike, Hood left the field without seeing that his orders were carried out. By 5:00 P.M., Cheatham had failed to capture the pike and was instead planning a full-scale assault on Spring Hill. Brown's men were to initiate the attack, with the sound of their musketry being the cue for Cleburne and Bate to advance. Strahl's brigade, including the Nineteenth, was on the extreme right of Brown's line. When Strahl spied Federals on his right, he informed Brown, who in turn advised Cheatham that the assault was ill-advised. Not only was the Confederate right not supported as planned, Brown argued, but also his men were worn out from their cross-country march in support of the main column.[18]

It was now after 6:00 P.M., and darkness was falling. As a new corps commander, Cheatham was unwilling to risk an assault without Hood's approval. He therefore postponed the attack and rode to Hood's headquarters. Inexplicably, Hood allowed both Cheatham and Stewart to bivouac their men, leaving Schofield's route of retreat open. When dawn arrived, broken-down wagons and abandoned equipment along the Columbia Pike bore witness to Schofield's escape. An irate Hood now lashed out at his subordinates (especially Cleburne, Brown, and Cheatham), blaming them for the mismanagement of the battle and Schofield's escape.[19]

Forrest's troopers pursued Schofield's column, and Hood ordered Cheatham and Stewart to advance toward Franklin, some twelve miles away. The clear, balmy weather and the sight of abandoned Yankee equipment raised the Confederates' spirits as they marched along the Columbia Pike. Local citizens lined the road and shouted encouragement. By noon, Forrest's troopers and the leading units of Stewart's corps had overtaken Schofield at Franklin. When the Rebels arrived, the Federals were trying frantically to bridge the Harpeth River. During the next couple of hours, all of Stewart's and Cheatham's men arrived on the field. From atop Winstead Hill, Hood and his generals could look across a two-mile open plain to the Yankee positions around the town. A sharp bend in the Harpeth protected Franklin's western, northern, and eastern

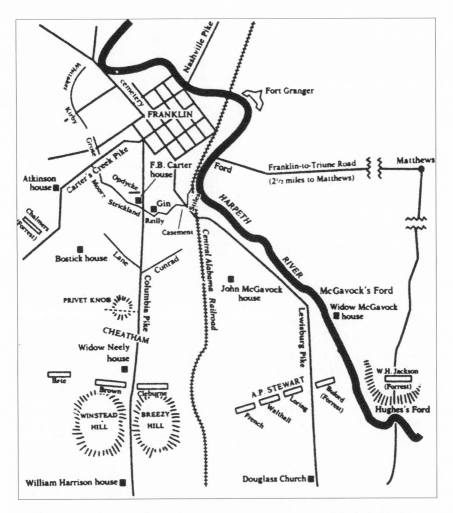

The Rebel Assault at Franklin. Page 181 from Embrace an Angry Wind (The Confederacy's Last Hurrah) *by Wiley Sword. Copyright © 1990 by Wiley Sword. Reprinted by permission of HarperCollins Publishers Inc.*

approaches, and an extensive line of earthworks guarded its southern approach. Union artillery was in place that could sweep the plain in front of Franklin with deadly accuracy.[20]

Despite the obvious strength of Schofield's position, Hood directed his generals to prepare to storm the town. His subordinates were stunned. Forrest, Cheatham, and Cleburne protested the order and advocated instead another flanking march. However, Hood remained adamant. There would be no more intricate flanking maneuvers. The Army of Tennessee would now go head-on against the enemy, and Cheatham's men would lead the way.[21]

The only apparent weak spot in the Federal works was in the center, where the Nashville-Columbia Pike passed through the entrenchments. There Hood concentrated his main effort. The "honor" of assaulting this position fell to two of Cheatham's divisions. Brown's men would advance northward on the left side of the pike and Cleburne's on the right. Brown's division was Cheatham's old command and arguably the toughest in the Army of Tennessee—rivaled only by Cleburne's stout veterans. These two crack divisions, the army's shock troops, would contend side by side. Meanwhile, on the Confederate left, cavalry, along with Bate's division of Cheatham's corps, would assail the Yankee works while Stewart's corps would assault the Federals on the Rebel right.[22]

Around 2:45 P.M., the Confederate regiments crossed Breezy and Winstead Hills. As the Nineteenth moved down the slope toward the plain below, General Strahl rode by, remarking, "boys, this will be short but desperate." At the base of the hills, the men chatted and rested while awaiting the order to advance. At approximately 4:00 P.M., as the late afternoon shadows crept across Franklin, the order came. Over twenty thousand ragged but determined Rebels surged forward, the sun glinting off their bayonets and a warm breeze catching their tattered battle flags. Bands struck up "The Bonnie Blue Flag" and "Dixie" as the last great spectacle of the Civil War unfolded.[23]

About half a mile in front of the main Federal line, the men halted and formed into two battle lines. In Brown's division, the brigades of Brigadier Generals States Rights Gist and George W. Gordon aligned in front, with the brigades of Brigadier Generals John C. Carter and Strahl behind them in support. The order to charge came, and the Rebel yell echoed over the plain.[24]

Several hundred yards in front of the main Federal works, Brown and Cleburne encountered a Yankee division entrenched on high ground across the Columbia Pike. The Federals loosed a fusillade into the onrushing Rebels, but it did not stop them. Brown's and Cleburne's men overran the position and sent the Federals fleeing along the pike and through the gap in the main fieldworks. The Rebels, now a yelling mass of intermixed units, were close behind. The Federals occupying the main line held their fire as long as possible for fear of hitting their retreating comrades, but as the Confederates drew closer they unleashed a withering mixture of artillery and musketry. Twenty-five-year-old Sergeant Major Arthur Fulkerson of the Nineteenth fell just before reaching the fieldworks, his body torn by sixteen bullets.[25]

During the charge, Gordon's brigade had shifted from its proper alignment, crossing the pike and blending with Cleburne's men. Therefore, Brown's division hit the Federal works with only one brigade in its first line. Immediately,

Strahl and Carter moved forward, hopelessly commingling the units of the division.[26]

Brown's and Cleburne's men surged across a large ditch fronting the entrenchments and breached the Federal works on both sides of the pike. Pushing the dazed Yankees back, Brown's men advanced beyond the Carter farmhouse while Cleburne's soldiers halted at a nearby cotton gin. A savage hand-to-hand struggle ensued. The Rebels, however, could not expand their breakthrough. Federal counterattacks gradually forced Brown's and Cleburne's men back with heavy casualties—including both division commanders.[27]

Brown's men retreated to the outer edge of the fieldworks, where they halted and exchanged fire with Federal troops behind a hastily constructed barricade some two hundred yards away in the Carter House garden. With the intermingling of regiments and the loss of many officers, command and control broke down completely. Instinct and experience took over as small groups began to operate independently.[28]

The works held by Strahl's brigade were so high in places that many Rebels had to stand on the dead to fire at the enemy. Others climbed the works for clearer shots, while their comrades passed up loaded rifles. Strahl moved along the fieldworks, encouraging his men and handing rifles to those on the works. He boosted two members of the Nineteenth to the top, only to see them quickly hit by the intense Federal fire. When Tom Alexander of Company H approached him, saying, "General, help me up," Strahl demurred, replying, "No, I have helped my last man up on the works to be shot in my hands." The general eventually climbed the breastworks himself to fire at the Yankees. He was joined by Private Zack Smith of Company A. Strahl recently had punished the private for insubordination, but now, impressed by his bravery, he patted his shoulder, saying "[g]o it, Zack. I will never forget you for this." Strahl, however, did not remember Zack's deeds for long. He was shot three times and died.[29]

Against all odds, Brown's men continued to launch uncoordinated assaults against the Federals in the garden. The color bearer of the Nineteenth's sister unit, the Forty-First, had his arm torn off, leaving the rumpled battle flag lying in the garden. In the Nineteenth, Lieutenant William W. Etter of Company K crossed the works and reached a brick smokehouse without being shot, earning cheers from the enemy. He remained there until the end of the battle. Lieutenant Frank H. Hale and Sergeant Lum Waller, both of Company H, scaled the works and advanced toward the Carter House. Waller took shelter behind a smokehouse, where he was wounded, and Hale reached an outbuilding, where he was tragically "filled with bullets from the guns of his own regiment."[30]

Uncoordinated assaults by Brown's men continued into the night but to no avail. The Rebels could neither advance nor retreat without subjecting themselves to Federal fire. Worse still, as long as they remained in their present position along the fieldworks, they were exposed to enfilading fire from their right because of an angle in the Federal line east of the pike. By nightfall, Brown's division was decimated. While the bravest continued to scale the works and fire at the Yankees, most huddled in the large ditch at the base of the works among the piles of dead and groaning wounded. Across the road, Cleburne's division and Gordon's brigade suffered such slaughter from enfilading fire that the proud veterans called for mercy and many surrendered.[31]

In the meantime, the Rebel assaults against the Federal flanks failed. These attacks did not even take place until Brown's and Cleburne's men had been forced back to the outer earthworks. Moreover, they were disjointed and failed to relieve the pressure on the Confederate center. A night assault by one of Lee's divisions near Brown's position likewise accomplished nothing. Bereft of support, Brown's and Cleburne's divisions—the finest in the army—were torn to shreds.[32]

Meanwhile, Hood remained at his headquarters on Winstead Hill, oblivious to his army's condition. Around midnight, he met with his corps commanders and outlined his plan to renew the attack in the morning. Mercifully, however, there would not be another assault. Around 2:00 A.M., a burning bridge announced the Federal withdrawal. Two hours later, Rebel forces entered the town. A cold wind blew across the battlefield, carrying the cries of the wounded. Cheatham walked over the field where Brown's men had stormed the works. There, by the glare of torchlight, members of the Nineteenth watched as "great big tears ran down his cheeks and he sobbed like a child." All around Cheatham lay "his boys."[33]

As dawn broke, the true dimensions of the tragedy became apparent. The Confederates had suffered over 6,200 casualties—1,750 of them killed. Moreover, the army's officer cadre, especially in Cheatham's and Stewart's corps, was decimated. The greatest single loss was the death of Patrick Cleburne, arguably the most capable officer ever to serve in the Army of Tennessee. In all, six generals were killed, five wounded, and one captured. Fifty-four regimental commanders were killed, wounded, or captured. The losses in Brown's division were particularly severe. Brown himself was badly wounded, and all four of his brigade commanders were killed or captured. Colonel Tillman of the consolidated Nineteenth/Twenty-Fourth/Forty-First was now the division's ranking officer and assumed temporary command. Colonel Andrew Kellar took command of Strahl's brigade, and Captain Daniel A. Kennedy of the Nineteenth assumed command of the regiment and her sister units.[34]

The Nineteenth lost about 40 percent of its strength at Franklin. Among the casualties was Charlotte Miller's brother, William Phipps, who suffered his first wound of the war. Charlotte could lavish all of her anxiety on William because her husband, Daniel Miller, managed to avoid the battle by obtaining leave—or perhaps deserting the ranks—to visit his dying father in upper East Tennessee. Although Phipps recovered from his head injury and continued to serve with the regiment, Miller did not return. His intermittent service with

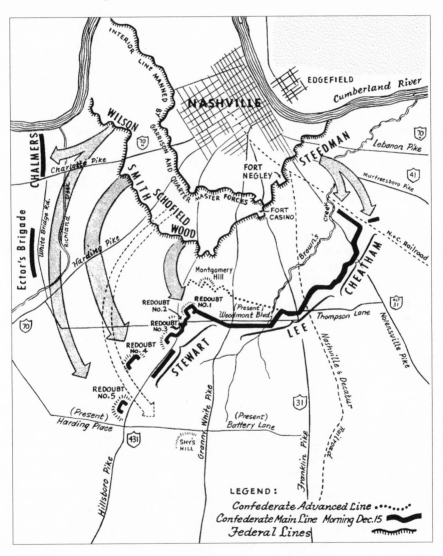

The Battle of Nashville, December 15, 1864. From Stanley F. Horn, The Decisive Battle of Nashville (Baton Rouge: Louisiana State University Press, 1956; reprint, Knoxville: University of Tennessee Press, 1978), 94–95.

the Nineteenth was now over. Meanwhile, the Nineteenth and the rest of the army buried their dead and billeted the wounded throughout the town.[35]

Even by Civil War standards the carnage was extraordinary. Private Sam Watkins, who served in Carter's brigade of Brown's division, was touched forever by what he experienced at Franklin. Decades later he reflected: "I was there. I saw it. My flesh trembles, and creeps, and crawls when I think of it today. My heart almost ceases to beat at the horrid recollection. Would to God that I had never witnessed such a scene!" Private Worsham declared, "Oh! this one scene of butchery will go down the ages in history as a black page in the memory of our lost cause."[36]

Despite wrecking his army at Franklin, Hood clung to the delusion of capturing Nashville and ordered an immediate pursuit of Schofield. The Nineteenth and the rest of Cheatham's battered corps set out on December 2, arriving at Nashville the following afternoon. There, seventy thousand Federals under the command of Thomas manned extensive fortifications protecting the city. Viewing the Federal dispositions, Hood now realized that attacking was out of the question. But unwilling to admit defeat, he decided to take a defensive position and invite a Federal assault.[37]

The Rebels entrenched along a five-mile line south of the city with Cheatham's corps on the right. The line covered only three of the seven major routes running south from Nashville, leaving the army vulnerable to a Federal turning movement. Worse still, Hood weakened his army by sending Forrest's cavalry and some infantry to harass the Federal garrison at Murfreesboro.[38]

The army's situation deteriorated during the second week of December when a winter storm descended on the region. Rain, sleet, and eventually snow pelted the men of the Nineteenth and the rest of the army, and frigid winds buffeted their camps. Private Worsham vividly recalled the scene: "We were out in the open fields on an elevation, without protection from the wintry blasts, and were thinly clad—many of us without shoes—with nothing whatever to keep our sore and bleeding feet from the cold and frozen ground. We were without tents, and with but one old worn blanket to each man, with which to cover at night, and our only bed the frozen ground, and that covered with ice and snow."[39]

On the fourteenth, however, the temperature rose, the weather began to clear, and the Federals prepared to attack. The next morning at 8:00 A.M., as a thick mist lifted, Union troops hit Cheatham's extreme right near the Nolensville Pike. The Confederates shifted to prepared positions, however, and stopped the attempted flanking movement cold. Many of the Union troops were African Americans—the first that the Nineteenth had encountered in battle. Although no record exists of the reaction of the men of the Nineteenth

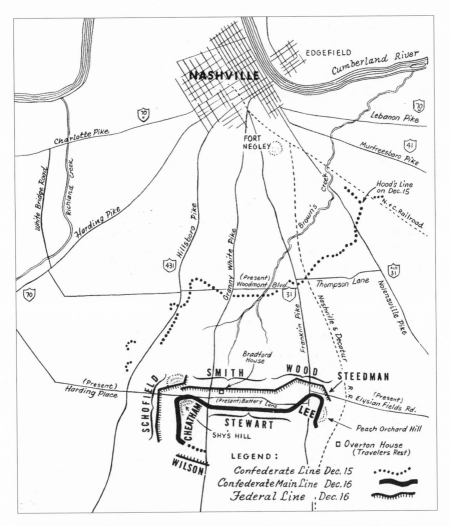

The Battle of Nashville, December 16, 1864. From Stanley F. Horn, The Decisive Battle of Nashville *(Baton Rouge: Louisiana State University Press, 1956; reprint, Knoxville: University of Tennessee Press, 1978), 110–11.*

to fighting "the dark brigade," their attitude was probably no different from that of another of Cheatham's veterans, who looked across the field littered with Federal dead and remarked scornfully that "all that remained on the ground were good niggers."[40]

Around 9:00 A.M., the Federals launched a massive wheeling maneuver aimed at Hood's left flank. By 11:00 A.M., the outnumbered defenders in that sector began to give way. About 3:00 P.M., Hood ordered Cheatham to send reinforcements to the collapsing flank. Brown's division was among these. The early winter darkness suspended the Federal advance, giving Hood the opportunity to pull back to a new defensive position two miles to the south. By 8:00 P.M., the exhausted men of the Army of Tennessee were at work digging entrenchments along a three-mile line. Cheatham's troops, including the Nineteenth, anchored the left on Shy's Hill.[41]

The Nineteenth and the rest of Kellar's brigade were on the extreme right of Brown's division (now commanded by Brigadier General Mark P. Lowrey) in a line running south from Shy's Hill. Although the troops tried to erect breastworks, the lack of tools and the frozen ground limited their efforts. The same problems plagued entrenching attempts all around Shy's Hill. The next morning, the Federals opened a barrage on the Confederate left from several directions, and shells rained on the line all day. The hastily dug works offered the Rebels little protection and in several places were simply obliterated.[42]

Throughout the morning and afternoon, Hood pulled units away from Cheatham's sector to reinforce other parts of the line. At 4:00 P.M., as icy rain drenched the field, the Yankees unleashed a terrific assault on Cheatham's weakened line from the north, west, and south. Bate's division atop Shy's Hill disintegrated. When the Nineteenth and the rest of Kellar's brigade saw Bate's men break without a struggle, they also fled. Indeed, Cheatham's whole line gave way.[43]

Eager to press their advantage, screaming Federals chased the routed Confederates. The Nineteenth attempted to escape through a large cornfield. One Yankee soldier caught up with Sergeant John Mason, the color bearer, who frantically ripped the battle flag from its staff, stuffed it in his shirt, and fled through the muddy field. He was lucky; many of his winded comrades could not elude the onrushing Federals.[44]

When Stewart's men saw Cheatham's corps dissolving, they also broke and fled southward. As Federal cavalry blocked the Confederate line of withdrawal, the retreating troops panicked and became a rabble. Cheatham tried to rally his men, but could not. The ordeal of the Tennessee campaign had robbed them of their strength and spirit; they simply had no fight left in them. Lee's corps maintained cohesion, however, and slowly pulled back, shielding the rest of the army from further assaults.[45]

The army retreated several miles before bivouacking along the road to Franklin. The disaster at Nashville had cost it sixty-seven hundred casualties and had destroyed it as a viable combat force. The Army of Tennessee was finished, and the war in the western theater was essentially over.[46]

Among the thousands of prisoners taken at Nashville were eighteen members of the Nineteenth, including the regiment's commander, Captain Daniel

A. Kennedy, and the adjutant, First Lieutenant Warren F. Hooper. Over the next two days, the Federals captured seventeen other members of the Nineteenth as Hood's army fled southward. In all, over one-third of the regiment was captured around Nashville.[47]

The thirty-five men overtaken by the victors were among the last of the Nineteenth's men to be taken prisoner during the war. Unfortunately, the conditions that they and those captured before them encountered in the Union prison camps made their survival precarious at best. Neither the Union nor the Confederacy was prepared for the flood of captives that began to accumulate by 1862. To ease the burden of caring for them, the two sides agreed to a prisoner exchange program that year. Many of the first prisoners from the Nineteenth benefited from this program, which quickly returned them to the regiment. Altogether, fifty-one members of the Nineteenth were repatriated during the war. The exchange system collapsed in the summer of 1863, however, and was not reinstated until February 1865. In the meantime, Rebel prisoners by the tens of thousands were immured in Northern prison camps.[48]

Conditions in these prisons varied greatly from camp to camp. On the whole, however, Confederate prisoners of war received adequate food, clothing, and shelter—up to December 1863, at least. But from that point until the end of the war, conditions deteriorated. In retaliation for the alleged mistreatment of Union soldiers in Confederate hands, Federal authorities cut the rations of Confederate prisoners and reduced fuel, clothing, and blankets to levels supposedly endured by Federal inmates. These orders resulted in much suffering and mortality among the captive Rebels.[49]

The experience of Private Joseph H. Warner of Company A illustrates the worsening conditions. Warner was captured at Missionary Ridge in November 1863. His captors immediately shipped him northward, and he eventually arrived at Rock Island prison on the Mississippi River in northern Illinois. The island was "naturally beautiful," Warner recalled, but the weather was extremely cold. He judged the barracks to be roughly built but satisfactory and was grateful for the rations, which were by regulation the same as Union soldiers received. Warner also experienced good treatment from the guards, which he attributed to their having served in combat (unlike most military prison guards). The prisoners were allowed to supplement their diets and improve their living conditions with items bought from the camp sutler or packages sent from home. The worst aspect of Warner's early captivity was an outbreak of smallpox about six months after his arrival.[50]

Abrupt changes came when the authorities decided to retaliate for the Confederacy's treatment of Federal prisoners. The Rock Island commandant ordered rations cut and prohibited the sutler from selling provisions to the prisoners. The standard daily ration now consisted of four ounces of "salt meat" and six ounces of cornbread. The prisoners grew ravenous. Warner remembered an inmate who searched waste barrels for bones and then boiled and mashed whatever he found to create a disgusting broth. One enterprising group of prisoners trapped and ate a guard's dog. The men then brazenly tacked the animal's hide to a tree with a placard underneath that read, "Bring in another dog." This episode angered the other Rebel prisoners—not because of any sentiment for the animal but because the "syndicate" had been selfish in not sharing the rich feast. Warner also remembered vicious fights between prisoners over mere scraps of food. Malnutrition led to outbreaks of scurvy and other diseases. To add to the misery, the original guards were replaced by "ninety-day men, enlisted for guard duty only—not soldiers at all." These new guards often abused the prisoners; some would fire their muskets at the inmates for the slightest infraction of camp regulations.[51]

Warner's experiences were typical of those of Rebel prisoners during the war's last years. Forced by starvation to eat garbage, rats, and dogs, and living in filthy conditions, the weakened men succumbed to a variety of diseases, including malaria, dysentery, anemia, consumption, scurvy, bronchitis, and pneumonia. In all, twenty-eight members of the Nineteenth died in Federal custody. Already underfed and poorly clad before being captured, the men of Hood's army were hit particularly hard. For example, Privates J. M. Herrold of Company F and J. J. Triplet of Company H, along with Second Corporal John Trusley of Company D, all died of pneumonia at Camp Chase in February 1865 after being captured around Nashville in December.[52]

The harsh conditions pushed many prisoners beyond their endurance and drove them to seek any means to alleviate their suffering. For some, this was accomplished by taking the loyalty oath to the Union—"swallowing the eagle," as the prisoners termed it. A Confederate soldier who took the oath and was judged sincere by an interviewing Federal officer could be released, provided that he stayed north of the Ohio River or at least behind Federal lines. No less than ninety-one members of the Nineteenth took the oath, seventy-five of whom were released.[53]

The will to survive drove nearly six thousand Rebel prisoners not only to take the oath but also to volunteer for service in the Federal navy or army. Forty-one prisoners from the Nineteenth volunteered for such service (two of whom were rejected because of poor health). Most of the volunteers were sent west for frontier service so they would not have to fight against the Confederacy, but a handful joined units that were assigned to duty in the South. Among those willing to endure the humiliation of becoming a "galvanized Yankee" was Private David Shell of Company F. Captured at Missionary Ridge in November 1863, Shell joined Private Warner at the Rock Island prison. He became ill several times while in captivity and concluded that he would not survive if he did not get out of Rock Island. He joined the Federal Army in late 1864 and was sent to Kansas, where he remained until the end of the war.[54]

According to Shell's comrade Private Warner, around fifteen hundred Rock Island inmates joined the Federal forces. Warner could not bring himself to do so, but he sympathized with those who did. He realized that most of the turncoats lived inside Federal lines and "had families who needed the money that Federal service provided." Others at Rock Island shared his view, he recalled, and were inclined to be charitable rather than bitter toward the "galvanized Yankees."[55]

For those prisoners unwilling to take the Yankee oath but determined to gain their freedom, escape was the only option. Extraordinary guile and luck were needed to slip out of camp, evade pursuit, and return to Confederate territory, but a number of enterprising souls managed the feat, including two members of the Nineteenth. One was Private Jacob Williford of Company H, who was captured at Missionary Ridge and subsequently imprisoned at Rock Island. There he took the Federal oath, convinced an interviewer of his sincerity, and volunteered for service in the Union Navy. However, once he arrived at the naval training center at Camp Douglas in Chicago, he slipped away, headed south, and amazingly avoided capture, rejoining the regiment in Georgia in June 1864. Private Henry S. Burem of Company K was even bolder. Captured at Brownsville, Mississippi, in 1862, he was transported to Cairo, Illinois. There he subdued one guard, killed another, stole a horse, and eventually rejoined the Nineteenth at Vicksburg. Burem fell into enemy hands again, however, after he was wounded at Franklin. This time he did not escape. He remained in Federal custody until the end of the war.[56]

Apparently Burem was not punished for his earlier escape when he was recaptured. He was fortunate, because Yankee discipline became increasingly brutal as the war continued. Even those who simply aided an escape attempt were subject to harsh retribution. First Lieutenant Amos C. Smith of Company B, for example, was placed in solitary confinement at Johnson's Island prison for assisting an escaped prisoner. Smith had answered roll call for the absent man, and the prison commandant decided to make an example of him. Smith's fellow inmates wrote an impassioned letter to the commandant requesting his release and pointing out the "right" and "duty" of prisoners to try to escape. Smith's plight caught the attention of Federal Lieutenant Colonel E. A. Scovill, an inspecting officer of the prison, and Robert Ould, a Confederate prisoner exchange agent, both of whom urged that Smith be released from solitary confinement. Although it is unclear when Smith's punishment ended, he remained a captive until February 1865, when he was exchanged. He

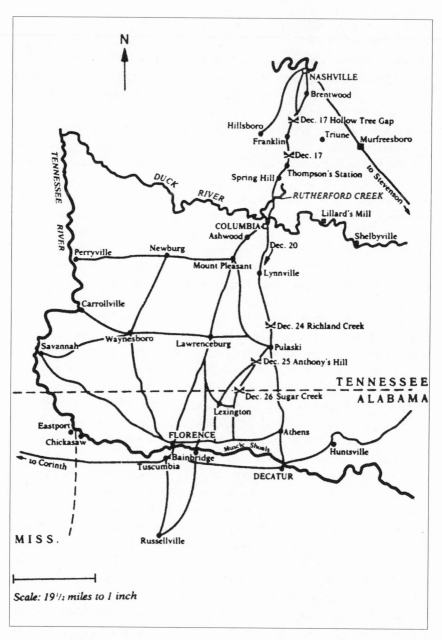

The Retreat from Tennessee. Page 409 from Embrace an Angry Wind (The Confederacy's Last Hurrah) by Wiley Sword. Copyright © 1990 by Wiley Sword. Reprinted by permission of HarperCollins Publishers Inc.

was put in a hospital immediately after his release and remained there until the end of the war.[57]

Those Rebels not fortunate enough to be exchanged, clever enough to escape, or desperate enough to "swallow the eagle" had to withstand the hardships of prison until the war's end. In all, fifty-five members of the Nineteenth were repatriated at the close of the conflict. Most were given a few days' rations and transportation south. Many, like Smith, required hospitalization. Others avoided the hospital but found themselves so debilitated that the trip home was a struggle. Private John H. House of Company E, for example, weighed a mere ninety pounds when he finally left Johnson's Island and headed home to Knoxville.[58]

While the members of the Nineteenth who were captured at Nashville traveled north to begin their stint as prisoners, the rest of the regiment joined the remnants of the Army of Tennessee and trudged southward along the road to Franklin. Cheatham's corps, including the Nineteenth, reached the vicinity of Spring Hill on the evening of December 17. On the next day's march, the corps served as the army's rear guard. December 19 found Cheatham and his veterans holding the south bank of the Rutherford Creek against the pursuing Federal cavalry. That afternoon, the corps disengaged and marched to the Duck River.[59]

There an ugly incident took place. Cheatham's men had been scheduled to cross the river early that day but arrived late because of their skirmishing. Forrest's troopers were already at the pontoons and ready to cross. An argument erupted between Cheatham and Forrest, and Forrest drew a pistol. Cheatham's veterans were outraged and determined that no harm would come to their beloved general. Members of the Nineteenth cocked their rifles and whispered the threat, "if he touch[es] old Mars Frank we will shoot him and his command into eternity." Fortunately, General Stephen D. Lee stepped in and defused the situation.[60]

By the time the army reached Columbia, Hood had decided to abandon the state and move south of the Tennessee River. Forrest agreed to act as the army's rear guard but insisted on infantry support. Hood chose Major General Edward C. Walthall to command the infantry, which consisted of the remnants of eight brigades totaling fewer than two thousand men. Kellar's brigade, containing the Nineteenth, was among those selected and charged with the task of protecting the retreat of the army. At Columbia, Colonel Heiskell rejoined his troops and replaced Kellar as brigade commander. The unit Heiskell inherited numbered fewer than two hundred effectives and was consolidated with another brigade under the command of Colonel Hume R. Feild.

Forrest's troopers and Walthall's tiny force would be all that stood between Hood's army and annihilation.[61]

On the morning of the twentieth, before the Army of Tennessee left Columbia, Hood rode among these rear guards, hoping to inspire them. After speaking with Colonel Heiskell, he turned to Heiskell's men and said, "Boys, the cards were fairly dealt at Nashville and Thomas beat the game." Among the remaining men of the Nineteenth was Second Sergeant James Stevenson of Company E, who stood directly under Hood. Looking up in disgust, the sergeant remarked, "Yes General, but the cards were d[amne]d badly shuffled." A stunned Hood rode away to the jeers of his soldiers.[62]

Nature gave no respite to the men of the Nineteenth and the rest of Walthall's rear guard. Temperatures again plunged, and a mixture of cold rain, sleet, and snow fell almost daily. Hundreds of the men were still without shoes or proper clothing. The icy and rocky roads often sliced the naked feet of the retreating Rebels, leaving a bloody trail for the Yankees to follow. However, the miserable weather served as their ally in one respect—mud and swollen streams slowed the enemy's pursuit.[63]

For several days, Forrest's and Walthall's men skirmished continually, holding the pursuing Federal cavalry at bay. As the troops retreated southward, they passed the debris of the main column. Frozen horses and mules lay by the roadside, and broken-down wagons and cast-off accouterments littered the ground. On Christmas Eve, the rear guard occupied Pulaski and destroyed much abandoned equipment. The rear guard had by now overtaken the retreating army, which was crawling, and there were still forty miles to march before reaching the Tennessee River. To relieve pressure on the main column, Forrest and Walthall devised a Christmas present for the Federals in the form of an ambush.[64]

The site chosen for the trap was Anthony's Hill, about seven miles south of Pulaski. The broken ground and dense woods there could screen Walthall's men until the last possible moment. The Nineteenth and the rest of Feild's command were placed in reserve, and the Rebels waited. When the Federal cavalrymen encountered Confederate pickets, they dismounted and charged. Hidden Rebel batteries then opened fire and Walthall's men countercharged, driving the Federals back in disorder. At sunset, the elated Rebels retired and marched toward Sugar Creek, Alabama.[65]

The Nineteenth trudged along the slushy roads in an icy rain. Colonel Heiskell was in a playful mood. For some time the men of the regiment had been asking the colonel to convert them into a cavalry unit. Watching his foot-sore soldiers splashing along, Heiskell called out, "Boys, how do you like the cavalry?" Several men replied that this was not the "regular cavalry," to

which one disgruntled veteran responded, "I think this has been pretty
d[amne]d regular for the past forty months." The spirit of these men and others like them, who could suffer so, joke about it, and march on, was all that
held Hood's battered army together.[66]

Reaching Sugar Creek around 11:00 P.M., the men came upon part of the
army's ordnance train that had been left behind. The wagons' mules had been
taken in order to speed the pontoon train forward to the Tennessee River, and
they would not be returned until the next morning. To protect the ammunition from capture by the Yankee cavalry, who were less than a mile away, the
rear guard would again have to make a stand.[67]

At sunrise, the Nineteenth was waiting along the creek with the rest of
Walthall's units. A thick mist concealed the Rebels. Once again, when the
Federal cavalrymen collided with the picket line, they dismounted and rushed
forward. What occurred next Colonel Heiskell recalled as "[t]he most striking
spectacle he witnessed during the whole war." The seemingly unstoppable
Federals advanced toward the eight weakened Rebel brigades. "Yet when the
command 'charge' was given [to the Confederates], as one man they sprang at
the on-coming foe, and with the rebel yell ringing loud above the din of battle
they swept the . . . Federal force from the field." Walthall's men again had
routed the Federals. For the rest of the retreat, the pursuers shadowed the
Rebels from a safe distance.[68]

On December 28, the Nineteenth and the rest of the rear guard crossed the
Tennessee River on a pontoon bridge at Bainbridge, safe at last from Federal
pursuit. The men of the regiment could look back with pride at their accom-
plishment. They and the other stalwart veterans of Walthall's and Forrest's
command had saved what remained of the Army of Tennessee.[69]

Once across the river, the army continued south, finally establishing a new
base at Tupelo, Mississippi, on January 13. There the men of the Nineteenth
rejoined their former command, and the true magnitude of the disaster in
Tennessee became clear. Only seven thousand effective infantry remained with
the army, most of the artillery was gone, and the wagon transportation system
had practically ceased to exist. Food, clothing, and shelter were scarce. In the
Nineteenth, many still had no shoes, and many had nothing to cover themselves with but a "piece of coat" or a crownless hat. To ease the logistical burden, Hood furloughed many of the men from Alabama, Mississippi, and Middle
Tennessee. Some, believing the war lost, would never return.[70]

Broken emotionally and physically, Hood asked to be relieved—a request
that the War Department quickly granted. Lieutenant General Richard Taylor
was placed in temporary command while Richmond decided the fate of the
army. The wait was short. With Sherman poised for a march through the

Carolinas, some units of the Army of Tennessee, including the Nineteenth, were ordered to proceed eastward where they would join an amalgamation of units under the command of Joseph E. Johnston.[71]

Cheatham's corps left Tupelo on January 25 to begin the first leg of a difficult journey across the Confederate heartland using the nearly collapsed Southern rail system. By February 13, the men of the Nineteenth had reached Demopolis, Alabama. They then traveled to Selma and from there took a steamboat to Montgomery. At Selma, Private Zack Smith, whose bravery at Franklin had so impressed General Strahl, stole a mule and took it aboard the boat. He sold the animal in Montgomery for sixteen hundred dollars and invited the regiment to join him on a "big drunk"—much to his comrades' delight.[72]

Recovering from their merriment, the men left Montgomery and passed through Georgia and South Carolina, finally arriving at Salisbury, North Carolina, in the second week of March. Nearby at Bentonville, Johnston was pulling together his scattered forces for one last attempt to stop Sherman's advance. However, the Nineteenth and the rest of Cheatham's corps were detained for a week at the Salisbury railyards, waiting for transportation. The delay in getting to Johnston exasperated Cheatham, who finally snapped when he saw a fully loaded troop train standing idle and blocking the tracks. Private Worsham saw Cheatham accost the conductor and demand an explanation. When the conductor replied, "I am running that part of the business, sir," Cheatham responded with a savage blow that leveled the man. Recovering himself, the conductor quickly moved the loaded train.[73]

It was too late, however. Cheatham's men did not arrive on the Bentonville battlefield until around 5:00 P.M. on March 20—too late to do anything but prepare entrenchments and make camp. The next day the regiment skirmished with the Federals, but no major action occurred. That night, fearing the encirclement of his small army, Johnston withdrew northward across the Neuse River.[74]

The Confederates moved to Smithfield, where Johnston waited to unite with Robert E. Lee's army. While at Smithfield, Johnston reorganized the motley assortment of units under his command into what was designated the Army of Tennessee. Because there was an overabundance of general officers, Cheatham was reduced to division command and given a consolidated force consisting of the army's remaining Tennessee units, including the Nineteenth. As part of the reorganization, the Nineteenth was consolidated with the Fourth, Fifth, Twenty-Fourth, Thirty-First, Thirty-Third, Thirty-Fifth, Thirty-Eighth, and Forty-First Tennessee to create the Third Consolidated Tennessee Infantry Regiment under Colonel James D. Tillman. The Nineteenth now numbered only sixty-four men, organized in two companies commanded by

Captains Jake Waller and Jake Kimbrough. Although Heiskell returned to the regiment, he was superfluous. Like the whole of Johnston's command, the Nineteenth had too many officers and not enough combat soldiers.[75]

Although Johnston's efforts may have improved his army's administration, they could not increase its strength. Anxious to link up with Lee, he moved his army toward Raleigh. On April 9, he learned that Lee had surrendered. With hope of Southern independence now gone, he ordered his troops to Greensboro and met there with Jefferson Davis. Johnston requested permission to negotiate with Sherman for the surrender of his army. A shaken Davis agreed. For a week and a half, Johnston and Sherman met intermittently. For the men of the Nineteenth, the prospect of the war's end brought a flood of emotions. Private Worsham remembered that "[t]he news of Lee's surrender and Johns[t]on's negotiations produced a feeling of sadness throughout the army. Although we were anxious for the war to end, yet we were hardly prepared for a surrender. We had not calculated and looked into the depth of a surrender, the giving up as lost that for which we had fought for long and for which so many had given their lives, was indeed hard, and the idea grated like harsh thunder, on our nerves." Johnston's situation was hopeless, however, and on April 26, the Army of Tennessee, the last major Confederate force east of the Mississippi, capitulated.[76]

In the Nineteenth's camp, excitement ran high over the announcement, and the men were unable to sleep or to talk of anything else. Johnston attempted to keep the army together until a formal disbanding, but many men slipped off and headed for home. By May 3, the Confederates had stacked their arms and received paroles. The army then marched to Salisbury, fifty miles to the southwest, to disband officially. At Salisbury, Cheatham drew up his division for one last inspection. As tears coursed down his broad face, he moved down the line, shaking hands with each of his remaining veterans. The men of the Nineteenth openly wept when he passed them.[77]

Who were these men who had fought to the bitter end? This is an intriguing question. Historian Fred Bailey maintains that the Tennessee Confederates who persevered until the surrender were generally those with the most to lose in terms of slaves and wealth. By constructing a socioeconomic profile of the men remaining in the Nineteenth, Bailey's hypothesis can be tested.[78]

Although Private Worsham and Colonel Heiskell recalled that the regiment had only sixty-four men present at Johnston's surrender, the Compiled Service Records list seventy-eight men paroled at Greensboro. These seventy-eight came from seventy-five households, fifty-three of which have been found in the 1860 census. The average real wealth for these households was $3,681, the average personal wealth $3,061, and the average aggregate wealth

$6,742—all well above the regional average for East Tennessee in 1860. In fact, these fifty-three households had greater average wealth ($688 higher in real and $350 higher in personal property) than the original regimental sample of 1861. Likewise, the median aggregate wealth was also higher—$850 compared to $650.[79]

Several of the regiment's last remaining members came from wealthy and influential households. First Lieutenant Richard W. Colville, for example, came from a family whose total wealth in 1860 stood at $36,000, including five slaves; his father had formed Company D and served as its captain until his retirement in 1862. Second Lieutenant William Phipps, who had remained with the Nineteenth throughout the war, rising from the rank of private, came from a family that held $22,150 in total property, including eleven slaves. Perhaps the best example in the regiment of the strong commitment of the upper class to Southern independence was John M. McDermott, who joined the regiment in 1863 as a seventeen-year-old private. The young man rose steadily through the ranks and at the war's end was the first lieutenant of Company H. McDermott's household in 1860 held $90,000 in aggregate wealth, including thirty-seven slaves, and the family's 1,900-acre plantation placed it among the largest landholders in Monroe County.[80]

Certainly, the presence of such wealthy slaveholders among the last remaining members of the Nineteenth lends credence to Bailey's thesis. However, there were others paroled at Greensboro who came from modest circumstances. Thirty of the fifty-three households held aggregate wealth below the regional average—fourteen of them, in fact, listed no property of any kind in the 1860 census. Forty-five of the households held no slaves.[81]

If a desire to protect substantial property—especially slave property—motivated the elite to fight to the war's end, what motivated the middling and poor? No answer covers every case, but it appears that the same factors that influenced the men to join the regiment initially (especially community pressure and patriotism) were integral to their decision to stay until the end.

Fifty-eight of the seventy-eight last remaining members had joined the Nineteenth in 1861. Of the remaining twenty, several were too young to volunteer in 1861 but had family members who did so. It seems fair to conclude, therefore, that on the whole the last remaining men of the Nineteenth were committed Confederate patriots, long dedicated to Southern independence and loath to admit defeat. They, like other Confederate soldiers who endured to the end, still fought for the ideals of 1861—liberty and republicanism, defense of homeland and family, personal pride and honor.[82]

An analysis of the ages of the last members of the Nineteenth suggests another possible motivation. Of the fifty-six whose ages are known, thirty were twenty-five years old or younger in 1865, and thus would have been no older than twenty-one when the war began. Not surprisingly, almost all of these thirty young men were not listed as heads of a household in the 1860 census. The army, then, marked their first experience of being on their own as adults, free from parental control. It is plausible to surmise that at least some of these Rebels continued to fight for the Confederacy because in a sense they had grown up in the army. The struggle for Southern independence had become part of their adult identity, and the Confederate army had become their world. Had the Confederacy been victorious, these men might well have become members of the new republic's regular army—especially those whose impoverished families had nothing to offer them at home.[83]

Regardless of motivation and irrespective of class, the survivors of the Nineteenth still had a personal cause to fight for after the surrender. They now had to come to terms with defeat and rebuild their lives. What those lives would be like and where they would be lived remained to be seen.

8 ✎

"There May Be Some Chance for a Reb. after Awhile"

The Postwar World

On a cold December morning in 1866, Daniel Miller looked out over the snow-covered mountains that surrounded his home in Smyth County, Virginia. After contemplating the serenity of the landscape, he sat down and wrote his wife Charlotte a letter, reflecting on their situation. Since the end of the war, the two had been forced to live apart. Facing prosecution in East Tennessee for actions he had taken while serving in the Confederate provost marshal's department, Daniel fled to Virginia as "a political refugee."[1]

For the next four years, Daniel continued to live alone. "I am an exile from the home of my fathers," he lamented, "and almost a stranger to the 'dear ones at home.'" Although Charlotte visited her husband periodically, she chose to live in Hawkins County, Tennessee, with the couple's two children, Kate and Phipps. Perhaps it was fear for the safety of her children that prompted Charlotte to remain in East Tennessee. Daniel was aware of the possibility of his being kidnapped by unionists who wanted to return him to Tennessee to stand trial. Nonetheless, he became acclimated to his new life as a teacher in a small subscription school, and after the Tennessee legislature disfranchised former Confederates in 1865, he begged Charlotte to leave Tennessee and join him in Virginia. He predicted that "[w]e can live [here] four or five years and then probably we can move back to Tenn. if we see proper. I don't know that I can do better anywhere else . . . and I have determined to remain." Daniel hoped that Charlotte would help him with his school by teaching embroidery and painting. He reminded her of their wedding vows: "'[w]hat God has joined together let no man put asunder.' So don't let us live asunder much longer."[2]

Despite Daniel's plea, Charlotte would not move to Virginia. She would only take the children for brief visits. As the spring of 1867 approached, Daniel became despondent. He wrote Charlotte that "[s]ometimes I think that if I could see father [his father-in-law], I would persuade him to sell his premises in Tenn. and move to the Northwest where we could live together and away from all the prejudices and bickering that is going on in the South. The Southern people are in a forlorn condition." Daniel also expressed fear for his future and that of all former Confederates under Congress's military reconstruction program: "the South is reduced to territories and subjected to the government of Military *Satraps;* from under the control so to speak of the federal head. The next thing will be a sweeping confiscation act. The South is already impoverished, then we will be poor indeed. . . . In the Northwest we could enjoy political privileges, and be out of the way of the negro element. Name it to him and see what are his notions."[3]

Apparently Charlotte's father rejected the idea, and Daniel remained in Virginia alone. The separation from Charlotte and the children took a heavy toll on Daniel's spirit. Writing to his wife in May 1867, he warned, "I want to see you so badly that I am almost crazy. I believe that if you don't exhibit yourself in Smythe [sic] Co. soon that I will commit suicide or some other desperate thing. So come along and by that means save your devoted husband from utter ruin and despair." Although Charlotte continued to visit Daniel, she would not move.[4]

In the summer of 1867, still fearing mob violence or arrest, Daniel told his wife that "[m]y hopes are not the brightest as regard my future home in Tenn. I expect that the best plan after all will be [for you] to remove to Virginia and become a fixture." But by late summer, news of conservative resistance to Tennessee governor William Brownlow's Radical agenda prompted Daniel to write his wife, optimistically predicting that "there may be some chance for a Reb. after awhile."[5]

Daniel's hunch was essentially correct. Although he would spend three more years as an exile, the hostility toward former Confederates in East Tennessee began to wane in 1870 with the "redemption" of the state. Only then did Charlotte join Daniel, who elected not to return to his native Hawkins County but to stay in Virginia.[6]

The postwar experience of Daniel and Charlotte was not unique. All across East Tennessee, ex-Confederates endured fear, anguish, and uncertainty as they struggled to rebuild their lives in the aftermath of the Civil War. Despite the "official peace," the unionist-secessionist conflict continued unabated in the coves, mountains, and villages of eastern Tennessee.[7]

Since the Federal "liberation" of the region in 1863, militant unionists led by Brownlow had sought vengeance against East Tennessee's Confederates for real and imagined wrongs inflicted on the loyalist population during the first two years of the war. Moving into Knoxville on the heels of Federal forces in the fall of 1863, Brownlow reestablished his newspaper, christening it the *Knoxville Whig and Rebel Ventilator*. For the next two years this ultra-unionist organ championed the destruction of the Confederacy and the severest punishment for Rebels, especially those of East Tennessee. "We endorse all that Lincoln has done," wrote Brownlow, "and we find fault with him for not having done more. The Federal Government has been too slow and lenient to punish rebels, and crush out this wicked, abominable, and uncalled for rebellion from its very commencement." The fiery editor went on to declare that "[t]he mediation we shall advocate is that of the cannon and the sword, and our motto is – no armistice on land or sea until all rebels, both front and rear, in arms and in ambush, are subjugated or exterminated." Brownlow's hatred for the Confederacy was surpassed only by his disgust for East Tennessee Rebels. A year before the end of the war, he advised his fellow loyalists that "it is proper and right for union men to shoot down upon sight, each and all of these murderers [Confederate soldiers] and that it is the duty that East Tennessee union men owe to their abused relatives to see that these men, each, anyone of them, or all, die violent deaths, if they shall dare to show themselves in East Tennessee during the present century."[8]

In 1865, when Federal troops native to the region began returning home, a systematic and ruthless campaign of terror was unleashed on the former Rebels. The Federal veterans planned not only to avenge the mistreatment they and their families had experienced under Confederate rule but also to drive the Rebels out of the region permanently. Brownlow's election to the governorship by the state's unionist oligarchy in 1865 only exacerbated the situation. Determined that only ardent unionists would control Tennessee, Brownlow and his Radical supporters enacted an extensive reconstruction plan for Tennessee. Over the next several years, they initiated legislation designed to humiliate, punish, and drive away the Rebel population. The cornerstone of the Radical effort was a series of franchise acts aimed at preventing ex-Confederates from voting and hence keeping control of the state government in the hands of the unionists. The franchise acts, however, were only one part of a far-reaching official and unofficial campaign of terror and intimidation. For the next several years, ex-Confederates like Daniel Miller faced beatings, looting, criminal and civil suits, and even indictments for treason. Unlike Confederates elsewhere in the South, those from East Tennessee found it difficult and even dangerous to return home.[9]

While Brownlow's exhortations generally fell on receptive ears in East Tennessee, not all of the region's unionists were as virulent as the governor toward their Rebel neighbors. Indeed, a sizable population of the region's unionists, known as Conservatives, hoped to follow Lincoln's and later Johnson's call for leniency and a spirit of reconciliation. Greenvillian Samuel Milligan, a member of the state supreme court, wrote President Andrew Johnson complaining that "[n]o part of the Country is in worse disorder than parts of E. Ten. not to be sure, from a spirit of rebellion but from the lawless conduct of the returned [Federal] soldiers. Not a day passes but some man or family is either beaten almost to death, or driven from the country, and all as it would seem, from the Governor's organ under his sanction."[10]

Milligan was correct in his estimation of the source of partisan fervor. Throughout the summer of 1865, Governor Brownlow used his newspaper to encourage violence against the returning Rebels. As conditions in East Tennessee deteriorated, a group of one hundred "union men" from Knox County petitioned the governor to issue a proclamation urging the citizens of the region to refrain from violence. Instead of calming the unionists, however, Brownlow launched into another tirade against the former Confederates. Advising his followers to seek first redress in civil courts, the governor declared that "[s]hould the guilty be shielded by the corruption of civil or judicial officers, or justice to the injured be refused in the courts, it will then be impossible to prevent the injured and oppressed from taking their remedies into their own hands." Brownlow had even more to add:

> I am not among those who would restrain their [unionists']
> vengeance against their oppressors, so long as their vengeance
> is kept within reasonable bounds and sought through legitimate
> channels. . . . Intelligent, influential men of wealth, who insti-
> gated this rebellion—who seized and imprisoned Union men,
> and sent them by hundreds and thousands to the grave—and then
> to crown their work of infamy, deprived their helpless families of
> all they had—have forfeited all right to protection and life, and
> merit the vigorous and undying opposition of loyal men. Still they
> must be punished in a legitimate way. And in the judgement of
> the Executive of this State, the disposition manifested by many
> of our loyal citizens to shield from justice the chief actors in these
> revolting scenes, is cause of serious alarm. Leniency, without a
> distinction between loyalty and treason, is more certain to subvert
> the Government than is rebellion itself. Clemency, at the sacrifice
> of justice, is the abandonment of government, and the overthrow
> of law and order. The treason of the rebellion is a crime against
> law, liberty, and humanity. They who are guilty of it have forfeited
> all rights to citizenship, and to life itself. Every field of carnage,

every rebel prison, every Union man's grave unite with a violated law and demand penalty, and if the courts do not administer it, an outraged people will.[11]

Conservative unionists were appalled by Brownlow's "proclamation." Thomas A. R. Nelson, whose son had served briefly in the Nineteenth, was a leader of the conservative movement in East Tennessee. Nelson received a letter from ex-Confederate Bird G. Manard, a resident of Morristown, who was thoroughly disgusted with the violence. Manard pleaded with Nelson to start a Conservative newspaper to compete with Brownlow's *Whig* and to advocate peace. Manard warned that "anarchy reigned" in East Tennessee and that each day another ex-Rebel was beaten or killed.[12]

Until Conservatives like Nelson attempted to stop the violence, the region's secessionists remained at the mercy of enraged unionists who wanted revenge and the removal of the Confederate population. While some ex-Rebels received individual warnings, others took heed to blanket warnings posted in public places. One such open letter illustrates the attitudes of the returning Union soldiers.

Spetial Order No 1

In the Woods near NewMarket Tenn
July the 24th 65

All *damed* Rebels are *hereby* notified to *lieve at wonce*, if found
her at the experation of ten days from the date of this order and
no *preparation to lieve Thrashing mashiens* will *sit at wonce* enough
to *thrash* all crops with the *usal tole hickry* withs and *cowhides* or
anything *els* that may be required on the occasion. We are working
by the order that you *theving* God forsaken helldeserving Rebels
issued four years ago Union men and Rebels cannot live together
which we find not altogether bogus

We are vary
respectively
Old Soldier[13]

The experience of Henry M. Doak, a former sergeant major in the Nineteenth, is illustrative of the tense and dangerous situation. He returned to his old home in Washington County in the spring of 1865, surprised to be "kindly, even cordially received by old Union neighbors." Doak soon discovered, however, that he had a "lower stratum" to contend with. On the second morning after his return, he found "a badly-scrawled and worse-spelled notice to quit [i.e., leave the region]." The determined Rebel decided to stay. "That night," he recalled, "roused by commotion among the horses, I found myself buckling on a revolver before leaving the house. So it would be for months to come." Eventually the strain wore down Doak, who "could not cope with the riffraff of that country—especially with midnight assassination." He pondered his options. "With neither country nor flag left," he thought of going to Mexico, but "[u]pon reflection . . . deemed it best to stay with companions in misfortune and to endure with them." He met in Knoxville with David Cummings, the Nineteenth's first colonel, who invited him to stay at "Chalk Level," one of the plantations owned by Cummings and his brother on the Red River in Louisiana. Doak accepted the offer, and although he eventually returned to Tennessee, he never again lived in the eastern portion of the state.[14]

John House, a former private in the Knoxville Grays, received a mortal wound during an ambush as he made his way to a wedding party just outside of Nashville. His sister, Ellen Renshaw House, hurriedly left Knoxville hoping to find him still alive. As the train neared Murfreesboro, she overheard two men laughing about the incident. One even commented that "he was only a Reb." Ellen was thankful her mother had not been present to hear the taunts. Her trip was in vain, however. Her brother was dead and so was part of Ellen.[15]

William Vestal, a former private in the Nineteenth, made the serious mistake of becoming intoxicated and wandering the streets of Knoxville. Standing in the middle of Gay Street one day in September 1865, he swore out loud that "he had fought three years against the d[amne]d Yankees, and was ready to fight that much longer in the same cause." An angry unionist ended Vestal's tirade with a rock that struck him down.[16]

East Tennessee Confederates made few attempts to fight back against their unionist persecutors. Although the Ku Klux Klan originated in Tennessee and became a powerful weapon of the ex-Confederates, it had virtually no impact on the eastern part of the state. While areas of Middle and West Tennessee were essentially controlled by the Klan by 1868, and while other areas of the South witnessed the birth of Klan chapters or similar groups during Reconstruction, East Tennessee remained under the unchallenged control of the region's unionist population.[17]

Klan pamphlets did appear in Knoxville and Chattanooga in 1868 amid threats to unionist leaders—but such threats were hollow. There were also periodic raids into East Tennessee from former Rebels hiding out in the border counties of Virginia. On one such occasion in the winter of 1869, a band of armed and mounted men rode into Tazewell in Claiborne County to threaten unionists and support local secessionists in their efforts to prevent blacks from registering to vote. While such raids were dramatic, they had no real effect on the control of the region. Indeed, such incidents only encouraged the governor to send members of the State Guard to the area.[18]

The only areas of East Tennessee that appear to have offered the former Rebels a safe haven and a modicum of support were the pro-secession counties of Sullivan and Hawkins. In Sullivan, a group of secessionists assaulted a justice of the peace for attempting to prosecute former Rebels. The county also witnessed during the elections of August 1868 a skirmish between Klansmen and members of the Loyal League, an antisecessionist group determined to prevent former Confederates from voting. A brazen assault against a unionist preacher in Hawkins County prompted a Federal veteran, Martin L. Helton, to write the governor requesting permission to form a company of "loyal" men to chase away the Rebels, some from Virginia and North Carolina, and restore order. Helton reported to the governor that a band of men wielding clubs robbed, stripped, and beat the minister of a mixed white and black congregation; they then ordered him to leave and told him that if he returned they would kill him. Helton complained that the county's civil officers were intimidated by the Rebels and would not punish them. Helton himself was intimidated and asked that his name not be used if the governor had the letter published.[19]

Despite these scattered incidents, in most counties secessionists were outnumbered and more likely to flee than attempt to fight the unionists. Even in Sullivan and Hawkins Counties, the presence of the State Guard and raids by unionists prevented the secessionist majority from reestablishing control.[20]

Less dramatic than violence but no less serious were the legal actions brought against ex-Confederates. Daniel Miller was but one example. The Reverend David Sullins, the Nineteenth's former chaplain, also fled East Tennessee under threat of prosecution. Sullins was indicted for treason in 1865 simply for counseling Thomas A. R. Nelson and Andrew Johnson not to speak at Blountville during the secession crisis. Already a refugee in Virginia, Sullins did not return to East Tennessee until 1868. Years afterward, he remained bitter, recalling Tennessee's reconstruction period as "days of relentless hate and bitter cruelty and revenge and robbery, rapine and murder."[21]

Several members of the Nineteenth facing charges of treason sought the protection of President Andrew Johnson in the form of an executive pardon. Some of those seeking pardons had been instrumental in creating the Nineteenth. Former First Lieutenant Charles St. John and Captain James P. Snapp had organized Company C, while Abraham Gammon had organized Company G and served as its first captain. James A. and John L. Rhea's father Samuel had aided Gammon in forming his company, and both young men served in the unit. Most such pardon seekers tried to explain away their apparent dedication to the Confederacy. James Rhea told President Johnson that his immaturity was to blame for his decision to support the Southern republic, and he promised henceforth to be "truly loyal to the United States." James's brother John L. went so far as to declare that "to avoid service in the armies of the so-called Confederate States I accepted . . . the office of Register for the County of Sullivan State of Tenn." Even the vocal William Vestal applied for a pardon. Governor Brownlow had to endorse all pardon applications before they were sent to Johnson. His endorsement of Abraham Gammon's application warned President Johnson that Gammon was "a bad case of rebellion." Despite such skepticism, Gammon and all other members of the Nineteenth who requested pardons received them and were able to remain in East Tennessee and avoid persecution by the loyalist population.[22]

For other ex-Confederates, readjustment would not be that easy. Facing violence and uncertainty, many like Daniel Miller and David Sullins fled the region. The magnitude of this exodus was staggering. Indeed, most of East Tennessee's secessionist leaders, as well as a great number of their followers, left the area. Although some returned after 1870 when conditions improved, most never did. What about the men of the Nineteenth? Did they remain in East Tennessee? If not, where did they go? Did they ever return? Tracing every surviving member of the regiment has proved impossible, but information on enough of the men was found to offer some answers to these questions.[23]

A search through the 1870 Tennessee census for members of the regiment uncovered only 131 members of the Nineteenth, out of the 800 to 1,000 or so who apparently survived the war. All but four were in East Tennessee. Not surprisingly, the counties with the greatest number of veterans were Sullivan (39), Rhea (18), and Hawkins and Washington (13 each). These were not only enlistment counties for the regiment but also counties that had strongly supported secession in 1861. Sullivan County, in particular, became something of a haven for ex-Confederates during the violence of the immediate post-war period.[24]

The 1870 census data point to two conclusions concerning the surviving veterans of the Nineteenth. First, given that most could not be located, it is a fair assumption that the majority either did not return to East Tennessee or did so but then left during the unionist onslaught. Second, those few veterans who could be found lived primarily in the pro-secessionist areas of the region, undoubtedly because of the safety that these enclaves offered. Likewise, an examination of the Tennessee Confederate Pension Applications reveals that of the 108 veterans of the Nineteenth who filed for a pension, 93 lived in East Tennessee, and 88 of those lived in the counties of enlistment. Sullivan County contained 34 ex-members filing for a pension—about a third of the total number for the regiment.[25]

What about those who fled Tennessee? Where did they go? And did they stay away for the remainder of their lives? In an appendix to his 1902 history of the Nineteenth, William Worsham listed 97 surviving members of the regiment. Seventy-five of those lived in Tennessee, most in the eastern portion of the state. This suggests that many returned to Tennessee in their later years, for it is a far larger proportion than the 1870 data suggest. However, the vast majority of the original membership apparently never returned. Twenty-two members listed by Worsham lived in other parts of the South—Alabama, Arkansas, Georgia, Kentucky, Virginia, and Texas. Only two members lived outside the South, one in Colorado and another in California. Evidence gleaned from obituaries and other sources corroborates Worsham's data. The members of the Nineteenth who left East Tennessee for good generally migrated to the pro-Confederate areas of the Volunteer State or to other parts of the former Confederacy, especially the Deep South.[26]

How did the veterans fare in the New South? Historian Fred Bailey has argued that returning Tennessee Confederates of all classes faced hardship and adversity. However, the elites were able to "reestablish their dominance in society" because of their wealth, education, and family connections. But do the veterans of the Nineteenth conform to Bailey's findings?[27]

To assess the economic condition of the Nineteenth's veterans following the war, the family property recorded in the 1860 Tennessee census was compared to that recorded in the 1870 census for the 131 members who were found in both. The analysis reveals an enormous decline in wealth. Overall, real wealth for the group fell 53 percent and personal wealth a staggering 73 percent. These figures are much higher than the median decline of wealth for the region, which stood at 60 percent for real and 19 percent for personal property.[28]

It must be remembered that most of these men were listed as heads of household in 1870; however, in 1860 most were not. Therefore, it is plausible that the decline in wealth resulted from the men leaving prosperous homes to begin their own lives with the modest wealth of young adults. However, when one focuses on those men who were heads of household both in 1860 and 1870 (a total of 58), a significant drop in personal wealth (63 percent) still appears. Clearly then, the veterans of the Nineteenth who remained in Tennessee were on average substantially poorer in 1870 than before the war.[29]

This decline in wealth affected the merchants, lawyers, doctors, and commercial farmers of the regiment's elite as well as the poor and middling artisans, yeomen, and tenants. The decline was based on several interrelated factors, especially the war. Fighting and foraging had produced widespread destruction and disrupted the economy of East Tennessee. The Confederate and Union forces' three-year struggle for control of the region and the savage guerrilla war between the area's unionists and secessionists had devastated the countryside. In addition, between 1860 and 1870, increased landlessness among the region's inhabitants, shrinking farm size, and soil depletion played a role in reducing real wealth, while emancipation and the destruction and looting of homes may explain the drop in personal wealth.[30]

The emancipation of slaves apparently was a significant factor in the decline of personal wealth for several of the veteran households. For example, William Phipps's father James listed $12,150 in personal property in the 1860 census along with eleven slaves. According to the 1870 census, he possessed only $1,500 in personal property. Likewise, Robert Clack held $3,000 in personal property in 1860, including three slaves, but in 1870 he possessed only $200 in personal property. Dr. John Paxton listed $13,000 in personal property and eleven slaves in the 1860 census yet only $5,000 in personal property in the 1870 census. As it did to other slaveholders throughout the South, the end of slavery delivered a sharp blow to the wealth of the regiment's elite.[31]

Another indicator of the relative poverty of many of the Nineteenth's veterans is the Confederate Pension Applications. In 1891, the Tennessee General Assembly passed an act appropriating funds for the maimed and indigent soldiers of the state whose families could not support them. The annual stipends were small; the largest amount given was $300 for a soldier who had lost both eyes, arms, or legs. Nevertheless, 108 members of the regiment applied for a pension. Their applications reveal extreme poverty. Most of the men owned less than $100 in real or personal property. For example, Madison Carrol, a former private in Company C, listed $100 worth of property on his application. His lawyer, W. A. Owens, wrote a letter entreating the Pension Board to provide Carrol a stipend: "This old rebel is in a pitiable condition. He is old and blind. His wife is old and feeble, and is unable to earn support for herself and the old man. If this old man could get $10 a month it would support he and his wife in their declining years. . . . This old man actually suffers at times. He and his wife go hungry. . . ." M. S. Holloway, the Commissioner of Poor for Rhea County, wrote the Pension Board on behalf of W. J. McLarrin, stating that he "needs aid badly to live" and is "dependent on our County for help to keep him from suffering." When asked if his children could not support him, pension applicant James A. Love informed the Pension Board, "No, They are very poor. . . . We are all living in almost absolute poverty."[32]

Not all of the Nineteenth's veterans fared poorly after the war. The experience of some does seem to confirm Bailey's conclusions regarding the elite following the conflict. Samuel J. A. Frazier, a former captain of Company D, studied law while a prisoner at Johnson's Island. Frazier had suffered a serious throat wound at Chickamauga that led to his capture. Admitted to the Tennessee Bar in 1866, Frazier built a lucrative practice and eventually retired from the legal profession. He then moved to Chattanooga where he established the Hill City suburb. He even donated ten thousand dollars toward the building of a suspension bridge that connected his development with Chattanooga. Frazier also developed a beach property named for him near Tampa, Florida. Frazier's comrade Richard W. Colville served as first lieutenant of Company D. A severe leg wound received at Murfreesboro put Colville in the hospital for an extended period. However, after the war Colville returned to Tennessee and in 1868 received a degree from the Nashville medical college. After retiring from his large practice, he moved to Hill City where, like Samuel Frazier, he held large real estate interests. William Brown Tate, a wealthy private in Company I, was discharged because of poor health in 1863. After the war, through frugality and shrewd investing, Tate became part owner of a bank. He built such a large fortune that he was able to purchase artificial arms and legs for forty-one ex-Confederates in East Tennessee at the cost of around twenty thousand dollars. Daniel Miller never returned to live in Hawkins County. He continued to teach at Liberty Academy until 1870. That year a public school system for Smyth County was instituted, and he became the superintendent. He remained involved in education throughout the 1870s and 1880s, eventually becoming principal of Marion High School in Virginia. He also returned to the practice of law, becoming a county judge in 1880. Overall then, it appears that although most of the Nineteenth's veterans who remained in Tennessee were worse off financially than before the war, certain members of the elite retained their status or actually prospered.[33]

If the men of the regiment for the most part struggled economically, how did they do politically? Did they hold any elected or appointed offices? Were they able to establish or reestablish themselves as community leaders? The answers to these questions offer insight into the ex-Rebels' reassimilation into the county's and state's political life and their postwar relations with the unionists of East Tennessee. Several of the ex-Confederates did indeed become politically active, primarily in the areas of strong Democratic/secessionist tradition. Charles St. John, for example, was appointed chancellor of Hawkins County in 1884 to serve out an unexpired term. He later served as quartermaster general of the state militia under Democratic governor James David Porter. William H. Watterson served as clerk and master of the chancery court of Hawkins County, while Thomas N. L. Cunnyngham held the office of mayor of Dayton in Rhea County. Cunnyngham also served as recorder, treasurer, and tax collector for the city at various times. J. C. Hodges was elected state senator from the second senatorial district in 1874. Carrick White Heiskell served as a judge of the Circuit Court in Memphis as well as city attorney. Henry Doak became a circuit and district court clerk in Nashville. Charles E. Vance served as a Democratic elector for Tennessee during the election of 1876. Nathan Gregg was elected sheriff of Sullivan County in 1870, 1872, and 1874 and also represented the county in the state legislature from 1876 to 1882, becoming a legislative leader. Abram Fulkerson was elected to the Virginia House of Delegates on four separate occasions, serving in the House and Senate. In 1880, he was elected to Congress to represent Virginia's Ninth Congressional District.[34]

In each of the aforementioned cases, the officeholder was a Democrat. However, two ex-members of the regiment in Hawkins County became Republicans. William P. Gillenwaters began a successful law practice following the war and became an ardent and active Republican. Christopher C. Spears ran as an independent and was elected sheriff of Hawkins County in 1870, 1872, and 1874. He then switched to the Republican ticket and became Circuit Court clerk in 1878 and 1882 and coroner in 1887. Clearly, political office, whether elected or appointed, was available to members of the regiment. However, such positions generally went to the old elite and were available only in areas of Democratic strength.[35]

By holding political office, the veterans of the Nineteenth proved that pockets of Democratic/secessionist sympathy still existed in East Tennessee and that former Rebels still had a place and a voice in those communities. In these enclaves the region's Confederates attempted to reconstruct their lives and commemorate their sacrifices for Southern independence. However, surrounded by unionists and few in number, the ex-Rebels made feeble attempts to join the South's celebration of the "Lost Cause." By 1893, only fifteen United Confederate Veterans (UCV) camps existed in East Tennessee, most in the pro-secessionist areas between Knoxville and Chattanooga. The only Rebel organization in the counties north of Knoxville was the Confederate Veterans Association of Upper East Tennessee. The UCV's sister organization, the United Daughters of the Confederacy (UDC), became the primary organization promoting the Confederate cause in East Tennessee. By 1920, sixteen chapters had been formed in the region, including one in Chattanooga named for Colonel Francis Walker of the Nineteenth. In 1924, a Bristol chapter was christened the "19th Tennessee Regiment Chapter." Thirty-one chapters dotted the Great Valley, but they had only a few hundred members altogether, and many chapters quickly disappeared for lack of interest. Today there are sixty-three Sons of Confederate Veterans (SCV) camps across Tennessee but only seven in East Tennessee. Likewise, the UDC has fifty-one chapters statewide but only twelve in the eastern counties with approximately three hundred members. Not surprisingly, the remaining camps and chapters are located primarily in the old secessionist areas of the region.[36]

The motto of the UDC's now defunct 19th Tennessee Regiment Chapter was "Faithful to Our Heroes of '61 and '65." However, this faithfulness proved difficult. As a distinct and often despised minority, the region's Confederates either had to leave or find ways to readjust their allegiances in the postwar world, which is not to say that the East Tennessee Confederates or the veterans of the Nineteenth repudiated their Confederate service. Rather, they merged it with their new loyalty to the United States. This is perhaps best exemplified by Colonel Carrick Heiskell, who at age seventy-five looked back over his life with pride at being *both* a Confederate soldier and a U.S. citizen.[37]

Over time the ex-Confederates began to slip into the background of the region's history. Ironically, most East Tennesseans today, even those with Confederate ancestors, have forgotten the region's secessionists, and until recent years historians relegated them to obscurity. This is unfortunate, for no Confederates suffered and sacrificed more for their commitment to southern independence than those from East Tennessee. More importantly, until the story of these forgotten Rebels is fully told, our understanding of the Civil War is incomplete. Their experiences tell us much about East Tennessee, the southern mountain region, and the conflict that tore apart a nation. By viewing the war through the eyes of these men, it becomes less abstract and more personal, and we come closer to capturing the essence of the time. We learn what it meant to be a mountain secessionist, a soldier, a deserter, a casualty, a prisoner, a survivor. Each of these little stories makes up the history of the Nineteenth, and the regiment's collective history, in turn, provides another piece of the ever-emerging mosaic of the Civil War.

Notes ✎

Preface

1. While this work is not a community study in the traditional sense of the term (i.e., it does not examine a specific town or county), it does, however, examine groups of citizen soldiers from several communities across East Tennessee. Important traditional community studies include Randolph B. Campbell, *A Southern Community in Crisis: Harrison County, Texas, 1850–1880* (Austin: Texas State Historical Association, 1983); Robert C. Kenzer, *Kinship and Neighborhood in a Southern Community: Orange County, North Carolina, 1849–1881* (Knoxville: Univ. of Tennessee Press, 1987); Stephen V. Ash, *Middle Tennessee Society Transformed, 1860–1870: War and Peace in the Upper South* (Baton Rouge: Louisiana State Univ. Press, 1988); Wayne K. Durrill, *War of Another Kind: A Southern Community in the Great Rebellion* (New York: Oxford Univ. Press, 1990); and Daniel W. Crofts, *Old Southampton: Politics and Society in a Virginia County, 1834–1869* (Charlottesville: Univ. Press of Virginia, 1992).

   Significant recent examinations of the experiences and thoughts of the common soldier include Reid Mitchell, *Civil War Soldiers: Their Expectations and Their Experiences* (New York: Viking, 1988); Gerald F. Linderman, *Embattled Courage: The Experience of Combat in the American Civil War* (New York: The Free Press, 1987); James M. McPherson, *For Cause and Comrades: Why Men Fought in the Civil War* (New York: Oxford Univ. Press, 1997); James I. Robertson Jr., *Soldiers Blue and Gray* (Columbia: Univ. of South Carolina Press, 1988); B. P. Gallaway, *The Ragged Rebel: A Common Soldier in W. H. Parsons' Texas Cavalry, 1861–1865* (Austin: Univ. of Texas Press, 1988); and Larry J. Daniel, *Soldiering in the Army of Tennessee: A Portrait of Life in a Confederate Army* (Chapel Hill: Univ. of North Carolina Press, 1991).

   Significant recent studies of the Southern mountain region during the war include W. Todd Groce, *Mountain Rebels: East Tennessee Confederates and the Civil War, 1860–1870* (Knoxville: Univ. of Tennessee Press, 1999); Noel C. Fisher, *War at Every Door: Partisan Politics and Guerilla Violence in East Tennessee, 1860–1869* (Chapel Hill: Univ. of North Carolina Press, 1997); John C. Inscoe and Gordon B. McKinney, *The Heart of Confederate Appalachia: Western North Carolina in the Civil War* (Chapel Hill: Univ. of North Carolina Press, 2000); Kenneth W. Noe and Shannon H. Wilson, eds., *The Civil War in Appalachia: Collected Essays* (Knoxville: Univ. of Tennessee Press, 1997); and

Martin Crawford, *Ashe County's Civil War: Community and Society in the Appalachian South* (Charlottesville: Univ. Press of Virginia, 2001).

2. A handful of other historians have attempted modern scholarly regimental studies. Leslie Anders's two books, *The Eighteenth Missouri* (Indianapolis: The Bobbs-Merrill Company, 1968) and *The Twenty-first Missouri: From Home Guard to Union Regiment* (Westport, Conn.: Greenwood Press, 1975), are both first rate in their use of sources and their emphasis on the experiences of the common soldier. Likewise, Edward J. Hagerty's *Collis' Zouaves: The 114th Pennsylvania Volunteers in the Civil War* (Baton Rouge: Louisiana State Univ. Press, 1996) and Douglas Hale's *The Third Texas Cavalry in the Civil War* (Norman: Univ. of Oklahoma Press, 1993) are studies that go beyond the "bugles and bullets" to discuss motivation, socioeconomic status, war weariness, and the daily routine and struggles of ordinary combat soldiers; Gay Wilson Allen and Sculley Bradley, eds., *The Collected Writings of Walt Whitman*, 2 vols., *Prose Works 1892: Specimen Days* (New York: New York Univ. Press, 1963), 115–18.

3. Historians have produced very little research on East Tennessee Confederates. The most important work is Groce, *Mountain Rebels*.

4. Anders, *Eighteenth Missouri*, vii.

5. Daniel E. Sutherland, "Getting The 'Real War' into the Books," *The Virginia Magazine of History and Biography* 98 (1990): 220.

Chapter 1 ✁ A Land Apart

1. Stanley John Folmsbee, Robert E. Corlew, and Enoch L. Mitchell, *Tennessee: A Short History* (Knoxville: Univ. of Tennessee Press, 1976), 5–11; Paul H. Bergeron, Stephen V. Ash, and Jeanette Keith, *Tennesseans and Their History* (Knoxville: Univ. of Tennessee Press, 1999), 1–2; Harry L. Law, *Tennessee Geography* (Norman, Okla.: Harlow Publishing Corporation, 1964), 15–18; Charles Faulkner Bryan Jr., "The Civil War in East Tennessee: A Social, Political, and Economic Study" (Ph.D. diss., Univ. of Tennessee, 1978), 8; Donald L. Winters, *Tennessee Farming, Tennessee Farmers: Antebellum Agriculture in the Upper South* (Knoxville: Univ. of Tennessee Press, 1994), 1–2, 4.

2. Donald W. Buckwalter, "Effects of Early Nineteenth Century Transportation Disadvantage on the Agriculture of Eastern Tennessee," *Southeastern Geographer* 27 (1987): 21–23; Winters, *Tennessee Farming*, 31–36, 48, 191; J. B. Killebrew, *Introduction to the Resources of Tennessee* (Nashville: Tavel, Eastman & Howell, 1874; reprint, Spartanburg: The Reprint Company, 1974), 6–25, 277–78, 432–33; Folmsbee et al., *Tennessee*, 244; Bergeron et al., *Tennesseans and Their History*, 113.

3. All figures can be found in the appendix; Folmsbee et al., *Tennessee*, 249; James W. Holland, "The East Tennessee and Georgia Railroad, 1836–1860,"

East Tennessee Historical Society's Publications 3 (1931): 89–107; James W. Holland, "The Building of the East Tennessee and Virginia Railroad," *East Tennessee Historical Society's Publications* 4 (1932): 83–101; Buckwalter, "Transportation Disadvantage," 33; Bergeron et al., *Tennesseans and Their History*, 115–17; Philip M. Hamer, ed., *Tennessee: A History, 1673–1932*, 4 vols. (New York: The American Historical Society, Inc., 1933), 1:262–63, 399–420, 448–54; Winters, *Tennessee Farming*, 84–87.

4. Groce, *Mountain Rebels*, 9–12; Killebrew, *Resources*, 433; Buckwalter, "Transportation Disadvantage," 32–35; Blanche Henry Clark, *The Tennessee Yeomen, 1840–1860* (Nashville: Vanderbilt Univ. Press, 1942), 117–18, 127, 156–57, 161; J. D. B. DeBow, *The Seventh Census of the United States: 1850— An Appendix* (Washington, D.C.: Robert Armstrong, Public Printer, 1853), 586; Joseph C. G. Kennedy, *Agriculture of the United States in 1860; Compiled from the Original Returns of the Eighth Census* (Washington, D.C.: Government Printing Office, 1864), 132–33, 136–37.

5. Groce, *Mountain Rebels*, 14–15.

6. Ibid., 16–20; Winters, *Tennessee Farming*, 51, 61–62, 76–79.

7. Groce, *Mountain Rebels*, 12; Winters, *Tennessee Farming*, 137.

8. Jonathan Atkins, *Parties, Politics, and the Sectional Conflict in Tennessee, 1832–1861* (Knoxville: Univ. of Tennessee Press, 1997), 20; William J. Cooper Jr. and Thomas E. Terrill, *The American South: A History*, 2d ed. (Boston: McGraw Hill, 1996), 194; Bryan, "Civil War in East Tennessee," 19–22.

9. Robert Tracy McKenzie, "Wealth and Income: The Preindustrial Structure of East Tennessee in 1860," *Appalachian Journal* 21 (1994): 271–74; David C. Hsiung, *Two Worlds in the Tennessee Mountains: Exploring the Origins of Appalachian Stereotypes* (Lexington: Univ. Press of Kentucky, 1997), 128, 162–63; Robert Tracy McKenzie, *One South or Many? Plantation Belt and Upcountry in Civil War–Era Tennessee* (New York: Cambridge Univ. Press, 1994), 53–54.

10. Atkins, *Parties, Politics*, 15, 87–88; Paul H. Bergeron, *Antebellum Politics in Tennessee* (Lexington: Univ. Press of Kentucky, 1982), 9–34, 64–102, 152, 156; Noel C. Fisher, *War at Every Door: Partisan Politics and Guerrilla Violence in East Tennessee, 1860–1869* (Chapel Hill: Univ. of North Carolina Press, 1997), 15; Bryan, "Civil War in East Tennessee," 12; Folmsbee et al., *Tennessee*, 178–94; Hamer, *Tennessee*, 1:277–94; Daniel W. Crofts, *Reluctant Confederates: Upper South Unionists in the Secession Crisis* (Chapel Hill: Univ. of North Carolina Press, 1989), 47.

11. Hamer, *Tennessee*, 1:265; Atkins, *Parties, Politics*, 2–3; Crofts, *Reluctant Confederates*, 47, 49.

12. Atkins, *Parties, Politics*, 163–73; Bergeron, *Antebellum Politics*, 103–6; Hamer, *Tennessee*, 1:479–85.

13. Atkins, *Parties, Politics*, 181–214; Bergeron, *Antebellum Politics*, 102–47; Folmsbee et al., *Tennessee*, 233–39; Hamer, *Tennessee*, 1:487–516.

14. Crofts, *Reluctant Confederates*, 54, 56.

15. Bergeron, *Antebellum Politics*, 163; Hamer, *Tennessee*, 1:516–19. For an in-depth analysis of the political polarization of the nation in the 1850s, see Eric Foner, *Free Soil, Free Labor, Free Men: The Ideology of the Republican Party before the Civil War* (Oxford: Oxford Univ. Press, 1970); David M. Potter, *The Impending Crisis, 1848–1861* (New York: Harper & Row, 1976); and Michael F. Holt, *The Political Crisis of the 1850s* (New York: Wiley, 1978).

16. James M. McPherson, *Battle Cry of Freedom: The Civil War Era* (New York: Ballantine Books, 1988), 232; Atkins, *Parties, Politics*, 227–28; Bergeron, *Antebellum Politics*, 163–66; Hamer, *Tennessee*, 1:519.

17. McPherson, *Battle Cry*, 241.

18. Folmsbee et al., *Tennessee*, 317; Mary Emily Robertson Campbell, *The Attitude of Tennesseans toward the Union, 1847–1861* (New York: Vantage Press, 1961), 159; Robert H. White and Stephen V. Ash, eds., *Messages of the Governors of Tennessee* (11 vols. to date, Nashville: Tennessee Historical Commission, 1952–), 5:265; Hamer, *Tennessee*, 1:522–32.

19. Campbell, *Attitude*, 136; *Knoxville Whig*, 19 Jan. 1861.

20. *Memphis Appeal*, 22 Jan. 1861, quoted in Crofts, *Reluctant Confederates*, 100; Atkins, *Parties, Politics*, 234; Hamer, *Tennessee*, 1:531–32.

21. Crofts, *Reluctant Confederates*, 104–29; *Knoxville Whig*, 28 Jan. 1861; Hamer, *Tennessee*, 1:532.

22. Oliver P. Temple, *East Tennessee and the Civil War* (Cincinnati: The Robert Clarke Company, 1899), 147–78; Bryan, "Civil War in East Tennessee," 34–35; Crofts, *Reluctant Confederates*, 130; Fisher, *War at Every Door*, 26–27.

23. Campbell, *Attitude*, 175–76, 288–90; Atkins, *Parties, Politics*, 241; Hamer, *Tennessee*, 1:532–33.

24. McPherson, *Battle Cry*, 255.

25. Fisher, *War at Every Door*, 27–28; Hamer, *Tennessee*, 1:534–35.

26. Crofts, *Reluctant Confederates*, 195–288.

27. Ibid., 289–333, 358.

28. Ibid., 334–52; Hamer, *Tennessee*, 2:537–39; James Welch Patton, *Unionism and Reconstruction in Tennessee, 1860–1869* (Chapel Hill: Univ. of North Carolina Press, 1934; repr. Gloucester, Mass.: Peter Smith, 1966), 14.

29. Hamer, *Tennessee*, 2:540–42; *Patriot* (Nashville), 24 Apr. 1861, quoted in Campbell, *Attitude*, 193–94; Patton, *Unionism and Reconstruction*, 15–19.

30. Atkins, *Parties, Politics*, 247; Hamer, *Tennessee*, 2:545–46; Fisher, *War at Every Door*, 29; Bryan, "Civil War in East Tennessee," 37–38.

31. Fisher, *War at Every Door*, 29; *Knoxville Whig*, 2 Apr. 1861; Hamer, *Tennessee*, 2:542; Bryan, "Civil War in East Tennessee," 38–39.

32. Fisher, *War at Every Door*, 29–30; Bryan, "Civil War in East Tennessee," 40–42; Hamer, *Tennessee*, 2:549; *Knoxville Whig*, 26 Jan. 1861, quoted in Fisher, *War at Every Door*, 30; Temple, *East Tennessee*, 588; Atkins, *Parties, Politics*, 252; *Knoxville Whig*, 25 May 1861, quoted in Atkins, *Parties, Politics*, 252; William Randolph Carter, *History of the First Regiment of Tennessee Volunteer Cavalry in the Great War of the Rebellion* (Knoxville: Gant-Ogden, 1902), 14–15, quoted in Fisher, *War at Every Door*, 30; D. Young to Governor William B. Campbell, June 3, 1861, quoted in Fisher, *War at Every Door*, 31.

33. *Knoxville Whig*, 26 Jan. 1861.

34. Fisher, *War at Every Door*, 33.

35. Ibid.; Temple, *East Tennessee*, 184–86; Thomas William Humes, *The Loyal Mountaineers of Tennessee* (Knoxville: Ogden Brothers & Company, 1888), 100, 347.

36. Fisher, *War at Every Door*, 34; Temple, *East Tennessee*, 192–94; Humes, *Loyal Mountaineers*, 120–21; William Phipps to Charlotte Phipps, 8 June 1861, Charlotte A. Phipps Miller and Daniel Chambers Miller Papers (#10287), Special Collections Department, Alderman Library, Univ. of Virginia, Charlottesville (hereinafter Miller Papers).

37. Fisher, *War at Every Door*, 34; Patton, *Unionism and Reconstruction*, 22.

38. Fisher, *War at Every Door*, 34–35; Temple, *East Tennessee*, 340–43; Humes, *Loyal Mountaineers*, 105–15; Bryan, "Civil War in East Tennessee," 43–51.

39. Fisher, *War at Every Door*, 35; Atkins, *Parties, Politics*, 247; Campbell, *Attitude*, 291–94; Hamer, *Tennessee*, 2:550–51; Bryan, "Civil War in East Tennessee," 53–55.

40. Fisher, *War at Every Door*, 37–40; Temple, *East Tennessee*, 343–65, 565–73; Patton, *Unionism and Reconstruction*, 24–25; Humes, *Loyal Mountaineers*, 115–19; Bryan, "Civil War in East Tennessee," 55–63.

41. John C. Inscoe, "Mountain Unionism, Secession, and Regional Self Image: The Contrasting Cases of Western North Carolina and East Tennessee," in Winfred B. Moore Jr. and Joseph F. Tripp, eds., *Looking South: Chapters in the Story of an American Region* (New York: Greenwood, 1989), 115.

Chapter 2 ✤ Southern Independence Is My Sentiment

1. Diary of Charlotte Phipps, 11 May 1861, Miller Papers.

2. Ibid., 17 May 1861.

3. Daniel C. Miller to Charlotte Phipps, 13 May 1861, Miller Papers.

4. *Knoxville Daily Register*, 2, 29 May 1861; W. J. Worsham, *Old Nineteenth Tennessee Regiment, CSA* (Knoxville: Press of Paragon Printing Company, 1902), 8; Eighth Census, 1860, Manuscript Returns of Productions of

Agriculture, Tennessee, Anderson County; D. H. Cummings to wife, 25 Sept., 28, 29 Dec. 1861, Colonel David H. Cummings and Family Personal Papers, private collection of Richard Cummings, St. Louis, Missouri, photocopies in possession of author (hereinafter Cummings Papers); *Knoxville Whig*, 15 June 1861; military medical report on D. H. Cummings, 30 Nov. 1847, Cummings Papers.

5. *Tennesseans in the Civil War: A Military History of Confederate and Union Units with Available Rosters of Personnel*, Part I (Nashville: Civil War Centennial Commission, 1964), 9; John B. Lindsley, *Military Annals of Tennessee, Confederate* (Nashville: J. M. Lindsley and Company, 1886), 521.

6. Clement A. Evans, ed., *Confederate Military History, Extended Edition*, 12 vols. (Atlanta: Confederate Publishing Company, 1899), 8:339; *Tennesseans in the Civil War*, 1:178–80.

7. Worsham, *Old Nineteenth*, 8; *Tennesseans in the Civil War*, 1:214–16; Lindsley, *Military Annals*, 372–73; *Knoxville Daily Register*, 29 May 1861; *The Athens Post*, 7 June 1861; *Knoxville Daily Register*, 24, 25 Apr., 2 May, 13 June, 4 July 1861.

8. Fisher, *War at Every Door*, 37–40; Atkins, *Parties, Politics*, 247; Campbell, *Attitude*, 291–94. The new infantry regiments were the Twenty-Sixth, Twenty-Ninth, Thirty-Seventh, and Forty-Third Tennessee. The cavalry units were the Third, Fourth, and Fifth Tennessee Cavalry Battalions. The artillery units consisted of McClung's, Burrough's and Lynch's batteries. *Tennesseans in the Civil War*, 1:24–27, 127–28, 134–35, 139–40, 228–30, 235–37, 252–55, 268–70. A standard cavalry battalion contained approximately five hundred men, an artillery battery one hundred men, and an infantry regiment one thousand men. However, both Confederate and Union units were frequently understrength.

9. See especially the following: Paul D. Escott, *After Secession: Jefferson Davis and the Failure of Confederate Nationalism* (Baton Rouge: Louisiana State Univ. Press, 1978); Phillip Shaw Paludan, *Victims: A True Story of the Civil War* (Knoxville: Univ. of Tennessee Press, 1981); John C. Inscoe, *Mountain Masters, Slavery, and the Sectional Crisis in Western North Carolina* (Knoxville: Univ. of Tennessee Press, 1989); Inscoe, "Mountain Unionism, Secession, and Regional Self-Image," 115–32; Martin Crawford, "Political Society in a Southern Mountain Community: Ashe County, North Carolina, 1850–1861," *Journal of Southern History* 55 (1989): 373–90; Martin Crawford, "Confederate Volunteering and Enlistment in Ashe County, North Carolina, 1861–1862," *Civil War History* 37 (1991): 29–50; Kenneth Noe, *Southwest Virginia's Railroad: Modernization and the Sectional Crisis* (Urbana: Univ. of Illinois Press, 1994); Inscoe and McKinney, *The Heart of Confederate Appalachia*; Peter Wallenstein, "Which Side Are You On? The Social Origins of White Union Troops from Civil War Tennessee," *Journal of East Tennessee History* 63 (1991):

72–103; Groce, *Mountain Rebels*; Fisher, *War at Every Door*; Kenneth W. Noe and Shannon H. Wilson, eds., *The Civil War in Appalachia: Collected Essays* (Knoxville: Univ. of Tennessee Press, 1997).

10. *Nashville Republican Banner*, 11, 13 June 1861; Temple, *East Tennessee*, 187; *Knoxville Whig*, 4 May 1861.

11. Groce, *Mountain Rebels*, 2, 15–20, 39, 43–45, 47–54.

12. Ibid., 47–54; Atkins, *Parties, Politics*, 234.

13. Family history, Cummings Papers; Evans, *Confederate Military History*, 8:339; Eighth Census, 1860, Manuscript Returns of Free Inhabitants, Tennessee, counties of Hamilton, Hawkins, Knox, McMinn, Polk, Rhea, Sullivan, Washington. Compiled Service Records of Confederate Soldiers Who Served in Organizations from the State of Tennessee, M268, Rolls 196–99, RG 109, National Archives, Washington, D.C. (hereinafter C.S.R.). The eight counties of enlistment listed above were home to most of the men of the Nineteenth, but sixty-three members of the 1861 regimental sample resided in the following counties: Anderson, Bedford, Benton, Bledsoe, Blount, Campbell, Carter, Claiborne, Grainger, Greene, Hancock, Jefferson, Marion, Meigs, Monroe, Montgomery, Roane, Sevier, Smith, Warren, and Wilson.

In preparing this study, an effort was made to match all the names on the C.S.R. for the Nineteenth with the corresponding 1860 census entries, but it proved impossible to positively identify every member of the regiment in the census. However, enough of the 1861 enlistees were found (602 of 1,009, or 59.7 percent) to justify conclusions concerning the socioeconomic make-up of the regiment. Throughout this chapter, the term "sample" will be used to denote the men who are shown in the C.S.R. as having enlisted in 1861 and who have been located in the 1860 population schedule.

After obtaining the civil district of residence from the census, maps were used to locate the general whereabouts of the various households. A collection of 1836 Civil District Maps from the County Map Collection in the Archives Search Section of the Tennessee State Library and Archives in Nashville for the counties of Hamilton (#1066), Hawkins (#1080), Knox (#1109), McMinn (#1137), Rhea (#1196), Sullivan (#1229), and Washington (#1252) was the most helpful. Other maps aiding in the search include the following: State of Tennessee, United States Department of the Interior Geological Survey, Reston, Virginia, compiled 1957, revised 1973; Tennessee, United States Department of Commerce, Bureau of the Census, U.S. Government Printing Office, Washington, D.C., 1980; Road Map of Meigs, Monroe, McMinn Counties: With Indexed Maps of Athens, Decatur, Madisonville, Sweetwater, JSK Map Services, 1989; Map NJ 17-10 Johnson City, Transverse Mercator Projection U.S. Geological Survey, Reston, Virginia, 1957, limited revision 1966; Map NI 16-3 Chattanooga, Transverse Mercator Projection, U.S. Geological Survey, Washington, D.C., 1966; Map

NI 17-1 Knoxville, Transverse Mercator Projection, U.S. Geological Survey, Reston, Virginia, 1959, revised 1972; Tennessee Transportation Map, United States Department of Commerce, Bureau of Public Roads, Superintendent of Documents, U.S. Government Printing Office, 1950; Tennessee: Chattanooga Sheet, U.S. Geological Survey Reconnaissance Map, 1893; Tennessee–North Carolina: Murphy Sheet, U.S. Geological Survey Reconnaissance Map, 1893; Tennessee: Kingston Sheet, U.S. Geological Survey Reconnaissance Map, 1893; Tennessee: Cleveland Sheet, U.S. Geological Survey Topography Map, 1895; Tennessee–North Carolina: Knoxville Quadrangle, U.S. Geological Survey Reconnaissance Map, 1901, reprinted 1910.

14. Aggregate data from C.S.R.; Eighth Census, 1860, Free Inhabitants, Tennessee, counties of Hamilton, Knox, Polk, Rhea, Sullivan, Washington; Mary U. Rothrock, ed., *The French Broad–Holston Country: A History of Knox County, Tennessee* (Knoxville: East Tennessee Historical Society, 1946), 127–29; T. J. Campbell, *Records of Rhea: A Condensed County History* (Dayton, Tenn.: Rhea Publishing Company, 1940), 126.

15. Eighth Census, 1860, Free Inhabitants, Tennessee, counties of Hawkins, McMinn.

16. Eighth Census, 1860, Free Inhabitants; Productions of Agriculture; Manuscript Returns of Slaves, Tennessee, counties of Anderson, Bedford, Benton, Bledsoe, Blount, Campbell, Carter, Claiborne, Grainger, Greene, Hamilton, Hancock, Hawkins, Jefferson, Knox, Marion, McMinn, Meigs, Monroe, Montgomery, Polk, Rhea, Roane, Sevier, Smith, Sullivan, Warren, Washington, Wilson.

Occupations of the sample Nineteenth members in the 1860 census were categorized as follows:

Professional: Baptist preacher, clerk (noncommercial establishment), county court clerk, druggist, editor, mail agent, mail carrier, Methodist minister, officer, physician, postmaster, student, teacher.

Commercial: clerk (at store or other commercial establishment), jeweler, merchant, salesman, trader.

Agricultural: day laborer (rural district), farm laborer, farmer, hired hand (rural district), laborer (rural district).

Skilled Labor: apprentice blacksmith, apprentice carpenter, apprentice plasterer, blacksmith, brick mason, bricklayer, carpenter, carriage maker, fireman (at foundry), machinist, miller, molder (at foundry), painter, plasterer, saddler, shoemaker, tailor, tanner, tinner.

Unskilled Labor: collier, day laborer (urban district), ditcher, drayman, hack driver, hired hand (urban district), laborer (urban district), mine laborer, miner, quarry hand, railroad hand, sawyer, server.

17. Eighth Census, 1860, Free Inhabitants, Tennessee, counties of Hamilton, Knox.

18. Stuart C. McGehee, "Wake of the Flood: A Southern City in the Civil War: Chattanooga, 1838–1878" (Ph.D. diss., Univ. of Virginia, 1978), 1–78; *Knoxville Whig*, 4 May 1861.

19. *Knoxville Daily Register*, 12 Dec. 1862.

20. Groce, *Mountain Rebels*, 43–45.

21. Eighth Census, 1860, Productions of Agriculture, Tennessee, counties of Anderson, Bedford, Benton, Bledsoe, Blount, Campbell, Carter, Claiborne, Grainger, Greene, Hamilton, Hancock, Hawkins, Jefferson, Knox, Marion, McMinn, Meigs, Monroe, Montgomery, Polk, Rhea, Roane, Sevier, Smith, Sullivan, Warren, Washington, Wilson; McKenzie, *One South*, 20–21.

22. Eighth Census, 1860, Productions of Agriculture, Tennessee, Sullivan County.
    In order to ascertain whether a household was producing for the market, Sam Bowers Hilliard's work *Hog Meat and Hoecake: Food Supply in the Old South, 1840–1860* (Carbondale: Southern Illinois Univ. Press, 1972) was used as a guide. Hilliard's figures on the average southerner's and average animal's consumption of corn (158), pork (56, 102), dairy products (119), beef (129), mutton (45–46, 141–44), wheat (167), and other selected foodstuffs such as peas, poultry, fruit, and potatoes (37, 46, 175–81) make it possible to identify market producers. Production of two or more times the amount able to be consumed by the household can be considered the result of a conscious decision to engage in commercial agriculture, whether for local, regional, or national markets. This criterion was applied to all farm households of the Nineteenth sample.

23. Eighth Census, 1860, Productions of Agriculture, Tennessee, counties of Anderson, Bedford, Benton, Bledsoe, Blount, Campbell, Carter, Claiborne, Grainger, Greene, Hamilton, Hancock, Hawkins, Jefferson, Knox, Marion, McMinn, Meigs, Monroe, Montgomery, Polk, Rhea, Roane, Sevier, Smith, Sullivan, Warren, Washington, Wilson.

24. Eighth Census, 1860, Productions of Agriculture, Tennessee, counties of Anderson, Blount, Hawkins, Roane, Washington.

25. Groce, *Mountain Rebels*, 41; Fisher, *War at Every Door*, 20; Atkins, *Parties, Politics*, 20; Bryan, "Civil War in East Tennessee," 19–22.

26. Eighth Census, 1860, Slaves, Tennessee, counties of Anderson, Blount, Campbell, Carter, Grainger, Greene, Hamilton, Hawkins, Knox, McMinn, Rhea, Roane, Sullivan; Kennedy, *Agriculture of the United States in 1860*, 238–39.

27. Eighth Census, 1860, Slaves, Tennessee, counties of Blount, Hawkins, Roane, Sullivan.

28. Eighth Census, 1860, Slaves, Tennessee, counties of Anderson, Blount, Campbell, Carter, Grainger, Greene, Hamilton, Hawkins, Knox, McMinn, Rhea, Roane, Sullivan, Washington; Family History, Cummings Papers.

29. James B. Campbell, "East Tennessee during the Federal Occupation, 1863–1865," *East Tennessee Historical Society's Publications* 19 (1947): 65; Humes, *Loyal Mountaineers*, 91.

30. Wallenstein, "Which Side Are You On?" 72–103.

31. Walter Lynn Bates, "Southern Unionists: A Socio-Economic Examination of the Third East Tennessee Volunteer Infantry Regiment, U.S.A., 1862–1865," *Tennessee Historical Quarterly* 50 (1991): 226–39.

32. Ibid., 229–30, 238; Eighth Census, 1860, Free Inhabitants, Tennessee, counties of Anderson, Bedford, Benton, Bledsoe, Blount, Campbell, Carter, Claiborne, Grainger, Greene, Hamilton, Hancock, Hawkins, Jefferson, Knox, Marion, McMinn, Meigs, Monroe, Montgomery, Polk, Rhea, Roane, Sevier, Smith, Sullivan, Warren, Washington, Wilson. While some of the sample members had their 1861 age listed in the C.S.R., most ages had to be approximated by adding one year to the age found in the 1860 census; Groce, *Mountain Rebels*, 55–56.

33. Groce, *Mountain Rebels*, 55; Thomas Alexander, *Thomas A. R. Nelson of East Tennessee* (Nashville: Tennessee Historical Commission, 1956), 113 n. 13; David Sullins, *Recollections of an Old Man, Seventy Years in Dixie, 1827–1897* (Bristol, Tenn.: King Printing Company, 1910), 202–4; Henry Melville Doak Memoirs, unpublished typescript, Civil War Collection, Tennessee State Library and Archives, Nashville (hereinafter Doak Memoirs), 9; Evans, *Confederate Military History*, 8:532–35.

34. Bates, "Third East Tennessee," 233; Eighth Census, 1860, Free Inhabitants, Tennessee, counties of Anderson, Bedford, Benton, Bledsoe, Blount, Campbell, Carter, Claiborne, Grainger, Greene, Hamilton, Hancock, Hawkins, Jefferson, Knox, Marion, McMinn, Meigs, Monroe, Montgomery, Polk, Rhea, Roane, Sevier, Smith, Sullivan, Warren, Washington, Wilson; Fred Arthur Bailey, *Class and Tennessee's Confederate Generation* (Chapel Hill: Univ. of North Carolina Press, 1987), 45–57.

35. Bates, "Third East Tennessee," 231; Eighth Census, 1860, Free Inhabitants, Tennessee, counties of Anderson, Bedford, Benton, Bledsoe, Blount, Campbell, Carter, Claiborne, Grainger, Greene, Hamilton, Hancock, Hawkins, Jefferson, Knox, Marion, McMinn, Meigs, Monroe, Montgomery, Polk, Rhea, Roane, Sevier, Smith, Sullivan, Warren, Washington, Wilson; *Statistics of the United States (Including Mortality, Property, &c.,) in 1860; Compiled from the Original Returns and Being the Final Exhibit of the Eighth Census*, under the direction of the Secretary of Interior (Washington, D.C.: Government Printing Office, 1866), 312, 348.

36. Eighth Census, 1860, Free Inhabitants, Tennessee counties of Hamilton, Hawkins, Rhea, Sullivan.

37. Eighth Census, 1860, Free Inhabitants, Tennessee, counties of Anderson, Bedford, Benton, Bledsoe, Blount, Campbell, Carter, Claiborne, Grainger,

Greene, Hamilton, Hancock, Hawkins, Jefferson, Knox, Marion, McMinn, Meigs, Monroe, Montgomery, Polk, Rhea, Roane, Sevier, Smith, Sullivan, Warren, Washington, Wilson; *Statistics of The United States*, 312, 348.

38. This question has generated some of the fiercest debate and finest scholarship in Southern history. Notable works touching on the issue include the following: Wilbur J. Cash, *The Mind of the South* (New York: Knopf, 1941); Avery Craven, *The Coming of the Civil War* (New York: Scribner, 1942); Frank L. Owsley, *Plain Folk of the Old South* (Baton Rouge: Louisiana State Univ. Press, 1949); Eugene Genovese, *The Political Economy of Slavery: Studies in the Economy and Society of the Slave South* (New York: Random House, Pantheon, 1965); Eugene Genovese and Elizabeth Fox-Genovese, *The Fruits of Merchant Capital: Slavery and Bourgeois Property in the Rise and Expansion of Capitalism* (New York: Oxford Univ. Press, 1983); Steven Hahn, *The Roots of Southern Populism: Yeomen Farmers and the Transformation of the Georgia Upcountry, 1850–1890* (New York: Oxford Univ. Press, 1983); J. William Harris, *Plain Folk and Gentry in a Slave Society: White Liberty and Black Slavery in Augusta's Hinterlands* (Middletown, Conn.: Wesleyan Univ. Press, 1985); Bailey, *Class and Tennessee's Confederate Generation*; Robert C. Kenzer, *Kinship and Neighborhood in a Southern Community: Orange County, North Carolina, 1849–1881* (Knoxville: Univ. of Tennessee Press, 1987); Inscoe, *Mountain Masters*; Wayne K. Durrill, *War of Another Kind: A Southern Community in the Great Rebellion* (New York: Oxford Univ. Press, 1990); Crofts, *Old Southampton*; James M. McPherson, *What They Fought For, 1861–1865* (Baton Rouge: Louisiana State Univ. Press, 1994); James M. McPherson, *For Cause and Comrades: Why Men Fought in the Civil War* (New York: Oxford Univ. Press, 1997).

39. Ronald D Eller, "Land and Family: An Historical View of Preindustrial Appalachia," *Appalachian Journal* 5 (1979): 83–109.

40. Crawford, "Confederate Volunteering," 31–36, 39–47; Inscoe, *Mountain Masters*, 7, 24–25, 37–38, 112–13; Hahn, *Roots*, 94–95, 117; Kenzer, *Kinship and Neighborhood*, 3; Crofts, *Old Southampton*, 19, 186.

41. Crawford, "Confederate Volunteering," 31–36, 39–47; Inscoe, *Mountain Masters*, 7, 24–25, 37–38, 112–13; Hahn, *Roots*, 94–95, 117. Such deference was common throughout the South. For examples, see the following: Crofts, *Old Southampton*, xi, 19–20, 77, 176, 186–87; Kenzer, *Kinship and Neighborhood*, 3; Durrill, *War of Another Kind*, 5, 14, 37, 229–41.

42. C.S.R. of Abraham L. Gammon, #648, Roll 197; Robert M. McBride and Dan M. Robison, eds., *Biographical Directory of the Tennessee General Assembly*, 6 vols. to date (Nashville: Tennessee State Library and Archives and Tennessee Historical Commission, 1975–), 1:272–74.

43. C.S.R. of James A. Rhea, #1487, Roll 198; McBride and Robison, *Biographical Directory*, 1:617; Rhea Family Papers, Special Collections, Hoskins Library, Univ. of Tennessee, Knoxville; Evans, *Confederate Military History*, 8:681–82;

Oliver Taylor, *Historic Sullivan: A History of Sullivan County, Tennessee* (Bristol, Tenn.: King Publishing Company, 1909), 143.

44. C.S.R. of James P. Snapp, #1683, Roll 199; C.S.R. of Charles St. John, #1744, Roll 199; Taylor, *Historic Sullivan*, 143–44, 162, 210, 279–80; Eighth Census, 1860, Free Inhabitants, Tennessee, Sullivan County.

45. C.S.R. of Carrick White Heiskell, #828, Roll 197; McBride and Robison, *Biographical Directory*, 1:353–55; John Trotwood Moore and Austin P. Foster, *Tennessee: The Volunteer State, 1796–1923, Deluxe Supplement* (Nashville: S. J. Clarke Publishing Company, 1923), 677–80; Evans, *Confederate Military History*, 8:532–35.

46. C.S.R. of Robert D. Powell, #1442, Roll 198; C.S.R. of Samuel Powell, #1443, Roll 198; C.S.R. of Thomas Powell, #1444, Roll 198; McBride and Robison, *Biographical Directory*, 1:597–98; Eighth Census, 1860, Free Inhabitants, Tennessee, Hawkins County; Charles A. Miller, *The Official and Political Manual of the State of Tennessee* (Nashville: Marshall and Bruce, 1890; reprint, Spartanburg: The Reprint Company, 1974), 180.

47. Doak Memoirs, 9; Eighth Census, 1860, Free Inhabitants, Tennessee, Knox County; C.S.R. of John W. Paxton, #1388, Roll 198.

48. C.S.R. of Warren E. Colville, #358, Roll 196; C.S.R. of Samuel Josiah Abner Frazier, #624, Roll 197; Eighth Census, 1860, Free Inhabitants, Tennessee, Rhea County; *A History of Tennessee* (Nashville: Goodspeed's Publishing Company, 1886; reprint: *Goodspeed's History of Tennessee: Containing Historical and Biographical Sketches of Thirty East Tennessee Counties* [Nashville: Charles and Randy Elder Booksellers, 1972]), 819; McBride and Robison, *Biographical Directory*, 1:263–65; Campbell, *Records of Rhea*, 125–28; Moore and Foster, *Tennessee: The Volunteer State, Deluxe Supplement*, 2:210; Evans, *Confederate Military History*, 8:480–81.

49. C.S.R. of Francis Marion Walker, #1870, Roll 199; C.S.R. of John D. Powell, #1441, Roll 198; Zella Armstrong, *The History of Hamilton County and Chattanooga, Tennessee*, 2 vols. (Chattanooga: Lookout Publishing Company, 1931), 2:6, 290–91, 466; Eighth Census, 1860, Free Inhabitants, Tennessee, Hamilton County.

50. C.S.R. of Joseph Dulany, #458, Roll 196; Taylor, *Historic Sullivan*, 220; Eighth Census, 1860, Free Inhabitants, Tennessee, Sullivan County.

51. C.S.R. of Daniel C. Miller, #1270, Roll 198; C.S.R. of Nicholas Fain, #555, Roll 197; C.S.R. of Samuel Fain, #556, Roll 197; McBride and Robison, *Biographical Directory*, 1:517–18; Eighth Census, 1860, Free Inhabitants; Agricultural Productions, Tennessee, Hawkins County; various letters, Miller Papers.

52. Aggregate data from C.S.R.; Eighth Census, 1860, Free Inhabitants, Tennessee, Knox County.

53. C.S.R. of Robert L. Blair, #127, Roll 196; C.S.R. of David Sullins, #1761, Roll 199; McBride and Robison, *Biographical Directory*, 1:51–52; Eighth Census, 1860, Free Inhabitants, Tennessee, Washington County; Sullins, *Recollections*, 197–99.

54. C.S.R. of Joseph Conley, #362, Roll 196; C.S.R. of James Crawford, #403, Roll 196; C.S.R. of John Mason, #1146, Roll 198; C.S.R. of Robert Crouch, #416, Roll 196; C.S.R. of Alexander Nelson, #1342, Roll 198; Eighth Census, 1860, Free Inhabitants, Tennessee, Washington County; Alexander, *Thomas A. R. Nelson*, 113; Doak Memoirs, 9.

55. C.S.R. of Daniel Kennedy, #1006, Roll 198; C.S.R. of Francis Foust, #610, Roll 197; C.S.R. of Summerfield Key, #1017, Roll 198; C.S.R. of George Massingale, #1147, Roll 198; C.S.R. of Beriah F. Moore, #1293, Roll 198; C.S.R. of V. Q. Johnson, #967, Roll 198; C.S.R. of Addison D. Taylor, #1777, Roll 199; Eighth Census, 1860, Free Inhabitants, Tennessee, Hamilton County; Armstrong, *Hamilton County*, 2:6, 290, 466.

    Some of the information on members of the Nineteenth Tennessee from Hamilton County is based on genealogical research by John Wilson of the *Chattanooga Free Press* and historian Nathaniel Hughes, a resident of Chattanooga. The two researchers are planning a book on Hamilton County Confederates, and Dr. Hughes was gracious enough to allow the author access to their typescript notes.

56. Aggregate data from C.S.R.; Groce, *Mountain Rebels*, 59–60; Atkins, *Parties, Politics*, 87–88, 212–13, 248, 250, 260; Eric Russell Lacy, *Vanquished Volunteers: East Tennessee Sectionalism from Statehood to Secession* (Johnson City: East Tennessee State Univ. Press, 1965), 121–29, 180, 184–89; Anne H. Hopkins and William Lyons, *Tennessee Votes, 1799–1976* (Knoxville: Bureau of Public Administration, Univ. of Tennessee, 1978); Crofts, *Reluctant Confederates*, 377; Bergeron, *Antebellum Politics*, 148–62; J. Mills Thornton III, "The Ethic of Subsistence and the Origins of Southern Secession," *Tennessee Historical Quarterly* 48 (1989): 67–85.

57. Groce, *Mountain Rebels*, 59–60; Evans, *Confederate Military History*, 8:339; LeRoy P. Graf, Ralph W. Haskins, and Paul H. Bergeron, eds., *The Papers of Andrew Johnson*, 16 vols. (Knoxville: Univ. of Tennessee Press, 1967–2000), letter from John C. Vaughn to Andrew Johnston [sic], 15 Mar. 1860, 2:469–70 (hereinafter cited as *Johnson Papers*); biographical sketch of D. H. Cummings, Cummings Papers; Moore and Foster, *Tennessee: The Volunteer State, Deluxe Supplement*, 679; *Knoxville Daily Register*, 4 Apr. 1861; McGehee, "Wake of the Flood," 52.

58. Thornton, "Ethic of Subsistence," 67–85; Temple, *East Tennessee*, 539–42; Hopkins and Lyons, *Tennessee Votes*, 20–43; Atkins, *Parties, Politics*, 248; Lacy, *Vanquished Volunteers*, 180, 217.

59. Eighth Census, 1860, Free Inhabitants, Tennessee, counties of Hamilton, Hawkins, Knox, McMinn, Polk, Rhea, Sullivan, Washington.

60. Thornton, "Ethic of Subsistence," 67–85; Atkins, *Parties, Politics*, 248–52; Crofts, *Reluctant Confederates*, 323–30, 334–52; Reid Mitchell, *Civil War Soldiers* (New York: Viking, 1988), 4, 16.

61. Mitchell, *Civil War Soldiers*, 18–19; Bell Wiley, *The Life of Johnny Reb: The Common Soldier of the Confederacy* (Indianapolis: The Bobbs-Merrill Company, 1943), 21–22; Gerald F. Linderman, *Embattled Courage: The Experience of Combat in the American Civil War* (New York: The Free Press, 1987), 87–89; Harris, *Plain Folk and Gentry*, 141–42; Armstrong, *Hamilton County*, 2:7.

62. Daniel Miller to Charlotte Phipps, 3 May 1861, Miller Papers; Armstrong, *Hamilton County*, 2:291.

63. Eighth Census, 1860, Free Inhabitants, Tennessee, counties of Anderson, Bedford, Benton, Bledsoe, Blount, Campbell, Carter, Claiborne, Grainger, Greene, Hamilton, Hancock, Hawkins, Jefferson, Knox, Marion, McMinn, Meigs, Monroe, Montgomery, Polk, Rhea, Roane, Sevier, Smith, Sullivan, Warren, Washington, Wilson; Aggregate data from C.S.R.; Genealogy and Family History, Rhea Family Papers; List of Descendants of John Breden and Reverend Joseph Rhea who served the Confederacy, in Tennessee Historical Records Survey, *Civil War Records of Tennessee*, 3 vols. (Nashville: The Historical Records Survey, 1939), 1:147–49 (hereinafter *Civil War Records of Tennessee*).

64. Bailey, *Class and Tennessee's Confederate Generation*, 78; Crawford, "Confederate Volunteering," 35–36; George C. Rable, *Civil Wars: Women and the Crisis of Southern Nationalism* (Urbana: Univ. of Illinois Press, 1989), 1–72; *Knoxville Daily Register*, 5 June 1861; Sullins, *Recollections*, 197–98.

65. Daniel Miller to Charlotte Phipps, 21 Apr., 3 May 1861, Miller Papers; Eighth Census, 1860, Free Inhabitants, Tennessee, Polk County; C.S.R. of John Alaway, #31, Roll 196.

66. Temple, *East Tennessee*, 188.

67. Gardiner H. Shattuck Jr., *A Shield and Hiding Place: The Religious Life of the Civil War Armies* (Macon: Mercer Univ. Press, 1987), 36–37.

68. Bryan, "Civil War in East Tennessee," 262–96. For an example from elsewhere in the South, see Stephanie McCurry, *Masters of Small Worlds: Yeoman Households, Gender Relations, and the Political Culture of the Antebellum South Carolina Low Country* (New York: Oxford Univ. Press, 1995), 290–92. Sullins, *Recollections*, 197–99; Eighth Census, 1860, Free Inhabitants, Tennessee, counties of Hawkins, Rhea; *Knoxville Daily Register*, 2 May 1861.

69. McPherson, *What They Fought For*, 1–25; McPherson, *For Cause and Comrades*, 90–116; Mitchell, *Civil War Soldiers*, 1–3; James I. Robertson, *Soldiers Blue and Gray* (Columbia: Univ. of South Carolina Press, 1988), 3.

70. McPherson, *What They Fought For*, 30; Mitchell, *Civil War Soldiers*, 4–8; Atkins, *Parties, Politics*, 233; Thornton, "Ethic of Subsistence," 72, 80–84.

71. *Knoxville Daily Register,* 29, 25 May, 5 June, 11 July 1861.
72. *Nashville Republican Banner,* 26 May 1861; *Knoxville Daily Register,* 3 Oct. 1861.
73. Will Phipps to Charlotte Phipps, 8 June 1861, Miller Papers.

Chapter 3 ✠ We Are the Pick Regiment of Tennessee

1. William Phipps to Charlotte Phipps, 4 June 1861. Other references to home-sickness include Daniel C. Miller to Charlotte Phipps, 16 May 1861; William Phipps to Charlotte Phipps, 23 May 1861, Miller Papers.
2. Robertson, *Soldiers Blue and Gray,* 3–18, 41–59.
3. *Knoxville Daily Register,* 2 May 1861; Worsham, *Old Nineteenth,* 9; Daniel C. Miller to Charlotte Phipps, 16 May 1861; William Phipps to Charlotte Phipps, 23 May 1861, 4 June 1861, Miller Papers.
4. Robertson, *Soldiers Blue and Gray,* 47–53; Paddy Griffith, *Battle Tactics of the Civil War* (New Haven, Conn.: Yale Univ. Press, 1989), 91–115, 137–63; Worsham, *Old Nineteenth,* 10; William Phipps to Charlotte Phipps, 23 May 1861; Daniel C. Miller to Charlotte Phipps, 16 May 1861, Miller Papers.
5. Robertson, *Soldiers Blue and Gray,* 48–49, 124; David Donald, "The Confederate as a Fighting Man," *Journal of Southern History* 25 (1959): 180–81; Moore and Foster, *Tennessee: The Volunteer State, Deluxe Supplement,* 389; Doak Memoirs, 8–9; Evans, *Confederate Military History,* 8:448; Armstrong, *Hamilton County,* 2:6, 290–91, 466; genealogical research of John Wilson and Nathaniel Hughes (see chap. 2, note 55); military records and various letters concerning David H. Cummings's career in the Mexican War, Cummings Papers; Graf et al., *Johnson Papers,* letter from Zadoc T. Willett to Andrew Johnson, 20 Apr. 1860, 3:571–72; Paul M. Fink, *Jonesborough: The First Century of Tennessee's First Town* (Johnson City, Tenn.: Upper East Tennessee Office of Tennessee State Planning Commission, 1972), 142; Lindsley, *Military Annals,* 380; *Knoxville Daily Register,* 22 May 1862; bibliographical note, Fulkerson Family Papers, *Webpage of the Virginia Military Institute Archives, Lexington, Virginia,* http://www.vmi.edu/archives/Manuscripts/ms 0363.html, accessed Dec. 23, 1998.
6. Robertson, *Soldiers Blue and Gray,* 122–26; Donald, "Confederate as a Fighting Man," 179–82.
7. Robertson, *Soldiers Blue and Gray,* 124–25; Donald, "Confederate as a Fighting Man," 181–82; William Phipps to Charlotte Phipps, 4 June 1861, Daniel C. Miller to Charlotte Phipps, 7 June 1861, Miller Papers.
8. Robertson, *Soldiers Blue and Gray,* 123; Wiley, *Life of Johnny Reb,* 337–39; Bailey, *Class and Tennessee's Confederate Generation,* 34, 74–79; Donald, "Confederate as a Fighting Man," 182–91; Daniel C. Miller to Charlotte Phipps Miller, 22 Oct. 1862, Miller Papers.

9. Daniel C. Miller to Charlotte Phipps, 16 May 1861, 17 Aug. 1861, Miller Papers; Bailey, *Class and Tennessee's Confederate Generation*, 78–79; aggregate data from C.S.R.; Eighth Census, 1860, Free Inhabitants, Productions of Agriculture, Slaves, Tennessee, counties of Anderson, Bedford, Benton, Bledsoe, Blount, Campbell, Carter, Claiborne, Grainger, Greene, Hamilton, Hancock, Hawkins, Jefferson, Knox, Marion, McMinn, Meigs, Monroe, Montgomery, Polk, Rhea, Roane, Sevier, Smith, Sullivan, Warren, Washington, Wilson; *Statistics of the United States*, 312, 348.

10. Bailey, *Class and Tennessee's Confederate Generation*, 85; Worsham, *Old Nineteenth*, 10, 181 (Worsham recalled that "Old Mungy" belonged to Colonel Cummings); Doak Memoirs, 20; William Phipps to Charlotte Phipps, 4 June 1861, Miller Papers.

11. Daniel C. Miller to Charlotte Phipps, 16 May 1861; William Phipps to Charlotte Phipps, 4 June 1861, 8 June 1861, Miller Papers; Wiley, *Life of Johnny Reb*, 36–58; Robertson, *Soldiers Blue and Gray*, 81–101; Ella Lonn, *Desertion during the Civil War* (New York: The Century Co., 1928; reprint, Lincoln: Univ. of Nebraska Press, 1998), 3–6; aggregate data from C.S.R.

12. William Phipps to Charlotte Phipps, 23 May 1861, 4 June 1861; Daniel C. Miller to Charlotte Phipps, 7 June 1861, 28 June 1861, 11 July 1861, 21 July 1861, 4 Aug. 1861, 4 Oct. 1861, Miller Papers; Paul E. Steiner, *Disease in the Civil War: Natural Biological Warfare in 1861–1865* (Springfield, Ill.: Charles C. Thomas, 1968), 3–49; aggregate data from C.S.R.

13. William Phipps to Charlotte Phipps, 23 May 1861, 4 June 1861; Daniel C. Miller to Charlotte Phipps, 7 June 1861, 28 June 1861, 3 July 1861, 7 July 1861, 11 July 1861, Miller Papers.

14. William Phipps to Charlotte Phipps, 8 June 1861; Daniel C. Miller to Charlotte Phipps, 29 June 1861, Miller Papers; Worsham, *Old Nineteenth*, 11; Sullins, *Recollections*, 201; Fisher, *War at Every Door*, 41–44; Colonel D. H. Cummings to General William R. Caswell, 16 July 1861, William G. Brownlow Papers, Special Collections, Hoskins Library, Univ. of Tennessee, Knoxville.

15. *The War of the Rebellion: A Compilation of the Official Records of the Union and Confederate Armies, 1861–1865*, 128 vols. (Washington, D.C.: Government Printing Office, 1880–1901), Series One, 4:374 (hereinafter *O.R.*). For a discussion of Zollicoffer's life prior to the Civil War, see James C. Stamper, "Felix K. Zollicoffer: Tennessee Editor, Politician, and Soldier" (M.A. thesis, Univ. of Tennessee, Knoxville, 1967), 1–68.

16. *O.R.*, Series One, 4:377; Circulars, Letters, Orders Issued by Various Commands, Brigadier General Felix K. Zollicoffer, East Tennessee Brigade, 1861, RG 109, National Archives, Washington, D.C.; General Orders No. 5, 23 Aug. 1861, Orders and Letters Sent, Brigadier General Felix K. Zollicoffer, Aug. 1861–Jan. 1862, RG 109, National Archives, Washington, D.C.; Fisher, *War at Every Door*, 44–48.

17. *O.R.*, Series One, 4:201, 374, 377.
18. Worsham, *Old Nineteenth*, 12; C.S.R. of Daniel C. Miller, #1270, Roll 198; C.S.R. of William Phipps, #1416, Roll 198; Daniel C. Miller to Charlotte Phipps, 21 July 1861, 4 Aug. 1861, and military records of Daniel C. Miller, Miller Papers.
19. Worsham, *Old Nineteenth*, 11–13; aggregate data from C.S.R.; Daniel C. Miller to Charlotte Phipps, 21 July 1861, 4 Aug. 1861, 17 Aug. 1861, Miller Papers.
20. Fisher, *War at Every Door*, 47–48; Atkins, *Parties, Politics*, 253–58; Temple, *East Tennessee*, 224–44; Worsham, *Old Nineteenth*, 12; Sullins, *Recollections*, 202; Alexander, *Thomas A. R. Nelson*, 87–93, 113 n. 13.
21. Fisher, *War at Every Door*, 48–50; Daniel C. Miller to Charlotte Phipps, 7 Aug. 1861, Miller Papers.
22. *O.R.*, Series One, 3:149–50; 4:179–80, 190, 193–94, 402, 404, 406; Zollicoffer to Col. Statham, 14 Sept. 1861, Orders and Letters Sent, Brigadier General Felix K. Zollicoffer, Aug. 1861–Jan. 1862, RG 109, National Archives, Washington, D.C.; Thomas Lawrence Connelly, *Army of the Heartland: The Army of Tennessee, 1861–1862* (Baton Rouge: Louisiana State Univ. Press, 1967), 65; Worsham, *Old Nineteenth*, 13; Daniel C. Miller medical records, Miller Papers.
23. W. J. McMurray, *History of the Twentieth Tennessee Regiment Volunteer Infantry, C.S.A.* (Nashville: Privately published, 1904), 192; Worsham, *Old Nineteenth*, 14; Sullins, *Recollections*, 204. McMurray insists that only "a few volunteers" from the Nineteenth, such as Lieutenant Robert Powell, participated in the raid at Barbourville but better evidence indicates a more substantial presence. D. H. Cummings to his wife, 25 Sept. 1861, Cummings Papers; *O.R.*, Series One, 4:199.
24. McMurray, *Twentieth Tennessee*, 192; Worsham, *Old Nineteenth*, 14; Sheila Weems Johnston, ed., *The Blue and Gray from Hawkins County (Includes Hancock County), Tennessee, 1861–1865* (Rogersville, Tenn.: The Hawkins County Genealogical and Historical Society, 1995), 123–24; Doak Memoirs, 16–17; Sullins, *Recollections*, 204.
25. *O.R.*, Series One, 4:202–3, 418–19, 424–25, 429.
26. Ibid., 4:202–3, 418–19, 429; Worsham, *Old Nineteenth*, 14–15, 182; Doak Memoirs, 17.
27. *O.R.*, Series One, 4:209–13, 409, 423–25, 435, 439, 462–63; 52(2):176; aggregate data from C.S.R.; D. H. Cummings to wife, 3 Oct. 1861, 16 Oct. 1861, Cummings Papers; General Order, 16 Oct. 1861, Orders and Letters Sent, Brigadier General Felix K. Zollicoffer, Aug. 1861–Jan. 1862, RG 109, National Archives, Washington, D.C.
28. *O.R.*, Series One, 4:209–13, 310, 313, 319, 439; 82; Doak Memoirs, 17; Worsham, *Old Nineteenth*, 16–17; McMurray, *Twentieth Tennessee*, 82–84, 119–20, 193–94.

29. Doak Memoirs, 17–18; Worsham, *Old Nineteenth*, 16–17; D. H. Cummings to wife, 27 Oct. 1861, Cummings Papers; *O.R.*, Series One, 4:205–13, 323, 336, 340–41, 347, 483.

30. Fisher, *War at Every Door*, 51–54; *O.R.*, Series One, 4:231, 239, 243, 317, 320, 482–83, 510; 52(1):191–92, (2):209–10, 214, 228–29, 232; Temple, *East Tennessee*, 370–77.

31. Worsham, *Old Nineteenth*, 17–18; Doak Memoirs, 18; *O.R.*, Series One, 4:211, 477–78, 482–83, 486–88, 490, 493, 501–2, 516–17, 520–21, 527, 530–31; 7:712–13, 734; 52(2):201.

32. *O.R.*, Series One, 4:211, 487, 490, 502, 511, 520–21, 524, 527, 530; 7:777–79; 52(2):201, 205; Sullins, *Recollections*, 207–8; McMurray, *Twentieth Tennessee*, 121.

33. *O.R.*, Series One, 4:232, 237, 241–44, 246–47, 511, 515–16, 524, 529–30; 7:686–87, 704–5, 712–13, 760; Temple, *East Tennessee*, 366–411.

34. *O.R.*, Series One, 4:244, 246–47; 7:453, 686, 690, 697, 715, 721–22; Fisher, *War at Every Door*, 57–61.

35. W. W. Etter to Mr. Harvey, 29 Dec. 1861, Private collection of George E. Webb Jr., Rogersville, Tennessee; *O.R.*, Series One, 7:10–12, 458, 474–76, 536–37, 725, 753, 786–87, 946; Connelly, *Army of the Heartland*, 90. A *chevaux de frise* is a log with projecting spikes used to hinder enemy assaults, especially that of cavalry.

36. Aggregate data from C.S.R.; *O.R.*, Series One, 4:517; 7:7, 10, 105, 697, 753; McMurray, *Twentieth Tennessee*, 122; military and medical records of Daniel C. Miller, Miller Papers.

37. *O.R.*, Series One, 7:753; Worsham, *Old Nineteenth*, 19.

38. David H. Cummings to wife, 28 Dec. 1861, Cummings Papers; *O.R.*, Series One, 7:105, 686, 715, 725, 753, 764–66, 780; General Order, 5 Dec. 1861, Orders and Letters Sent, Brigadier General Felix K. Zollicoffer, Aug. 1861–Jan. 1862, RG 109, National Archives, Washington, D.C.

39. *O.R.*, Series One, 4:533; 7:530, 715, 753, 764, 780, 786; 52(2):219; Worsham, *Old Nineteenth*, 18.

40. *O.R.*, Series One, 7:753, 838–39.

41. Ibid., 7:79, 96, 98, 105, 558.

42. Ibid., 7:105; Worsham, *Old Nineteenth*, 19.

43. Worsham, *Old Nineteenth*, 19–20; *O.R.*, Series One, 7:105–6; Cummings's report on the Battle of Mill Springs, 31 Jan. 1862, Cummings Papers.

44. *O.R.*, Series One, 7:106, 111; Worsham, *Old Nineteenth*, 21; Raymond E. Myers, *The Zollie Tree* (Louisville, Ky.: Filson Club Press, 1964), 91, 93–94; Cummings's report on the Battle of Mill Springs, 31 Jan. 1862, Cummings Papers; T. H. Moore, Untitled Journal, Eleanor S. Brockenbrough Library, Museum of the Confederacy, Richmond, Virginia (hereinafter Untitled Journal).

45. *O.R.*, Series One, 7:106, 111; Myers, *Zollie Tree*, 94.

46. *O.R.*, Series One, 7:112; Cummings's report on the Battle of Mill Springs, 31 Jan. 1862, Cummings Papers; Worsham, *Old Nineteenth*, 21–22; Myers, *Zollie Tree*, 94–95.

47. Myers, *Zollie Tree*, 95–96; Worsham, *Old Nineteenth*, 22; Doak Memoirs, 20; Cummings's report on the Battle of Mill Springs, 31 Jan. 1862, Cummings Papers.

48. Cummings's report on the Battle of Mill Springs, 31 Jan. 1862, Cummings Papers; Myers, *Zollie Tree*, 96, 119–29; Doak Memoirs, 21; Worsham, *Old Nineteenth*, 22–23; *O.R.*, Series One, 7:107; Moore, Untitled Journal.

49. *O.R.*, Series One, 7:107; Cummings's report on the Battle of Mill Springs, 31 Jan. 1862, Cummings Papers; Myers, *Zollie Tree*, 97; Worsham, *Old Nineteenth*, 23.

50. *O.R.*, Series One, 7:107, 112–13; Myers, *Zollie Tree*, 97–100; Worsham, *Old Nineteenth*, 22–23; McMurray, *Twentieth Tennessee*, 123, 202.

51. *O.R.*, Series One, 7:104–10, 114, 766, 780; Myers, *Zollie Tree*, 73; Worsham, *Old Nineteenth*, 22.

52. *O.R.*, Series One, 7:107, 112–13; Myers, *Zollie Tree*, 100.

53. *O.R.*, Series One, 7:107–8, 112–13, 115–16; Worsham, *Old Nineteenth*, 23; Myers, *Zollie Tree*, 100–101; Moore, Untitled Journal.

54. Worsham, *Old Nineteenth*, 23–24, 26; Myers, *Zollie Tree*, 105–6; *O.R.*, Series One, 7:109.

55. Worsham, *Old Nineteenth*, 26; Joseph Allan Frank and George A. Reaves, *"Seeing the Elephant": Raw Recruits at the Battle of Shiloh* (New York: Greenwood Press, 1989) offers insight from two sociologists into what Civil War combat was like for raw volunteers (see especially 87–128).

56. *O.R.*, Series One, 7:108–9, 114; Doak Memoirs, 22–23; Worsham, *Old Nineteenth*, 27–28; Myers, *Zollie Tree*, 106–7; Moore, Untitled Journal.

57. *O.R.*, Series One, 7:81, 110–14; Myers, *Zollie Tree*, 107–10.

58. *O.R.*, Series One, 7:110, 114; D. H. Cummings to wife, 22 Jan. 1861, 26 Jan. 1861, Cummings Papers; aggregate data from C.S.R.; Doak Memoirs, 23; Myers, *Zollie Tree*, 110 n. 25; Worsham, *Old Nineteenth*, 29–30, 182–83; McMurray, *Twentieth Tennessee*, 124; Peter Franklin Walker, "Holding the Tennessee Line: Winter, 1861–62," *Tennessee Historical Quarterly* 16 (1957): 248.

59. *O.R.*, Series One, 7:108, 110; Worsham, *Old Nineteenth*, 30; Myers, *Zollie Tree*, 110.

60. *Knoxville Daily Register*, 31 Jan. 1862; 4, 6, 7, 8 Feb. 1862; Daniel C. Miller to Charlotte Phipps, 23 Jan. 1862, Miller Papers; D. H. Cummings to wife, 4 Feb. 1862, Cummings Papers; Myers, *Zollie Tree*, 112.

61. Worsham, *Old Nineteenth*, 31–33; Augustus Henvey Mecklin Diary, 18–19 Feb. 1862, Augustus Henvey Mecklin Papers, Mississippi Department of Archives and History, Jackson, Mississippi (hereinafter Mecklin Diary). For a

detailed account of the Confederate collapse in the Western Theater, see Connelly, *Army of the Heartland*, 103–25.

62. Worsham, *Old Nineteenth*, 31; Daniel C. Miller to Charlotte A. Phipps, 2, 5, 15 Dec. 1861; 2, 23 Jan. 1862; 26 Mar. 1862, Miller Papers.

63. *O.R.*, Series One, 7:904; Worsham, *Old Nineteenth*, 32.

64. Connelly, *Army of the Heartland*, 139–42; Sullins, *Recollections*, 213–17; Worsham, *Old Nineteenth*, 34–35; Mecklin Diary, 1–13 Mar. 1862.

65. Larry J. Daniel, *Shiloh: The Battle That Changed the Civil War* (New York: Simon & Schuster, 1997), 88–90; McMurray, *Twentieth Tennessee*, 125; Worsham, *Old Nineteenth*, 35.

66. Daniel, *Shiloh*, 96–98; Worsham, *Old Nineteenth*, 35; Mecklin Diary, 15–20 Mar. 1862.

67. Connelly, *Army of the Heartland*, 145–52.

68. Ibid., 152–55.

69. Ibid., 155–57; Daniel, *Shiloh*, 123–30; Mecklin Diary, 3–4 Apr. 1862.

70. Wiley Sword, *Shiloh: Bloody April* (New York: William Morrow & Co., 1974), 106; Mecklin Diary, 5 Apr. 1862; Daniel, *Shiloh*, 125, 129; Connelly, *Army of the Heartland*, 156, Worsham, *Old Nineteenth*, 36–37; Frank and Reaves, "*Seeing the Elephant*," 93–94.

71. *O.R.*, Series One, 10(1):454; D. W. Reed, *The Battle of Shiloh and the Organizations Engaged* (Washington, D.C.: Government Printing Office, 1902; reprinted 1913), 84.

72. Connelly, *Army of the Heartland*, 158–65; Doak Memoirs, 25–26. A good, detailed analysis of the early part of the battle is in Sword, *Bloody April*, 141–245, 308–29; and Daniel, *Shiloh*, 143–202.

73. *O.R.*, Series One, 10(1):454; Doak Memoirs, 26.

74. *O.R.*, Series One, 10(1):438–39; 454–55.

75. Ibid., 10(1):339, 445; Sam R. Watkins, "*Co. Aytch*": *A Side Show of the Big Show* (New York: Collier Books, 1962 [1882]), 40–41; Reed, *The Battle of Shiloh*, 85, 88.

76. *O.R.*, Series One, 10(1):438–39, 455; biographical sketch of David H. Cummings, Cummings Papers; Doak Memoirs, 26; Sullins, *Recollections*, 225. The Sunken Road was an old wagon road running parallel to the Federal lines.

77. *O.R.*, Series One, 10(1):455; Daniel, *Shiloh*, 235; Mecklin Diary, 6 Apr. 1862; Frank and Reaves, "*Seeing the Elephant*," 98, 100–110; Reed, *The Battle of Shiloh*, 85.

78. *O.R.*, Series One, 10(1):409, 418, 525–56; Daniel, *Shiloh*, 235–37; Mecklin Diary, 6 Apr. 1862. There is a good deal of controversy over which Confederate officer actually received Prentiss's sword. See Daniel, *Shiloh*, 236; Worsham; *Old Nineteenth*, 39–41; Doak Memoirs, 26–27; Edward O. Cunningham, "Shiloh and the Western Campaign of 1862" (Ph.D. diss., Louisiana State Univ., 1966), 412.

79. O.R., Series One, 10(1):334, 387, 410, 466–67, 550–51, 559, 562, 569, 616; Daniel, *Shiloh*, 245–61; Sword, *Bloody April*, 339–68; Doak Memoirs, 27; Worsham, *Old Nineteenth*, 41; Mecklin Diary, 6 Apr. 1862.

80. O.R., Series One, 10(1):518; Worsham, *Old Nineteenth*, 41–42; Sullins, *Recollections*, 217–20 (quotation 217–18); Sword, *Bloody April*, 372–73; Daniel, *Shiloh*, 262–63; Mecklin Diary, 6 Apr. 1862.

81. Daniel, *Shiloh*, 263; Sword, *Bloody April*, 373–75; Mecklin Diary, 6 Apr. 1862.

82. Daniel, *Shiloh*, 265, 267–69; Sword, *Bloody April*, 376–86.

83. Daniel, *Shiloh*, 269–71, 278–83; Sword, *Bloody April*, 384–87; O.R., Series One, 10(1):388; Mecklin Diary, 7 Apr. 1862.

84. Doak Memoirs, 27–28; Mecklin Diary, 7 Apr. 1862.

85. Daniel, *Shiloh*, 268–69; Sword, *Bloody April*, 388; Mecklin Diary, 7 Apr. 1862.

86. Daniel, *Shiloh*, 271–72; Doak Memoirs, 28; Sword, *Bloody April*, 388–91; Sullins, *Recollections*, 222–24. Sullins remembered the Nineteenth and the Crescent Regiment charging Federal artillery together on the first day's fighting at the Hornet's Nest. However, a careful examination of the historical record and the battlefield leads to the conclusion that the charge could have taken place only on the second day of the battle. Mecklin Diary, 7 Apr. 1862.

87. Daniel, *Shiloh*, 275–77, 283–87; Sword, *Bloody April*, 391–413; O.R., Series One, 10(1):120, 251, 318; Worsham, *Old Nineteenth*, 43; Mecklin Diary, 7 Apr. 1862.

88. Doak Memoirs, 28–29.

89. Daniel, *Shiloh*, 287–91, 294–97; Sword, *Bloody April*, 410–16; Worsham, *Old Nineteenth*, 43; Mecklin Diary, 7–10 Apr. 1862.

90. Worsham, *Old Nineteenth*, 44; Joseph H. Crute Jr., *Units of the Confederate States Army* (Midlothian, Va.: Derwent Books, 1987), 293; Lindsley, *Military Annals*, 374–75.

91. Sullins, *Recollections*, 225–26.

92. O.R., Series One, 10(1):395; "Report of Killed, Wounded & Missing, Battle of Shiloh," Chap. II, vol. 220 1/2, RG 109, National Archives, Washington, D.C.; Doak Memoirs, 29; Sullins, *Recollections*, 226–28; Worsham, *Old Nineteenth*, 44–45.

93. James Lee McDonough, *Shiloh: In Hell before Night* (Knoxville: Univ. of Tennessee Press, 1977), 225.

Chapter 4 ✆ Fortunes of War

1. James M. McPherson, *Ordeal by Fire: The Civil War and Reconstruction*, 2d ed. (New York: McGraw Hill, 1992), 232.

2. O.R., Series One, 10(1):771; Kate Cumming, *Kate, The Diary of a Confederate Nurse* (Baton Rouge: Louisiana State Univ. Press, 1959), 14.

3. Ibid.; Steiner, *Disease*, 161–67; Sword, *Bloody April*, 427; Worsham, *Old Nineteenth*, 48–49.

4. McMurray, *Twentieth Tennessee*, 129; aggregate data from C.S.R.; E. Merton Coulter, *The Confederate States of America, 1861–1865* (Baton Rouge: Louisiana State Univ. Press, 1950), 313–14; Albert Burton Moore, *Conscription and Conflict in the Confederacy* (New York: MacMillan Company, 1924), 13–15; Mecklin Diary, 19 Apr. 1862.

5. Moore, *Conscription*, 16; Wiley, *Life of Johnny Reb*, 129–30.

6. Worsham, *Old Nineteenth*, 46; Moore, *Conscription*, 14; Bailey, *Class and Tennessee's Confederate Generation*, 78–79; Hale, *Third Texas Cavalry*, 28–31; Paul D. Escott, *Many Excellent People: Power and Privilege in North Carolina, 1850–1900* (Chapel Hill: Univ. of North Carolina Press, 1985), 37; Harris, *Plain Folk and Gentry*, 143–44, 241; Crawford, "Confederate Volunteering," 39. For an alternative view, see Roger L. Hart, "Social Structure and Confederate Army Rank in Lincoln County, Tennessee," *Locus* 3 (1991): 157–75.

7. David H. Cummings biography, Cummings Papers; *Knoxville Daily Register*, 20 May 1862; Worsham, *Old Nineteenth*, 46–48; C.S.R. of David H. Cummings, #428, Roll 196; C.S.R. of Francis M. Walker, #1870, Roll 199; C.S.R. of Beriah F. Moore, #1293, Roll 198.

8. Worsham, *Old Nineteenth*, 8–9, 47–48; aggregate data from C.S.R.

9. Worsham, *Old Nineteenth*, 48; C.S.R. of Abraham Fulkerson, #637, Roll 197; C.S.R. of Henry M. Doak, #474, Roll 196; Doak Memoirs, 30; Evans, *Confederate Military History*, 8:448–49; *Knoxville Daily Register*, 22 May 1862.

10. Aggregate data from C.S.R.

11. Ibid.; Eighth Census, 1860, Free Inhabitants, Productions of Agriculture, Slaves, Tennessee, counties of Anderson, Hamilton, Hawkins, Knox, McMinn, Polk, Rhea, Sullivan, Washington.

12. C.S.R. of Thomas Carney, #277, Roll 196; C.S.R. of Nicholas P. Nail, #1338, Roll 198; Eighth Census, 1860, Free Inhabitants, Tennessee, Hamilton County.

13. Aggregate data from C.S.R.; Eighth Census, 1860, Free Inhabitants, Productions of Agriculture, Tennessee, counties of Hamilton, Hawkins, Knox, McMinn, Polk, Rhea, Sullivan, Washington.

14. Connelly, *Army of the Heartland*, 176–77; Worsham, *Old Nineteenth*, 49.

15. O.R., Series One, 15:15, 758, 769–70; Connelly, *Army of the Heartland*, 181; Worsham, *Old Nineteenth*, 50; Mecklin Diary, 23 June 1862.

16. McMurray, *Twentieth Tennessee*, 216; O.R., Series One, 15:9; Worsham, *Old Nineteenth*, 51–52.

17. Worsham, *Old Nineteenth*, 55; Samuel Carter III, *The Final Fortress: The Campaign for Vicksburg 1862–1863* (New York: St. Martin's Press, 1980), 65, 76.

18. Worsham, *Old Nineteenth*, 52–55; O.R., Series One, 15:11; McMurray, *Twentieth Tennessee*, 220; Lindsley, *Military Annals*, 375–76.

19. Worsham, *Old Nineteenth*, 51, 57; McMurray, *Twentieth Tennessee*, 129, 217; Steiner, *Disease*, 193; aggregate data from C.S.R.

20. William Johnston Worsham Memoir, Special Collections, Hoskins Library, Univ. of Tennessee, Knoxville, 84 (hereinafter Worsham Memoir); aggregate data from C.S.R.; *Knoxville Daily Register*, 22 July, 14 Aug. 1862.

21. Aggregate data from C.S.R.; Eighth Census, 1860, Free Inhabitants, Tennessee, counties of Benton, Bledsoe, Campbell, Grainger, Hamilton, Hawkins, Knox, Marion, McMinn, Polk, Rhea, Roane, Smith, Sullivan, Washington.

22. Moore, *Conscription*, 27–28; Coulter, *Confederate States*, 314–15.

23. C.S.R. of Thomas Crawford, #405, Roll 196; C.S.R. of Wade P. Rutledge, #1583, Roll 199; C.S.R. of Powell H. George, #661, Roll 197; C.S.R. of James Smith, #1672, Roll 199; C.S.R. of Nathan Galloway, #647, Roll 197; Eighth Census, 1860, Free Inhabitants, Productions of Agriculture, Slaves, Tennessee, counties of McMinn, Rhea, Sullivan.

24. C.S.R. of F. D. Faulkner, #563, Roll 197; C.S.R. of John McNabb, #1236, Roll 198; C.S.R. of Aaron McNabb, #1235, Roll 198; C.S.R. of William J. Tate, #1775, Roll 199; Eighth Census, 1860, Free Inhabitants, Tennessee, Hamilton County; Moore, *Conscription*, 29–51; Coulter, *Confederate States*, 318–19.

25. O.R., Series One, 15:16, 775–79, 785–86.

26. Worsham, *Old Nineteenth*, 59; Lindsley, *Military Annals*, 376.

27. O.R., Series One, 15:14–19, 76–82, 1124.

28. Ibid., 15:76–78.

29. Ibid.

30. Ibid., 15:76–79.

31. Ibid., 15:34, 77, 104; Worsham, *Old Nineteenth*, 61; Steiner, *Disease*, 204–8. The Federal garrison at Baton Rouge was not in much better shape. Although aware of Breckinridge's presence and imminent attack, Brigadier General Thomas Williams could only count on half of his five-thousand-man force for action. The other half filled the Federal hospitals in the city, suffering, like their Rebel counterparts, from dysentery and malaria. Edwin C. Bearss, "The Battle of Baton Rouge," *Louisiana History* 3 (1962): 95; Steiner, *Disease*, 204–5.

32. For a good description of the battle, see Bearss, "Baton Rouge," 95–97; O.R., Series One, 15:77, 89.

33. For a good description of the battle, see Bearss, "Baton Rouge," 99, 101–10; O.R., Series One, 15:78.

34. Worsham, *Old Nineteenth*, 60–61; O.R., Series One, 15:79; *Official Records of the Union and Confederate Navies in the War of the Rebellion*, Series One, 19:114 (hereinafter O.R.N.).

35. Worsham, *Old Nineteenth*, 60–61; O.R., Series One, 15:79.

36. O.R., Series One, 15:79.

37. Ibid., 15:79, 81, 89; Worsham, *Old Nineteenth*, 61.

38. O.R., Series One, 15:80–81; 800–801; Worsham, *Old Nineteenth*, 61.

39. O.R., Series One, 16(2):771–72, 995; Connelly, *Army of the Heartland*, 207–8.

40. O.R., Series One, 16(2):809–10, 840, 995–97; 17(2):897; 52(2):350; Connelly, *Army of the Heartland*, 239; Worsham, *Old Nineteenth*, 61–62.

41. Worsham, *Old Nineteenth*, 61.

42. Ibid., 62.

43. O.R., Series One, 17 (2):692–93, 701, 897–99; Worsham, *Old Nineteenth*, 63.

44. O.R., Series One, 16(2):809–10, 815, 840–41, 852, 862, 996–97; 17(2):703, 706–7, 900; Worsham, *Old Nineteenth*, 61–64.

45. Worsham, *Old Nineteenth*, 64.

46. O.R., Series One, 17 (2):900; Worsham, *Old Nineteenth*, 64–65; *Chattanooga Daily Rebel*, 1 Oct. 1862; McMurray, *Twentieth Tennessee*, 222.

47. Griffith, *Battle Tactics*, 92–93.

48. The new infantry regiments were the Thirty-Sixth (which was disbanded), the Thirty-Ninth, Fifty-Ninth, and Sixty-Third. Additional East Tennessee Confederate units formed in the first half of 1862 include Captain D. Breck Ramsey's Tennessee Battery, Pickett's Company of sappers and miners, and some independent cavalry companies. Altogether, the region contributed about forty-five hundred new troops to the Confederate war effort, a large portion of the region's available pro-Confederate populace of military age. *Tennesseans in the Civil War*, 1:11, 45–46, 60, 145–47, 251–52, 259–61, 298–300, 305–7; Groce, *Mountain Rebels*, 81–82; Fisher, *War at Every Door*, 68–78.

49. Moore, *Conscription*, 140–61; Coulter, *Confederate States*, 314; Groce, *Mountain Rebels*, 91–94; *Tennesseans in the Civil War*, 1:300–305; Fisher, *War at Every Door*, 110–11, 115–16, 118; O.R., Series One, 16(2):851, 953–55. The new infantry regiments were the Sixtieth, Sixty-First, and Sixty-Second. The new cavalry battalions were the Twelfth and Sixteenth, and the new cavalry regiments were the First (Roger's), First (Carter's), Second, and Fifth. Both the First (Carter's) and the Second Cavalry were organized from preexisting cavalry battalions, and the First (Roger's) formed the basis for the Fifth Cavalry when it was created. Therefore, while new units were being created, many preexisting units were incorporated into the new commands. The pro-Confederate population of military age was now all but exhausted. No new Confederate units would be formed in the region, meaning that conscripts, many if not most of them unionists, would be all the Confederacy could now obtain from East Tennessee.

50. *Tennesseans in the Civil War*, 1:300–303, 305; Lindsley, *Military Annals*, 572–74, 585; Johnston, *Blue and Gray*, 228–30.

51. Aggregate data from C.S.R.; Fisher, *War at Every Door*, 111, 115–16.

52. *Chattanooga Daily Rebel*, 26, 27, 28 Sept. 1862; William Phipps to Charlotte Phipps Miller, 16 Oct. 1862; Daniel C. Miller to Charlotte Phipps Miller, 17 Oct. 1862, 22 Oct. 1862, Miller Papers; aggregate data from C.S.R.

53. O.R., Series One, 20(1):709; aggregate data from C.S.R.; Eighth Census, 1860, Free Inhabitants, Productions of Agriculture, Slaves, Tennessee, counties of Anderson, Bradley, Carter, Greene, Hamilton, Hancock, Hawkins, Johnson, Knox, McMinn, Monroe, Polk, Rhea, Roane, Sullivan, Washington.

54. O.R., Series One, 16(2):930, 933–34, 937–38, 997, 999.

55. Ibid., 16(2):1000–1003; McMurray, *Twentieth Tennessee*, 223.

56. Worsham, *Old Nineteenth*, 65; Daniel C. Miller to Charlotte Phipps Miller, 17, 22 Oct. 1862, Miller Papers.

57. Daniel C. Miller to Charlotte Phipps Miller, 23 Oct. 1862, Miller Papers; O.R., Series Two, 4:899–900; *Knoxville Daily Register*, 15 Oct. 1862; Bailey, *Class and Tennessee's Confederate Generation*, 81; Kenneth Radley, *Rebel Watchdog: The Confederate States Army Provost Guard* (Baton Rouge: Louisiana State Univ. Press, 1989), 14–15.

58. Worsham, *Old Nineteenth*, 65, 67; *Chattanooga Daily Rebel*, 17 Dec. 1862; O.R., Series One, 20(1):658; (2):411, 417–20, 447–48.

59. Thomas Connelly, *Autumn of Glory: The Army of Tennessee, 1862–1865* (Baton Rouge: Louisiana State Univ. Press, 1971), 44 n. 1.

60. Ibid., 45–54.

61. Peter Cozzens, *No Better Place to Die: The Battle of Stones River* (Urbana: Univ. of Illinois Press, 1990), 76.

62. Ibid.; Christopher Losson, *Tennessee's Forgotten Warriors: Frank Cheatham and His Confederate Division* (Knoxville: Univ. of Tennessee Press, 1989), 80–81.

63 McDonough, *Bloody Winter*, 78; Worsham, *Old Nineteenth*, 69; Losson, *Tennessee's Forgotten Warriors*, 80.

64. Cozzens, *No Better Place to Die*, 81–83.

65. Ibid., 85–109.

66. O.R., Series One, 20(1):724, 728; Worsham, *Old Nineteenth*, 71; Unidentified Nineteenth Tennessee Veteran Reminiscence, Stones River Regimental Files, Nineteenth Tennessee, Confederate States of America, Stones River National Battlefield (hereinafter Stones River Regimental Files).

67. O.R., Series One, 20(1):724–25, 728–30; Worsham, *Old Nineteenth*, 71; Stones River Regimental Files.

68. Cozzens, *No Better Place to Die*, 155–56; O.R., Series One, 20(1):715, 726, 729; Stones River Regimental Files.

69. Cozzens, *No Better Place to Die*, 156–57; O.R., Series One, 20(1):725, 729.

70. Cozzens, *No Better Place to Die*, 156–58; O.R., Series One, 20(1):726, 730; Worsham, *Old Nineteenth*, 72.

71. O.R., Series One, 20(1):716, 725, 729; Cozzens, *No Better Place to Die*, 158.

72. For a good discussion of the fighting at the Round Forest, see Connelly, *Autumn of Glory*, 56–61.
73. *O.R.*, Series One, 20(1):676, 725–26, 729; Worsham, Old *Nineteenth*, 72; Stones River Regimental Files.
74. *O.R.*, Series One, 20(1):726, 729–30; Worsham, *Old Nineteenth*, 71–72; Stones River Regimental Files; *List of Casualties in the Second Brigade, First Division. Battle Before Murfreesboro. Nineteenth Regiment*, M836, Roll 4, RG 109, National Archives, Washington, D.C.
75. Cozzens, *No Better Place to Die*, 167, 169, 171, 203; *O.R.*, Series One, 20(1):726; Stones River Regimental Files; Worsham, *Old Nineteenth*, 73.
76. Cozzens, *No Better Place to Die*, 174; Connelly, *Autumn of Glory*, 61.
77. *O.R.*, Series One, 20(1):726, 729; Worsham, *Old Nineteenth*, 73; Cozzens, *No Better Place to Die*, 172–76.
78. Connelly, *Autumn of Glory*, 61–65.
79. Ibid., 66–67.
80. Ibid., 68–69.
81. Cozzens, *No Better Place to Die*, 201–2, 218; J. H. Warner, *Personal Glimpses of the Civil War* (no place or publisher, 1914), 8; Chickamauga and Chattanooga Regimental Files, Nineteenth Tennessee, Confederate States of America, Chickamauga and Chattanooga National Battlefield (hereinafter Chickamauga and Chattanooga Regimental Files).
82. Worsham, *Old Nineteenth*, 76; Daniel C. Miller to Charlotte Phipps Miller, 26 Nov., 6 Dec. 1862, Miller Papers.

Chapter 5 A Nobler Spirit

1. C.S.R. of A. L. Gammon, #648, Roll 197; A. L. Gammon to Landon C. Haynes, 28 May 1863, in C.S.R. of J. K. P. Gammon, #649, Roll 197.
2. A. L. Gammon to Landon C. Haynes, 28 May 1863, in C.S.R. of J. K. P. Gammon, #649, Roll 197.
3. B. F. Moore to Adjutant General's Office, 18 June 1863, in C.S.R. of J. K. P. Gammon, #649, Roll 197.
4. Ibid.
5. A. L. Gammon to Landon C. Haynes, 28 May 1863, in C.S.R. of J. K. P. Gammon, #649, Roll 197.
6. B. F. Moore to Adjutant General's Office, 18 June 1863, in C.S.R. of J. K. P. Gammon, #649, Roll 197.
7. C.S.R. of R. L. Blair, #127, Roll 196; C.S.R. of J. K. P. Gammon, #649, Roll 197.
8. *O.R.*, Series One, 20(1):682–84, 698–99, 701–2; 23(2):677, 684–85, 698, 708, 745–46. For insights into the fighting and recriminations within the Army of Tennessee concerning Bragg's campaign in Kentucky, see *O.R.*, Series One, 16(1):1097–1107.

A good discussion of the bickering of the Army of Tennessee's high command during this period can be found in Connelly, *Autumn of Glory*, 70–92.

9. Connelly, *Autumn of Glory*, 112–16.

10. O.R., Series One, 30(3):48, 276, (4):518–19; 23(1):585.

11. Aggregate data from C.S.R.

12. Ibid.; Eighth Census, 1860, Free Inhabitants, Productions of Agriculture, and Manuscript Returns of Slaves, Tennessee, counties of Bradley, Carter, Claiborne, Cocke, Greene, Hamilton, Hancock, Hawkins, Jefferson, Johnson, Knox, McMinn, Monroe, Polk, Rhea, Sevier, Sullivan, Union, Washington; *Statistics of the United States*, 312, 348.

13. C.S.R. of Wiley B. Moseley, #1326, Roll 198; Eighth Census, 1860, Free Inhabitants, Slaves, Tennessee, Sullivan County; O.R., Series Four, 1:409; Richard Rollins, ed., *Black Southerners in Gray: Essays on Afro-Americans in Confederate Armies* (Redondo Beach, Calif.: Rank and File Publications, 1994), 75. There is an error on page 89 of the Rollins book: no pension records exist for an African American serving in the Nineteenth Tennessee Infantry. Other works mentioning African Americans serving in the Confederate military include the following: Charles Kelly Barrow et al., eds., *Forgotten Confederates: An Anthology about Black Southerners*, Journal of Confederate History Series 15 (1995); Bell I. Wiley, *Southern Negroes, 1861–1865* (New Haven, Conn.: Yale Univ. Press, 1965); Hubert C. Blackerly, *Blacks in Blue and Gray: Afro-American Service in the Civil War* (Tuscaloosa, Ala.: Portals, 1979); Ervin L. Jordan Jr., *Black Confederates and Afro-Yankees in Civil War Virginia* (Charlottesville: Univ. Press of Virginia, 1995).

14. Connelly, *Autumn of Glory*, 113–15.

15. Ibid., 116–19.

16. Steven E. Woodworth, *Jefferson Davis and His Generals: The Failure of Confederate Command in the West* (Lawrence: Univ. Press of Kansas, 1990), 223.

17. Worsham, *Old Nineteenth*, 77.

18. Woodworth, *Jefferson Davis*, 223; Worsham, *Old Nineteenth*, 77.

19. Shattuck, *Shield and Hiding Place*, 39–41, 96, 100–104; G. Clinton Prim Jr., "Born Again in the Trenches: Revivals in the Army of Tennessee," *Tennessee Historical Quarterly* 42 (1984): 250; Drew Gilpin Faust, "Christian Soldiers: The Meaning of Revivalism in the Confederate Army," *Journal of Southern History* 53 (1987): 63–64, 67, 82–83, 86; Samuel J. Watson, "Religion and Combat Motivation in the Confederate Armies," *Journal of Military History* 58 (1994): 29–55; Sidney J. Romero, *Religion in the Rebel Ranks* (Lanham: Univ. Press of America, 1983), 70, 72–75, 128–30.

20. Connelly, *Autumn of Glory*, 121; Worsham, *Old Nineteenth*, 78.

21. O.R., Series One, 23(1):402–6, 583–84, 618–20, 627; Worsham, *Old Nineteenth*, 79; Dieter C. Ullrich, ed., *The Civil War Diaries of Van Buren Oldham: Company G, Ninth Tennessee Volunteer Infantry, C.S.A.* (Martin, Tenn.: D. Ullrich, 1999), 24 June 1863 (hereinafter *Oldham Diary*).

22. Worsham, *Old Nineteenth*, 79.
23. O.R., Series One, 23(1):621–27.
24. Losson, *Tennessee's Forgotten Warriors*, 98; Worsham, *Old Nineteenth*, 80–81.
25. O.R., Series One, 23(1):424; Connelly, *Autumn of Glory*, 133–34, 137.
26. Connelly, *Autumn of Glory*, 164–65; Worsham, *Old Nineteenth*, 82.
27. O.R., Series One, 30(2):26–27; Connelly, *Autumn of Glory*, 148–49, 156–59.
28. Connelly, *Autumn of Glory*, 166–71; O.R., Series One, 30(1):678–79; Chattanooga *Sunday Times*, 2 Aug. 1936; Worsham, *Old Nineteenth*, 83; *Oldham Diary*, 21 Aug. 1863.
29. Worsham, *Old Nineteenth*, 83–84; Chattanooga *Sunday Times*, 2 Aug. 1936; Eighth Census, 1860, Free Inhabitants, Tennessee, Hamilton County; Chattanooga *Sunday Times*, 2 Aug. 1936.
30. O.R., Series One, 30(2):27; Connelly, *Autumn of Glory*, 171–73; O.R., Series One, 30(4):599–600, 610–11; *Oldham Diary*, 27, 29 Aug., 8 Sept. 1863.
31. Cozzens, *This Terrible Sound*, 39, 57; O.R., Series One, 30(3):367; aggregate data from C.S.R.
32. Aggregate data from C.S.R. Although dated, the best general work on the subject is still Lonn, *Desertion during the Civil War*. It was often difficult to determine the difference between a straggler or absentee and a deserter. While Confederate authorities labeled a deserter as "a soldier who left the army with no intention of returning," knowing "intention" was next to impossible. See Coulter, *Confederate States*, 463. In the present study, any soldier listed in the Compiled Service Records as having deserted and not returned, or being absent without leave with no record of returning, is considered a deserter.
33. Lonn, *Desertion during the Civil War*, 3, 6–13, 123; Coulter, *Confederate States*, 463–66; Bailey, *Class and Tennessee's Confederate Generation*, 100, 103–4; Mitchell, *Civil War Soldiers*, 168–73, 177–78; Wiley, *Life of Johnny Reb*, 132–39; Moore, *Conscription*, 359–60.
34. Aggregate data from C.S.R.; Eighth Census, 1860, Free Inhabitants and Products of Agriculture, Tennessee, counties of Anderson, Bedford, Blount, Campbell, Claiborne, Grainger, Hamilton, Hancock, Hawkins, Jefferson, Knox, Marion, McMinn, Meigs, Monroe, Polk, Rhea, Roane, Sullivan, Washington; *Statistics of the United States*, 312, 348. For information on the 1861 regimental average see chap. 2.
35. Aggregate data from C.S.R.; Eighth Census, 1860, Free Inhabitants and Productions of Agriculture, Tennessee, counties of Anderson, Bradley, Hamilton, Hancock, Hawkins, Johnson, McMinn, Monroe, Polk, Rhea, Roane, Sullivan, Washington; *Statistics of the United States*, 312, 348.
36. Aggregate data from C.S.R.; Eighth Census, 1860, Free Inhabitants and Productions of Agriculture, Tennessee, counties of Bradley, Carter, Claiborne, Greene,

Hamilton, Hancock, Jefferson, Johnson, McMinn, Monroe, Polk, Rhea, Sevier, Sullivan, Union, Washington; *Statistics of the United States*, 312, 348.

37. Aggregate data from C.S.R.; Eighth Census, 1860, Free Inhabitants, Productions of Agriculture, and Manuscript Returns of Slaves, Tennessee, counties of Anderson, Bedford, Blount, Campbell, Carter, Claiborne, Grainger, Greene, Hamilton, Hancock, Hawkins, Jefferson, Johnson, Knox, Marion, McMinn, Meigs, Monroe, Polk, Rhea, Roane, Sevier, Sullivan, Union, Washington. See chap. 2 for information on how market-producing household status was determined.

38. C.S.R. of Cyrus Depew, #463, Roll 196; C.S.R. of Lilburn Depew, #464, Roll 196; C.S.R. of Robert E. Depew, #465, Roll 196; C.S.R. of Samuel P. Depew, #466, Roll 196; C.S.R. of W. F. Leath, #1068, Roll 198; C.S.R. of T. J. Leath, #1069, Roll 198; C.S.R. of W. A. Leath, #1070, Roll 198; C.S.R. of J. F. M. Newport, #1345, Roll 198; C.S.R. of Robert P. Short, #1639, Roll 199.

39. Aggregate data from C.S.R. For insight into conditions in East Tennessee during this period, see Bryan, "Civil War in East Tennessee"; Fisher, *War at Every Door*; Campbell, "East Tennessee during the Federal Occupation," 64–80; and Daniel E. Sutherland, ed., *A Very Violent Rebel: The Civil War Diary of Ellen Renshaw House* (Knoxville: Univ. of Tennessee Press, 1996).

40. Coulter, *Confederate States*, 469; Lonn, *Desertion during the Civil War*, 18, 21–27, 93–96; *O.R.*, Series One, 31(3):396; 46(2):828–29, Series Two, 6:680–82, 943, 988; 7:225–26; Series Three, 4:118; C.S.R. of Joseph E. Spurgin, #1700, Roll 199.

41. Lonn, *Desertion during the Civil War*, 97–99; *O.R.*, Series Three, 3:353; aggregate data from C.S.R.

42. Lonn, *Desertion during the Civil War*, 18, 99–124; Moore, *Conscription*, 202, 332, 359–60; Wiley, *Life of Johnny Reb*, 143; Mitchell, *Civil War Soldiers*, 168–70; Richard E. Beringer et al., *Why the South Lost the Civil War* (Athens: Univ. of Georgia Press, 1986), 266, 327, 334, 435, 439.

43. Coulter, *Confederate States*, 467–68; Wiley, *Life of Johnny Reb*, 225–27; Lonn, *Desertion during the Civil War*, 46–60, 123–24; Worsham, *Old Nineteenth*, 77; C.S.R. of Alvin P. Underwood, #1849, Roll 199; C.S.R. of John A. Martin, #1141, Roll 198; aggregate data from C.S.R.

44. *O.R.*, Series One, 30(2):28.

45. Ibid., 30(2):27–31, 43–45, (3):49–50, (4):640–41; *Oldham Diary*, 11–12 Sept. 1863.

46. *O.R.*, Series One, 30(1):447, (2):31; Cozzens, *This Terrible Sound*, 84–85; Worsham, *Old Nineteenth*, 86; *Oldham Diary*, 13 Sept. 1863.

47. *O.R.*, Series One, 30(1):31, 451–53, 922–23, (2):239, (4):645; *Oldham Diary*, 14–15 Sept. 1863.

48. Worsham, *Old Nineteenth*, 88.

49. *O.R.*, Series One, 30(2):32, 77–78, 240, 524.

50. Ibid., 30(2):78; Worsham, *Old Nineteenth*, 88–89. George Maney had been promoted to Brigadier General and brigade command by this time.

51. Worsham, *Old Nineteenth*, 88–89; *O.R.*, Series One, 30(2):77–79, 82–84, 94, 106–7, 118–19, 127, 129–30.

52. *O.R.*, Series One, 30(2):78, 94–95, 118–19, 130–31, 134.

53. Ibid., 30(2):131, 134; Worsham, *Old Nineteenth*, 89–91; "Capt. S. J. A. Frazier," *Confederate Veteran* 30 (Nashville: S. A. Cunningham, 1922): 188; Evans, *Confederate Military History*, 8:480–81; John Euclid Magee Diary, Duke Univ., Durham, North Carolina.

54. *O.R.*, Series One, 30(2):95–96, 99, 102–3, 131–32, 135–36, 362, 401.

55. Ibid., 30(2):95, 99, 102–3, 132, 135.

56. Ibid., 30(2):78, 95–96, 105, 107.

57. Ibid., 30(2):135.

58. Ibid., 30(2):79, 107–8, 112–13, 132.

59. Cozzens, *This Terrible Sound*, 280–81, 283–85; Glenn Tucker, *Chickamauga: Bloody Battle in the West* (Indianapolis: The Bobbs-Merrill Company, Inc., 1961), 190–91; Worsham, *Old Nineteenth*, 91–92.

60. Connelly, *Autumn of Glory*, 208.

61. *O.R.*, Series One, 30(2):52–63, 79, 141; James Longstreet, *From Manassas to Appomattox: Memoirs of the Civil War in America* (Philadelphia: J. B. Lippincott Co., 1896), 448–50, 452.

62. *O.R.*, Series One, 30(2):80, 96–97, 120; Watkins, *"Co. Aytch,"* 96; Longstreet, *From Manassas to Appomattox*, 455–56.

63. Connelly, *Autumn of Glory*, 226–30; Worsham, *Old Nineteenth*, 92.

64. *O.R.*, Series One, 30(2):80, 97, 113, (4):691–92.

65. Connelly, *Autumn of Glory*, 232–34.

66. Losson, *Tennessee's Forgotten Warriors*, 112–13. For a good discussion of Bragg's deteriorating relationship with his generals, see Connelly, *Autumn of Glory*, 235–50, and Woodworth, *Jefferson Davis*, 238–45.

67. Losson, *Tennessee's Forgotten Warriors*, 116–19; Worsham, *Old Nineteenth*, 97; *O.R.*, Series One, 31(2):658–64.

68. Cozzens, *Shipwreck of Their Hopes*, 28–32; Worsham, *Old Nineteenth*, 97; J. P. Edwards, 26 Dec. 1863, chap. 1, vol. 196, Records of Courts-Martial, RG 109, National Archives, Washington, D.C., 234.

69. Connelly, *Autumn of Glory*, 234; *O.R.*, Series One, 31(3):576, 600–601.

70. Connelly, *Autumn of Glory*, 258, 262–63.

71. Cozzens, *Shipwreck of Their Hopes*, 116–19.

72. Connelly, *Autumn of Glory*, 272–74.

73. *O.R.*, Series One, 31(2):673, 676, 679; Cozzens, *Shipwreck of Their Hopes*, 141–42, 196–97; McDonough, *Chattanooga*, 140, 174, 182–85.

74. Worsham, *Old Nineteenth*, 98–99; reports of O. F. Strahl, J. J. Lamb, and A. P. Stewart in C.S.A. Records, Collection 169, Georgia Historical Society, Savannah, Georgia (hereinafter C.S.A. Records).

75. For a detailed analysis of the Federal assault on the Confederate right flank, see Cozzens, *Shipwreck of Their Hopes*, 207–43, 255–56; reports of A. P. Stewart and O. F. Strahl in C.S.A. Records.

76. Worsham, *Old Nineteenth*, 99–100; report of F. M. Walker in C.S.A. Records; Cozzens, *Shipwreck of Their Hopes*, 245.

77. Reports of F. M. Walker and J. S. McCall in C.S.A. Records.

78. Cozzens, *Shipwreck of Their Hopes*, 262–65.

79. Ibid., 169–72, 302–3; report of O. F. Strahl in C.S.A. Records.

80. Reports of F. M. Walker and A. P. Stewart in C.S.A. Records.

81. Cozzens, *Shipwreck of Their Hopes*, 307; Lindsley, *Military Annals*, 198; reports of J. J. Lamb, F. M. Walker, and O. F. Strahl in C.S.A. Records.

82. Cozzens, *Shipwreck of Their Hopes*, 355; reports of F. M. Walker and O. F. Strahl in C.S.A. Records; Worsham, *Old Nineteenth*, 99, 101.

83. Reports of F. M. Walker and O. F. Strahl in C.S.A. Records.

84. Ibid.

85. Reports of O. F. Strahl and A. P. Stewart in C.S.A. Records; Worsham, *Old Nineteenth*, 101.

86. Report of O. F. Strahl in C.S.A. Records; Worsham, *Old Nineteenth*, 101.

87. Worsham, *Old Nineteenth*, 101–2.

88. Report of O. F. Strahl in C.S.A. Records.

89. Ibid.; Worsham, *Old Nineteenth*, 102–3; *O.R.*, Series One, 31(2):753–58.

90. *O.R.*, Series One, 31(2):681, 775–76.

Chapter 6 ✒ A Wise & Just Providence

1. Connelly, *Autumn of Glory*, 281, 290–92; Albert Castel, *Decision in the West: The Atlanta Campaign of 1864* (Lawrence: Univ. Press of Kansas, 1992), 30–31; *O.R.*, Series One, 31(3):795, 850, 860, 883; 52(2):573–74; Watkins, "Co. Aytch," 131–32.

2. C.S.R. of Edward F. Lyons, #1115, Roll 198, and aggregate data from C.S.R.; R. W. Colville to W. E. Colville, 29 Apr. 1864, Civil War Collection (Confederate), Microfilm Accession No. 824, Reel 3, Tennessee State Library and Archives, Nashville, Tennessee. On Confederate manpower problems late in the war, see Moore, *Conscription*, 305–53.

3. Connelly, *Autumn of Glory*, 291; Castel, *Decision in the West*, 31; Worsham, *Old Nineteenth*, 105; Watkins, "Co. Aytch," 126; *Oldham Diary*, 24–26, 28 Dec. 1863.

4. *O.R.*, Series One, 32(2):530–35, 548–49, 591–92, 603–4; Watkins, "Co. Aytch," 126; Connelly, *Autumn of Glory*, 313–14; Worsham, *Old Nineteenth*, 105–6; Lindsley, *Military Annals*, 162, 199, 218.

   For a detailed analysis of Johnston's problems in feeding his army via the Western and Atlantic Railroad, see Jeffrey N. Lash, *Destroyer of the Iron Horse: General Joseph E. Johnston and Confederate Rail Transport, 1861–1865* (Kent, Ohio: Kent State Univ. Press, 1991), 104–30.

5. Worsham, *Old Nineteenth*, 106; Watkins, "Co. Aytch," 128.

6. *O.R.*, Series One, 32(2):662, 700, 716, 752, 755; 52(2):621, 624, 627; Lindsley, *Military Annals*, 162, 199, 298, 310; Melancthon Smith, "Journal of Campaign from Dalton to Atlanta," 18–19 Feb. 1864, Cheatham Papers, Tennessee State Library and Archives, Nashville, Tennessee (hereinafter Smith Journal).

7. Worsham, *Old Nineteenth*, 107.

8. Ibid.; *O.R.*, Series One, 52(2):627–28; Smith Journal, 3 Mar. 1864.

9. Worsham, *Old Nineteenth*, 107.

10. McMurray, *Twentieth Tennessee*, 307; Watkins, "Co. Aytch," 116–17; Smith Journal, 7 Apr. 1864; Losson, *Tennessee's Forgotten Warriors*, 135; Prim, "Born Again in the Trenches," 257–65; Watson, "Religion and Combat Motivation," 31, 34–55; Faust, "Christian Soldiers," 64, 67, 83; Shattuck, *Shield and Hiding Place*, 100–106. While many Rebel soldiers used religion as a bulwark, some historians have stressed the negative impact of religious fatalism on the Southern homefront's morale as hardships intensified and defeat loomed closer. See Shattuck, *Shield and Hiding Place*, 40–44; Beringer et al., *Why the South Lost the Civil War*, chaps. 5, 12, 14. Linderman, in *Embattled Courage*, 252–57, contends that religious fervor among Confederate soldiers declined as defeat became certain.

11. Worsham, *Old Nineteenth*, 108–9; *Oldham Diary*, 1–2 May 1864; Lindsley, *Military Annals*, 278; Watkins, "Co. Aytch," 116–17, 131.

12. Worsham, *Old Nineteenth*, 107–8; Lindsley, *Military Annals*, 199; Smith Journal, 22 Mar. 1864; B. L. Ridley, "Camp Scenes around Dalton," *Confederate Veteran* 10 (1902): 66–67; Ben LaBree, ed., *Camp-Fires of the Confederacy* (Louisville, Ky.: Courier-Journal Job Printing Co., 1898), 48–51; *Oldham Diary*, 22 Mar. 1864.

13. Worsham, *Old Nineteenth*, 108; Watkins, "Co. Aytch," 135–36; *Oldham Diary*, 15, 20, 28, 30, 31 Mar.; 7 Apr. 1864; Smith Journal, 7 Apr. 1864; *O.R.*, Series One, 32(3):865–66, 38(3):676; Castel, *Decision in the West*, 105–12; R. W. Colville to W. E. Colville, 29 Apr. 1864, Civil War Collection (Confederate), Microfilm Accession No. 824, Reel 3, Tennessee State Library and Archives, Nashville, Tennessee.

14. *O.R.*, Series One, 38(4):659–63, 669–70.

15. Connelly, *Autumn of Glory*, 326–29; Castel, *Decision in the West*, 127–28.

16. B. F. Cheatham, "Journal of Military Maneuvers around Atlanta, 1864" (hereinafter Atlanta Military Journal), Cheatham Papers, Tennessee State Library and Archives, Nashville, Tennessee; Connelly, *Autumn of Glory*, 334; Worsham, *Old Nineteenth*, 111; Watkins, "*Co. Aytch*," 128–29; Smith Journal, 7–8 May 1864.

17. O.R., Series One, 38(4):672–77; Worsham, *Old Nineteenth*, 110; Connelly, *Autumn of Glory*, 335–38; Lindsley, *Military Annals*, 189, 199.

There is some confusion as to whether the Nineteenth was present in the action at Dug Gap; see Losson, *Tennessee's Forgotten Warriors*, 144. Worsham claims the regiment was present, and the *Official Records* do not refute his contention.

18. O.R., Series One, 38(3):678; Worsham, *Old Nineteenth*, 111; Connelly, *Autumn of Glory*, 338–40.

19. O.R., Series One, 38(4):686–89, 692–97; Connelly, *Autumn of Glory*, 340–42.

20. O.R., Series One, 38(3):615, 722, 761, 874–75; (4):705–8; Connelly, *Autumn of Glory*, 342; Worsham, *Old Nineteenth*, 112; Losson, *Tennessee's Forgotten Warriors*, 145.

21. O.R., Series One, 38(3):704, (4):706–7, 711; Losson, *Tennessee's Forgotten Warriors*, 144–46; Worsham, *Old Nineteenth*, 112–15; Smith Journal, 15 May 1864.

22. O.R., Series One, 38(3):615, 704, (4):719.

23. Worsham, *Old Nineteenth*, 116; *Oldham Diary*, 17–18 May 1864; Lindsley, *Military Annals*, 163; Watkins, "*Co. Aytch*," 134–35; Smith Journal, 16–17 May 1864.

24. O.R., Series One, 38(3):616, 983–84; *Oldham Diary*, 19–20, 22 May 1864.

25. O.R., Series One, 38(3):705–6; Worsham, *Old Nineteenth*, 117; Cheatham, Atlanta Military Journal; Smith Journal, 25 May 1864; *Oldham Diary*, 23–24 May 1864.

26. O.R., Series One, 38(3):705–6; Cheatham, Atlanta Military Journal; Smith Journal, 26–27 May 1864; *Oldham Diary*, 25–27 May 1864; Worsham, *Old Nineteenth*, 117–18.

27. O.R., Series One, 38(3):706–7; Cheatham, Atlanta Military Journal; Smith Journal, 28 May–8 June 1864; Connelly, *Autumn of Glory*, 355–57.

28. *Oldham Diary*, 17, 20 June 1864; Castel, *Decision in the West*, 272.

29. Cheatham, Atlanta Military Journal; Smith Journal, 10–14 June 1864; *Oldham Diary*, 15–16 June 1864; Worsham, *Old Nineteenth*, 119; Watkins, "*Co. Aytch*," 138–39.

30. Worsham, *Old Nineteenth*, 119; Evans, *Confederate Military History*, 8:533; O.R., Series One, 38(3):654.

31. Losson, *Tennessee's Forgotten Warriors*, 152; Worsham, *Old Nineteenth*, 119–20; Smith Journal, 15–26 June 1864.

32. *O.R.*, Series One, 38(1):68–69.

33. Cheatham, Atlanta Military Journal; Smith Journal, 27 June 1864.

34. *O.R.*, Series One, 38(1):295–96, 632–33, 680; Cheatham, Atlanta Military Journal; Smith Journal, 27 June 1864; McMurray, *Twentieth Tennessee*, 317; B. H. Harmon, "Dead Angle," *Confederate Veteran* 11 (1903): 219; J. L. W. Blair, "The Fight at Dead Angle," *Confederate Veteran* 12 (1904): 533; Lindsley, *Military Annals*, 164, 299; Richard A. Baumgartner and Larry M. Strayer, *Kennesaw Mountain, June 1864: Bitter Standoff at the Gibralter of Georgia* (Huntington, W. Va.: Blue Acorn Press, 1998), 141, 144; Losson, *Tennessee's Forgotten Warriors*, 155.

35. Watkins, "*Co. Aytch*," 158; Worsham, *Old Nineteenth*, 121–22.

36. *O.R.*, Series One, 38(1):680, 693, 698, 711, 724; *Chattanooga Daily Rebel*, 28, 29 June; 1 July 1864; Lindsley, *Military Annals*, 219; W. D. Pickett, "The Dead Angle," *Confederate Veteran* 14 (1906): 458–59; T. H. Maney, "Battle of Dead Angle on Kennesaw Line," *Confederate Veteran* 11 (1903): 159; H. K. Nelson, "Dead Angle, Or Devil's Elbow, Ga.," *Confederate Veteran* 11 (1903): 321; Watkins, "*Co. Aytch*," 157–58, 163; Worsham, *Old Nineteenth*, 121–22.

37. *O.R.*, Series One, 38(1):69, 637, (3):703; Watkins, "*Co. Aytch*," 159–60, 162–63 (quotation on 160); Worsham, *Old Nineteenth*, 121; Cheatham, Atlanta Military Journal; Smith Journal, 27 June 1864; Lindsley, *Military Annals*, 299; *Chattanooga Daily Rebel*, 2 July 1864.

38. Cheatham, Atlanta Military Journal; Smith Journal, 30 June 1864; B. H. Harmon, "Dead Angle," *Confederate Veteran* 11 (1903): 219; Pickett, "The Dead Angle," 459; Maney, "Battle of Dead Angle on Kennesaw Line," 160; Nelson, "Dead Angle, Or Devil's Elbow, Ga.," 321; T. G. Dabney, "Fight at Dead Angle in Georgia," *Confederate Veteran* 14 (1906): 312; Blair, "The Fight at Dead Angle," 533.

39. Cheatham, Atlanta Military Journal; *Chattanooga Daily Rebel*, 4 July 1864; Lindsley, *Military Annals*, 299; Pickett, "The Dead Angle," 459; Maney, "Battle of Dead Angle on Kennesaw Line," 159; Nelson, "Dead Angle, Or Devil's Elbow, Ga.," 321; Worsham, *Old Nineteenth*, 122; Watkins, "*Co. Aytch*," 159.

40. Worsham, *Old Nineteenth*, 123.

41. Edward Hagerman, *The American Civil War and the Origins of Modern Warfare: Ideas, Organization, and Field Command* (Bloomington: Indiana Univ. Press, 1988), xi, 192–98, 207–19, 221–25, 292–98; Thomas Vernon Moseley, "Evolution of the American Civil War Infantry Tactics" (Ph.D. diss., Univ. of North Carolina, 1967), 401; Griffith, *Battle Tactics*, 123–35; Worsham, *Old Nineteenth*, 123.

42. Castel, *Decision in the West*, 228; Griffith, *Battle Tactics*, 128–32.

43. Losson, *Tennessee's Forgotten Warriors*, 150; Griffith, *Battle Tactics*, 135, 153–55, 175, 185; Worsham, *Old Nineteenth*, 123.

44. Losson, *Tennessee's Forgotten Warriors,* 150; Worsham, *Old Nineteenth,* 123–24; Castel, *Decision in the West,* 264.

45. Worsham, *Old Nineteenth,* 204–5.

46. Ibid.; Steiner, *Disease,* 8.

47. Aggregate data from C.S.R.

48. Steiner, *Disease,* 3; H. H. Cunningham, *Doctors in Gray: The Confederate Medical Service* (Baton Rouge: Louisiana State Univ. Press, 1958), 5; Stewart Brooks, *Civil War Medicine* (Springfield, Ill.: Charles C. Thomas, 1966), 6.

49. Steiner, *Disease,* 12–25; Cunningham, *Doctors in Gray,* 184–211; Brooks, *Civil War Medicine,* 106–21; Wiley, *Life of Johnny Reb,* 244–55; Robertson, *Soldiers Blue and Gray,* 148–56.

50. Ledger 4L223 (vol. 1), Fairground Hospital #2 [*sic:* actually #1], Hospital Register, Sept. 1862–Oct. 17, 1863; Ledger 2G384, Fairground Hospital #2, Hospital Register, Feb. 15, 1863–Sept. 22, 1863; Ledger 4L221, Fairground Hospital #1, Hospital Register, Aug. 23, 1863–Nov. 14, 1864; and Ledger 4L223 (vol. 2), Fairground Hospital #2, Hospital Register, Oct. 21, 1863–May 24, 1864, all in Samuel Hollingsworth Stout Papers, Center for American History, Univ. of Texas at Austin (hereinafter Stout Papers).

51. Ibid.

52. Ibid.; Robertson, *Soldiers Blue and Gray,* 161; Cunningham, *Doctors in Gray,* 219–20; Brooks, *Civil War Medicine,* 74–75; Samuel D. Moore, #1936, in Tennessee Confederate Soldiers' Pension Applications, Tennessee State Library and Archives, Nashville (hereinafter Pension Applications).

53. Joseph Britton, #114, George W. Roller, #7654, J. T. Ensminger, #3294, in Pension Applications; C.S.R. of Joseph Britton, #189, Roll 196; C.S.R. of George W. Roller, #1546, Roll 199; C.S.R. of Thomas Ensminger, #538, Roll 197.

54. John Basket, #323, Allen Christian, #9083, Silas Riggins, #365, Hiram D. Hawk, #15924, in Pension Applications; C.S.R. of John Basket, #94, Roll 196; C.S.R. of Allen Christian, #334, Roll 196; C.S.R. of Silas Riggins, #1509, Roll 199; C.S.R. of Hiram D. Hawk, #810, Roll 197.

55. Brooks, *Civil War Medicine,* 90–105; Cunningham, *Doctors in Gray,* 222–27, 236–42; Steiner, *Disease,* 11–12.

56. Cunningham, *Doctors in Gray,* 45–50, 57–62, 66–69, 70–98, 134–62; aggregate data from C.S.R. See especially Glenna R. Schroeder-Lein, *Confederate Hospitals on the Move: Samuel H. Stout and the Army of Tennessee* (Columbia: Univ. of South Carolina Press, 1994).

57. Cunningham, *Doctors in Gray,* 39–42; aggregate data from C.S.R.

58. C.S.R. of A. B. Hodge, #867, Roll 197; C.S.R. of Daniel C. Miller, #1270, Roll 198; C.S.R. of Robert L. Blair, #127, Roll 196; Cunningham, *Doctors in Gray,* 39–43; Radley, *Rebel Watchdog,* 19, 22–30.

59. C.S.R. of Robert J. Tipton, #1821, Roll 199; C.S.R. of Lewis Rowe, #1560, Roll 199; C.S.R. of James Powers, #1445, Roll 198; C.S.R. of Thomas Stevens, #1732, Roll 199; C.S.R. of N. P. Frazier, #622, Roll 197; C.S.R. of Michael Wagner, #1865, Roll 199; C.S.R. of Henry A. Parrott, #1375; C.S.R. of Roll 198, William R. Stewart, #1737, Roll 199; C.S.R. of Richard Lions, #1083, Roll 198; C.S.R. of William H. Patterson, #1385, Roll 198; C.S.R. of H. B. Mullins, #1329, Roll 198; J. T. Barnes, #4633, N. P. Frazier, #4605, Michael Wagner, #2713, Henry A. Parrott, #9381, W. R. Stuart, #12704, Richard Lyons, #1557, William H. Patterson, #6316, H. B. Mullins, #5771, in Pension Applications.

60. Aggregate data from C.S.R.; Cunningham, *Doctors in Gray*, 167; Bailey, *Class and Tennessee's Confederate Generation*, 84–86; David H. Cummings to his wife, 3 Oct. 1861, Cummings Papers.

61. Aggregate data from C.S.R.; McPherson, *For Cause and Comrades*, 80; Watkins, "Co. Aytch," 7. For the tactical problems faced by Civil War commanders and how they sought to solve them, see Albert Castel, "Mars and the Reverend Longstreet: Or, Attacking and Dying in the Civil War," *Civil War History* 33 (1987): 103–14. See also Thomas V. Moseley, "Evolution of the American Civil War Infantry Tactics" (Ph.D. diss., Univ. of North Carolina, 1967). On nineteenth-century honor and southern heritage, see Linderman, *Embattled Courage*, and Grady McWhiney and Perry D. Jamieson, *Attack and Die: Civil War Military Tactics and the Southern Heritage* (Tuscaloosa: Univ. of Alabama Press, 1982).

62. Aggregate data from C.S.R.

63. *O.R.*, Series One, 38(2):514–15, (5):3, 14–25, 29–30, 33–34, 860; 52(2):704–7; Connelly, *Autumn of Glory*, 392; Smith Journal, 1–4 July 1864.

64. *O.R.*, Series One, 38(5):871–73; Connelly, *Autumn of Glory*, 392–97; Worsham, *Old Nineteenth*, 124–25; *Oldham Diary*, 5 July 1864; Smith Journal, 5–9 July 1864.

65. *O.R.*, Series One, 38(5):878–85; Smith Journal, 17 July 1864.

66. *O.R.*, Series One, 38(5):987–88; 39(2):713–14; 52(2):645, 707; *Chattanooga Daily Rebel*, 20 July 1864; Watkins, "Co. Aytch," 156–58, 164; Lindsley, *Military Annals*, 96–97, 165, 310, 426; *Oldham Diary*, 18 July 1864; T. G. Dabney, "When Hood Superceded Johnston," *Confederate Veteran* 22 (1914): 406–7; Cheatham, Atlanta Military Journal; Worsham Memoir, 204; Worsham, *Old Nineteenth*, 125, 127. At least two scholars question the initial negative impact Hood's assumption of command had on Confederate morale in the Atlanta campaign. See Richard M. McMurry, "Confederate Morale in the Atlanta Campaign," *Georgia Historical Quarterly* 54 (1970): 227–43, and William J. McNeill, "A Survey of Confederate Soldier Morale during Sherman's Campaign through Georgia and the Carolinas," *Georgia Historical Quarterly* 55 (1971): 1–25.

67. O.R., Series One, 38(3):630, (5):892–94; John Bell Hood, *Advance and Retreat* (New Orleans: Published for Hood Orphan Memorial Fund, 1880), 162–66; Connelly, *Autumn of Glory*, 439–40.

68. Connelly, *Autumn of Glory*, 432; Castel, *Decision in the West*, 372.

69. *Oldham Diary*, 20 July 1864; Worsham, *Old Nineteenth*, 128; Connelly, *Autumn of Glory*, 439–44.

70. Connelly, *Autumn of Glory*, 442–43; *Oldham Diary*, 20 July 1864.

71. Connelly, *Autumn of Glory*, 443–44; *Oldham Diary*, 29 July 1864; Grand Summary of Casualties in Cheatham's Division during the First Campaign of 1864, to include July 22nd, Cheatham Papers, Tennessee State Library and Archives, Nashville, Tennessee (hereinafter Summary of Casualties).

72. O.R., Series One, 38(3):544, 631, (5):219–20, 898–99; Connelly, *Autumn of Glory*, 445–46.

73. J. B. Heiskell to J. A. Seddon, 28 Feb. 1863, 1 Aug. 1863 (quotation); William G. Swan to J. A. Seddon, 5 Feb. 1863; William J. Hardee to Samuel Cooper, 16 July 1864; O. F. Strahl to J. A. Seddon, 14 Dec. 1863 (quotation), envelope endorsed by Alexander P. Stewart, all in C.S.R. of Francis M. Walker, #1870, Roll 199.

74. Cheatham, Atlanta Military Journal; Smith Journal, 22 July 1864; *Oldham Diary*, 21–22 July 1864; O.R., Series One, 38(3):631; Connelly, *Autumn of Glory*, 444–45, 447; Castel, *Decision in the West*, 385–86, 388–89.

75. O.R., Series One, 38(3):631; Connelly, *Autumn of Glory*, 447–49; Castel, *Decision in the West*, 389–98; Smith Journal, 22 July 1864.

76. Castel, *Decision in the West*, 404–7, 409–10 (quotation on 409); Connelly, *Autumn of Glory*, 449–50; McMurray, *Twentieth Tennessee*, 321; Worsham, *Old Nineteenth*, 128–29, 205–6, 209, 213; *Oldham Diary*, 22 July 1864; Lindsley, *Military Annals*, 377; Summary of Casualties, Cheatham Papers.

77. Castel, *Decision in the West*, 423–24; Daniel C. Miller to Charlotte Phipps Miller, 14 Aug. 1864, Miller Papers; Worsham, *Old Nineteenth*, 190. East Tennessee was under Federal occupation at this time, but a small section around Bristol was still under Confederate control.

78. O.R., Series One, 38(5):987–88; 39(2):832, 837; 52(2):729–30; Connelly, *Autumn of Glory*, 451.

79. Connelly, *Autumn of Glory*, 452–58; *Oldham Diary*, 26–29 July 1864.

80. Connelly, *Autumn of Glory*, 458–62.

81. Ibid., 462–63.

82. Connelly, *Autumn of Glory*, 464–66; Castel, *Decision in the West*, 505–7, 509–22, 524–25; Losson, *Tennessee's Forgotten Warriors*, 192–93.

83. Connelly, *Autumn of Glory*, 466–68; Castel, *Decision in the West*, 522–24, 536–37; Losson, *Tennessee's Forgotten Warriors*, 193; Worsham, *Old Nineteenth*, 190 (quotation).

84. Castel, *Decision in the West*, 548–49; Daniel C. Miller to Charlotte Phipps Miller, 13 Sept. 1864, Miller Papers.
85. Daniel C. Miller to Charlotte Phipps Miller, 13 Sept. 1864, Miller Papers; aggregate data from C.S.R.
86. Daniel C. Miller to Charlotte Phipps Miller, 13 Sept. 1864, Miller Papers; Connelly, *Autumn of Glory*, 470; Castel, *Decision in the West*, 550–51; Losson, *Tennessee's Forgotten Warriors*, 194.

Chapter 7 ✖ A Black Page in the Memory of Our Lost Cause

1. Connelly, *Autumn of Glory*, 470–71.
2. Ibid., 470; Worsham, *Old Nineteenth*, 134 (quotation).
3. Connelly, *Autumn of Glory*, 471–73.
4. Ibid., 476–80; Watkins, "Co. Aytch," 203–4.
5. Worsham, *Old Nineteenth*, 133–34, 211, 214; Connelly, *Autumn of Glory*, 320–21.
6. O.R., Series One, 39(1):582–84, 588, 718–22, 800–803, 806–10; Connelly, *Autumn of Glory*, 480–83.
7. O.R., Series One, 39(1):797–98; Connelly, *Autumn of Glory*, 483–85.
8. Connelly, *Autumn of Glory*, 484, 486–87; H. K. Nelson, "Tennessee, A Grave or a Free Home," *Confederate Veteran* 15 (1907): 508; Enoch Mitchell, ed., "Letters from a Confederate Surgeon in the Army of Tennessee to His Wife," *Tennessee Historical Quarterly* 5 (1946): 174.
9. Worsham, *Old Nineteenth*, 137 (quotation).
10. Connelly, *Autumn of Glory*, 490–91; Worsham, *Old Nineteenth*, 137; H. K. Nelson, "Tennessee, A Grave or a Free Home": 508; O.R., Series One, 45(1):657, 669–70, 730, 752.
11. O.R., Series One, 45(1):669, 730, 736.
12. Ibid., 45(1):657, 670, 1243.
13. Connelly, *Autumn of Glory*, 491; J. P. Young, "Hood's Failure at Spring Hill," *Confederate Veteran* 16 (1908): 25; Watkins, "Co. Aytch," 216–17; Hood, *Advance and Retreat*, 283; O.R., Series One, 45(1):657, 670, 687, 693, 720–21, 730–31, 742, 752–53, 769, 1243, 1254–55.
14. Watkins, "Co. Aytch," 217; O.R., Series One, 45(1):742.
15. Connelly, *Autumn of Glory*, 494; O.R., Series One, 45(1):753–54, 763.
16. O.R., Series One, 45(1):712; Losson, *Tennessee's Forgotten Warriors*, 204; Connelly, *Autumn of Glory*, 495.
17. Losson, *Tennessee's Forgotten Warriors*, 204–5; O.R., Series One, 45(1):670, 742, 753.
18. Losson, *Tennessee's Forgotten Warriors*, 205–7; B. F. Cheatham, "The Lost Opportunity at Spring Hill, Tennessee—General Cheatham's Reply to

Hood," *Southern Historical Society Papers*, 52 vols. (Richmond, 1881), 9:525–26, 537–38.

19. O.R., Series One, 45(1):653, 657, 713; Hood, *Advance and Retreat*, 287–90, 356; Connelly, *Autumn of Glory*, 497–502.

20. O.R., Series One, 45(1):653, 712–13, 731, 753–54, 756; Watkins, "Co. Aytch," 217; Tillman H. Stevens, "'Other Side' in Battle of Franklin," *Confederate Veteran* 11 (1903): 165; Cheatham, "The Lost Opportunity," 530–32; Connelly, *Autumn of Glory*, 502–3.

21. O.R., Series One, 45(1):731; Hood, *Advance and Retreat*, 290; Irving A. Buck, "Military View of the Battle of Franklin," *Confederate Veteran* 17 (1909): 383; Connelly, *Autumn of Glory*, 503–4.

22. O.R., Series One, 45(1):653, 678–79, 708, 736–37; Connelly, *Autumn of Glory*, 503–4.

23. Wiley Sword, *Embrace an Angry Wind; The Confederacy's Last Hurrah: Spring Hill, Franklin, and Nashville* (New York: Harper Collins, 1992), 180, 183–84, 187; Worsham, *Old Nineteenth*, 141; Connelly, *Autumn of Glory*, 504.

24. James Lee McDonough and Thomas L. Connelly, *Five Tragic Hours: The Battle of Franklin* (Knoxville: Univ. of Tennessee Press, 1983), 89; Connelly, *Autumn of Glory*, 504; Lindsley, *Military Annals*, 301, 427.

25. Connelly, *Autumn of Glory*, 504; McDonough and Connelly, *Five Tragic Hours*, 109–14; Worsham, *Old Nineteenth*, 145–46, 190; Lindsley, *Military Annals*, 222, 301, 378; O.R., Series One, 45(1):232, 421.

26. Losson, *Tennessee's Forgotten Warriors*, 225.

27. O.R., Series One, 45(1):239–41; Connelly, *Autumn of Glory*, 504–5; McDonough and Connelly, *Five Tragic Hours*, 115–19; Lindsley, *Military Annals*, 221–23, 302.

28. O.R., Series One, 45(1):241, 354, 395; Worsham, *Old Nineteenth*, 143; Watkins, "Co. Aytch," 219; Connelly, *Autumn of Glory*, 505; McDonough and Connelly, *Five Tragic Hours*, 119.

29. McDonough and Connelly, *Five Tragic Hours*, 129; Worsham, *Old Nineteenth*, 144–46 (quotation, 144); Lindsley, *Military Annals*, 377–78 (quotation).

30. Lindsley, *Military Annals*, 378; Worsham, *Old Nineteenth*, 145.

31. Losson, *Tennessee's Forgotten Warriors*, 224–25.

32. Connelly, *Autumn of Glory*, 505–6.

33. Sword, *Embrace an Angry Wind*, 255–57; Worsham, *Old Nineteenth*, 146.

34. Connelly, *Autumn of Glory*, 506; O.R., Series One, 45(1):344, 356, 654, 658, 667, 684–86, 720–21.

35. Worsham, *Old Nineteenth*, 149–50, 190–91; Lindsley, *Military Annals*, 378; Daniel C. Miller to Charlotte Phipps Miller, 15 Dec. 1864, Miller Papers.

36. Worsham, *Old Nineteenth*, 146; Watkins, "Co. Aytch," 232.

37. O.R., Series One, 45(1):654, 731; Connelly, *Autumn of Glory*, 506–8.

38. O.R., Series One, 45(1):731, 744–46, (2):640–41, 654; Connelly, *Autumn of Glory*, 508.

39. *O.R.*, Series One, 45(1):747, (2):685; Connelly, *Autumn of Glory*, 508–9; Worsham, *Old Nineteenth*, 152 (quotation); Watkins, "*Co. Aytch*," 221–25.

40. Connelly, *Autumn of Glory*, 509; Worsham, *Old Nineteenth*, 152; Charles B. Martin, "Jackson's Brigade in the Battle of Nashville," *Confederate Veteran* 17 (1909): 12 (quotation).

41. *O.R.*, Series One, 45(1):654–55, 709–10, 747–48; Connelly, *Autumn of Glory*, 509–10; Worsham, *Old Nineteenth*, 153–54; M. B. Morton, "Battle of Nashville," *Confederate Veteran* 17 (1909): 18. For a detailed account of the fighting on 15 Dec. 1864, see Stanley F. Horn, *The Decisive Battle of Nashville* (Baton Rouge: Louisiana State Univ. Press, 1956; reprint, Knoxville: Univ. of Tennessee Press, 1978), 77–109.

42. *O.R.*, Series One, 45(1):748–49; Connelly, *Autumn of Glory*, 510–11; Horn, *Battle of Nashville*, 109–12, 118–19; Worsham, *Old Nineteenth*, 154.

43. *O.R.*, Series One, 45(1):749–50, (2):707, 774–75; Connelly, *Autumn of Glory*, 511. For a detailed account of the fighting on 16 Dec. 1864, see Horn, *Battle of Nashville*, 120–44.

44. Worsham, *Old Nineteenth*, 154–55.

45. *O.R.*, Series One, 45(1):689; Connelly, *Autumn of Glory*, 511–12; Horn, *Battle of Nashville*, 144–46.

46. Connelly, *Autumn of Glory*, 511; Horn, *Battle of Nashville*, 146–53; *The Battle Atlas of the Civil War* (New York: Barnes and Noble, 1996; originally published as *Echoes of Gray*, Henry Woodhead, ed. [New York: Time Life Books, 1991]), 267.

47. Aggregate data from C.S.R.

48. Ibid.; Phillip R. Shriver and Donald J. Breen, *Ohio's Military Prisons in the Civil War* (Columbus: Ohio State Univ. Press, 1964), 3–5; Philip Burnham, "The Andersonvilles of the North," *Quarterly Journal of Military History* 10 (1997): 54.

49. Shriver and Breen, *Ohio's Military Prisons*, 5–6; Burnham, "Andersonvilles of the North," 51, 54.

50. Warner, *Personal Glimpses*, 13–15; C.S.R. of Joseph H. Warner, #1896, Roll 199.

51. Warner, *Personal Glimpses*, 16–19.

52. Burnham, "Andersonvilles of the North," 54; aggregate data from C.S.R.; William H. Knauss, *The Story of Camp Chase: A History of the Prison and Its Cemetery Together with Other Cemeteries Where Confederate Prisoners Are Buried, etc.* (Nashville and Dallas: Publishing House of the Methodist Episcopal Church, South, 1906), 376, 384; Frances Ingmire and Carolyn Ericson, *Confederate P.O.W.'s: Soldiers and Sailors Who Died in Federal Prisons and Military Hospitals in the North* (Nacogdoches, Tex.: Ericson Books, 1984), 82, 89.

53. Burnham, "Andersonvilles of the North," 53; aggregate data from C.S.R.

54. Burnham, "Andersonvilles of the North," 53–54; aggregate data from C.S.R.

55. Burnham, "Andersonvilles of the North," 54; Warner, *Personal Glimpses*, 18–19 (quotation).

56. C.S.R. of Jacob Williford, #1954, Roll 199; C.S.R. of Henry S. Burem, #229, Roll 196.

57. Burnham, "Andersonvilles of the North," 52; Baxter Smith, W. A. Williamson, and J. N. McCain to Charles W. Hill, 5 Dec. 1864, in C.S.R. of Amos C. Smith, #1667, Roll 199; O.R. Series Two, (8):41, 87–88.

58. Aggregate data from C.S.R.; Sutherland, *A Very Violent Rebel*, xx.

59. O.R., Series One, 45(1):731, 750; Horn, *Battle of Nashville*, 159–60; Worsham, *Old Nineteenth*, 156.

60. Worsham, *Old Nineteenth*, 156–57 (quotation), 191.

61. Ibid., 241; O.R., Series One, 45(1):724, 726–27, 729, 757.

62. O.R., Series One, 45(1):673; Lindsley, *Military Annals*, 378; Worsham, *Old Nineteenth*, 158 (quotation).

63. Connelly, *Autumn of Glory*, 512; Worsham, *Old Nineteenth*, 158; O.R., Series One, 45(1):729, (2):351, 423, 721.

64. Worsham, *Old Nineteenth*, 158–60, 163–64; Watkins, "Co. Aytch," 225; Lindsley, *Military Annals*, 190–92, 223–24, 378; O.R., Series One, 45(1):164, 673, 727–28, 758–59.

65. Worsham, *Old Nineteenth*, 160; O.R., Series One, 45(1):567, 603–7, 727–28, 757–59, (2):331; Lindsley, *Military Annals*, 190–92, 223–24, 378.

66. Worsham, *Old Nineteenth*, 160 (quotation); Lindsley, *Military Annals*, 378.

67. O.R., Series One, 45(1):608, 727, 758, 772; Worsham, *Old Nineteenth*, 160–61.

68. O.R., Series One, 45(1):608, 727–28, 758, 772; Lindsley, *Military Annals*, 378; Worsham, *Old Nineteenth*, 161 (quotation), 192.

69. Worsham, *Old Nineteenth*, 161–62; O.R., Series One, 45(1):674, 728, 732.

70. O.R., Series One, 45(2):778–79, 781; Watkins, "Co. Aytch," 230; Luke W. Finlay, "Another Report on Hood's Campaign," *Confederate Veteran* 15 (1907): 406; Connelly, *Autumn of Glory*, 513; Worsham, *Old Nineteenth*, 166 (quotation).

71. O.R., Series One, 45(2):771, 778–79, 781–82, 784–85, 791–96, 800–805; 47(2):1043, 1060, (3):716; Connelly, *Autumn of Glory*, 513; Worsham, *Old Nineteenth*, 166.

72. Connelly, *Autumn of Glory*, 514; Worsham, *Old Nineteenth*, 167.

73. O.R., Series One, 47(1):1082–83, (2):1174, 1184, 1186–87, 1199, 1206–10, 1224, 1238, 1246, 1257–59, 1261–62, 1269, 1272, 1274–75, 1314, 1319; Connelly, *Autumn of Glory*, 526; Worsham, *Old Nineteenth*, 171–72 (quotation).

74. Worsham, *Old Nineteenth*, 173, 193; Connelly, *Autumn of Glory*, 527–28; Nathaniel Cheairs Hughes Jr., *Bentonville: The Final Battle of Sherman and Johnston* (Chapel Hill: Univ. of North Carolina Press, 1996), 171, 207.

75. Connelly, *Autumn of Glory*, 528–31; Worsham, *Old Nineteenth*, 174–75; *Tennesseans in the Civil War*, 1:174, 193, 200; Evans, *Confederate Military History*, 8:176–77.

76. Connelly, *Autumn of Glory*, 531–34; Losson, *Tennessee's Forgotten Warriors*, 248; Worsham, *Old Nineteenth*, 175–76 (quotation).

77. Connelly, *Autumn of Glory*, 534–35; Worsham, *Old Nineteenth*, 176–78.

78. Bailey, *Class and Tennessee's Confederate Generation*, 86, 99, 103–4.

79. Worsham, *Old Nineteenth*, 175, 194; aggregate data from C.S.R.; Eighth Census, 1860, Free Inhabitants, Tennessee, counties of Greene, Hamilton, Hawkins, Knox, McMinn, Monroe, Polk, Rhea, Roane, Sullivan, Washington; *Statistics of the United States*, 312, 348. See chap. 2 of this study for the 1861 regimental sample's averages of real and personal property.

80. C.S.R. of Richard W. Colville, #357, Roll 196; C.S.R. of William Phipps, #1416, Roll 198; C.S.R. of John M. McDermott, #1196, Roll 198; Eighth Census, 1860, Free Inhabitants, Productions of Agriculture, Slaves, Tennessee, counties of Hawkins, Monroe, Rhea.

81. Aggregate data from C.S.R.; Eighth Census, 1860, Free Inhabitants, Productions of Agriculture, Slaves, Tennessee, counties of Greene, Hamilton, Hawkins, Knox, McMinn, Polk, Rhea, Roane, Sullivan, Washington.

82. McPherson, *For Cause and Comrades*, 21–25, 85–89, 95, 114–16, 134–37, 148–51, 170; Mitchell, *Civil War Soldiers*, 168, 173–77.

83. Historian Tracy McKenzie noted an overabundance of white labor in East Tennessee during the era, which would have hurt the chances of landless and unskilled members of the remaining regiment in finding employment in their old communities. See McKenzie, "Wealth," 269; aggregate data from C.S.R.; Eighth Census, 1860, Free Inhabitants, Tennessee, counties of Greene, Hamilton, Hawkins, Knox, McMinn, Polk, Rhea, Roane, Sullivan, Washington.

Chapter 8 ✎ There May Be Some Chance

1. Daniel Miller to Charlotte Phipps Miller, 1 Dec. 1866, Miller Papers.

2. Ibid., 1 Dec. 1866, 28 Dec. 1865, 25 Feb. 1866, 11 Mar. 1866; Fisher, *War at Every Door*, 167–68.

3. Daniel Miller to Charlotte Phipps Miller, 8 Mar. 1867, Miller Papers.

4. Ibid., 7 May 1867.

5. Ibid., 7 May 1867, 5 July 1867, 3 Aug. 1867.

6. Ibid., 17, 19 Aug. 1867; 7 Oct. 1867, 22 Aug. 1869, 4 Sept. 1869; Groce, *Mountain Rebels*, 150–51.

7. For a general overview of conditions in postwar East Tennessee, see the following works: Groce, *Mountain Rebels*, 127–51; Fisher, *War at Every Door*, 154–77; Bryan, "The Civil War in East Tennessee," 160–86; Thomas B. Alexander, *Political Reconstruction in Tennessee* (Nashville: Vanderbilt Univ. Press, 1950), 58–68.

8. Groce, *Mountain Rebels*, 129; Fisher, *War at Every Door*, 135; *Knoxville Whig and Rebel Ventilator*, 11 Nov. 1863, 9 Apr. 1864.

9. Groce, *Mountain Rebels*, 132–45; Fisher, *War at Every Door*, 156; Alexander, *Political Reconstruction*, 58–59.

10. Groce, *Mountain Rebels*, 132–33; Samuel Milligan to Andrew Johnson, 1 Sept. 1865, *Johnson Papers*, 9:41.

11. Petition to Brownlow, 22 May 1865, William G. Brownlow Papers, Tennessee State Library and Archives, Nashville, Tennessee; *Knoxville Whig and Rebel Ventilator*, 7 June 1865.

12. Bird G. Manard to Thomas A. R. Nelson, 28 June 1865, Nelson Papers, McClung Collection, Lawson McGhee Library, Knoxville, Tennessee.

13. "Special Order No. 1," 24 July 1865, Nelson Papers.

14. Doak Memoirs, 46–50.

15. Sutherland, *A Very Violent Rebel*, 193–94, quote on 193.

16. *Knoxville Whig and Rebel Ventilator*, 20 Sept. 1865.

17. Fisher, *War at Every Door*, 158; Allen W. Trelease, *White Terror: The Ku Klux Klan Conspiracy and Southern Reconstruction* (New York: Harper & Row, 1971), 3–46.

18. Fisher, *War at Every Door*, 158–59; Trelease, *White Terror*, 27; *Knoxville Whig*, 12 June 1867.

19. Fisher, *War at Every Door*, 159; Martin L. Helton to DeWitt Senter, 5 June 1869, DeWitt C. Senter Papers, Tennessee State Library and Archives, Nashville, Tennessee.

20. Nashville *Daily Press and Times*, 19 Apr. 1867; H. Wax to "Cousin App," 25 Feb. 1865, H. G. Wax Papers, Special Collections Library, Univ. of Tennessee, Knoxville, Tennessee.

21. Sullins, *Recollections*, 195, 262–95.

22. Charles R. Vance to Andrew Johnson, 30 June 1865, Amnesty Papers (M1003, Roll 51), Tenn.; amnesty oath of Joseph A. Conley, 20 May 1865, Amnesty Papers (M1003, Roll 48), Tenn.; amnesty oath of J. G. Deaderick, 14 July 1865, Amnesty Papers (M1003, Roll 48), Tenn.; John M. Morrow to Andrew Johnson, 21 Aug. 1865, Amnesty Papers (M1003, Roll 50), Tenn.; Charles St. John to Andrew Johnson, 19 July 1865, Amnesty Papers (M1003, Roll 51), Tenn.; James P. Snapp to Andrew Johnson, 27 June 1865, Amnesty Papers (M1003, Roll 51), Tenn.; A. L. Gammon to Andrew Johnson, 28 June 1865, Amnesty Papers (M1003, Roll 49), Tenn.; James A. Rhea to Andrew Johnson, 27 June 1865, Amnesty Papers (M1003, Roll 50), Tenn.; John L. Rhea to Andrew Johnson, 10 May 1865, Amnesty Papers (M1003, Roll 50), Tenn.; amnesty oath of William P. Vestal, 13 Nov. 1865, Amnesty Papers (M1003, Roll 51), Tenn., RG 94, National Archives, Washington, D.C.

23. Groce, *Mountain Rebels*, 145–49; Fisher, *War at Every Door*, 163–64.

24. Eighth Census, 1860, Free Inhabitants, Tennessee, counties of Bedford, Blount, Carter, Greene, Hamilton, Hawkins, Johnson, Knox, McMinn, Monroe, Polk,

Rhea, Roane, Sullivan, Washington; Ninth Census, 1870, Inhabitants, Tennessee, counties of Bedford, Bradley, Carter, Cumberland, Davidson, Greene, Hamilton, Hancock, Hawkins, Jefferson, Johnson, Knox, Lincoln, Marion, McMinn, Polk, Rhea, Roane, Sullivan, Washington; aggregate data from C.S.R.; Worsham, *Old Nineteenth*, 204–5; Groce, *Mountain Rebels*, 149.

25. Aggregate data from Pension Applications.

26. Obituary of D. A. Wilkins, *Confederate Veteran* 6 (1898): 133; Obituary of W. W. Etter, *Confederate Veteran* 6 (1898): 277; John C. Cates, "Disaster at Zollicoffer Barracks," *Confederate Veteran* 9 (1901): 554; Obituary of Capt. J. F. Tatham, *Confederate Veteran* 13 (1905): 514; Obituary of A. Clarke Brewer, *Confederate Veteran* 15 (1907): 240ii; "Deaths in Camp in McKinny, Tex.," *Confederate Veteran* 15 (1907): 511; "Eight Members of a Georgia Camp," *Confederate Veteran* 16 (1908): 285; A. J. Hord advertisement, *Confederate Veteran* 19 (1911): 100; Obituary for James Howe Moore, *Confederate Veteran* 26 (1918): 263; Obituary for Capt. Arthur V. Deaderick, *Confederate Veteran* 37 (1929): 386–87; Evans, *Confederate Military History*, 8:532–34, 681–82.

27. Bailey, *Class and Tennessee's Confederate Generation*, 89–90, 104–6, 118–22, 127–28.

28. Eighth Census, 1860, Free Inhabitants, Tennessee, counties of Bedford, Blount, Carter, Greene, Hamilton, Hawkins, Johnson, Knox, McMinn, Monroe, Polk, Rhea, Roane, Sullivan, Washington; Ninth Census, 1870, Inhabitants, Tennessee, counties of Bedford, Bradley, Carter, Cumberland, Davidson, Greene, Hamilton, Hancock, Hawkins, Jefferson, Johnson, Knox, Lincoln, Marion, McMinn, Polk, Rhea, Roane, Sullivan, Washington.

29. Eighth Census, 1860, Free Inhabitants, Tennessee, counties of Bedford, Carter, Greene, Hamilton, Hawkins, Jefferson, Johnson, Knox, McMinn, Monroe, Polk, Rhea, Roane, Sullivan, Washington; Ninth Census, 1870, Inhabitants, Tennessee, counties of Bedford, Blount, Bradley, Carter, Cumberland, Greene, Hamilton, Hawkins, Johnson, Knox, McMinn, Polk, Rhea, Roane, Sullivan, Washington; McKenzie, *One South*, 96.

30. Eighth Census, 1860, Free Inhabitants, Tennessee, counties of Greene, Hawkins, McMinn, Rhea, Sullivan, Washington; Ninth Census, 1870, Inhabitants, Tennessee, counties of Greene, Hancock, Hawkins, Jefferson, Knox, McMinn, Rhea, Sullivan, Washington; McKenzie, *One South*, 89, 96, 152, 154–55, 172, 186–87.

31. Eighth Census, 1860, Free Inhabitants, Slaves, Tennessee, counties of Hawkins, McMinn, Rhea, Sullivan, Washington; Ninth Census, 1870, Inhabitants, Tennessee, counties of Hancock, Hawkins, Knox, McMinn, Rhea, Sullivan, Washington.

32. W. A. Owens to Frank Moses, 16 July 1909, in Madison Carrol, #683; M. S. Holloway to State Board of Pensions, 9 Feb. 1892, in W. J. McLarrin, #849; James A. Love, #7008, all in Pension Applications.

33. "Capt. S. J. A. Frazier," *Confederate Veteran* 30 (1922): 188; J. W. Godwin, "W. B. Tate, Donor to Comrades," *Confederate Veteran* 3 (1895): 300; Obituary for William Brown Tate, *Confederate Veteran* 12 (1904): 191; Evans, *Confederate Military History*, 8:427–28, 480–81; Biographical Sketch of Daniel C. Miller, Miller Papers.

34. *Goodspeed's History of Tennessee*, 1311, 1237–38, 1052–53, 1206; Evans, *Confederate Military History*, 8: 448–49, 532–34; Obituary of Abram Fulkerson, *Confederate Veteran* 11 (1903): 124–25; Obituary of Col. Charles Robertson Vance, *Confederate Veteran* 20 (1912): 80; Taylor, *Historic Sullivan*, 201–2.

35. *Goodspeed's History of Tennessee*, 1227–28, 1236.

36. *Confederate Veteran* 1 (1893): 343; "Confederates in East Tennessee," *Confederate Veteran* 3 (1895): 277; J. W. Lillard, "Confederates in East Tennessee," *Confederate Veteran* 5 (1897): 593–94; George Moorman, "Reorganization of Georgia Division," *Confederate Veteran* 8 (1900): 17–18; J. C. Hodges, "Model Camp at Morristown, Tenn.," *Confederate Veteran* 15 (1907): 28–29; James L. Douthat, *Roster of Upper East Tennessee Confederate Veterans* (Signal Mountain, Tenn.: Mountain Press, Inc., no date); Groce, *Mountain Rebels*, 156–57; Anne Cody, *History of the Tennessee Division of the United Daughters of the Confederacy* (Nashville: no publisher or date), 259–336; *Minutes of the One Hundred and Ninth Annual General Convention of the United Daughters of the Confederacy Incorporated Held at Richmond, Virginia, October 31–November 5, 2002* (Richmond: no publisher or date), 207; *Minutes of the One Hundred and Fifth and One Hundred and Sixth Annual Conventions, Tennessee Division 2000–2002, United Daughters of the Confederacy* (Nashville: no publisher or date), 27–28; *Webpage of the Sons of Confederate Veterans*, http://www.scv.org., accessed Apr. 15, 2003.

37. Cody, *United Daughters of the Confederacy*, 323; "Distinguished Surviving Confederates," *Confederate Veteran* 19 (1911): 420–21. For a discussion of how the South attempted to come to grips with the Confederacy's defeat, see Gaines M. Foster, *Ghosts of the Confederacy: Defeat, The Lost Cause, and the Emergence of the New South, 1865 to 1913* (New York: Oxford Univ. Press, 1987), and Charles Regan Wilson, *Baptized in Blood: The Religion of the Lost Cause, 1865–1920* (Athens: Univ. of Georgia Press, 1980).

Bibliography ✄

Primary Sources

Manuscripts

Eleanor S. Brockenbrough Library, Museum of the Confederacy, Richmond, Virginia
> T. H. Moore, Untitled Journal

Chickamauga and Chattanooga National Military Park, Longstreet/Thomas Library Unit Files
> J. H. Warner, *Personal Glimpses of the Civil War: Nineteenth Tennessee.* No place or publisher, 1914.

Cumberland Gap National Historical Park
> Letters of James C. Holt

Duke Univ., Durham, North Carolina
> John Euclid Magee Diary

Georgia Historical Society, Savannah, Georgia
> Report of J. J. Lamb. C.S.A. Records, Collection 169.
> Report of J. S. McCall. C.S.A. Records, Collection 169.
> Report of Alexander P. Stewart. C.S.A. Records, Collection 169.
> Report of O. F. Strahl. C.S.A. Records, Collection 169.
> Report of F. M. Walker. C.S.A. Records, Collection 169.

Lawson McGhee Library, McClung Collection, Knoxville, Tennessee
> T. A .R. Nelson Papers

National Archives, Washington, D.C.
> Amnesty Papers (M1003, Rolls 48–51), Tenn., RG 94.

Circulars, Letters, Orders Issued by Various Commands, Brigadier General Felix K. Zollicoffer, East Tennessee Brigade, 1861, RG 109

Compiled Service Records of Confederate Soldiers Who Served in Organizations from the State of Tennessee, M268, Rolls 196–99, RG 109
> Tennessee Muster Rolls, RG 109 (microfilm copy).
> Eighth Census, 1860. Manuscript Returns of Free Inhabitants, Tennessee.
> Eighth Census, 1860. Manuscript Returns of Productions of Agriculture, Tennessee.
> Eighth Census, 1860. Manuscript Returns of Slaves, Tennessee.
> Eighth Census, 1860. Manuscript Returns of Social Statistics, Tennessee.

List of Casualties in the Second Brigade, First Division. Battle Before Murfreesboro. Nineteenth Regiment. M836, Roll 4, RG 109

Ninth Census, 1870. Manuscript Returns of Inhabitants, Tennessee.
Ninth Census, 1870. Manuscript Returns of Productions of Agriculture,
    Tennessee.
Ninth Census, 1870. Manuscript Returns of Social Statistics, Tennessee.
Orders and Letters Sent, Brigadier General Felix K. Zollicoffer, Aug. 1861–
    Jan. 1862, RG109
Private Collection of Richard Cummings, St. Louis, Missouri
    Col. D. H. Cummings and Family Personal Papers
Private Collection of George E. Webb Jr., Rogersville, Tennessee
    W. W. Etter Letter
Samuel Hollingsworth Stout Papers. Center for American History,
    Univ. of Texas at Austin
Special Collections, Hoskins Library, Univ. of Tennessee, Knoxville.
    William G. Brownlow Papers
    Confederate History of Hawkins County, Tennessee
    Rhea Family Papers
    H. G. Wax Papers
    William Johnston Worsham Memoirs
Special Collections Library, Univ. of Virginia, Charlottesville
    Charlotte A. (Phipps) Miller and Daniel Chambers Miller Papers (#10287)
Stone's River National Battlefield, Regimental Files
    Miscellaneous papers relating to Nineteenth Tennessee
Tennessee State Library and Archives, Nashville
    Antebellum civil district maps for the counties of Hamilton, Hawkins,
    Knox, Polk, Rhea, Sullivan, Polk
    William G. Brownlow Papers
Journal of B. F. Cheatham, B.F. Cheatham Papers
    Civil War Veterans Pension Records
    Henry Melville Doak Memoirs
    History of Company D, Nineteenth Tennessee Regiment
    Miscellaneous military records of Nineteenth Tennessee Regiment
    DeWitt C. Senter Papers
Journal of Melancthon Smith, B.F. Cheatham Papers
    Summary of Casualties, B.F. Cheatham Papers

Websites

Fulkerson Family Papers. Webpage of the Virginia Military Institute Archives,
    Lexington, Virginia, http://www.vmi.edu/archives/Manuscripts/ms 0363.html,
    accessed December 23, 1998.
Webpage of the Sons of Confederate Veterans, http://www.scv.org, accessed
    Apr. 15, 2003.

Published Works

Caldwell, Joshua W. *Sketches of the Bench and Bar of Tennessee*. Knoxville: Ogden Brothers & Co., printers, 1898.

Confederate Veteran. 40 vols. Nashville: S. A. Cunningham, 1883–1932.

DeBow, J. D. B. *The Seventh Census of the United States: 1850—An Appendix*. Washington, D.C.: Robert Armstrong, Public Printer: 1853.

Dyer, Gustavus W., and John Trotwood Moore, comps. *The Tennessee Civil War Veterans Questionnaires*. 5 vols. Easley, S.C.: Southern Historical Press, 1985.

Evans, Clement A., ed. *Confederate Military History, Extended Edition*. 12 vols. Atlanta: Confederate Publishing Company, 1899.

Graf, LeRoy P., Ralph W. Haskins, and Paul H. Bergeron, eds. *The Papers of Andrew Johnson*. 16 vols. Knoxville: Univ. of Tennessee Press, 1967–2000.

A History of Tennessee. Nashville: Goodspeed's Publishing Co., 1886; reprint, *Goodspeed's History of Tennessee: Containing Historical and Biographical Sketches of Thirty East Tennessee Counties*. Nashville: Charles and Randy Elder Booksellers, 1972.

Hood, John Bell. *Advance and Retreat*. New Orleans: Published for Hood Orphan Memorial Fund, 1880.

Horn, Stanley F., ed. and comp. *Tennessee's War: 1861–1865, Described by Participants*. Nashville: Tennessee Civil War Centennial Commission, 1965.

Humes, Thomas W. *The Loyal Mountaineers of Tennessee*. Knoxville, Tenn.: Ogden Brothers & Co., 1888.

Johnson, Robert Underwood, and Clarence Clough Buel, eds. *Battles and Leaders of the Civil War: Being for the most part contributions by Union and Confederate officers*. 4 vols. New York: Century Company, 1884–87.

Kennedy, Joseph C. G. *Agriculture of the United States in 1860; Compiled from the Original Returns of the Eighth Census*. Washington, D.C.: Government Printing Office, 1864.

Killebrew, J. B. *Introduction to the Resources of Tennessee*. Nashville: Tavel, Eastman & Howell, 1874; reprint, Spartanburg: The Reprint Company, 1974.

Lindsley, John B. *Military Annals of Tennessee, Confederate*. Nashville: J. M. Lindsley & Co., 1886.

Longstreet, James. *From Manassas to Appomattox: Memoirs of the Civil War in America*. Philadelphia: J. B. Lippincott Co., 1896.

Miller, Charles A. *The Official and Political Manual of the State of Tennessee*. Nashville: Marshall and Bruce, 1890; reprint, Spartanburg: The Reprint Company, 1974.

Minutes of the One Hundred and Fifth and One Hundred and Sixth Annual Conventions, Tennessee Division 2000–2002, United Daughters of the Confederacy. Nashville: No publisher or date.

Minutes of the One Hundred and Ninth Annual General Convention of the United Daughters of the Confederacy Incorporated Held at Richmond, Virginia, October 31–November 5, 2002. Richmond: No publisher or date.

Southern Historical Papers. 52 vols., Richmond, 1881.

Statistics of the United States (Including Mortality, Property, &c.) in 1860; Compiled from the Original Returns and Being the Final Exhibit of the Eighth Census, under the direction of the Secretary of Interior. Washington, D.C.: Government Printing Office, 1866.

Sullins, David. *Recollections of an Old Man, Seventy Years in Dixie, 1827–1897.* Bristol, Tenn.: King Printing Co., 1910.

Sutherland, Daniel E., ed. *A Very Violent Rebel: The Civil War Diary of Ellen Renshaw House.* Knoxville: Univ. of Tennessee Press, 1996.

Temple, Oliver P. *East Tennessee and the Civil War.* Cincinnati: The Robert Clarke Company Publishers, 1899.

Tennessee Historical Records Survey. *Civil War Records of Tennessee.* 3 vols. Nashville: Historical Records Survey, 1939.

Tennesseans in the Civil War: A Military History of Confederate and Union Units with Available Rosters of Personnel. Part 1. Nashville: Civil War Centennial Commission, 1964.

Ullrich, Dieter C., ed. *The Civil War Diaries of Van Buren Oldham: Company G, Ninth Tennessee Volunteer Infantry, C.S.A.* Martin, Tenn.: D. Ullrich, 1999.

United States War Department, comp. *The War of the Rebellion: A Compilation of the Official Records of the Union and Confederate Armies, 1861–1865.* 128 vols. Washington, D.C.: Government Printing Office, 1880–1901.

Watkins, Sam R. *"Co. Aytch": A Side Show of the Big Show.* New York: Collier Books, 1962 [1882].

Whitman, Walt. *The Collected Writings of Walt Whitman.* vol. 1, *Prose Works 1892: Specimen Days,* edited by Gay Wilson Allen and Sculley Bradley. New York: New York Univ. Press, 1963.

Worsham, W. J. *Old Nineteenth Tennessee Regiment, CSA.* Knoxville, Tenn.: Press of Paragon Printing Company, 1902.

Newspapers

Athens Post
Chattanooga Daily Rebel
Daily Press and Times (Nashville)
Knoxville Daily Register
Knoxville Whig
Knoxville Whig and Rebel Ventilator
Memphis Appeal
Nashville Republican Banner

Patriot (Nashville)
Sunday Times (Chattanooga)

Secondary Sources

Books

Abernethy, Thomas Perkins. *From Frontier to Plantation in Tennessee: A Study in Frontier Democracy.* University, Alabama: Univ. of Alabama Press, 1967 (orig. pub. Univ. of North Carolina Press, 1932).

Alexander, Thomas B. *Political Reconstruction in Tennessee.* Nashville: Vanderbilt Univ. Press, 1950.

————. *Thomas A. R. Nelson of East Tennessee.* Nashville: Tennessee Historical Commission, 1956.

Allen, Valentine Collins. *Rhea and Meigs Counties in the Confederate War.* No publisher, 1908.

Anders, Leslie. *The Eighteenth Missouri.* Indianapolis: The Bobbs-Merrill Company, 1968.

————. *The Twenty-first Missouri: From Home Guard to Union Regiment.* Westport: Greenwood Press, 1975.

Armstrong, Zella. *The History of Hamilton County and Chattanooga, Tennessee.* 2 vols. Chattanooga: Lookout Publishing Co., 1931.

Ash, Stephen V. *Middle Tennessee Society Transformed 1860–1870: War and Peace in the Upper South.* Baton Rouge: Louisiana State Univ. Press, 1988.

Atkins, Jonathan. *Parties, Politics, and the Sectional Conflict in Tennessee, 1832–1861.* Knoxville: Univ. of Tennessee Press, 1997.

Bailey, Fred Arthur. *Class and Tennessee's Confederate Generation.* Chapel Hill: Univ. of North Carolina Press, 1987.

Barney, William. *The Secessionist Impulse: Alabama & Mississippi in 1860.* Princeton: Princeton Univ. Press, 1974.

Barrett, John Gilchrist. *Sherman's March through the Carolinas.* Chapel Hill: Univ. of North Carolina Press, 1956.

Barrow, Charles Kelly, J. H. Segars, and R. B. Rosenburg, eds. *Forgotten Confederates: An Anthology About Black Southerners. Journal of Confederate History Series* 14. Atlanta: Southern Heritage Press, 1995.

Barton, Michael. *Goodmen: The Character of Civil War Soldiers.* University Park: Pennsylvania State Univ. Press, 1981.

Battle Atlas of the Civil War. New York: Barnes and Noble, 1996; originally published as *Echoes of Gray.* Henry Woodhead, ed. New York: Time Life Books, 1991.

Baumgartner, Richard A., and Larry M. Strayer. *Kennesaw Mountain, June 1864: Bitter Standoff at the Gibralter of Georgia.* Huntington, W. Va.: Blue Acorn Press, 1998.

Bearss, Edwin C. *Rebel Victory at Vicksburg*. Vicksburg: Vicksburg Centennial Commemoration Commission, 1963.

Beitzell, Edwin W. *Point Lookout Prison Camp for Confederates*. Leonard Town, Md.: St. Mary's County Historical Society, 1972.

Bergeron, Paul H. *Antebellum Politics in Tennessee*. Lexington: Univ. Press of Kentucky, 1982.

————. *Paths of the Past: Tennessee, 1770–1970*. Tennessee Three Star Books Series. Knoxville: Univ. of Tennessee Press, 1979.

Bergeron, Paul H., Stephen V. Ash, and Jeanette Keith. *Tennesseans and Their History*. Knoxville: Univ. of Tennessee Press, 1999.

Beringer, Richard E., Herman Hattaway, Archer Jones, and William N. Still Jr. *Why the South Lost the Civil War*. Athens: Univ. of Georgia Press, 1986.

Blackerly, Hubert C. *Blacks in Blue and Gray: Afro-American Service in the Civil War*. Tuscaloosa, Ala.: Portals, 1979.

Bowman, John S., ed. *The Civil War Day by Day*. New York: Barnes & Noble, 1996.

Brooks, Stewart. *Civil War Medicine*. Springfield, Ill.: Charles C. Thomas, 1966.

Burton, William L. *Melting Pot Soldiers: The Union's Ethnic Regiments*. Ames, Iowa: Iowa State Univ. Press, 1988.

Campbell, Mary Emily Robertson. *The Attitude of Tennesseans toward the Union, 1847–1861*. New York: Vantage Press, 1961.

Campbell, Randolph B. A Southern Community in Crisis: Harrison County, Texas, 1850–1880. Austin: Texas State Historical Association, 1983.

Campbell, T. J. *Records of Rhea: A Condensed County History*. Dayton, Tenn.: Rhea Publishing Company, 1940.

Carter, Samuel III. *The Final Fortress: The Campaign for Vicksburg, 1862–1863*. New York: St. Martin's Press, 1980.

Cash, Wilbur J. *The Mind of the South*. New York: Knopf, 1941.

Castel, Albert. *Decision in the West: The Atlanta Campaign of 1864*. Lawrence: Univ. Press of Kansas, 1992.

Cimprich, John. *Slavery's End in Tennessee, 1861–1865*. Tuscaloosa: Univ. of Alabama Press, 1985.

Clark, Blanche Henry. *The Tennessee Yeomen, 1840–1860*. Nashville: Vanderbilt Univ. Press, 1942.

Cody, Anne. *History of the Tennessee Division of the United Daughters of the Confederacy*. Nashville: No publisher or date.

Connelly, Thomas Lawrence. *Army of the Heartland: The Army of Tennessee, 1861–1862*. Baton Rouge: Louisiana State Univ. Press, 1967.

————. *Autumn of Glory: The Army of Tennessee, 1862–1865*. Baton Rouge: Louisiana State Univ. Press, 1971.

Cooper, William J., Jr., and Thomas E. Terrill. *The American South: A History*. 2d ed. Boston: McGraw Hill, 1996.

Coulter, E. Merton. *The Confederate States of America, 1861–1865*. Baton Rouge: Louisiana State Univ. Press, 1950.

Cozzens, Peter. *No Better Place to Die: The Battle of Stones River*. Urbana: Univ. of Illinois Press, 1990.

———. *The Shipwreck of Their Hopes: The Battles for Chattanooga*. Urbana: Univ. of Illinois Press, 1990.

———. *This Terrible Sound: The Battle of Chickamauga*. Urbana: Univ. of Illinois Press, 1992.

Craven, Avery. *The Coming of the Civil War*. New York: Scribner, 1942.

Crawford, Martin. *Ashe County's Civil War: Community and Society in the Appalachian South*. Charlottesville: Univ. Press of Virginia, 2001.

Crofts, Daniel W. *Old Southampton: Politics and Society in a Virginia County, 1834–1869*. Charlottesville: Univ. Press of Virginia, 1992.

———. *Reluctant Confederates: Upper South Unionists in the Secession Crisis*. Chapel Hill: Univ. of North Carolina Press, 1989.

Crute, Joseph H., Jr. *Units of the Confederate States Army*. Midlothian, Va.: Derwent Books, 1987.

Cunningham, H. H. *Doctors in Gray: The Confederate Medical Service*. Baton Rouge: Louisiana State Univ. Press, 1958.

Daniel, Larry J. *Cannoneers in Gray: The Field Artillery of the Army of Tennessee, 1861–1865*. Tuscaloosa: Univ. of Alabama Press, 1984.

———. *Shiloh: The Battle That Changed the Civil War*. New York: Simon & Schuster, 1997.

———. *Soldiering in the Army of Tennessee: A Portrait of Life in a Confederate Army*. Chapel Hill: Univ. of North Carolina Press, 1991.

Degler, Carl N. *The Other South: Southern Dissenters in the Nineteenth Century*. New York: Harper & Row, 1974.

Donnelly, Ralph W. *The History of the Confederate States Marine Corps*. Washington, N.C.: Ralph W. Donnelly, 1976.

Douthat, James L. *Roster of Upper East Tennessee Confederate Veterans*. Signal Mountain, Tenn.: Mountain Press, Inc., no date.

Dunkelman, Mark H., and Michael J. Winey. *The Hardtack Regiment: An Illustrated History of the 154th Regiment, New York State Infantry Volunteers*. London: Associated Univ. Press, 1981.

Durrill, Wayne K. *War of Another Kind: A Southern Community in the Great Rebellion*. New York: Oxford Univ. Press, 1990.

Escott, Paul D. *After Secession: Jefferson Davis and the Failure of Confederate Nationalism*. Baton Rouge: Louisiana State Univ. Press, 1978.

———. *Many Excellent People: Power and Privilege in North Carolina, 1850–1900*. Chapel Hill: Univ. of North Carolina Press, 1985.

Fink, Paul M. *Jonesborough: The First Century of Tennessee's First Town*. Johnson City: Upper East Tennessee Office of Tennessee State Planning Commission, 1972.

Fisher, Noel C. *War at Every Door: Partisan Politics and Guerrilla Violence in East Tennessee, 1860–1869*. Chapel Hill: Univ. of North Carolina Press, 1997.

Folmsbee, Stanley John. *Sectionalism and Internal Improvements in Tennessee, 1796–1845*. Knoxville: The East Tennessee Historical Society, 1939.

Folmsbee, Stanley John, Robert E. Corlew, and Enoch L. Mitchell. *Tennessee: A Short History*. Knoxville: Univ. of Tennessee Press, 1976.

Foner, Eric. *Free Soil, Free Labor, Free Men: The Ideology of the Republican Party before the Civil War*. New York: Oxford Univ. Press, 1970.

Foote, Shelby. *The Civil War: A Narrative*. 3 vols. New York: Vintage Books, 1986 [1963].

Foster, Gaines M. *Ghosts of the Confederacy: Defeat, The Lost Cause, and the Emergency of the New South, 1865 to 1913*. New York: Oxford Univ. Press, 1987.

Frank, Joseph Allan, and George A. Reaves. *"Seeing the Elephant": Raw Recruits at the Battle of Shiloh*. New York: Greenwood Press, 1989.

Gaines, George. *Fighting Tennesseans*. Kingsport, Tenn.: Kingsport Press, 1931.

Gallaway, B. P. *The Ragged Rebel: A Common Soldier in W. H. Parsons' Texas Cavalry, 1861–1865*. Austin: Univ. of Texas Press, 1988.

Genovese, Eugene. *The Political Economy of Slavery: Studies in the Economy and Society of the Slave South*. New York: Random House, Pantheon, 1965.

Genovese, Eugene, and Elizabeth Fox-Genovese. *The Fruits of Merchant Capital: Slavery and Bourgeois Property in the Rise and Expansion of Capitalism*. New York: Oxford Univ. Press, 1983.

Glatthaar, Joseph T. *The March to the Sea and Beyond: Sherman's Troops in the Savannah and Carolinas Campaign*. New York: New York Univ. Press, 1985.

Govan, Gilbert E., and James W. Livingood. *The Chattanooga Country, 1540–1951: From Tomahawks to TVA*. New York: E. P. Dutton & Company, Inc., 1952.

Gray, Lewis Cecil. *History of Agriculture in the Southern United States to 1860*. 2 vols. New York: Peter Smith, 1941.

Griffith, Paddy. *Battle Tactics of the Civil War*. New Haven: Yale Univ. Press, 1989.

Groce, W. Todd. *Mountain Rebels: East Tennessee Confederates and the Civil War, 1860–70*. Knoxville: Univ. of Tennessee Press, 1999.

Hagerman, Edward. *The American Civil War and the Origins of Modern Warfare: Ideas, Organization, and Field Command*. Bloomington: Indiana Univ. Press, 1988.

Hagerty, Edward J. *Collis' Zouaves: The 114th Pennsylvania Volunteers in the Civil War*. Baton Rouge: Louisiana State Univ. Press, 1996.

Hahn, Steven. *The Roots of Southern Populism: Yeomen Farmers and the Transformation of the Georgia Upcountry, 1850–1890*. New York: Oxford Univ. Press, 1983.

Hale, Douglas. *The Third Texas Cavalry in the Civil War*. Norman: Univ. of Oklahoma Press, 1993.

Hamer, Philip M., ed. *Tennessee: A History, 1673–1932*. 4 vols. New York: The American Historical Society, Inc. 1933.

Harris, J. William. *Plain Folk and Gentry in a Slave Society: White Liberty and Black Slavery in Augusta's Hinterlands*. Middletown, Conn.: Wesleyan Univ. Press, 1985.

Harrison, Lowell H. *The Civil War in Kentucky*. Lexington: Univ. Press of Kentucky, 1975.

Hesseltine, William B., ed. *Civil War Prisons*. Kent, Ohio: Kent State Univ. Press, 1972.

Hilliard, Sam Bowers. *Atlas of Antebellum Southern Agriculture*. Baton Rouge: Louisiana State Univ. Press, 1984.

———. *Hog Meat and Hoecake: Food Supply in the Old South, 1840–1860*. Carbondale: Southern Illinois Univ. Press, 1972.

Holt, Michael F. *The Political Crisis of the 1850s*. New York: Wiley, 1978.

Hopkins, Anne H., and William Lyons. *Tennessee Votes: 1799–1976*. Knoxville: Bureau of Public Administration, Univ. of Tennessee, 1978.

Horn, Stanley F. *The Army of Tennessee*. Norman: Univ. of Oklahoma Press, 1941.

———. *The Decisive Battle of Nashville*. Baton Rouge: Louisiana State Univ. Press, 1956; reprint, Knoxville: Univ. of Tennessee Press, 1978.

Hsiung, David C. *Two Worlds in the Tennessee Mountains: Exploring the Origins of Appalachian Stereotypes*. Lexington: Univ. Press of Kentucky, 1997.

Hughes, Nathaniel Cheairs, Jr. *Bentonville: The Final Battle of Sherman and Johnston*. Chapel Hill: Univ. of North Carolina Press, 1996.

Ingmire, Frances T., and Carolyn Ericson. *Confederate Prisoners of War: Soldiers and Sailors Who Died in Federal Prisons and Military Hospitals in the North*. Nacogdoches, Tex.: Ericson Books, 1984.

Inscoe, John C. *Mountain Masters, Slavery, and the Sectional Crisis in Western North Carolina*. Knoxville: Univ. of Tennessee Press, 1989.

———. "Mountain Unionism, Secession, and Regional Self-Image: The Contrasting Cases of Western North Carolina and East Tennessee." In *Looking South: Chapters in the Story of an American Region*, eds. Winfred B. Moore Jr. and Joseph F. Tripp (New York: Greenwood, 1989), 115–29.

Inscoe, John C., and Gordon B. McKinney. *The Heart of Confederate Appalachia: Western North Carolina in the Civil War*. Chapel Hill: Univ. of North Carolina Press, 1997.

Jewell, Carey C. *Harvest of Death: A Detailed Account of the Army of Tennessee at the Battle of Franklin*. Hicksville, New York: Exposition Press, 1976.

Jimerson, Randall C. *The Private Civil War: Popular Thought during the Sectional Conflict*. Baton Rouge: Louisiana State Univ. Press, 1988.

Johnston, Sheila Weems, ed. *The Blue and Gray from Hawkins County (Includes Hancock County), Tennessee, 1861–1865*. Rogersville, Tenn.: The Hawkins County Genealogical and Historical Society, 1995.

Jordan, Ervin L., Jr. *Black Confederates and Afro-Yankees in Civil War Virginia*. Charlottesville: Univ. Press of Virginia, 1995.

Kenzer, Robert C. *Kinship and Neighborhood in a Southern Community: Orange County, North Carolina, 1849–1881*. Knoxville: Univ. of Tennessee Press, 1987.

Knauss, William H. *The Story of Camp Chase: A History of the Prison and Its Cemetery Together with Other Cemeteries Where Confederate Prisoners Are Buried, etc.* Nashville and Dallas: Publishing House of the Methodist Episcopal Church, South, 1906.

LaBree, Ben, ed. *Camp-Fires of the Confederacy*. Louisville, Ky.: Courier-Journal Job Printing Co., 1898.

Lacy, Eric Russell. *Vanquished Volunteers: East Tennessee Sectionalism from Statehood to Secession*. Johnson City: East Tennessee State Univ. Press, 1965.

Lash, Jeffrey N. *Destroyer of the Iron Horse: General Joseph E. Johnston and Confederate Rail Transport, 1861–1865*. Kent, Ohio: Kent State Univ. Press, 1991.

Law, Harry L. *Tennessee Geography*. Norman, Oklahoma: Harlow Publishing Corp., 1964.

Linderman, Gerald F. *Embattled Courage: The Experience of Combat in the American Civil War*. New York: The Free Press, 1987.

Livingood, James W. *Hamilton County*. Memphis, Tenn.: Memphis State Univ. Press, 1981.

Logue, Larry M. *To Appomattox and Beyond: The Civil War Soldier in War and Peace*. Chicago: Ivan R. Dee, 1996.

Lonn, Ella. *Desertion during the Civil War*. New York: The Century Co., 1928; reprint, Lincoln: Univ. of Nebraska Press, 1998.

Losson, Christopher. *Tennessee's Forgotten Warriors: Frank Cheatham and His Confederate Division*. Knoxville: Univ. of Tennessee Press, 1989.

McBride, Robert M., et al., eds. *Biographical Directory of the Tennessee General Assembly*. 6 vols. to date. Nashville: Tennessee State Library and Archives and Tennessee Historical Commission, 1975–.

McCurry, Stephanie. *Masters of Small Worlds: Yeoman Households, Gender Relations, and the Political Culture of the Antebellum South Carolina Low Country*. New York: Oxford Univ. Press, 1995.

McDonough, James Lee. *Chattanooga: A Death Grip on the Confederacy*. Knoxville: Univ. of Tennessee Press, 1984.

———. *Shiloh: In Hell Before Night*. Knoxville: Univ. of Tennessee Press, 1977.

———. *Stones River: Bloody Winter in Tennessee*. Knoxville: Univ. of Tennessee Press, 1980.

McDonough, James Lee, and James Pickett Jones. *War So Terrible: Sherman and Atlanta*. New York: W. W. Norton, 1987.

McDonough, James Lee, and Thomas Lawrence Connelly. *Five Tragic Hours: The Battle of Franklin*. Knoxville: Univ. of Tennessee Press, 1983.

McKenzie, Robert Tracy. *One South or Many? Plantation Belt and Upcountry in Civil War–Era Tennessee*. New York: Cambridge Univ. Press, 1994.

McMurray, W. J. *History of the Twentieth Tennessee Regiment Volunteer Infantry, C.S.A.* Nashville: Privately published, 1904.

McMurry, Richard M. *Two Great Rebel Armies: An Essay in Confederate Military History*. Chapel Hill: Univ. of North Carolina Press, 1989.

McPherson, James M. *Battle Cry of Freedom: The Civil War Era*. 2d ed. New York: Ballantine Books, 1988.

———. *For Cause and Comrades: Why Men Fought in the Civil War*. New York: Oxford Univ. Press, 1997.

———. *Ordeal by Fire: the Civil War and Reconstruction*. New York: Alfred A. Knopf, 1982.

———. *What They Fought For, 1861–1865*. Baton Rouge: Louisiana State Univ. Press, 1994.

McWhiney, Grady, and Perry D. Jamieson. *Attack and Die: Civil War Military Tactics and the Southern Heritage*. Tuscaloosa: Univ. of Alabama Press, 1982.

Mitchell, Reid. *Civil War Soldiers: Their Expectations and Their Experiences*. New York: Viking, 1988.

Moe, Richard. *The Last Full Measure: The Life and Death of the First Minnesota Volunteers*. New York: Henry Holt and Company, 1993.

Mooney, Chase C. *Slavery in Tennessee*. Westport, Conn.: Negro Universities Press, 1971 (reprint: orig. pub. Indiana Univ. Press, 1957).

Moore, Albert Burton. *Conscription and Conflict in the Confederacy*. New York: Macmillan Company, 1924.

Moore, John Trotwood, and Austin P. Foster, ed. *Tennessee: The Volunteer State, 1769–1923—Deluxe Supplement*. Nashville: S. J. Clarke Publishing Company, 1923.

Myers, Raymond E. *The Zollie Tree*. Louisville, Ky.: Filson Club Press, 1964.

Noe, Kenneth W. *Southwest Virginia's Railroad: Modernization and the Sectional Crisis*. Urbana: Univ. of Illinois Press, 1994.

Noe, Kenneth W., and Shannon H. Wilson, eds. *The Civil War in Appalachia: Collected Essays*. Knoxville: Univ. of Tennessee Press, 1997.

Norton, Herman. *Rebel Religion: The Story of Confederate Chaplains*. St. Louis: The Bethany Press, 1961.

Otto, John Solomon. *Southern Agriculture during the Civil War Era, 1860–1880*. Westport, Conn.: Greenwood Press, 1994.

Owsley, Frank Lawrence. *Plain Folk of the Old South*. Baton Rouge: Louisiana State Univ. Press, 1949.

Patterson, Caleb Perry. *The Negro in Tennessee, 1790–1865*. New York: Negro Universities Press, 1968 (orig. pub. Univ. of Texas, 1922).

Patton, James Welch. *Unionism and Reconstruction in Tennessee, 1860–1869*. Chapel Hill: Univ. of North Carolina Press, 1934; reprint, Gloucester, Mass.: Peter Smith, 1966.

Potter, David M. *The Impending Crisis, 1848–1861*. New York: Harper & Row, 1976.

Rable, George C. *Civil Wars: Women and the Crisis of Southern Nationalism*. Urbana: Univ. of Illinois Press, 1989.

Radley, Kenneth. *Rebel Watchdog: The Confederate States Army Provost Guard*. Baton Rouge: Louisiana State Univ. Press, 1989.

Reed, D. W. *The Battle of Shiloh and the Organizations Engaged*. Washington, D.C.: Government Printing Office, 1902; reprint, 1913.

Ridley, Bromfield Lewis. *Battles and Sketches of the Army of Tennessee*. Mexico, Mo.: Missouri Printing and Publishing Co., 1906.

Robertson, James I., Jr. *Soldiers Blue and Gray*. Columbia: Univ. of South Carolina Press, 1988.

Rogan, James Woods. *Historical Sketches of Hawkins County, Tennessee*. Rogersville, Tennessee: Hawkins Co. Genealogical and Historical Society, 1989.

Rollins, Richard, ed. *Black Southerners in Gray: Essays on Afro-Americans in Confederate Armies*. Redondo Beach, Calif.: Rank and File Publications, 1994.

Romero, Sidney J. *Religion in the Rebel Ranks*. Lanham: Univ. Press of America, 1983.

Rothrock, Mary U., ed. *The French Broad-Holston Country: A History of Knox County, Tennessee*. Knoxville: East Tennessee Historical Society, 1946.

Schroeder-Lein, Glenna R. *Confederate Hospitals on the Move: Samuel H. Stout and the Army of Tennessee*. Columbia: Univ. of South Carolina Press, 1994.

Seymour, Digby Gordon. *Divided Loyalties: Fort Sanders and the Civil War in East Tennessee*. Knoxville: Univ. of Tennessee Press, 1963.

Shattuck, Gardiner H., Jr. *A Shield and Hiding Place: The Religious Life of the Civil War Armies*. Macon, Ga.: Mercer Univ. Press, 1987.

Shriver, Phillip R., and Donald J. Breen. *Ohio's Military Prisons in the Civil War*. Columbus: Ohio State Univ. Press, 1964.

Sifakis, Stewart. *Compendium of the Confederate Armies: Tennessee*. New York: Facts on File, 1991.

Steiner, Paul E. *Disease in the Civil War: Natural Biological Warfare in 1861–1865*. Springfield, Ill.: Charles C. Thomas, 1968.

Swinfen, David B. *Ruggles' Regiment: The 122nd New York Volunteers in the American Civil War*. London: Univ. Press of New England, 1982.

Sword, Wiley. *Embrace an Angry Wind: The Confederacy's Last Hurrah: Spring Hill, Franklin, and Nashville*. New York: Harper Collins, 1992.

—————. *Mountains Touched with Fire: Chattanooga Besieged, 1863*. New York: St. Martin's Press, 1995.

—————. *Shiloh: Bloody April*. New York: William Morrow & Co., 1974.

Taylor, Oliver. *Historic Sullivan: A History of Sullivan County, Tennessee*. Bristol, Tenn.: The King Printing Co., 1909.

Temple, Oliver P. *East Tennessee and the Civil War*. Cincinnati: The Robert Clarke Company, 1899.

Tennesseans in the Civil War: A Military History of Confederate and Union Units with Available Rosters of Personnel. Nashville: Civil War Centennial Commission, 1964.

Trelease, Allen W. *White Terror: The Ku Klux Klan Conspiracy and Southern Reconstruction*. New York: Harper & Row, 1971.

Tucker, Glenn. *Chickamauga: Bloody Battle in the West*. Indianapolis: The Bobbs-Merrill Company, Inc., 1961.

White, Robert H., and Stephen V. Ash, eds., *Messages of the Governors of Tennessee*. 11 vols. to date. Nashville: Tennessee Historical Commission, 1952– .

Wiley, Bell Irvin. *The Life of Billy Yank: The Common Soldier of the Union*. Baton Rouge: Louisiana State Univ. Press, 1952.

—————. *The Life of Johnny Reb: The Common Soldier of the Confederacy*. Indianapolis: The Bobbs-Merrill Company, 1943.

—————. *Southern Negroes, 1861–1865*. New Haven, Conn.: Yale Univ. Press, 1965.

Wilson, Charles Reagan. *Baptized in Blood: The Religion of the Lost Cause, 1865–1920*. Athens: Univ. of Georgia Press, 1980.

Winters, Donald L. *Tennessee Farming, Tennessee Farmers: Antebellum Agriculture in the Upper South*. Knoxville: Univ. of Tennessee Press, 1994.

Williams, A. J. *A Confederate History of Polk County, Tennessee, 1860–1866*. Nashville: McQuiddy, 1923.

Winslow, Hattie Lou, and Joseph R. H. Moore. *Camp Morton, 1861–1865, Indianapolis Prison Camp*. Indianapolis: Indiana Historical Society, 1940.

Woodworth, Steven E. *Jefferson Davis and His Generals: The Failure of Confederate Command in the West*. Lawrence: Univ. Press of Kansas, 1990.

—————. *Six Armies in Tennessee: The Chickamauga and Chattanooga Campaigns*. Lincoln: Univ. of Nebraska Press, 1998.

Articles

Alexander, Thomas B. "Neither Peace Nor War: Conditions in Tennessee in 1865." *East Tennessee Historical Society's Publications* 21 (1949): 33–51.

Bates, Walter Lynn. "Southern Unionists: A Socioeconomic Examination of the Third East Tennessee Volunteer Infantry Regiment, U.S.A., 1862–1865." *Tennessee Historical Quarterly* 50 (1991): 226–39.

Bearss, Edwin C. "The Battle of Baton Rouge." *Louisiana History* 3 (1962): 77–128.

Boone, Jennifer K. "'Mingling Freely': Tennessee Society on the Eve of the Civil War." *Tennessee Historical Quarterly* 51 (1992): 137–46.

Breeden, James D. "A Medical History of the Later Stages of the Atlanta Campaign." *Journal of Southern History* 35 (1969): 31–59.

Bryan, Charles F. "A Gathering of Tories: The East Tennessee Convention of 1861." *Tennessee Historical Quarterly* 39 (1980): 27–48.

———. "'Tories' Amidst Rebels: Confederate Occupation of East Tennessee, 1861–1863." *East Tennessee Historical Society's Publications* 60 (1988): 3–22.

Buckwalter, Donald. "Effects of Early Nineteenth Century Transportation Disadvantage on the Agriculture of Eastern Tennessee." *Southeastern Geographer* 27 (1987): 18–37.

Burnham, Philip. "The Andersonvilles of the North." *Quarterly Journal of Military History* 10 (1997): 47–55.

Campbell, James B. "East Tennessee during the Federal Occupation, 1863–1865." *East Tennessee Historical Society's Publications* 19 (1947): 64–80.

———. "East Tennessee during the Radical Regime, 1865–1869." *East Tennessee Historical Society's Publications* 20 (1948): 84–102.

Clay, Cassius M. "Postscript to the Battle of Mill Springs." *Filson Club Historical Quarterly* 30 (1956): 103–14.

Crawford, Martin. "Confederate Volunteering and Enlistment in Ashe County, North Carolina, 1861–1862." *Civil War History* 37 (1991): 29–50.

———. "Mountain Farmers and the Market Economy: Ashe County During the 1850s." *North Carolina Historical Review* 71 (1994): 430–50.

———. "Political Society in a Southern Mountain Community: Ashe County, North Carolina, 1850–1861." *Journal of Southern History* 55 (1989): 373–90.

Crownover, Sims. "The Battle of Franklin." *Tennessee Historical Quarterly* 14 (1955): 291–322.

Cummings, Charles M. "Otho French Strahl: Choicest Spirit to Embrace the South." *Tennessee Historical Quarterly* 24 (1965): 341–55.

Donald, David. "The Confederate as a Fighting Man." *Journal of Southern History* 25 (1959): 178–93.

Downer, Edward T. "Johnson's Island." *Civil War History* 8 (1962): 202–17.

Eastwood, Bruce S. "Confederate Medical Problems in the Atlanta Campaign." *Georgia Historical Quarterly* 47 (1963): 276–92.

Edmund, C. "Hog Raising and Hog Driving in the Region of the French Broad River." *Journal of Agricultural History* 20 (1946): 87–98.

Eller, Ronald D. "Land and Family: An Historical View of Preindustrial Appalachia." *Appalachian Journal* 5 (1979): 83–109.

Faust, Drew Gilpin. "Christian Soldiers: The Meaning of Revivalism in the Confederate Army." *Journal of Southern History* 53 (1987): 63–90

Fink, Paul M. "The Railroad Comes to Jonesboro." *Tennessee Historical Quarterly* 36 (1977): 161–79.

Folmsbee, Stanley J. "The Beginnings of the Railroad Movement in East Tennessee." *East Tennessee Historical Society's Publications* 5 (1933): 81–104

Freeman, Frank R. "The Medical Support System for the Confederate Army of Tennessee during the Georgia Campaign, May–September 1864." *Tennessee Historical Quarterly* 52 (1993): 44–55.

Govan, Gilbert, and James W. Livingood. "Chattanooga Under Military Occupation, 1863–1865." *Journal of Southern History* 17 (1951): 23–47.

Gow, June I. "Military Administration in the Confederate Army of Tennessee." *Journal of Southern History* 40 (1974): 183–98.

Groce, W. Todd. "Confederate Faces in East Tennessee: A Photographic Essay." *Journal of East Tennessee History* 65 (1993): 3–33.

Hart, Roger L. "Social Structure and Confederate Army Rank in Lincoln County, Tennessee." *Locus* 3 (1991): 157–75.

Henry, J. Milton. "The Revolution in Tennessee, February, 1861 to June, 1861." *Tennessee Historical Quarterly* 18 (1959): 99–118.

Henry, Robert S. "Chattanooga and the War." *Tennessee Historical Quarterly* 19 (1960): 222–30.

Hesseltine, William B. "Civil War Prisons—Introduction." *Civil War History* 8 (1962): 117–20.

Holland, James W. "The Building of the East Tennessee and Virginia Railroad." *East Tennessee Historical Society's Publications* 4 (1932): 83–101.

———. "The East Tennessee and Georgia Railroad, 1836–1860." *East Tennessee Historical Society's Publications* 3 (1931): 89–107.

Hyman, Harold M. "Civil War Turncoats: A Commentary on a Military View of Lincoln's War Prisoner Utilization Program." *Military Affairs* 22 (1958): 134–38.

Jones, Archer. "The Vicksburg Campaign." *Journal of Mississippi History* 29 (1967): 12–27.

Keen, Nancy Travis. "Confederate Prisoners of War at Fort Delaware." *Delaware History* 13 (1968): 1–27.

Livingood, James W. "Chattanooga, Tennessee: Its Economic History in the Years Immediately Following Appomattox." *East Tennessee Historical Society's Publications* 15 (1943): 35–48.

Luvaas, Jay. "Johnston's Last Stand—Bentonville." *North Carolina Historical Review* 33 (1956): 332–58.

Lynne, Donald M. "The Confederate Chaplain." *Civil War History* (1955): 127–40.

Maslowski, Pete. "A Study of Morale in Civil War Soldiers." *Military Affairs* 34 (1970): 122–26.

McGehee, C. Stuart. "'The Property and Faith of the City': Secession and Chattanooga." *East Tennessee Historical Society's Publications* 60 (1988): 23–38.

McKee, James W., Jr. "Felix K. Zollicoffer: Confederate Defender of East Tennessee" (Part I). *East Tennessee Historical Society's Publications* 43 (1971): 34–58.

———."Felix K. Zollicoffer: Confederate Defender of East Tennessee" (Part II). *East Tennessee Historical Society's Publications* 44 (1972): 17–40.

McKenzie, Robert Tracy. "Civil War and Socioeconomic Change in the Upper South: The Survival of Local Agricultural Elites in Tennessee, 1850–1870." *Tennessee Historical Quarterly* 52 (1993): 170–84.

———. "Wealth and Income: The Preindustrial Structure of East Tennessee in 1860." *Appalachian Journal* 21 (1994): 260–79.

McMurry, Richard M. "The Atlanta Campaign of 1864: A New Look." *Civil War History* 22 (1976): 5–15.

———."Confederate Morale in the Atlanta Campaign of 1864." *Georgia Historical Quarterly* 54 (1970): 226–43.

———. "The Opening Phase of the 1864 Campaign in the West." *Atlanta Historical Journal* 27 (1983): 5–24.

McMurtry, Gerald R. "Zollicoffer and the Battle of Mill Springs." *Filson Club Historical Quarterly* 29 (1955): 303–19.

McNeill, William J. "A Survey of Confederate Soldier Morale During Sherman's Campaign Through Georgia and the Carolinas." *Georgia Historical Quarterly* 55 (1971): 1–25.

Miller, Robert Earnest. "War Within Walls: Camp Chase and the Search for Administrative Reform." *Ohio History* 96 (1987): 35–56.

Mitchell, Enoch, ed. "Letters from a Confederate Surgeon in the Army of Tennessee to His Wife." *Tennessee Historical Quarterly* 5 (1946): 142–81.

Nichols, William. "Some Foundations of Economic Development in the Upper East Tennessee Valley, 1850–1900." *Journal of Political Economy* 64 (1956): 277–302.

Norton, Herman. "Revivalism in the Confederate Armies." *Civil War History* 6 (1960): 410–24.

Osborn, George S. "The Atlanta Campaign, 1864." *Georgia Historical Quarterly* 34 (1950): 271–87.

Owsley, Frank, and Harriett C. Owsley. "The Economic Structure of Rural Tennessee, 1850–1860." *Journal of Southern History* 8 (1942): 161–82.

Prim, G. Clinton, Jr. "Born Again in the Trenches: Revivals in the Army of Tennessee." *Tennessee Historical Quarterly* 42 (1984): 250–72.

Riley, Harris D., Jr., and Amos Christie. "Deaths and Disabilities in the Provisional Army of Tennessee." *Tennessee Historical Quarterly* 43 (1984): 132–54.

Robinson-Durso, Pamela. "Chaplains in the Confederate Army." *Journal of Church and State* 33 (1991): 747–63.

Sutherland, Daniel. "Getting the 'Real War' into the Books." *The Virginia Magazine of History and Biography* 98 (1990): 220.

Thornton, J. Mills, III. "The Ethic of Subsistence and the Origins of Southern Secession." *Tennessee Historical Quarterly* 48 (1989): 67–85.

Walker, Peter Franklin. "Building a Tennessee Army: Autumn, 1861." *Tennessee Historical Quarterly* 16 (1957): 99–116.

———."Holding the Tennessee Line: Winter, 1861–62." *Tennessee Historical Quarterly* 16 (1957): 228–49.

Walker, T. R. "Rock Island Prison Barracks." *Civil War History* 8 (1962): 152–63.

Wallenstein, Peter. "Which Side Are You On? The Social Origins of White Union Troops from Civil War Tennessee." *Journal of East Tennessee History* 63 (1991): 72–103.

Watson, Samuel J. "Religion and Combat Motivation in the Confederate Armies." *Journal of Military History* 58 (1994): 29–55.

Winters, Donald L. "'Plain Folk' of the Old South Reexamined: Economic Democracy in Tennessee." *Journal of Southern History* 53 (1987): 565–86.

Theses and Dissertations

Bryan, Charles Faulkner, Jr. "The Civil War in East Tennessee: A Social, Political, and Economic Study." Ph.D. diss., Univ. of Tennessee, 1978.

Cunningham, Edward O. "Shiloh and the Western Campaign of 1862." Ph.D. diss., Louisiana State Univ., 1966.

Fisher, Noel Charles. "'War at Every Man's Door': The Struggle for East Tennessee, 1860–1869." Ph.D. diss., Ohio State Univ., 1993.

Hsiung, David. "Isolation and Integration in Upper East Tennessee, 1780–1860: Historical Origins of Appalachian Characterizations." Ph.D. diss., Univ. of Michigan, 1991.

Mason, Kevin George. "Black Sabbath: The Battle of Mill Springs." Master's thesis, Univ. of Tennessee, 1997.

McGehee, C. Stuart. "Wake of the Flood: A Southern City in the Civil War: Chattanooga, 1838–1878." Ph.D. diss., Univ. of Virginia, 1985.

Moseley, Thomas Vernon. "Evolution of the American Civil War Infantry Tactics." Ph.D. diss., Univ. of North Carolina, 1967.

Stamper, James C. "Felix K. Zollicoffer: Tennessee Editor, Politician, and Soldier." Master's thesis, Univ. of Tennessee, 1967.

Index ❧

Abernathy, S. G., 94
African Americans
  in Confederate Army, 102–3
  at Nashville, 172–73
  See Nineteenth Tennessee
    Volunteer Regiment—socioeco-
    nomic information
agricultural production
  See Nineteenth Tennessee
    Volunteer Infantry Regiment—
    socioeconomic information
Alabama Units
  Infantry regiment: Sixteenth, 57
Alaway, John, 36
American Party, 6
Anderson, Patton
  division of, 88, 121
  brigade of, 92
Athens, Tennessee, 21, 66
Atlanta, battle of
  See Bald Hill, battle of

Bald Hill, battle of, 152, 153–55
Barbourville, Kentucky, 46–47
Barnes, J. T., 147
Basket, John, 146
Bate, William
  division of: at Bald Hill, 153; at
    Dallas, 138; at Missionary Ridge,
    121; at Franklin, 168; at; Nash-
    ville, 174; at Spring Hill, 165–66
Battle, Joel A., 46
Baton Rouge, battle of, 79–83
Beauregard, P. G. T.
  at Corinth, 69
  meeting with Johnston, 58, 59

replacement of, 75
  at Shiloh, 63, 64, 66, 67
  takes command of Military
    Division of the West, 162
Beech Grove, Kentucky
  See Mill Springs, battle of
Bell, John
  election of 1860, 6
  on Lincoln's coercion of South, 10
  speaking for Confederacy, 13
Benton, Tennessee, 21
Blair, John, Jr., 32
Blair, John III, 32
Blair, Robert L., 32
  capture of, 67
  promotion of, 97–99
  at reorganization, 71
  transfer to Invalid Corps, 147
  wounded at Chickamauga, 115–16
Blountville Guards
  See Nineteenth Tennessee
    Volunteer Infantry Regiment—
    Company C
Blountville, Tennessee, 19, 21, 30,
  32, 33, 66, 193
Bowen, John S.
  brigade of, 59, 63, 65, 79
Bowers, Henry, 25
Bowles, William, 73, 74
Bragg, Braxton
  assumes command of Army of
    Tennessee, 75
  in Atlanta, 150
  corps of: at Chattanooga, 105–107,
    109, 118, 120; at Chickamauga,
    112–13, 116, 117, 118; at Mission-
    ary Ridge, 120–21, 123, 124; at